Living from Music in Salvador

Jeff Packman

LIVING FROM MUSIC
IN SALVADOR

Professional Musicians

and the Capital of Afro-Brazil

Wesleyan University Press   Middletown, Connecticut

Wesleyan University Press
Middletown CT 06459
www.wesleyan.edu/wespress
© 2021 Jeff Loren Packman
All rights reserved
Manufactured in the United States of America
Designed by Mindy Basinger Hill
Typeset in Minion Pro

Library of Congress Cataloging-in-Publication Data

Names: Packman, Jeff (Jeff Loren) 1964– author.

Title: Living from music in Salvador : professional
musicians and the capital of Afro-Brazil / Jeff Packman.

Description: [First.] | Middletown, Connecticut :
Wesleyan University Press, 2021. | Series: Music/culture |
Includes bibliographical references and index. | Summary:
"Ethnography on working musicians, musical production,
and labor in Salvador de Bahia, Brazil. Explores the concept
of musical labor in relation to conditions of race
and class"— Provided by publisher.

Identifiers: LCCN 2021017519 (print) | LCCN 2021017520
(ebook) | ISBN 9780819580498 (cloth) | ISBN 9780819580481
(trade paperback) | ISBN 9780819580504 (ebook)

Subjects: LCSH: Music—Social aspects—Brazil—Salvador. |
Musicians—Brazil—Salvador—Economic conditions. |
Music trade—Brazil—Salvador.

Classification: LCC ML3917.B6 P3 2021 (print) | LCC ML3917.
B6 (ebook) | DDC 306.4/842098142—dc23

LC record available at https://lccn.loc.gov/2021017519
LC ebook record available at https://lccn.loc.gov/2021017520

5   4   3   2   1

FOR DANI AND CUPCAKE

CONTENTS

AUTHOR'S NOTE

Living from Music in the Time of Covid-19

About a month and a half before my deadline to return the revised manuscript of this book, the University of Toronto (my employer) sent all faculty, staff, and students home out of concern for the rapid spread of what was then called "the novel coronavirus." At the time, few of us had any idea how grave the situation would become. Early discussions tended to focus on managing our circumstances until we could get back into the classroom, with time frames of a couple of weeks bandied about. Very quickly, though, the seemingly endless stream of online meetings I attended started shifting from short-term problem solving to longer-term planning. Even before we had a concrete sense of how to get our students and ourselves through the semester, our horizon for possible return was being discussed in terms of many months. Eight months later, we are still not back on campus, life has not returned to anything close to what it was before, and we are, in fact, seeing Covid-19 infection rates increase alarmingly fast where, once, many thought the situation was improving.

Not long after we saw widespread lockdown measures implemented in Toronto, the Covid-19 pandemic hit Brazil, which quickly became a global "hot spot." The national government was not much help in controlling the spread of the virus, with the president widely reported as asking rhetorically and indifferently "what do you want me to do?" (Farzan and Berger, 2020). While several friends in Bahia have told me about safety measures such as masking and limitations on public gatherings that have been implemented locally, they also mentioned seeing plenty of people not adhering to them.

In Brazil, Toronto, and as far as I can tell, many other places in the world, a significant loss of live music has accompanied countless losses of life, jobs, and overall well-being. In Salvador, a city that has long been a place where musicians' livelihoods have depended on live performance, restrictions on public gatherings and, indeed, the danger of gathering at all, has been nothing short of catastrophic for local music industries and workers. Along with the shuttering of venues that provided baseline income for many of the people discussed in this book, one of two major festivals that provide enhanced work opportunities for Salvador's music professionals, the *festas juninas*, was cancelled. Not long after that, it was announced that Carnaval, the backbone of Bahia's music industries, would not be held until the pandemic was under control. More recently, local officials offered the idea of postponing Carnaval 2021 until July, a tactical move likely aimed toward restarting the stalled tourism industry that is so vital to Bahia's economy. Holding these massive musical gatherings, however, is contingent on evidence that they can happen without becoming super spreader events, which would likely require an effective vaccine. Regardless, it is clear that, for the time being anyway, much of what I discuss in this book no longer exists.

On the other hand, one thing that I discuss throughout and that continues during the pandemic is that Salvador's musicians (and its residents in general) are incredibly resourceful and, often with the help of family, community, and other socio-professional networks, extremely adept at making it through very difficult times. Accordingly, when the gravity of Covid-19 and the necessary means to address its spread started to become apparent to several of the musicians I know, their fears and frustrations quickly gave way to various solutions. For instance, whereas so much performance activity and work geared toward securing those performances had been done in person, online activity is clearly on the increase, at least among the friends and collaborators with whom I have corresponded in the last several months. Despite unequal access to technology, many mentioned doing various "lives," streaming broadcasts on Facebook, YouTube, and other internet platforms. Further, one "live" that I watched was linked with a dona-tion site for a fund to help other local musicians who had suddenly lost their livelihoods and were still waiting for promised government relief to arrive. In support of such work, a sound production company owned by a friend that was built on providing sound systems, mixers, roadies, and DJs for live events, converted part of their headquarters into a studio for live musical broadcasts. A few musicians I know have also taken to internet-facilitated collaborations, especially visually and sonically multitracked recordings instead of co-present performances, which they have posted on YouTube and other social media. In several instances this has involved newly created accounts, thus suggesting a means of promoting and at times commodifying their work that they had not previously utilized much if at all.

New or not, and directly monetized or not, all of these activities have kept the music coming while also doing promotional work and, in several instances, fostering new professional alliances and thus future possibilities. As such, they are crisis-inspired, slightly adapted enhancements of the various kinds of work these musicians have been doing for years. I suspect that, despite the primacy of live performance I have seen for almost twenty years in Salvador, some of the pandemic-inspired changes might become permanent features of the portfolio of activities that most of my collaborators have used to live from their music since well before I met them.

On the other hand, I cannot help but think that most *baianos* would welcome a return to many aspects of musical life that were normal before any of us ever heard of "the novel coronavirus." At the same time, few would say that living from music or life in general in Salvador was without serious issues during the old normal. Perhaps, the exposing of the many inequities embedded in twenty-first-century neoliberal capitalism might provide some impetus for change. Daily news reports have shown in no uncertain terms how the poor and racially othered are disproportionately likely to be dispossessed or killed by Covid-19, and how the ranks of the poor are increasing with the cratering of labor markets worldwide. Unsurprisingly, these losses are even more common in occupations defined by so-called flexible employment practices, which feature in neoliberal economies and provide workers little or no protection from the brutal "logic" of the market. Yet as I discuss in the book, this is the precarious reality faced by most professional musicians and many *baiano*s long before neoliberalism or Covid-19 were common topics of discussion.

Notably, in the wake of widespread economic havoc wrought by a global pandemic, the silencing of in-person, collectively shared music is garnering attention, and not just because of lost revenue. Certainly, the numerous reports I have read on the cancellation of the *festas juninas* and Bahian Carnaval—as well as concert tours, opera productions, and local bar performances in any number of locations—do tend to focus on the financial implications. However, many implicitly and often explicitly broach topics such as rattled senses of identity as well as fears about group and individual well-being. The optimist in me hopes that this calamity-induced awareness of how much music actually matters might engender lasting changes in how people think about music and musicians. At the very least, we might hope for concerted efforts to bring back live performances as soon as possible. With or without such lessons learned, the ways Bahian musicians have adapted to current conditions and the ways they have navigated past challenges suggest that the vitality of Salvador's soundscape will return one day. Hopefully we won't be left waiting for too long.

JP

Toronto | November 1, 2020

NOTE

Farzan, Antonia Noori, and Miriam Berger. 2020. "Bolsonaro says Brazilians must not be 'Sissies' about Coronavirus, as 'All of Us are going to Die One Day.'" *Washington Post* November 11, 2020. https://www.washingtonpost.com/world/2020/11/11/bolsonaro -coronavirus-brazil-quotes/. Accessed November 19, 2020.

ACKNOWLEDGMENTS

Living from Music in Salvador is what it is thanks to scores of people who have generously given their time, wisdom, and care to me over many, many years. Without all of them, this book would not only look very different, but it might not exist at all. I would be a very different person too.

I am convinced that there are few better places than Salvador for doing field research, especially on music. My family and I were not only made to feel welcome, but I was also blessed with the support and friendship of a host of musicians and music industry personnel who brought me to rehearsals, recordings, and performances, answered my never-ending questions patiently and thoughtfully, and introduced me to their friends and colleagues as well. *Muito obrigado* to Carol di Roma; Papa Mel and Pingo; Eugênio Coelho, Marquinhos, Tiago, Rafa, Pinguim, and Candy from Funk 'n' Roll; Diqua, Fredson, Mala, Katia, Edson, Pastel Reis, and Edmar from Banda Patua; Nogueira, Jorge, Alison, and Tim from Salsalitro; Anderson, Marconi, Arão, and Wilton from Vox Pop; Leo, Jair, Marcelo, and the rest of the A Zorra team; Jorge Elaíde Gois and Iza; Ximbinha and Thais Mamede; Mauricio Almeida; Sueli Sodre; Márcia Castro; Dona Conceição; Elpidio Bastos; Henrique Rebouças; Vando Nery; Paulinho Baterista; Keiler Rego; Nestor Madrid; Márcio Dhiniz; Israel Baxista; Ivan Torres; Dino Reis; and Marilda Santanna.

There are many more people, too many to mention, whose small contributions and acts of kindness have made Bahia so special to my family and me. There are also several others who have became especially close to us and with whom we have been able to remain in contact during and between return visits to Bahia. These close collaborators and now friends include Zé Raimundo, Nadjaí Arraújo, Son Melo, Luciano Salvador Bahia, Kadija Telles, Josehr Santos, Laurinha Arantes, Junior Oliveiros, Roberval Santos, Yara Santiago, Márcio Valverde,

Lívia Milena, Edni Devay, and Luciano Caroso. Finally, and most of all, I would not know the vast majority of these people if not for Jorge Farofa, who taught me percussion and continues to teach me about music and life in Bahia. I am grateful beyond words to you all.

My gratitude to the many *baianos* who have been crucial to this project extends well beyond professional music makers. Manuel Viega and Milton Moura were the first Brazilian scholars I met and both supported my work in its early phases. Carlos Quícoli, who isn't a *baiano* but who oversaw the University of California's study abroad program in Salvador and Clara Ramos, the director of the host institution, ACBEU (Brazil-US Cultural Association), were also crucial for helping me get my research off the ground. Dance scholar Eloisa Domênici has been a colleague, friend, and occasional research partner since 2004. Subsequently, I met and had productive interactions with Angela Luhnig at the Federal University of Bahia (UFBA) and most recently, Rodrigo Herringer from the Federal University of the Bahian Recôncavo (UFRB), who invited me to participate in the online symposium on music and labor, which gave me the final energy and intellect boost to finalize the manuscript. Beyond the scholars who contributed to the research are the people who became part of my, my wife's, and later my daughter's everyday life in Bahia, much like a second family. They include Zenobia Quintela Nunes; Ana Helena Quintela; Gabriel Oliveira; Weliton Quintela Nunes; Ogvalda Devay and her (very large and wonderful) family; Martha Rocha; Dona Naná; Seu Raimundo; Flor and Gabriel Valverde; Brau; Laís Lima; Marcos "Porco Olho" Boa Morte; Raimunda Nadia; Lazinho Boa Morte; Zozo Boa Morte; Dona Nicinha; Sonia, Sandrina, and Renato dos Anjos; Lúcia, Luzia, Jô, and Alaíde from Privilege; and Marcos Silveira, my oldest friend in Bahia.

My route to Bahia was long and winding and has been facilitated by several agencies and institutions. Initial fieldwork was supported by the Fulbright Program, a Foreign Language Area Studies (FLAS) Fellowship, and the Music Department of the University of California–Berkeley. Subsequent trips were made possible by Canada's Social Sciences and Humanities Research Council (SSHRC) as well as SSHRC Institutional Grant (SIG) funds from the University of Toronto Faculty of Music.

Once again though, people, especially my many teachers, made research in Bahia, this book, and so much more, possible. David Goodman at Santa Monica College was crucial in helping me believe that academia was, in fact, a viable option for me and for giving me the basic tools to give it a go. At the University of California–Riverside, I had the privilege of studying with several scholars whose examples have inspired me for twenty years and counting. Philip Brett exemplified what a senior professor should be; Paul Gelles, Anna Scott, Sally Ness, and Ethan Nasreddin-Longo were all important mentors and friends. Most of all, Deborah Wong and René Lysloff challenged and encouraged me, and taught me more than I could ever have imagined. Good fortune, unflagging support, and inspiration continued at the University of California–Berkeley. Bonnie Wade encouraged me to consider Brazil as a research site and helped me always see the big picture. Ben Brinner has always been an important source of wisdom and encouragement, and his influence on my research (and teaching) has only increased over time. Percy Hintzen was one of the most generous scholars and teachers I have ever met, and remains central to how I have wrestled with issues of race. Olly Wilson encouraged me not to forget about the music and Michael Orland patiently helped bolster my ability to do it; and Richard Taruskin challenged me to be surprised when doing research, something that I still take with me to Bahia no matter how familiar it may seem. Finally, my dissertation advisor Jocelyne Guilbault's theoretical knowledge was and continues to be rivaled only by her warmth and energy. Many years on she still challenges and inspires me in my work.

I also was blessed with an unparalleled cohort of student colleagues while I was at UC–Berkeley. Among them are Christina Sunardi, Marié Abe, Eliot Bates, Patty Hsu, Francesca Rivera, Rebecca Bodenheimer, Bill Quillen, Charles Ferris, Lisa Mezzacappa, Shalini Ayyagari, Noel Verzosa, Tim Fuson, Alex Kahn, and perhaps most of all, Carla Brunet, each of whom has helped and in various ways continues to help me hone my thinking. Before that, Brian Bunker, Griffin Woodworth, and Chris Alberding were tremendous colleagues at UC–Riverside who helped make it clear that academia was the right path for me.

A host of other scholars have joined in the conversation since grad school, offering feedback on paper presentations and other bits of writing, much of which eventually became part of this book. Among them are Charles Perrone, Alex Dent, John Murphy, KE Goldschmitt, Gillian McGillivray, Bryan McCann, Esther Kurtz, Andrew Snyder, Rachel Beausoleil-Morrison, Schuyler Wheldon, Dan Sharp, Fred Moehn, Juan Diego Diaz, Noam Lemish, Ian Sinclair, Chris Wilson, Kevin Fellezs, Thomas Garcia, Suzel Reiley, Henrique Cazes, Marilia Figueredo, TM Scruggs, Henry Spiller, Travis Jackson, Sean Bellaviti, Tom Greenlund, Katherine Preston, Mark DeWitt, Steve Pond, Lucia Suarez, Xavier Livermon, Marlon Bailey, Juliet McMains, Laurence Robitaille, Mark Laver, Marco Túlio, Amy Medvick, Anna Hoefnagels, Louise Wrazen, Rob Sims, Michael Marcuzzi, Paul Lovejoy, Chris Innes, David Trotman, Pablo Idahosa, Judy Hellman, Rob

Bowman, George Sawa, Dorothy Deval, Tim Taylor, Evan Rapport, Harris Berger, and Paul Theberge.

I could not ask for a better place to work than the University of Toronto (U of T). Many thanks to Deans Gage Averill for hiring me, Russell Hartenberger for helping me stay, and Don McLean for trusting me with the challenges of administration. At U of T, I joined and was later joined by a spectacular group of people, musicologists, ethnomusicologists, music theorists, Music Education scholars, and librarians including Robin Elliott, Greg Johnston, Caryl Clark, Annette Sanger, Tim Neufeldt, Celia Cain, Estelle Joubert, Paul Doerwald, Mary Ann Parker, Ken McLeod, John Haines, Lori Dolloff, Liz Gould, Sherry Lee, Suzanne Meyers-Sawa, Ryan McClelland, Steven Vande Moortele, John Brownell, Sarah Gutsche-Miller, Ellen Lockhart, Nasim Nicknafs, Daphne Tan, James Mason, Bryan Martin, and Sebastian Biscigliano. I am grateful for their friendship and support. My involvement with U of T's vibrant performance programs was an unexpected and invaluable aspect of my job that has profoundly shaped my research. I have been able to think about musical labor in discussions with elite musicians who think about living from music performance for themselves and the next generation of performers they train every day. Among them are Midori Koga, Jeff Reynolds, Jeff McFadden, Lydia Wong, Hilary Apfelstadt, Terry Promane, Mike Murley, Jim Lewis, Lorna McDonald, Steven Philcox, Aiyun Huang, Mark Fewer, Uri Meyer, Mark Duggan, Alan Heatherington, and Gillian MacKay. My experiences at U of T are all the richer for having been able to work with them.

And then there are my colleagues in Ethnomusicology. Since I arrived at U of T, Jim Kippen has never stopped sharing his considerable wisdom while always encouraging me and my peers, Josh Pilzer and Farzi Hemmasi, to forge our own paths. He has been the ideal senior colleague and friend. Jim is now retired, but Josh and Farzi continue in the form he taught us by example. They are both brilliant, generous, and, well, just a joy to work and hang out with.

My support network at U of T extends beyond the Faculty of Music and even faculty members as well. I am grateful for the support from scholars in our small but vibrant program in Latin American Studies. In particular, Victor Rivas, Sanda Munic, and Berenice Villagomez have been consistent resources for coffee and opportunities to exchange ideas. Economist Beth Duhey has been not only a friend, but also provided me with an invaluable primer on economic theories, not the least of which was marginal revenue product. I cannot imagine trying to write (or teach) without the amazing staff at U of T's Faculty of Music, especially Nalayini Balasubramanium, Lisa Jack, Kevin Howey, Dina Garcia,

Mary-Beth Campbell, and Iliana Sztainbok. Likewise, my students have also shaped my thinking in profound ways. Two graduate seminars in particular, Music and the Racial/Ethnic Imaginations and Music, Capital, Markets, and Industries have provided opportunities to keep thinking about core issues central to this book, but all of my students have challenged and, indeed, taught me a tremendous amount.

As I worked toward putting together *Living from Music in Salvador*, many colleagues stressed the importance of the press that published it. Their advice has proven true, and working with Wesleyan University Press has been a pleasure and privilege. Editor-in-chief Suzanna Tamminen has been amazing in fielding my questions and organizing the many threads of the publishing process for me, and production editor Jim Schley has followed suit. Jackie Wilson leads a creative and responsive marketing team, and Alan Berolzheimer has been a more precise, attentive, and instructive copy editor than I could have asked for. The editors of the Music/Culture Series—Sherrie Tucker, Jeremy Wallach, and especially Deborah Wong—have been extremely supportive of the project since I first submitted materials some time ago. This support includes giving just the right amount of advice when needed and finding the right anonymous readers, whose critical feedback improved the final product in numerous ways. I thank them all for their expertise and generosity.

Some of the material presented here has benefitted from the process of publication in other venues. Parts of chapter 5 appeared in *Ethnomusicology* volume 55, issue 3 (2011), and portions of chapter 3 were published in *Black Music Research Journal* volume 29, number 1 (2009). I thank the University of Illinois Press for allowing me to include this writing here and also the anonymous readers and editors who shaped the articles as they initially appeared. Kristen Hoosen helped me with proofreading on those publications and this manuscript, and Kristen Graves is a recent addition to the team, lending her keen eye to the text and images presented here. JP Robinson was able to lend a professional look to my homemade diagrams, and Allison Sokil helped me bring my studio vocabulary into the twenty-first century.

Finally, there is my family, all of whom have supported me through the many excursions I have taken in my life. Vince Jordan has been a steadfast confidant since long before I ever heard of ethnomusicology or Bahia. VJ has been the brother I didn't have. I do have a sister, Jill Packman, a scholar herself, who I thank for enduring me as a big brother and for leading the way to graduate study. My parents, Paul and Sandy Packman, always encouraged me to spend my life doing something I love and taught me to value knowledge. My grandmother, Lottie Weingarten, was the lone other musician among us, leaving little doubt about the source of my love for music. Finally, my daughter Rebecca is the best reason I can think of for seeing this book to completion, and my wife, research partner, and best person I know, Danielle Robinson, is the reason I could complete it at all. *Living from Music in Salvador* is for them.

Living from Music in Salvador

INTRODUCTION

Mystique, Myths, and Materialities
of Professional Music Making and Bahia

They are either under no necessity to work for their living, or are enabled
to choose the sphere of activity that is really congenial to them, and gives
them pleasure. These are the poets, the philosophers, the men of science,
the men of culture—in a word, the real men, the men who have realised
themselves, and in whom all Humanity gains a partial realization.

Oscar Wilde, "The Soul of Man Under Socialism" (1891)

Não fui feito pro trabalho, eu nasci pra batucar
(I wasn't made for working, I was born to drum)
René Bittencourt and Noel Rosa, "Felicidade" (Happiness)

There is a saying in Bahia: "*O baiano não nasce. Estreia!*" (People from Bahia
aren't born. They debut!). This pithy nod to Bahians' expressive flair is supported by the fact that their state is the natal home of luminary musicians such
as Gilberto Gil, Caetano Veloso, Dorival Caymmi, João Gilberto, Maria Bethânia,
and Gal Costa to name but a few. The roots of samba, Brazil's national music
and dance, are in Bahia too, extended to Rio by Bahian migrants in the late
nineteenth century. The state's musical reputation is bolstered by a massive
pre-Lenten Carnaval in its capital city, Salvador. Often called the Carnaval of
Participation, the weeklong celebration features parading, dancing, and singing
"audiences" accompanying performances delivered from *trios elétricos*, semi
trucks outfitted with stages and PA systems. Attracting millions of tourists and

saturated media coverage, Bahian Carnaval's scope now rivals Rio de Janeiro's more famous spectacle.

In the 1980s Bahian Carnaval gave rise to a new genre, "*axé* music," that altered its soundscape and catalyzed the expansion of Salvador's music industries. Local artists began to attract national and international attention, whereas in the past, Bahian musicians typically won fame and fortune after relocating to more industrialized southern cities such as Rio and São Paulo. As the 1980s drew to a close, Bahian music *qua* Bahian music effectively had its own debut.

Audiences worldwide were soon introduced to Bahia-based musicians and several genres, including *axé*, that are now commonly glossed as *música baiana* (Bahian music). Many, including me, stopped in their tracks upon hearing drummers from *bloco afro* Olodum performing a precursor to *axé* know as samba-reggae on Paul Simon's 1990 album *Rhythm of the Saints*;[1] or they saw the group on Michael Jackson's 1996 video for "They Don't Care About Us." Others were captivated by Margareth Menezes's show-stealing performances across Europe and the U.S. during David Byrne's *Rei Momo* tour (c. 1989). The list of globally recognizable Bahian musics and artists has continued to grow, exemplified by years of headline shows on several continents by stars such as Daniela Mercury, Carlinhos Brown, and Ivete Sangalo.

I got my first, first-hand sample of Salvador's music during a short visit to the city in December 2002. The experience most likely to elicit enthusiasm from a fan of Brazilian music was watching Gal Costa greet the new year headlining a free multiact concert sponsored by the municipal government at the Farol da Barra, the lighthouse at the city's southern tip. Her midnight set was preceded by a succession of opening acts that were largely unknown to me, and, from what I could tell, much of the crowd. Though their numbers were relatively small and their level of enthusiasm rather middling, the initially sparse, mildly attentive hodgepodge of onlookers morphed into a tightly packed, energetically rapt mass over the course of the evening. It was diverse too. I saw men, women, boys, and girls ranging from toddlers to seniors; with dark skin, light skin, and everything in between; and wearing clothes spanning casual to casually chic to tattered. Gal and her backing quartet presented a cross-section of material recorded since her debut as part of the Tropicália movement in the 1960s and her subsequent career as an MPB (*música popular brasileira* — Brazilian popular music) artist.[2] Joining them, and seeming to me somewhat out of place, was a middle-aged man with long brown hair playing what looked like a miniature Stratocaster. The frenzied applause upon his introduction, however, told me that he was anything but extraneous—I learned later that he was Armandinho Maceda, the son of one of the inventors of the *trio elétrico* and a master of the *guitarra baiana*.[3] His blazing solos and distorted tone were a marked step away from Gal's gentle voice and her group's smoother, nylon string guitar-led sound. The contrast clearly appealed to the crowd, which danced and sang *en masse* to every song.

I was thrilled to have seen an MPB legend but nevertheless eager to see some of the *axé* artists whose music I had been exploring prior to coming. A tour guide waiting in the lobby of my hotel overheard me mention this and told me that none other than Margareth Menezes would be appearing in town later that week. A few days later, my family and I followed his tip and headed to Rock 'n' Rio, a ritzy club in what was then an upscale shopping complex. After passing an MPB trio performing in the mall's food court, we found the already substantial box office queue. So we waited, joined by well-dressed twenty- and thirtysomethings as well as a number of middle-aged women—a crowd that appeared both markedly more affluent and significantly less diverse than the one on New Year's Eve. We finally entered the club to see the last half of a set by an opening act that I described in my field notes as "disco" and "four female singers backed by an all-male band."[4] We took our place on the balcony overlooking them, by chance next to the tour guide from the hotel. Together we waited (again), listening half attentively to the band and watching the dancers on the semi-full dance floor below.

Well after midnight, Margareth and her (again, all-male) group finally took the stage. There was no longer open space on the dance floor or anywhere else in the venue, and the crowd responded with a fervor that belied the late hour. They (we) jumped up and down, danced, and sang along with each song, including several I recognized from my CD collection. The band was big and forceful, powered by electric guitar and bass, keyboards, horns, a drummer, and a percussion section pounding out variants of samba-reggae. Margareth was a dynamo delivering catchy tunes in a uniquely powerful and slightly husky voice. The show wrapped in the wee hours of the morning, and we headed home, tired and with ringing ears, but invigorated.

A third experience on that trip provided a provocative counterpoint to what I had seen emerge over the course of the Rock 'n' Rio and New Year's Eve shows. After a day meandering the cobblestone streets of the Historic District, my family and I were drawn to a restaurant by the sounds of *bossa nova* escaping through open windows. With a sparse early evening crowd,[5] we listened to a singer accompany himself on *violão* (acoustic guitar). Most patrons were all but indifferent to his performance, occasionally offering a smattering of applause, but mostly carrying on conversations while eating and drinking. The audience dissipated and became less attentive as the evening progressed. Yet the singer soldiered on, his subdued voice floating sinuously above the rich harmonies of classic tunes by the likes of João Gilberto and Tom Jobim. Despite his potentially demoralizing performance conditions the restaurant singer, like Margareth and Gal, left no doubt that he was a seasoned performer, indeed, a pro.

While these three experiences showed me that Bahia's reputation for music was well deserved,[6] another moment on that first visit called out its more insidious side. Stopped at a red light near the *Orixá* statues presiding over the Dique do Tororó,[7] a tour guide named Ed spoke passionately about perceptions of his hometown. He told us how numerous people dismissed it as a city of little substance, where residents only cared about having a good time, countering "but we work hard at entertainment!" In just a few words, Ed spoke back to two prevalent, entangled myths at issue in this book: 1) that *baianos* do not work, and 2) that "playing" music is not really working.

The traction of these misconceptions raises the stakes for a topic that might otherwise seem a pedestrian aspect of Brazilian music: the day-to-day work of making it.[8] *Living from Music in Salvador* is not about global industries, star performers, or the big money often discussed apropos of both. It is about people who support themselves creating music, usually in more limited contexts to little acclaim and often for low wages, as well as the variety of activities including and beyond performing onstage and making recordings that comprise the occupation of being a musician. Against tendencies among scholars, journalists, and fans to focus on "great artists" or celebrities and their "works," performances, and/or products, I want to illustrate how studying the quotidian *work processes* of local performers, "working musicians,"[9] provides a powerful means to understand them, their music, and the context in which they make it. As I argue throughout the book, their practices and productions are entangled with numerous issues at the fore of everyday life in Salvador, not the least of which are economics and various vectors of cultural politics. Bahian musicians' seemingly mundane practices, when ignored or misunderstood as they often are, can reify problematic stereotypes—of musicians and people from Bahia, a place where the economy once depended on the commodification and labor of enslaved African people and now relies heavily on the commodification of African expressive culture. Making their labors visible, then, not only points toward the material consequences of music for workers who are often "hidden" in plain sight within a highly racialized setting,[10] but also pushes against potentially dire, unintended, and broad-ranging consequences when they are noticed. Who was the singer in the restaurant? Who performed in the opening acts on New Year's Eve and at Rock 'n' Rio? Who were the musicians backing the headliners? What do their careers look and sound like? Do local players ever win wider acclaim? If so, how? What if they don't? How are their practices entangled with assumptions about musicians, music, and *baianos*? These types of questions underlie what follows.

MUSICIANS' HIDDEN WORK AND MUSIC'S HIDDEN WORKERS

Non/misrecognition of musical workers, be they singers, instrumentalists, or a host of other people whose labor makes music audible, persists for a number of reasons including wariness about the relationship between creative expression and economic activity common in cultures with ties to European Romanticism, Liberal Humanism, and Modernism. As part of these legacies, idealized notions of Art have long emphasized autonomy from everyday matters such as money. Optimistic in some ways (see the Oscar Wilde quotation, above), highly problematic in others, but rarely irrelevant, an enduring "ideology of autonomous art" (Wolfe 1987) is apparent in frequent and not always unfounded concerns expressed by scholars, producers of expressive culture, and audiences about the power of commerce to impede creative expression.

The conviction that music and money are irreconcilable is, paradoxically, evident in discussions of popular musics that are unequivocally commercial. Complaints often revolve around "the music itself" — too much repetition (it all sounds the same!), simplistic harmony (it's only three chords!), and problematic lyrics (another song about sex, drugs, and rock 'n' roll?!). Yet the art/commerce binary frequently looms despite scholarly critique (e.g., Frith 1987, Weinstein 1999, Taylor 2016), and as the tenets of neoliberalism, in particular the primacy of "the market," become increasingly naturalized on a global scale: do we not still hear (ex-)fans of marquee artists cry "sell out" when a new release features material accessible beyond the core audience and earns high revenues when new listeners respond with their pocketbooks?

The art/commerce opposition, however problematic, is one of several interrelated factors, including "the music itself," that feed the disjuncture between music and work. As historian Karl Miller (2008, 428) notes, performance conventions in many musical traditions require a "consciously contrived mask of effortlessness." Sambas such as "Felicidade" (see the epigraph) along with countless songs in multiple genres resituate notions of effortlessness with declarations that even professional musicians don't or can't really work. The statements may be ironic; or they might be earnest calls for artistic integrity. But either way, such (self) representations can obscure the very real work necessary to "play" music. This is exemplified in Brazil, where the icon of samba, the *malandro*, is infamous for living outside of societal norms, including holding a job.[11]

Mass media portrayals of stars' leisure-filled lifestyles also contribute to the disconnect. In addition to enhancing celebrity mystique, such imagery can also bolster their artistic credibility and, ironically, commercial appeal. Less cynically, it would be hard to deny that traveling the world performing for an adoring public while earning large sums of money might be pleasurable. Regardless, it is almost *de rigueur* that if the more job-like aspects of a successful musician's career are mentioned—in interviews, career retrospectives, biopics, and biographies—they are treated with at least a glint of nostalgia for bygone days of paying dues on the way to the big time or as evidence of sacrifices made and overcome.

Absent from such triumphant tales are accounts of the numerous musicians who are employed in local music industries, working without label support, world tours, or widespread adulation.[12] *Living from Music* is about them—working musicians who earn their living performing popular music primarily on a local scale. It asks how and to what effects such professionals in Salvador da Bahia, a city notable for its music and rich Afro-diasporic culture, make music, money, and meanings as laborers within industries of cultural production. While most of these performers do not earn acclaim or income remotely comparable to their star counterparts, they are in many ways the "faces," "bodies," and "voices" of music in their home town. Moreover, more than a few of them back high-profile performers; and some become stars in their own right. Regardless of their level of success, their practices, their music, and the meanings of both are inseparable from economics and an array of other issues, local and global, that inform life in Salvador.

FOUNDATIONS

In order to make sense of musicians' work as entangled with musical, financial, and sociocultural concerns in the Bahian context, I draw a great deal from "practice theory," especially the ideas of Pierre Bourdieu, Michel de Certeau, and Michel Foucault. Less a coherent theory than a number of perspectives on how and to what effects people navigate various structures of constraint and conditions of possibility, these ideas, informed by local knowledge, provide a useful framework for critically interpreting the practices of living from music in Salvador.[13]

For instance, working musicians' activities can productively be understood as what Bourdieu calls "position takings" (*prises de position*), "the structured system of practices and expressions of agents" (Bourdieu and Wacquant 1992, 105) in a particular "field." Accordingly, the music Salvador's musicians perform, their discourse, and their job-seeking efforts are informed by, and also help map out, a tangled network of popular music *scenes* (Straw 1991) that I treat as that field.[14] In keeping with Bourdieu's formulation, certain features of the Salvador Scenes as a field of practice are quite particular to it. An example would be specialized musical knowledge. Other structures, for instance, certain social hierarchies, are more intertwined with proximal fields such as Bahian society. Likewise, while the field as a composite of scenes shares some informing sensibilities with the various genre-specific (sub)scenes that comprise it,[15] others are more discrete. For instance, abilities that might place a musician at the top of their profession in one subfield might hold little sway beyond it. The point is that the practices, politics, and implications of professional music making are at once highly specific and also linked with an array of local and supralocal meanings and vectors of power. The organization and sensibilities of the Scenes introduced in chapter 1 are broader aspects of Bahian culture that come to bear on local musicians' and their audiences' habituses, the durable, embodied, dispositions that inform their musical and quotidian practices.

Various forms of capital, the third factor of Bourdieu's equation, practice = ([habitus × capital] + field) (1984, 101), are negotiated, accumulated, and exchanged in various ways in the Scenes. Obviously, economic capital is a central concern for people endeavoring to live from music. However, their ability to earn it, as Bourdieu's writing suggests, is entangled with the other capital types he theorized. For example, cultural capital in the form of particular valued skills and claims of participation is especially important for professional musicians as they work to advance their careers. Also crucial among Bahian musicians is social capital, contacts in the Scenes who can, among other things, help create conditions of possibility for paid musical work.

Many of the issues, conditions, and related actions I examine through practice theory are relevant to any number of locations — the importance of capitals is a standout, if somewhat obvious, example.[16] Related matters such as wage stagnation linked to an overabundance of capable workers in competition for limited jobs are, similarly, likely familiar to both scholars and members of many workforces. Also notable in a large and increasing number of contexts are the informal, precarious conditions of employment navigated by the majority of people I met who live from music.

While these concerns are not unique to Salvador, their local specificities intensify their importance both materially and conceptually. This becomes apparent if one considers the recent surge in public interest and scholarly debate on topics such as "the gig economy," "portfolio careers," flexible labor, and post-Fordism,[17] as well as new analytics such as "precarity" utilized by researchers to address their impact on workers. These important critiques should also be seen as responses to changes in what were once fairly conventional and reliable labor sectors. Indeed, that these "new" conditions are hardly novel to musicians is suggested by the fact that much of the language describing them, for example "gig" and even Richard Florida's (2012) application of "creativity" for knowledge economy workers, betrays links to musical work.

Such occlusions suggest other blind spots addressed in this study as well. Anthropologist Kathleen Millar (2014, 34) astutely notes that critical discussions of changing labor paradigms and their effects really took hold apropos of "post-industrial societies of Europe, North America, and Japan—places where Fordism was strongest in the twentieth century and which therefore have been most affected by its unraveling." Her point is that temporary and informal labor has long been disturbingly prevalent in the Global South—and not just among musicians. Cultural geographer Oli Mould (2018) contributes to this intervention "at home" with a biting critique of Florida's work and the correct observation that the benefits of "creativity" as an emblem of entrepreneurial savvy and a path to middle-class lifestyles are less available to those already marginalized by race, gender, disability, or current socioeconomic status. As portended by such writing, then, much of the increased attention to purportedly novel notions such as creativity, post-Fordism, and precarity risks either leapfrogging over or ignoring through normalization the long-standing precarious labor conditions that permeate the Global South,[18] the volatility endemic to professional music making, and many obstacles encountered by variously othered workers, all of which continue, even accelerate, in the global march of neoliberal capitalism.

Living from Music in Salvador aims to avoid such oversights by homing in on everyday musical work activities that might otherwise seem quite familiar and even common sense among people whose profession and racialized location limits their access to the rewards of being part of the so-called creative class.

It also localizes issues that are increasingly of global concern. Perhaps most saliently, precarious labor conditions, both old and new, contribute to jarringly stark disparities in quality of life among Salvador's residents. Such stratification is not only firmly entrenched, but it is inseparable from and continues to provide palpable evidence of the sediments of colonialism, the trans-Atlantic slave trade, and the plantation system. These dubious legacies, which manifest very visibly in articulations of "race" and "class," are profoundly entangled with local musical sensibilities in ways that inform and are informed by the practices of working musicians.

The local particularity of broadly shared concerns is, likewise, evident in many of the dominant "strategies" (De Certeau 1984) that structure the Scenes and that are, themselves, entangled with racialized and classed notions of music. This is especially apparent in local discourse about genre as well as in several conventions in Salvador's music industries such as shifting and differentiated involvement during an annual cycle of music participation. I introduce the genres most central to Bahian musicians' careers, typical discourse about them, and a number of implications related to the forms of capital as well as where and when musical work is done in the next chapter. This discussion then carries over into chapter 2, which looks closely at the processes and politics of the flexible, collaborative formations in which musicians do such work (e.g., Carnaval production companies, event venues, "bands"). My application of practice theory in these two chapters emphasizes De Certeau's notion of "tactics" for "making do" with dominant "strategies" as well as unintended consequences such as the reification of extant power relations, an undertheorized aspect of his exploration of agency.[19]

As the familiarity of some of the above suggests, a number of the local strategies and tactics discussed throughout the book resonate with issues addressed in foundational literature that has considered music making as labor. For example, flexibility in relation to employment conditions and, to varying degrees, musical versatility among performers who are, for the most part, unknown beyond their professional milieus underpins studies by sociologists Robert Faulkner (1971), H. Stith Bennett (1980), and Jon Frederickson and James Rooney (1993); economist Ruth Towse (1993); economic historian Cyril Ehrlich (1986); musicologist Katherine Preston (1988); and ethnomusicologists Bruce MacLeod (1993) and Steven Cottrell (2004, 2007). A fair number of these have focused on "classical music," perhaps in an effort to counter the tenacious traction of the ideology of autonomous art. A welcome recent contribution to this discussion is Marianna Ritchey's (2019) monograph, which adroitly analyzes the practices of several twenty-first-century American classical music makers (primarily composers and production-oriented entities) and their various entanglements with neoliberalism, as evidenced by, for instance, their overt embrace of market objectives and corporate sponsorship as well their adherence and valorization of "the dogma of flexibility" (76). Like Ritchey's work, finally, a significant portion of the extant research on music and labor has been based in the U.S. or Europe,[20] settings very different from Bahia, which is marked by entrenched precarity across labor sectors compounded by particular sedimented constructions of racialized social inequity that impinge profoundly on the practices and politics of music.

Certainly, critical engagements with issues entangled with the particularities of "cultural context" are the norm in ethnomusicology. Yet many genre histories, studies of notable performers, and ethnographies of non-Western (and popular) musics tend to treat as a given the fact that the musicians involved are professionals. Standing apart from such studies are a growing number of monographs (e.g., Baily 1988, Miller 2010, Requião 2010, Perullo 2011, Stahl 2012, Weaver Shipley 2013, Guilbault and Cape 2014, Hitchens 2014, Abé 2018, Whitmore 2020, Bellaviti 2020) that delve more fully into issues attendant to musicians' labor and thus intersect with several of my central concerns.[21] These include money, prestige, industry, race, professional networks, genre politics, and precarious employment, among others. Within this literature, ethnomusicologists Louise Meintjes's (2003) study of the production of *mbquanga* recordings in South Africa and Eliot Bates's (2016) ethnography of Turkish recording studio production resonate especially strongly with *Living from Music in Salvador* in their close attention to everyday music-making practices, albeit in recording studios rather than in the wide range of activities that comprise most musicians' careers. Their research is, further, a welcome complement to the large and ever-increasing number of music industry studies, which often, albeit understandably, limit or eschew detailed engagement with the work of musical performers in order to provide more overarching accounts and/or increased attention to perspectives of other kinds of musical workers whose labor is also central to the operations of recording companies,[22] which are often and erroneously assumed to be one and the same with "the music industry" (see Williamson and Cloonan 2007). That said, my up-close focus on multiple aspects of musicians' work within Salvador's multifaceted music *industries* is, likewise, interested in the politics and implications of genre that is often foregrounded in these studies.[23]

Similarly resonant with most contexts for musical labor addressed in prior research is the fact that the vast majority of instrumentalists, backing performers, and, therefore, musicians who live from music in Salvador are men. Thus, their voices are most prominent in my discussion. On the other hand, there are plenty of female musicians visible in the Scenes primarily as lead and background vocalists. Exceptions exist, such as the prominent *bloco afro*, Banda Femina Didá (see Haas 2010), which is comprised entirely of (Afro-descendant) women who play drums behind singers and dancers. Daniela Mercury employed a female dancer-percussionist who I saw working around 2005, and in 2014 I became aware of an all-female *samba de roda* group in which women handled all of the plucked strings and percussion. Yet in the rest of my many musical experiences in Bahia, I encountered only one other woman who supported herself as an instrumentalist in popular music, keyboardist and musical director Kadija Teles. Notable is that Kadija, presumably like one or more women in Didá and the *samba de roda* group as well as many other female musicians in Salvador, leads ensembles. In most instances, further, ensemble leadership was their primary basis of income rather than work as side musicians, especially when they were instrumentalists. This clearly suggests that certain avenues of labor are less available to women. On the other hand, the accomplishments of the female professionals I met illustrate their tactical ability to carve out careers despite habituated exclusions akin to those detailed in studies focused on female professional musicians (e.g., van Nieuwkerk 1995, Tucker 2000; in Brazil, Santanna 2009, Requião 2019).[24] The experiences of two female singers are presented variously throughout the book but, along with perspectives from several others, become especially important in chapter 2's discussion of ensemble leaders working to secure paid employment for their enterprise—yet another aspect of musical labor that is often unseen by audiences and many scholars.

Admittedly, my interest in and approach to these topics emerges from my history as a drummer in Los Angeles. There I connected with others who, like me, defined themselves as *professional* musicians. I also noticed that they called making music "working" and not "playing," as I had always done. Looking back, conversations in the LA scenes about who could and could not perform certain kinds of music "authentically" were also a starting point for thinking about the implications for music and musicians of what ethnomusicologists Ronald Radano and Philip Bohlman (2000, 5) have theorized as the "racial imagination . . . the shifting matrix of ideological constructions of difference associated with body type and color that have emerged as part of the discourse network of modernity." I brought this background with me to Salvador, which had become increasingly appealing as a research site following years of performing *bossa novas* in jazz bars and then becoming aware of, and developing an affinity for, the sounds and histories of the *blocos afro* and *axé* music after my turn to ethnomusicology.

My first trip to Bahia left me convinced about the perspectives that could be developed exploring small-scale, economically oriented aspects of music making there. Subsequent fieldwork reinforced for me how success, even survival, as a musical worker requires specialized and, frequently, locally specific skills, including many that are not obviously musical. This resonates with Bourdieu's writing on literature and art in which he asserts that their meanings and value are inseparable from the conditions of their production, the circumstances navigated by producers, and the producers themselves. Situating art objects analytically on par with attendant practices, he writes: "*position takings* . . . including literary or artistic works, obviously, but also political acts and discourses, manifestos or polemics, etc." correspond "to different positions, which, in a universe as little institutionalized as the literary or artistic field, can only be appreciated through the properties of their occupants" (1992, 231, emphasis in original). In other words, the sounds professional musicians make, the things they do to create them and live, and the meanings of all of their practices are inseparable from the specifics of their work, the settings in which it is done, and who they are.

In terms of making sense of Bahian musicians' professional practices and productions, my analysis of "properties" addresses various issues related to economics including class position, but as overarched by particular ideas about human difference based on inherited phenotypical characteristics, that is, "race." This articulation was driven by constant references to Salvador as Brazil's most African city and various other monikers (including my pun in the book's title) that speak to its racial past and present,[25] as well as "political processes of the construction of 'Black Bahia,' which today appears to 'naturally' define the identity of the state" (Teles dos Santos 2005, 22, my translation). Crucially, the construction to which Teles refers is supported by hard data, history, and experience. According to Brazil's 2010 census, 79.5 percent of Salvador's population self-identified as "Black" or "Brown" (IBGE 2010).[26] The city was also a center for the importation of enslaved African laborers, many of whom worked nearby plantations; and Afro-diasporic culture permeates everyday life and drives the tourism economy.

As I discuss below, however, this history and its presence can be contentious for a variety of reasons. Among them is that the very notion of "race" is especially vexed in Brazil owing to the ways that intellectuals, politicians, and Brazilians have wrestled with its meanings since the colonial encounter. Despite the problematics of "race," a crucial point for this study is that *baianos* repeatedly asserted linkages between specific groups of people and musical practices and proclivities in a manner akin to the homologies that are central to Bourdieu's theorizing. Whereas his primary concern was class, these linkages in Bahia have an unmistakable racial component even if the term itself, *raça*, is infrequently invoked.

The Brazilian census cited above provides some clarity on this omission. Instead of referring to race explicitly, *baianos*, like most other Brazilians, utilize an elaborate language of color (*cor*) to describe groups and individuals, others, and themselves.[27] They do so freely and in a manner akin to how North Americans discuss hair and eye color, but ostensibly in reference to skin tone. While such matter of fact-ness might register to some as evidence of "raceless-ness," processes of social stratification still track patterns rooted in phenotype and established by Brazil's *racial* history. What is more, even as the language of color deviates in some ways from typical discourses and attendant politics of race in places such as North America and Europe, it shows many similarities as well. I pursue this below, but for now it is important to state that hereditary physical characteristics, (racialized) understandings of cultural heritage, and notions of class based on economic, social, and racially rooted constructions of cultural capital are of great importance to a great many people in Salvador, shaping and being shaped by the practices of everyday life and living from music.[28]

The depth, breadth, and impact of the entanglements between music, race, and capital I noted eventually pushed me to think beyond the racial imagination toward what critical race theorist David Theo Goldberg deems "racial conception." Goldberg (2008, 4) writes:

> Racial conception, or what some such as Anthony Appiah have called racialism, is the view that groups of people are marked by certain generalizable visible and heritable traits. These generalized traits may be physical or psychological, cultural or culturally inscribed on the body, and the physical and psychological, bodily and cultural traits are usually thought somehow indelibly connected. Thus racialists more often than not think that racial group members share not only these traits but also behavioral dispositions and tendencies to think in certain ways those not so marked do not share.

In addition to his descriptive definition, his use of the term "conception" provocatively evokes how ideas about inherited phenotypical traits and their significance, whether given voice through the language of race or not, are in no way exterior to most *baianos'* social thinking, action, and interaction. Rather, they are a basis for them.

Importantly, for Goldberg, racial conception is multivalent and not one and the same with racism, which he characterizes as the belief that "racial difference warrants exclusion of those so characterized from elevation into the realm of protection, privilege, property, or profit" (2008, 5). Certainly, I saw racial conception emerge as overt racism in the form of, say, aggressive exclusions and verbal bigotry. And if I did not see it myself, friends and interlocutors shared their own troubling experiences. More often, though, I noted how racial conception informed subtler racist actions, for instance offhand comments and thinly veiled assertions of superiority that left little doubt about their genesis. On the other hand, racial conception was also evident in how *baianos* discussed themselves and each other in assertions of regional identity and pride as well as claims of musical authority and authenticity. Regardless of setting, outcome, or intent, it was abundantly clear on a daily basis that ideas about phenotypical similarities and differences along with related homologies of character, position, and practice were powerful social forces in the capital of Afro Brazil.

A CONFLUENCE OF CONCEPTIONS, IMAGININGS, AND ISSUES

Local discourse and widely circulated representations of Bahia, its residents, and its culture are difficult to separate from lingering racially conceived stereotypes, in particular, the durable belief that *baianos* are less than assiduous. The prominence of music and other forms of entertainment therein abets such misunderstanding, shifting attention and imaginings away from the many residents of Salvador who are employed in conventional sectors such as petroleum, finance, healthcare, manufacturing, retail/service (both formal and informal), and agriculture. Such material also conceals the fact that, as Ed the tour guide noted, those who work in entertainment, including musicians, work hard.

The ongoing stereotyping of Bahia and *baianos* owes a great deal to exterior forces, people, and practices. I have been told on numerous occasions in the U.S., Canada, and in cities such as Rio and São Paulo that people in Bahia do not work.[29] But detrimental imaginings also emerge from within and not necessarily out of malicious intent. Unintended consequences of musicians' career tactics are a concern throughout the book, but the risks of ostensibly tactical representations are well illustrated by a tourist trinket I was given by a Bahian friend. Almost certainly offered to me ironically—my friend is a physician, a professor of medicine, and an accomplished musician who rarely stops working—the mini t-shirt bearing the "Bahian 10 Commandments" nevertheless speaks volumes about how Bahia is imagined, how such imaginings are used to appeal to tourists, and how such tactics might go awry:

THE BAHIAN 10 COMMANDMENTS

(my translation)

1. Live to rest.
2. If you see someone resting, help him/her.
3. Love your bed. It's your temple.
4. Work is sacred. Don't touch it.
5. Love your work. Spend hours looking at it.
6. Rest by day for the strength to sleep at night.
7. Eat, sleep, and when you wake, rest.
8. Don't forget, work is health. Save it for the sick.
9. When you feel the urge to work, sit and wait. It will pass.
10. Never do tomorrow what you can do the day after tomorrow.

As a self-representation, these commandments exemplify the playful good humor for which Bahia is widely recognized—marketing material often calls it "*a terra de alegria*" (the land of happiness). They also speak to the relaxed approach many *baianos* take to certain aspects of their lives, another feature that can appeal to those looking for a vacation. This tempo, however, can also frustrate visitors and some locals, who cast it as evidence of backwardness or lack of a serious work ethic. Much as the city's laid-back and cheery atmosphere is both an effective marketing tactic and a target for condemnation, words and images portraying smiling, musicking *baianos* can have troubling consequences regardless of their intent or economic expedience. Moreover, in a place marked by striking inequality, questions remain about who speaks for *baianos*, who benefits, and at whose expense.

It was clear on many occasions that social positions were negotiated through less ironic discourse about local lifestyles, especially proclivities for leisure activities. For instance, members of the middle and upper classes often cast aspersions on the less affluent majority, the *povo* (the people), if they saw "them" socializing in a public space: "*they* are partying when they should be working" or "*those people* should be resting so they can work tomorrow."[30] Sentiments such as these were also evident when more affluent *baianos* discussed manual laborers, service industry workers, and their own domestic employees who, by the way, typically work long hours, six days per week. As one of many possible examples, a well-to-do woman from whom I rented a room said to me more than once, usually after she had fired yet another housekeeper, "they only care about money and samba!" Disturbing as such statements are in terms of class alone, they are all the more unsettling in light of Bahia's metonymy with Blackness and Brazil's location in the Global South. It is but a small step to concede that many references to pleasure-seeking, labor-avoiding *baianos* who readily sing and dance are conceived in enduring notions of layabout, naturally musical Black bodies.

Yet, some of these ideas can be hard to dispute. As I noted above, the majority of Salvador's population is visibly of (sub-Saharan) African descent.[31] Likewise, in keeping with tourist material, history books, and imaginings of Bahia, manifestations of Afro-diasporic expressive culture are everywhere in Salvador and its surrounding areas. Further affirming the happiness, relaxation, and party narrative that is so commodifiable is that, along with abundant hospitality and numerous festive events, I saw daily how Salvador is rich with *baianos* who dance and make music with remarkable facility.

Yet as several of my friends who identified as members of the *povo* told me, their smiles, laughter, and parties help keep them from crying. Bahia continues to suffer the ills of economic marginalization and inequality. Although I have noticed improvements in, for instance, infrastructure, the local jobless rate consistently exceeds the national average,[32] and many of the employed struggle to make ends meet with the wages they earn. Several of my closest collaborators confided to me that very little of the economic prosperity generated in Brazil early in the new millennium found its way to them, their families, or the majority in their circles. They also made it clear that subsequent economic decline and political scandals, including the divisive impeachment of President Dilma Rouseff in 2016, hit poorer, and darker-skinned Bahians particularly hard.

Thus, many *baianos* continue to lack adequate income and housing. People living on the streets are common, and many more live in slums referred to as *invasões* (invasions). Marked by exposed brick, do-it-yourself homes, and crumbling infrastructure,[33] *invasões* and slightly more affluent "popular neighborhoods" are occupied primarily by people with darker skin. Such living conditions likely contribute to stereotypes about Bahian attitudes toward work, since cramped homes in such areas — as well as a tradition of children living with their parents until marriage — leads many residents to "*ficar na rua*" (spend time on the street). Although understandable and usually innocuous, this can invite indictments of *baianos*', and especially *afro-baianos*' work habits.

The dangers of perpetuating such imaginings are pungently evident in a statement made by then candidate and, subsequently, president of Brazil, Jair Bolsonaro in 2018:

> I went to visit a *quilombo* [a settlement founded by the descendants of runaway slaves]. The lightest afrodescendant there weighed seven *arrobas* [more than 100 kg]. They don't do anything. I don't think they're even good for procreating anymore.[34]

That language such as this would be used by someone who would be elected president by a clear majority highlights the alarming potential for the misappropriation of otherwise tactical self-representations as well as everyday practices that are not only logical, but often necessary. Bolsonaro's vulgarity also indicates that much has deteriorated since my most concentrated and extended periods of fieldwork during the left-leaning presidency of Luis Inácio "Lula" da Silva (2003–2011). Lula's administration, which encompasses the analytical focus of the book, saw many societal reforms, economic ascendency, and a related sense of optimism among plenty of *baianos* in light of the many challenges that remained. Things turned markedly for the worse early into the term of his hand-picked successor, Rouseff, and, for a majority of my collaborators, have continued to deteriorate, putting increased pressure on their tactics, any long-term risks of which seem to be outweighed by short-term survival needs.

Like many *baianos*, musicians also face a double bind with respect to common tactics and unintended consequences. Despite ideologies that they should not work and the artistic and economic efficacy of narratives that they do not work, music makers often find themselves condemned as second rate or lazy if they cannot justify what they do with financial success. Compounding misunderstandings is that professional performers spend a great deal of time "working to work," that is, engaged in pursuits that do not look like labor or in some cases, music, but that are crucial to their careers. As cultural studies scholar Melissa Gregg (2011) has noted, such blurring of work and "leisure" activities is becoming increasingly endemic to how people in numerous sectors labor, in many instances increasing precarity and abetting abuses since such practices look, and often are, fun. And yet again, while somewhat new and understandably unsettling among white-collar professionals in the Global North, activities that look like leisure and can be pleasurable are and have always been the stuff of living from music, are often misappropriated to damaging ends, and are, as such, a central focus of my analysis.

RACE, CLASS, AND MUSIC IN BAHIA

As I have been suggesting, mappings of musicians' attitudes toward work compounded by racial conception as a basis of thinking and action in Bahia raise the stakes for mischaracterizations and misunderstandings of Salvador's musicians. The debates that gave rise to this racial epistemology have a long and broad history that is addressed in a vast literature, much of which resonates with my experiences.[35] Thus a brief overview of central issues discussed therein should suffice to frame life and musical work in Salvador as I came to understand it.

At the fore of many scholars' concern is the obfuscation and related perpetuation of racially rooted inequities through two durable and entangled discourses: *mestiçagem* (racial and cultural mixing) and subsequently *democracia racial* (racial democracy). Processes of *mestiçagem* have been prevalent in Brazil since the colonial period, with contestations over meanings and related politics raging for just as long. While there have been several shifts in how mixing has been interpreted, its implications remain quite consistent especially for people othered by phenotype.

Mixing among different peoples and cultures was initially seen as a problem, likened to contamination by Brazilian elites who looked to Europe as the benchmark for human worth and cultural value. A solution to this "problem" was offered by nineteenth-century nationalist intellectuals, who postulated that continued intermingling between Indigenous-, African-, and European-descended peoples would eventually eliminate the traces of "inferior" races thanks to the purported superiority of European blood and culture. Yet by its own logic, this idea, *branqueamento* (whitening), was limited in its ability to legitimize an extensively mixed emerging nation since an imagined European *purity* stood as its gold standard. Thus, *branqueamento* would ultimately be displaced, but not erased, in the first third of the twentieth century through overt efforts to valorize hybridity in and of itself.

Most famously Brazilian anthropologist Gilberto Freyre set the tone for enduring notions of *mestiçagem* and paved the way for a discourse of racial democracy to follow with the 1933 publication of *Casa Grande e Senzala* (in English, *The Masters and the Slaves*). Against aspirations to whiten Brazil, Freyre championed the idea that the blend of "the three races" was not a problem to be solved through purification but instead a source of uniqueness and strength for a new Brazilian "race." His argument and its subsequent applications put tremendous stock in the belief in intimate reciprocity between "the masters and the slaves."

Yet the underlying ideology behind *branqueamento* is plain to see in Freyre's (1933, 80) characterization:

> Hybrid from the beginning, Brazilian society is, of all those in the Americas, the one most harmoniously constituted so far as racial relations are concerned, within the environment of a practical cultural reciprocity that results in the advanced people deriving the maximum profit from the values and experiences of the backward ones, and in a maximum of conformity between the foreign and the native cultures, that of the conqueror and the conquered.

While not using the term "racial democracy," Freyre's language clearly alludes to the sentiment even as he betrays stark Eurocentrism. History bears out that his rose-tinted perspective would feed a powerful national narrative that Brazil has no racism. This notion of racial democracy is buttressed by color discourse, which, in addition to sidestepping the language of race, provides a sense that free and open discussions of phenotypical difference reference nothing more than skin-deep variations within a society, a race, unified by its mixed-ness.

Racial democracy has repeatedly been challenged—it is now commonly referred to as a myth—yet it continues to shape interactions on a daily basis. Furthermore, mixing *is* common and a point of pride for most people with whom I spoke. The key is that despite the overt embrace of *mestiçagem* in theory and in practice, and even among many people who were skeptical of racial democracy as *fait accompli*—not everyone was—I saw repeatedly that not all mixtures were valued equally. Instead, those that were seen as more "White" have continued to occupy privileged positions. Even referring to a person with a term "too dark" for their sense of self can be an affront.[36] Digging deeper and especially speaking with *baianos* who identify/are identified as Black(er)—and more recently, as *afro-descendentes* (African descendants)—left little doubt that, despite widespread mixing and pervasive use of a spectrum of color identification spanning from "*branco*" (White) to "*preto*" (Black) with hundreds of variations between, a racially conceived binary, "White/nonwhite," is still very much in play.[37]

Brazilianist Christopher Dunn (2007) has noted this duality, productively bringing it to bear on the particularities of Bahia by arguing that *baianidade* (Bahian-ness) accommodates both *mestiçagem* and a Black/White binary. This is especially significant because it allows for Bahia's fit within the Brazilian nationalist ideal of one Brazilian Race as well as its singularity (and I would add, marketability) as the capital of *Afro*-Brazil. It also simultaneously incorporates and occludes Indigeneity, yielding a notion of identity that glosses the marginalization of numerous darker-skinned *baianos* while also telling them that they belong, indeed, are vital to their nation-state, their city and state, and, in the case of those visibly of African descent, the local economy.[38]

This duality, the racial conception that underpins it, and the ambivalent implications of both are unmistakable features of music discourse. I met plenty of musicians, many of whom self-identified as "*negro*" (Black), "*pardo*" (Brown), "Black" (in English), or another of many terms used to indicate nonwhite identity, who told me that music was "in their blood." I have no doubt that theirs were statements of identity affirmation, cultural pride, and musical authority. Yet their references to "natural" musicality in a place so thoroughly defined by its African-ness risks supporting the belief that developing the skill to perform music, especially certain kinds of music, does not require work.

Most perilously, Bahian music was regularly described as "*mais afro*" (more African, and notably, not more Black).[39] It was also most frequently associated with natural musicality by musicians and nonmusicians alike—and usually not in positive terms. Bahian music was regularly cast as simplistic and its participants uncultivated. Such moments were also where *mestiçagem* and the duality of *baianidade* enabled obliviousness to racist logic and in some instances cover for outright racism. This is because most *baianos* can truthfully claim at least some African blood even if their appearance provides benefits of Whiteness. Thus, on several occasions I heard phenotypically privileged (i.e., "Whiter") people mention a Black relative when claiming their *baianidade*, asserting their authority with respect to Afro-Bahian culture, or denying racism. As such, even negative commentary about Bahian music and musicians, which was frequent, could be cast as self-critique aimed at betterment even as racial bias lurked just below the surface. Regardless of intent, much of the language surrounding Bahian music, be it tactical or strategic, also reified problematic, racialized stereotypes of Bahian musicians and Bahia itself. I explore this issue in chapter 3 through a discussion of musicians' narrative position taking as part of their tactical working to work.

It is difficult to deny that one of the most significant factors informing daily life and musical work in Salvador is lingering Eurocentrism alongside and often recalibrated through local pride in *mestiçagem* and assertions of or aspirations to *democracia racial*, a cultural politics Goldberg (2008, 217–18) distinguishes as "Euro-mimesis." Indeed, despite abundant rhetoric that might suggest some degree of racial parity, the most cursory investigation reveals that in "Black Rome" a disproportionate number of fair-skinned people hold positions of power while the lowest-paying jobs, the poorest neighborhoods, and the ranks of the unemployed are conspicuously dominated by those whose bodies leave little doubt about their African heredity. When grave social concerns are chalked up to economic inequality, little acknowledgment is paid, especially by Whiter elites, to the racial history that gave rise to it. Entangled with the maintenance of social and economic stratification held over from colonization and the slave era is a hegemonic Euro-mimetic cultural hierarchy in which music is deeply implicated.

In fact, music often showcases many of the points that *mestiçagem* and racial democracy apologists deploy to support their claims. Bands regularly feature a range of phenotypes and several stars, mostly men, have dark skin. Carlinhos Brown, Gilberto Gil, and Margareth Menezes (and the ensembles that back them) are three notable examples. More broadly, congenial relations between people of different colors are the norm and economic prosperity, high levels of education, and accomplishment in white-collar professions have all been achieved by a substantial number of nonwhite people. There are also plenty of impoverished people who look White(r).

Slippage and exceptions within an otherwise predictably racialized color hierarchy combined with entrenched, acknowledged, and often embraced economic stratification informs aggressive performances of class position, including numerous instances of conspicuous consumption. For instance, expensive imported whisky—Johnnie Walker was a favorite among those who could afford it—was commonly brought in the bottle and on a tray to purchasers' tables to be poured in ceremonial fashion. Doing so signaled to all present the *poder aquisitivo* (purchasing power) and "good taste" of the patron—their economic and cultural capital. I also saw ample evidence of cultural capital deployed through what Brazilian linguist Marcos Bagno (2002) calls "linguistic prejudice"—discrimination against those whose inability to speak "proper" Portuguese marked them as uneducated, poor, and thus inferior. Class policing was sometimes subtly apparent—a dismissive look or passing comment—but at other times it was disturbingly blatant—skipping ahead in a line of presumed subordinates or overt lack of attention from waiters or sales staff when a patron was assumed to be less affluent. While such incidents occasionally occurred between individuals of similar phenotypes, it was apparent—and confirmed by several interlocutors— that this type of behavior was much more common when the recipient mapped as more African than the transgressor. While a dark-skinned person can receive respectful treatment, those who map as Black(er) are more frequently burdened with having to demonstrate their deservedness through displays of their "class." Performances of *poder aquisitivo*, relationships with powerful people, education, linguistic skill, and "good" taste in matters of culture, especially music—in other words, economic, social, and cultural capital—were front and center in numerous daily interactions even crosscutting color identifications, albeit only to a point.

The limits of accumulated capital were evident to numerous *baianos* who told me that, regardless of money, connections, and accomplishments, life in Salvador is just easier if you have fairer skin (or straighter hair, light-colored eyes, a narrower nose, or thinner lips). Building upon Goldberg's (2002, 206) assertion that in Brazil "race becomes not so much reduced to class as rearticulated through it," a central concern of the book is exploring how notions and materialities of race and class are (re)articulated through musical practices in commercially driven contexts, to what effects, and for whom, even as race qua race is denied in assertions of racial democracy and occluded through discourses of *mesticagem* and *baianidade*. Indeed, I would go as far as to assert that hierarchical understandings of the latter two notions that privilege higher proportions of phenotypical, discursive, and musical "Whiteness" describe a hegemonic commonality across social positions and related differences in *baianos*' habituses.[40]

With this stratified understanding of foundational tenets of Brazilian and Bahian identity, the discontents typically associated with mixing that is "too African" resonate compellingly with anthropologist Michael Hertzfeld's notion of cultural intimacy. He defines his concept as "the recognition of those aspects of cultural identity that are considered a source of external embarrassment but that nevertheless provide insiders with their assurance of common sociality" (2005, 3). The culturally intimate, specifically the place of African-ness in the Bahian racial and cultural mix, permeates the meanings and sensibilities that bind *baianos* together on one hand and foment divisions among them on the other.

Although Hertzfeld's mention of recognition suggests reflexivity, discourse, and knowledge, I would counter that in Salvador, particular dispositions rooted in racial conception articulated with Euro-mimetic notions of class have become naturalized, embodied, and action shaping in a manner suggestive of the nonreflexiveness implied by habitus.[41] On the other hand, and as a nod to the importance of Michel Foucault's notion of discourse as "practices which systematically form the objects of which they speak" (1972, 49), practice at the intersection of habitus, capital, and field should not be assumed to be a one-way process. Rather, the meanings, politics, and embodied dispositions that inform music participants' actions, the value of different capitals, and the structure of the field are also shaped by the practices of professional musicians. Chief among them are the ways they make do with the cultural intimacy of *baianidade* through the sounds they make. This is the focus of chapter 5, which examines the most public (and profitable) aspects of doing musical work in Salvador, live performance.

SITUATING AN ANALYSIS OF MUSICAL WORK

I developed my general understanding of Salvador's popular music scenes by attending multiple performances and, beginning with my second field stay in 2003, attending rehearsals and participating to varying degrees in the daily lives of several collaborators. Though my attention remained focused primarily on professional performers, conversations with amateur musicians and members of a broadly construed audience (see below) have been vital for contextualizing work conditions and practices I observed and that local pros described during informal conversations and in formal interviews. To round out the picture, I also formally and informally interviewed other types of musical workers such as venue owners, producers, engineers, managers, and crew members. The perspectives I developed in these ways can be cautiously taken as representative of the Scenes.

On the other hand, much of what I came to understand is based on a particular subset of musical workers who were part of a network loosely centered around the person who would become my closest collaborator, Jorge "Farofa" (Jorge Luis dos Santos Boa Morte),[42] a percussionist who self-identifies as "Black" (in English) and a member of the *povo*. As a result of this and the timing of my most extended fieldwork, people I met who were involved with a project called Banda Patua that occupied much of Farofa's energy in 2004 and 2005 figure prominently in what follows. Among them are guitarist/composer and now ethnomusicologist Luciano Caroso, bassist and now professor of music theory Son Melo, singer Josehr Santos, drummer "Pastel" (Paulo Reis), and guitarist "Ximbinha" Mamede. Like most professional musicians I encountered, Farofa's income has depended on working with multiple ensembles and solo artists even when he has one project that is relatively consistent. A few of these more sporadic employers and coworkers became close collaborators for me as well. They include singer-bandleaders Márcia Castro and especially Laurinha Arantes, the latter of whom I have been able to maintain close contact with since we met in 2005. Both musicians facilitated meeting still more working players who became central to my research. For example, by attending Laurinha's rehearsals, performances, recording sessions, and after work hangouts, I developed a close relationship with percussionist and later, drummer, Junior Oliveira. Junior then introduced me to the musicians involved with the various projects in which he worked. This pattern repeated variously and thus my network grew. As a result of the varying degrees of connection evident in this process, a certain sharing of perspectives on music and life was evident, though they were not by any means uniform, and disagreement and debates certainly occurred.

I also encountered somewhat different viewpoints and practices thanks to connections I made parallel to those nurtured through Farofa and his peers. I met close collaborators, drummer Edni Devay and vocalist/guitarist Jorge Elaíde Gois, through nonmusician friends. Edni and I struck up a long-term friendship, and he introduced me to members of his *axé* band and a number of other colleagues, providing a key point of entry into the *axé* scene. Jorge, on the other hand, was a fixture in numerous local bars and clubs, supporting himself almost exclusively by providing music to accompany drinking and dancing. Edni and Jorge never worked together, and neither worked with Farofa. Still, their professional networks overlapped a great deal. I found this to be rather typical and indicative of the permeability of scene borders. Time and again, musicians I met shared mutual friends, colleagues, and work experiences; and few of the busier musicians in town were unbeknownst to most others. Such crossover facilitated commonalities of certain attitudes and perspectives despite frequent differences in age, color identification, socioeconomic background, and musical training both within the same ensemble and across broader professional networks. On the other hand, the differences expressed by musicians united by the fact that they all lived from music—in a sense, comprising a generation of fairly established musicians—helped me map the Scenes' contours and borders and understand the contestations within.

Methodologically, my fieldwork practice, and my representation of it, mirrors processes that a musician working in a scene would follow: through active efforts to meet people as well as chance encounters, I was able to connect with key people who were then willing to help me further my professional aims. In other words, my own social capital was vital to my fieldwork. The process was certainly dependent on the goodwill of the musicians I met and often affinities that enabled us to become friends. However, given Salvador's racial politics and the gendering of the Scenes, my identity, especially the fact that I map as a White male, facilitated a great deal. Other types of capital that I might have had or was thought to be able to provide also helped and were illuminating. For example, I was introduced on several occasions as a drummer from the U.S., suggesting the cachet an association with an international musician might hold. Some performers I met asked me about booking performances in the U.S. and, after my move, Canada; and many asked me to help them purchase instruments and other items that are hard to come by in Brazil (which I did whenever possible). As such, my collaborators were anything but random, and I cannot claim a "holistic" perspective as implied in studies based on a wide pool of interview and survey data (e.g., Faulkner 1974, Hesmondhalgh and Baker 2011). However, in addition to giving me a taste of, and in some instances implicating me in, networking processes in the Scenes, I was able to participate in aspects of musicians' work such as otherwise closed rehearsals, meetings, and recording sessions that aiming for a large "representative" sample would not.

Perhaps most valuable among all of these opportunities was riding to and from these events. Winding through the streets of Salvador and occasionally on the highway between the capital and other cities, I was able to speak at length with one or more of the musicians who I would soon see or had just seen work. Though I conducted over forty-five formal interviews both with close collaborators and many other musical workers with whom my relationship was more distant, much of my most useful understanding came from various types of informal (and not recorded) conversations in cars, buses, backstage, in studios, and over drinks and meals. Representationally, I lean on recounting such moments rather than on an abundance of extended quotations. Conducting interviews, indexing the recordings, and transcribing collaborators' words, nevertheless, proved to be a useful means of learning about the lives and labors of musical workers, especially, but not only, those more distant from me. But this was only a small part of a much larger picture. On the other hand, excerpts of formal interviews are presented in several instances when what was said and recorded is particularly illuminating.

Researching (with) Professional Makers of Popular Music

Flexibility, an increasingly prominent aspect of capitalism worldwide, is a central theme throughout the book owing to the employment strategies dominant in Salvador's music industries and musicians' tactics for navigating them. As such, I use the term to refer not only to the fact that musicians are archetypal flexible laborers—they are hired as needed without contracts and with little guarantee of future employment—but also with respect to the multiplicity of jobs, roles, and skills they must cultivate in order to survive in such an unstable context and that, in some instances, contributes to their precarity (see Requião 2016, Ritchey 2019). Musical flexibility in terms of genre versatility and the ability to work under varied conditions with different people, a topic frequently mentioned in the literature (e.g., Faulkner 1971; Preston 1992; MacLeod 1993; and especially Cottrell 2004, 2007, and Ritchey 2019), was especially crucial in the Scenes. Over the years, numerous performers at various levels characterized their careers with some form of the statement "*temos que tocar tudo*" (we have to play everything). Their claims were repeatedly borne out in practice. As one example, I have watched bassist Son Melo work with multiple artists, live and in the studio, performing music ranging from samba to rock, and we discussed his musical activities in even more diverse settings. Because of his instrument, exceptional abilities, and calm demeanor Son was perhaps more flexible than some local musicians. But nearly all of them spoke about and demonstrated some degree of flexibility in terms of musical abilities and employment.

It was also abundantly clear that musical flexibility among Bahian musicians (and audiences), however prevalent, was not limitless, unconditional, or in-discriminate. Thus, while attention to multiplicity of participation is definitive of this study, it is necessarily situated against the boundaries that musicians in particular observe. As I discuss, the extent to which a performer "played everything" was sometimes a matter of their ability; but in nearly all cases the relationship between flexibility and constraint in their careers was inseparable from the at times contradictory implications of economic, social, and especially, cultural capital. A framework for understanding these tensions is provided in the next chapter, where I introduce the primary genres heard in the Scenes, their associated meanings, and how they relate to conditions of musical labor including venue type, pay, and prestige.

My focus on flexible musical participation, while necessary and illuminating, also created practical difficulties. Equal attention to all genres and related work spaces in the Scenes was simply not possible. In terms of coverage, however, following the "pathways" (Finnegan 1989) by which my closest collaborators navigated their fields of practice led me across numerous genres and worksites while also helping me note the discursive boundaries of the various subscenes, including those with which I had only limited experiences.

Another issue that emerged more slowly is that several central people in the study changed career directions. Some became academics, other changed genre focus. Still others made more drastic moves to careers outside of music, usually continuing to make it for pleasure. On the other hand, many such as Farofa and composer, musical director, and guitarist/singer Luciano Salvador Bahia have continued to support themselves as creators of popular music in Salvador. Márcia Castro followed a well-worn path by moving south to São Paulo to further her career as an MPB singer and songwriter, while others such as Ximbinha left and returned, facing various challenges and sometimes benefits from their excursions

As this suggests, flexibility over time is also crucial for most professional musicians. This is particularly the case if they specialize in popular music, which tends to favor youth and rapid turnover. Though there are instances in which royalties from a hit song can provide a lifetime of income, nothing of the kind has happened to the musicians in my network. Nor have any of them established sustaining investment portfolios (and in many cases, retirement savings). Rather, all of them must keep working in order to keep earning.[43] The ways that they have continued to do this demonstrate tactical, long-term, "diachronic" flexibility on par with their short-term, "synchronic" flexibility exemplified by their simultaneous or rapidly sequential musical involvements and multigenre competences.

Multiple return visits and sustained contact with, among others, Farofa, Laurinha, Edni, Josehr, Junior, Son, and both Lucianos via Skype and email have allowed me to accompany various shifts in their lives and labors—economic ups and downs, political turmoil, new genres, changing perspectives on some old ones—while also pointing to a degree of stasis. Indeed, the precarious employment conditions they have faced for years not only persist, but have at times gotten worse. Also very much in place is the general organization of the industries in which they labor. Durable too are the typical gendering of musical work roles and, especially, racial conception, which continues to inform veiled and overt racist exclusions, particular notions of class position, and dominant musical sensibilities.

Continued contact has also shown me that a core of popular musical practices has remained fundamental to the Scenes. MPB is of particular concern here because it continues to be so highly esteemed across a wide spectrum of musicians and audiences while remaining less lucrative than several less well-regarded genres.[44] On the other hand, owing to their continued centrality during Carnaval, Salvador's most visible and lucrative genres were and are *axé* music and a local samba variant known as *pagode*. A close second in terms of audibility and income potential is Forró,[45] which is featured during a second series of public celebrations known as the *festas juninas* (June Festivals) or colloquially, São João. These seasonal, festival-related genres have figured into the work lives of a majority of my collaborators in important ways. They discussed them frequently—with me and with each other—but almost never in the glowing terms that were the norm when they talked about "alternative" genres such as MPB and to a slightly lesser degree, samba. Rather, *axé*, certain types of Forró, and especially *pagode* were regular targets of critique and condemnation by performers and audience members from a range of backgrounds. Yet most musicians told me that they had taken jobs performing one or more of them, usually "for the money." Thus, throughout my fieldwork, I noted patterns of association, both discursive and through participation, between these less esteemed but generally better-paying genres and *baianos* occupying and jockeying for positions in the professional scenes and in Salvador's societal hierarchy.

Audiences

At the risk of stating and oversimplifying the obvious, professional musicians' incomes are dependent on their ability to find people willing to pay to hear their music. Musicians' awareness of the importance of finding an audience, therefore, informed their tactical choices, and even if they did not respect the opinions of the public, very few disregarded them. Thus, audiences have a very real impact on the sounds of music in Salvador and the logics of the Scenes; that is, practices and discourses of consumption are not only informed by, but also inform the "field of cultural *production*." This means that conversations with self-described nonmusicians proved nearly as useful as speaking with musical workers in terms of understanding the sensibilities of the Scenes. This was both a benefit and a liability. One of the most convenient, pleasurable, and at times daunting aspects of doing fieldwork on music in Salvador is that so many people care deeply about it, know a great deal, and are eager to share their perspectives. Tapping into these multiple viewpoints was the basis of my rather amorphous notion of audience. Yet this loose conceptualization allowed me to venture away from my close network and gain a broader sense of the soundscape. Taking seriously the opinions of listeners also enabled me to better situate my closer collaborators' musical work in relation to the politics of local music practice in the context where, at least in terms of commodification processes, they mattered most.

Flexible participation in music also meant that systematically isolating and surveying clearly demarcated audiences with particular tastes proved difficult, if not misguided. But among the many rather randomly gathered opinions shared with me were strong views about who listened to certain genres and who would be present at specific performances. Whenever I could, I spoke with people about music. At public performances, I did so noting the genre, the location, and the costs while also taking stock of how each person with whom I spoke self-identified and how they identified fellow attendees, especially in terms of class and at times, color. Such conversations were not always possible, in which case I resorted to observation. This led to the unsurprising but overwhelming sense that patrons of expensive venues tended to be more European looking.

Everyday conversations on the street, in stores, on buses, in taxis, at restaurants, and in people's homes were also extremely informative. Interlocutors in these settings, regardless of whether they told me they were musicians, consistently positioned themselves in relation to specific kinds of music and events. Among this large and highly varied group of people there has been marked consistency of perspective over many years. The patterns that emerged were crucial for understanding the cultural capital associated with various genres and any related changes and contestations.[46]

As much as audience discourse coupled with spending habits, projected and actual, informed practice within the Scenes, music listeners' most interesting and dramatic impact could only be felt in moments of performance. As I saw at the Margareth Menezes and Gal Costa shows on my first trip, and at the vast majority of performances I attended since then, Bahian audience members dance. Even more commonly, they sing, usually without prompting, often at full volume, and typically with almost every word to almost every song. Such active participation might not seem especially unusual, but spontaneous embodied engagement was so prevalent across settings and genres in Salvador that I came to view it as an influence on how music is made rather than merely a result of it.[47] That is, I came to see participation as part of the aesthetics of popular music there.[48] This aesthetic of participation had numerous implications for working musicians in terms of the sound of their music as well as the money, esteem, and relationships that followed as a result of making it.

MATRICES OF CAPITAL, NETWORKS OF WORKERS

Despite my use of the term "aesthetic" and any sense of "autonomy" it might conjure, musical participation in Salvador is deeply political. Conventions and expectations about the ways audiences participate and their ability to do so inform how a particular musical practice might be valued in terms of its cultural capital, the price of a live presentation or recording, and the value of musicians' labor and their career direction. Farofa nicely encapsulated this:

JP: You told me before that it is difficult to become really successful playing music like bossa nova and MPB.

JF: Yes, very!

JP: Why?

JF: Why is it hard? Because, Jeff, it is music to which you have to pay more attention and for which you have to be more intelligent to be able to like and understand. Like I told you on the trip we took to the Chapada, there are three kinds of music: music that moves (*mexe com*) your mind, music that moves your heart, and music that moves your waist—that music for which you don't think about anything, but you dance . . . that is *axé* and *pagode*. (Salvador, September 21, 2005)[49]

Farofa's understanding was widely shared throughout the Scenes, expressed time and again in conversations with musicians and listeners.

In these conversations and at performances I also noted various nuances to this dominant perspective on musical use. For instance, *baianos* do dance to music for the mind, as I saw during Gal Costa's New Year's Eve show and multiple other MPB presentations. Farofa also told me that music for the waist *could* contain profound messages. However, he was resolved that most of it did not—and he was not alone in this. I also doubt that any of my collaborators would say that contemplative or dance music is unable to touch the emotions. Yet many of them also highlighted certain genres and subgenres that were viewed as especially emotional with terms such as *romântica* (romantic) and *dor de cotovelo* ("sore elbows," a reference to holding one's head in one's hands with elbows on the table in response to love lost).[50]

The specificity of terms such as romantic or sore elbow music as well as frequent suggestions that most dance music is not for thinking are just two of the many indications of strong linkages between genres and uses that serve as organizing strategies. Indeed, uses had a clear hierarchy, with music for the mind at the acme. This point has been addressed extensively in the research of Brazilian ethnomusicologist Martha Ulhôa de Carvalho (1995 and 2007 as Tupinambá de Ulhôa). Akin to the Euro-mimesis that profoundly informs everyday life, Ulhôa elaborates that despite extensive hybridity, musical characteristics that tend to be most appreciated in Western art music, for instance elaborated harmonies and arrangements, are frequently cited by Brazilians as definitive of quality *popular* music. She and many others (e.g., Stroud 2008) have also demonstrated convincingly how consumption of MPB, which is constantly praised for its harmonic complexity and its poetic sophistication and often simply called "quality music," is an important part of middle- and upper-class identity construction.[51]

This was very much my experience. I also heard countless musical workers and middle-class fans tell that me "the masses do not want quality music" (*O povo não quer música de qualidade*).

Assumed homologies such as these index a scale of musical cultural capital that overarched the Scenes—one that is deeply racialized. MPB sat squarely at the apex, but the sonic characteristics for which it was so frequently praised, its interesting harmonies, intricate arrangements, and especially poetic lyrics,[52] were also cited as part of the appeal of other well-regarded genres. Evidence of these characteristics also earned approval for songs, and occasionally artists who performed them, even if they were associated with genres typically mapped as lower quality. Crucial in terms of understanding the politics of genre is that such cases were usually posited as exceptions while entire genres were dismissed as inferior because of their purported inability to move the mind. In everyday discourse, participation in such music, especially *axé* and *pagode*, was typically qualified. Audience members told me "it's only good for dancing or a party," deeming it not worthy of purchasing, and rejecting it for at-home listening. Musicians nearly always cited their economic motivations for performing it.

Hovering over this pyramid of esteem and use is a Cartesian epistemology, a mind/body duality that privileges rational thought and relegates the body to secondary status. Although music marked for its abundance of emotionality such as *romântica* and *dor de cotovelo* were rarely praised in a manner akin to contemplative genres such as MPB, Bahian music, in its circumscription to dancing and partying, was constructed as the epitome of "body music." Its body centricity and its "African-ness" were conflated through a tautology that leaves its cultural capital diminished and its economic potential amplified.[53] The impact of capitalism and the ambivalence of the ideology of autonomous art were, on the other hand, evident in that a big enough paycheck and the trappings of fame could compensate, but from what I saw, not entirely overcome, the devalorization of music that moves the waist.

Thus, as I discuss in chapter 3, the ways working musicians discursively represented their musical participation, preferences, and experiences were crucial for their careers and also for shaping the sensibilities of the Scenes. Most discussions I had and heard about matters such as musical quality, furthermore, served to reify the cultural capital associated with MPB and other mind-oriented musics as well as a few international genres and samba, usually as a matter of its status as national music and dance.[54] So too did discourse about what kinds of people participated in different genres.

However common such associations and related hierarchies were in conversation, they did not always map neatly onto practice. Rather, I encountered fairly frequent breaks with assumed orthodoxy. For instance, although many venues for MPB are cost prohibitive for members of the *povo*, it is also a staple in numerous neighborhood *barzinhos* (little bars) that charge little or nothing for entry. The audience at Gal Costa's New Year's Eve show was also populated by plenty of people who, based on their attire and presence at a free event rather than a private party, were not affluent and who were of visible African descent. Conversely, Carnaval music is regarded as low quality across socioeconomic classes and color categories, but it attracts throngs of wealthy (and more European-looking) consumers, including hundreds of thousands of tourists, many of whom who pay steep prices to parade in big-name clubs animated by stars. Thus, in certain circumstances, elites participate in music assumed to be inferior or *déclassé*, and members of the *povo* enjoy "quality" genres typically assumed to be beyond their taste and understanding. I also spoke with a number of people who advocated for the legitimacy, or at least acceptability, of Bahian music, again usually in specific contexts such as Carnaval. I have even noted a degree of increasing tolerance for local popular music over the years. Nevertheless, the tendency to elevate contemplative, supralocal, national, international music over local dance-related genres has remained very pronounced in the face of any tendencies toward omnivorousness and change.[55]

Even more durable and of great import for working musicians is a pronounced and inverse relationship between cultural capital and earning potential. Since I began my fieldwork Salvador's professional musicians have navigated a field in which performances of the most esteemed genres tend to pay considerably less than performances of dance music during São João (Forró), and especially Carnaval (*axé* and *pagode*). When comparing conditions of the two major festivals, this tendency continues: Forró was much less frequently criticized than either *axé* or *pagode*, and it is generally less lucrative (for Bahian musicians) as well.[56]

Regardless of genre, live performances rather than sales of recordings, publishing rights, or other commodities are Bahian musicians' primary basis for income. The vast majority receive a fee (*cachê*) for each live presentation or recording session rather than a weekly, monthly, or yearly salary or any kind of royalty. Such "payment for each play" employment combined with minimal job security, and, in most cases, erratic performance scheduling led most musicians I met to work for an array of different employers. As I discuss throughout, this multiplicity has numerous implications for nearly all aspects of professional music making, not the least of which is the sound of their music, as I discuss in chapter 5, which focuses on musicians' flexible treatment of repertoire in the context of portfolio musical careers.

Most of the work local pros do—that which creates conditions of possibility for paid work—is much less audible, visible, or profitable than their on-stage labor time and the work to produce any recordings or merchandise they might be able to sell. One obvious example is rehearsal. Clearly effortful and musical, this vital work is often done for free or at a cost in hopes of future benefits. I address this and a number of other issues and processes related to preparing performances "off stage," including the rather private work of making recordings for the public, in chapter 4. Less immediately obvious are numerous other aspects of working to work, for instance project promotion, which are crucial for earning income making music and discussed in chapter 2.

Money for Musical Work

Understandably, a primary concern underpinning the practices of professional musicians is how musical labor is valued (or not), especially but not only in economic terms. Wide variations in musicians' pay are in part related to the contingent ways that their employers earn their own revenue. Most operators of bars, restaurants, theaters, Carnaval *blocos*, and festivals cover expenses, including performers' wages, and hopefully earn profit through fees charged for entry and whatever services and products are sold. Some musical enterprises and performers earn money through sponsorships and government support too; but all of them have to demonstrate that their musical production merits expenditure or investment, typically based on their ability to attract a paying audience. This comes to a head when an employer negotiates payment with a musical worker.

At issue in this process is what economists refer to as "marginal revenue product" (MRP), or the income associated with hiring an employee, which is measured against the wages they are paid. A logical and seemingly straightforward notion, MRP can be difficult to establish, and all the more so for musicians. In contexts such as restaurants or bars where music is bundled with other products and services, music makers are rather easily cast as nonessential. Even if music is part of the atmosphere that makes the venue appealing to patrons, a substantial chunk of income is usually derived from food and drink sales. This means that musicians' impact on profit is more abstract compared to employees such as cooks, bartenders, and servers. Even if a specific performer is a known draw for audiences, the argument can still be credibly made that many patrons came for the venue, the menu, or the company of other patrons.

This line of argumentation can be extended to events such as Carnaval parades or São João celebrations even though they are defined by live musical performances. Music remains part of a larger experience—parading, dancing, and partying—and many audience members turn up almost regardless of who performs, for instance, out of loyalty to a particular carnival club or for one artist out of the many who appear at the larger *forrós*. Thus, relatively few musicians can claim credit for a lucrative event and successfully demand commensurate pay. The situation is more challenging for supporting musicians whose MRP is difficult to assert even in situations when the ensemble in which they work is clearly the main driver of employer profit. Would audience members notice or be deterred from attending a performance if a star singer replaced her rhythm guitarist? Would the artist herself notice?

Furthermore, even if a star commands a high fee, there is not necessarily a "trickle down effect" in terms of pay, bargaining power, or job security. Exacerbating all of this is the intense competition for jobs compounded by the comparatively low barriers of entry for popular music participation. Many acceptably competent musicians are willing to labor for minimal or contingent pay (e.g., cover charges) or in some instances, no money at all. Among them are part-time performers who support themselves in other jobs, people who take low-paying musical employment as an alternative to unemployment or demanding physical labor, and new musicians eager to break into the Scenes. Their eagerness to perform provides employers with exceedingly favorable hiring conditions. Accordingly, several collaborators noted that wages for much of the work they do have declined over time, asserting that venue operators often prioritized profit over hiring the "best" musicians.

The pay gap between local musicians and stars has been, by all accounts, widening as well. This disparity hit backing musicians particularly hard since lower-level acts cannot pay high wages and some top acts feel little need to based on the belief that supporting musicians are easily replaced. Thus, several side musicians I know, including Edni, told me that they faced pay cuts during their tenures with well-capitalized artists. Decreased wages in such contexts can result from the employer's declining revenue. However, Edni told me in 2014 that one of Bahia's top *axé* artists had implemented a drastic pay decrease for members of her band even as her status as a premier artist remained very much intact.

A key defense against declining wages and employment instability in virtually any industry, including music, is for laborers to minimize their "substitutability" (see Towse 1993).[57] This term is used by economists to describe the degree to which an employee can be replaced without negatively impacting employer revenue. Within flexible employment schemes the assumption that most laborers are substitutable creates ample opportunity for wage stagnation or reduction as well as minimal commitment to employees. On the other hand, establishing oneself as less or unsubstitutable can provide leverage for increased pay and more assurance of long-term employment.

In economic terms, a musician is less substitutable when venue owners, producers, other musicians, and sponsoring entities believe that hiring them will directly or indirectly attract an audience that will spend more money than they would if they hired someone else. Since concerns other than money are presumably at issue in the music industries, reducing substitutability also often entails demonstrating that hiring another performer would be detrimental to the music. For all of the reasons mentioned above and more, this remains a constant battle, and most Bahian musicians I met were treated and behaved as though they were quite substitutable—a reasonable assumption since nearly all of them were not only aware of the competition in the Scenes, but also worked without contracts or union protections. Indeed, a saturated musical labor market as well as a history of alleged corruption and inefficacy impeded the few organization efforts among musical laborers I heard about, despite the fact that one such union, the OMB (Ordem dos Músicos do Brasil), was federally mandated and membership is technically required. Several interlocutors refused to join and those that did were not shy in expressing its many problems and their resentment at having to pay for what they saw as a useless affiliation.[58] Against this precarious backdrop, the existence of highly sought-after, well-compensated stars and the long-term careers maintained by several of my collaborators illustrate that through tactical navigation of the field—one overarched by the racialized and classed cultural politics of music in Salvador—it is possible to become established as less substitutable and in some rare instances, irreplaceable.

Contacts in the Scenes

Establishing a position as a less substitutable musical worker is vital for both keeping jobs and for getting them. Doing so, further, is necessarily a matter of cultural and economic capital: what skills does a musician have that make the ensemble sound better? Will hiring an ensemble attract a bigger audience? How much will they cost? But nonsubstitutability is also entangled with social capital in any number of ways. Bourdieu (1986, 51) defines social capital as "the aggregate of the actual or potential resources which are linked to possession of a durable network of more or less institutionalized relationships of mutual acquaintance and recognition—or in other words, to membership in a group." The notion has also been theorized by sociologist Robert Putnam (2000), who emphasizes matters of trust and shared values in relation to social cohesion that ring true with what I have experienced in Salvador. Several musicians mentioned the pleasure of making certain kinds of music with like-minded friends, and I saw repeatedly how doing so could fortify relationships; I also saw the opposite.[59] Yet Bourdieu's more instrumentalist concern with how relationships figure into efforts to improve social positions as well as how those positions are defined was especially prominent in working musicians' practices of finding jobs. In fact, the importance of connections in the Bahian job market in general is reflected in local slang: "QI" (*Quem indicou?* Who recommended you?).[60]

In simple terms, musicians who lack QI struggle to find employment. Beyond the clout of close association with an influential person or the credibility provided by a recommendation from a respected one—both of which are matters of what sociologist Mark Granovetter (1973) might call "strong ties"—"weak ties" or acquaintances outside of one's immediate network are also key. Notice of upcoming auditions are nearly always circulated by word of mouth rather than any formal process. While close friends and colleagues can be conduits for such information and perhaps open doors that might otherwise be closed, contact with people who move in distinct circles can be crucial for hearing about more and more varied opportunities.

Despite the pleasures of making music and the cohesion it can engender, I nevertheless privilege the notion that, as professionals trying to earn a living, most of my collaborators' actions were ultimately directed toward economic goals. This is not to say that aesthetic or social aims were not important to them. It is rather a reminder that, as a matter of practicality and survival, finances often take precedence. Yet in most instances the musicians with whom I consulted continually have sought manageable balances of income sufficiency, musical pleasure, and satisfying sociality. As the following chapters will show, finding such a balance is anything but simple. More often than not it involves working through a tangle of concerns related to various forms of capital, cultural and professional politics, and musical knowledge.

Music-Makers' Lives and Livings

When thinking about issues such as social power and practices of musical labor under capitalism, it is rather easy to fall back into a functionalist understanding: the need for money articulated with various hegemonic scene structures leads musicians to do this or that, with one or another implication for themselves and certain other people. In some ways, such causal linkages hold up in practice. Yet this understanding is too tidy. Professional musicians and their audiences, despite the force of particular discourses, industry efforts, and their own monetary conditions are still able to maneuver in sometimes surprising ways. Indeed, it was clear that music mattered to my collaborators in ways well beyond helping them resist, make do with, or exert power. Musical work, likewise, *is* a means of sustenance and survival; but it is also a source of pleasure, fear, and frustration. It is the basis of friendships and enmities; and is central to the formation of identities, both individual and collective. Even in instances when the musicians with whom I conducted fieldwork performed what might seem to be the most perfunctory musicking acts, they were rarely alienated from the basis of their labor, the music. This was the case when they were dissatisfied by the conditions of a particular job or the struggles they face to survive in the day-to-day—what they so often call *a luta* (the fight)—as well.

Thus, one final and overarching consideration for the book is how and to what effects the musicians I met maintain their emotional, social, and creative investments in music making at the same time that they strive to convert it into a source of income. Some have been more successful than others, and all have experienced ups and downs. However, in the end, my discussions of the musical lives and careers of Bahian musicians should be taken as an analysis of how, in the context of the numerous challenges they face as they try to live from their music, most have not stopped living for it.

ONE

Sounds and Circuits of Musical Work
in the Salvador Scenes

Salvador não é uma cidade . . . é uma gravadora!
(Salvador isn't a city . . . it's a record company!)
Mauricio Almeida, Brazilian music producer

My first trip to Salvador was in some ways much as I had expected. In a
short period of time I was able to take in an abundant variety of music and see
first-hand that plenty of people who appeared to be professional musicians were
working all around town. But there were also several surprises, not the least of
which was the relative difficulty I had finding *axé* music, the genre I, like many
others, had come to associate most strongly with the city. Where were Daniela
Mercury and Carlinhos Brown? Though their names came up from time to time,
their presence seemed remarkably muted. And Olodum? Each time I asked
about the famed *bloco afro* I was told I had just missed them (my wife and I
joked it was a lot like chasing Elvis). Other surprises followed too. Marcos, the
hotel receptionist I befriended, told me about newer Bahian music performers,
noting that those I had been asking about were considered somewhat passé,
and that there was "better" music to be heard in Salvador anyway. He and the
tour guide who told me about the Margareth Menezes performance also advised
me that rather than chase Olodum, I should check out Ilê Aiyê. They added,
though, that their non-Carnaval performances, if they were taking place at all
so far in advance of the official event, were held far from where we and most
other tourists were staying.

What I would realize on subsequent trips is not that my initial ideas about Salvador's soundscape were wrong. They just did not line up with the timing of my first visit or the areas I frequented. I would eventually learn that, depending on time and place, Salvador looks and sounds different. The entanglements between timing, location, musical sounds, and musicians' work are the overarching concern of this chapter.

Through multiple, differently scheduled trips and a stay of over a year, I saw how and to what effects certain kinds of music and contexts for performances take and then cede center stage as the calendar progresses. Effectively, three overlapping, but ultimately discrete, circuits of musical performance and related work operate: two that are directly tied to seasonal festivals, Carnaval and the *festas juninas*, and a third that is more constant. Temporal implications for music are crosscut by the cityscape, which differentially accommodates certain types of musical events, and in combination with the demographics associated with various parts of town, informs widely accepted musical mappings of places and people. In this, Bahia's circuits of musical work are reminiscent of the wedding/saint's day celebration circuit, night club circuit, and "performing arts" circuit in which Egyptian female singers and dancers work, as described by van Nieuwkerk (1995). However, the Bahian context is distinguished by its annual cycle, specific genres, and the primacy of racial conception, all of which hold profound implications for the challenges, possibilities, and meanings of living from music in Salvador.

Because of travel timing, Salvador's soundscape continued to defy my expectations until my third field stay in February 2003. Arriving just as official Carnaval celebrations began, I found the city almost dormant in terms of "normal" daily life and the music I heard previously. But it teemed with people, including numerous tourists—something that was suggested when I arrived at the apartment in which I had rented a room to find it packed to capacity with visitors from São Paulo and Brasília. Moreover, Bahian music sounded everywhere, and thus I started noting the signficance of what I would come to understand as the Carnaval Circuit.

In the heart of the city and across its various spaces, I heard songs and saw performers I had read about before ever setting foot in Bahia. I watched Ivete Sangalo and several other *axé* notables performing on *trios elétricos* for dense masses of people lining the streets and dancing alongside the trucks in matching shirts that marked them as members of a *bloco*. I also saw *blocos* parading with *trios* featuring *pagode*, which I had begun hearing about on my second trip, but had not yet experienced live. Interspersed were the Afro-centric groups, both *blocos* afro and *afoxés*,[1] as well as several *trios* that were not surrounded by any type of distinguishable club organization. The artists performing on these *trios independentes* (independent *trios*) lacked the elaborate production infrastructure I noted supporting the stars. However, there were enough of them to suggest that they might be a signficant basis of work for musicians who had not achieved a degree of elevated industry status. Still more sites where musicians worked during Carnaval came into view when I turned my attention away from the center of the action on the streets and toward venues alongside and well away from the parade routes. Thanks to Edni's invitation, I rode on my first *trio elétrico* during a Bahian Carnaval-like celebration in a nearby city several weeks after Ash Wednesday. Though many clubs and restaurants that host music in Salvador almost year-round shut their doors for the pre-Lenten week, as do most nonentertainment businesses, a few remained open either providing spaces for the alternative genres they featured throughout the year or adapting programming to suit the season.

In contrast to Carnaval, which leaves no doubt that the star of the show is Bahian music, a visit to Salvador during the month of June is a very different experience, as I would learn on my second trip in 2002. Still unaware of any seasonal implications or circuits and eager to find *axé*, my queries about where to hear it were met with a rather uniform answer: *"agora é São João—e a música é* Forró!" (It's São João now and the music for this celebration is Forró). Accordingly, the sounds of this accordion-based complex of genres complemented a soundscape already dense with music, other than *axé* and *pagode*, such as that which I heard in December, and that is, for all intents and purposes, nonseasonal.

Indeed, trips to Salvador in June and just before Ash Wednesday indicated that my December experience approximated musical activity between what were clearly two seasonal peaks. No one mentioned Forró or the *festas juninas* around the end of the year since they were six months in the future and preceded by Bahia's signature event. Carnaval too was temporally remote enough that it was not at the fore of many people's concerns. Related activities had only begun, though they ramp up steadily as the main event approaches. The slow build to a peak several months away helps account for the difficulty I had finding *axé* and *bloco afro* performances at the time. Instead, the music that was most audible between Carnaval and São João lacked association with a temporally defined celebration. Rather, it was taken as more "universal" and embraced as suitable for everyday participation regardless of time of year. Like Carnaval and São João, New Year's Eve does mark a surge in local musical activity. But as a globally celebrated event commemorated in settings from concerts to clubs to private homes, it more easily accommodates a range of music, including *axé, pagode,* and Forró, but especially genres such as MPB, samba, and bossa nova, as well as a fair bit of pop/rock and even straight-ahead jazz that, as I would learn, are fixtures of year-round music making and what comprises, for all intents and purposes, a nonseasonal circuit.

In what follows, I further survey the contours of Salvador's three circuits of musical performance as key organizational structures of the Scenes. They are foundational to the sounds that are most audible at any given time and are thus crucial for informing the work practices of most local musicians. In particular, the vast majority of the musicians I met who live from music move tactically between the circuits, and formations within them (see next chapter), in order to piece together their livings.

As is the case for most laborers, where a musician works is tremendously important. Unlike most conventionally employed people, occupational musicians generally do their jobs in a variety of settings *and* profoundly different setting types including studios, clubs, and concert halls. Differences between musical work sites can be very pronounced in any context, but they are amplified in Bahia because of the distinct musical seasons and specificities of the related circuits. All of these distinctions hold numerous implications for labor conditions including income potential, performance content, and presentational approach, as well as the meanings associated with musical genres, especially their mapping in terms of cultural capital.

A CITY OF CONTRASTS AND SITE FOR THE CIRCUITS

Before discussing the specifics of each circuit, it is important to contextualize them within Salvador's physical and social spaces to provide a framework for musical work and a sense of the stakes for the sounds and meanings that emerge from it. Perhaps most significant, in addition to the abundance of music and people of visible African descent, are ubiquitous signs of extreme poverty that frequently collide with the trappings of wealth and twenty-first-century urban convenience. Such disjunctures, which are inseparable from the city's colonial history, underpin the conditions of the circuits and the sensibilities of the Scenes.

Salvador sits on the eastern side of the entrance to Baía de Todos os Santos (All Saints Bay), the body of water for which the state is named. It was Brazil's first colonial capital and a focal point of the sugar industry, which was fundamental to the new colony's economy. Salvador's coastal location, the region's suitability for sugar cultivation, and the emergence of a plantation system reliant on forced labor conspired to establish it as the primary site for the importation of enslaved Africans. Material and ideological traces of this history permeate the city, touching the lives of its residents every day as evidenced by the city's architecture, demographics, and inequalities.

With the faltering of the Brazilian sugar industry in the late seventeenth century, the relocation of the capital to Rio de Janeiro in 1763, and abolition in 1888, Salvador became increasingly marginal to Brazil's social, political, and economic life.[2] It was slow to be industrialized, especially in comparison to southeastern cities such as Rio and São Paulo.[3] Even with increased industrialization in Bahia and much of the Northeast beginning in the middle of the twentieth century, Southeastern Brazil has remained more economically prosperous, more infrastructurally modernized, and more "European" in demographics and culture.[4] Comprising what is frequently called the *eixo* Rio/São Paulo—Rio/São Paulo Axis—the nation-state's two largest cities remain abriters of national culture and a home base for industries of cultural production. The centrality of African-ness to notions of *baianidade* (Bahian-ness) sets Salvador apart from the rest of Brazil and the rest of the Brazilian Northeast in many Brazilians' eyes—a distinction that is enacted musically and is of great significance (see below).

Within Salvador, Brazil's fourth-largest metropolis, any benefits from the mid-twentieth-century economic expansion were felt unevenly, to say the least. A large number of *soteropolitanos* (people from Salvador), especially those in the darker-skinned majority, continue to lack opportunities for significant social and economic advancement.[5] This situation persists due to a number of factors, including a high illiteracy rate among poorer residents who have limited access to quality schools and who often abandon formal education to take (low-wage) jobs to help support their families.[6] On the other hand, many old landowning families have retained their wealth since the plantation era. While some from the lower classes have worked their way up the socioeconomic ladder to become part of a middle class populated by white-collar professionals, many more remained on the disadvantaged side of long-standing, new, and newly fortified social and economic barriers, which are exacerbated by the city's particular spatiality—a process that Brazilian anthropologist Jeferson Bacelar (1999) refers to as "peripheralization."

Consistent with Bacelar's characterization, *baianos* consistently emphasized Salvador's contrasts. Most visible is the jarring distinction between the high-rise luxury apartment buildings in the center of town and the *invasões*, unzoned squatter settlements that lie in their shadows. Peripheralization's human toll can be seen during the morning and evening commutes, when buses and sidewalks are packed with people, primarily those of visible African descent, trekking from poor neighborhoods to more affluent ones where they labor at minimum-wage jobs such as *empregada* (maid) and *porteiro* (doorman) at posh and middle-class dwellings. The view is starkly different in the city's several upscale shopping malls that serve a decidedly more European-looking clientele. Complicating all of this is that putative separations are permeable and divisions are transgressed all of the time, as exemplified by the daily commute that often requires moving across and between very different spaces. Such moments of contact call attention to the disjunctures and put increased pressure on performances of social position that are already high stakes owing to classism (see DaMatta 1995) in the context of *mestiçagem* and the racial democracy myth.

Points of contact, contrast, and division are part and parcel of the physical layout of the city, which is subdivided into three primary areas: the Cidade Alta (Upper City), Cidade Baixa (Lower City), and Subúrbio (Suburbia), also commonly called the Periferia (Perifery). While these terms refer to geography, they also give insight into economic and social conditions. Each area is subdivided into multiple neighborhoods, nearly all of which carry certain connotations and characterizations of residents. But the general locale names serve as frequent points of reference for *soteripolitanos* when talking about their city, its people, and its music.

As might be surmised, the Upper City sits on Salvador's high ground. It begins at the mouth of the bay and extends northeast along the Atlantic coast via the Maritime Orla and the Paralela, a second northeast-southwest artery that sits inland. Further west, a long plateau stands as the peninsular divide between the Upper and Lower Cities. The Cidade Alta is home to most of Salvador's affluent neighborhoods, both old and new. It is also where one would expect to see the majority of well-restored historic buildings, tourist hotels, shopping centers, white-collar office complexes, gated apartment buildings, high-rise condominiums, tony restaurants, and trendy clubs.

At Salvador's Historical Center, which is commonly referred to as Pelourinho (pillory),[7] the city's high ground is linked to the Cidade Baixa in dramatic fashion by the Elevador Laçerda. This much-photographed outdoor lift juts out from a sheer cliff and presides over Comércio, the old financial district. Here the Lower City begins, extending northward between the eastern coastline of the bay and

Liberdade, often said to be Brazil's largest "Black" neighborhood, on the plateau adjacent to the Upper City. The Cidade Baixa is low in both elevation and in economic prosperity.[8] High-rise dwellings are few and far between, and though the commercial district's multistory office buildings resemble those of any other older urban downtown, decaying infrastructure betrays the fact that revitalization here has often taken a back seat to development projects in the Upper City. There are a few comparatively affluent areas in the Cidade Baixa along with plenty of business activity, but it tends toward smaller operations; and a majority of area residents are from the poorer classes and of visible African descent.

At the far north end of the Cidade Baixa are the twenty-two neighborhoods comprising Subúrbio. This area is especially underdeveloped and infrastructurally unsound. Yet as of 2014 it was home to approximately six hundred thousand people,[9] a majority of whom identify/are identified as Black or Brown. Subúrbio and its residents are frequently stigmatized, and municipal services including basic sanitation and police protection are lacking. Unemployment is high, and most residents who are employed work at low-income jobs. The area is served by buses and trains, but travel time to the Cidade Alta can still be well over an hour, often in hot, crowded conditions and at a price that is prohibitive for many residents.[10] Transportation becomes sparser at night and on weekends, compounding the area's peripheralization.

Impoverished neighborhoods are not limited to Subúrbio or the Cidade Baixa and can also be found throughout the Upper City. A major thoroughfare might separate a so-called noble neighborhood (*bairro nobre*) from a working-class area or an *invasão*, but in many other cases, the threshold is no more than the turn of a corner. Very quickly, storefronts and gated apartment complexes give way to the lower-lying, distressed housing that signals a less prosperous area.

The difference between so-called *bairros populares* (popular or working-class neighborhoods)[11] and *invasões* can be more subtle—many zoned areas, in fact, began as squatter settlements. Over time, residents managed to improve their environs, with some even securing middle-class conditions. On the other hand, numerous *invasões* still exist and crop up anew, marked by exposed brick or clapboard houses, glassless windows, and open sewers. Residents of these areas, and many in popular neighborhoods as well, continue to suffer the ills of chronic violence, drug use, crumbling infrastructure, and racism. Thus, the starkness of stratification and related discontents continue unabated and are even amplified.

MUSIC MAKING IN A DIVIDED CITY

The physical divisions, social contrasts, and peripherialization of the RMS, the Região Metropolitana Salvador (Greater Salvador), were of consequence to the professional musicians I met in a variety of ways. They lived and worked in various parts of the city, but few were from wealthy areas, and several described their home neighborhoods as popular. In contrast, most of the performances I attended, both by collaborators and on my own, were in the Cidade Alta, including the Historic District, and newer middle-class neighborhoods up the Orla. Performances in the Lower City tended to be less well publicized, and most I attended there and in Surbúrbio were in small, bare-bones settings. In general, more frequent, better-promoted, and higher-paid work in the Cidade Alta helped make it more appealing to musicians. Ritzier venues, better performance visibility, and stories about dangerous travel kept many middle-class Upper City residents closer to home for their live music participation. On the other hand, venue prices and the cost and risks of public transportation at night kept many residents of the Cidade Baixa and Subúrbio from patronizing Cidade Alta performances.

Still, events in the Cidade Baixa were not unknown or irrelevant to residents of the Upper City and vice versa. People in both locations frequently made pronouncements about what was happening "there"—in terms of music and life in general. At least some of what they said was rooted in assumption or imagination, but a fair bit of it was consistent with my experiences. Much as I was told, I heard some genres more regularly in certain areas, both in venues and, in the case of poorer neighborhoods, sounding in the open air on home, car, and business sound systems and sometimes performed by musicians in the street. By contrast, performances in more affluent areas tended to be more private, exclusive affairs, but since many of the venues were not fully enclosed, at least some music—usually more esteemed genres—was audible to passersby.

What all of this amounted to were frequent associations between music, people, and place, with issues of class and color never far behind. I saw exceptions, but a majority of the people I saw at most performances of music with high cultural capital, especially in costly venues, were more European in appearance. And, as I was often told would be the case, most events involving less valorized music, especially in economically accessible settings, involved large numbers of people of visible African descent. On the other hand, I saw plenty of evidence of multiplicity of musical participation that rendered asserted homologies problematic. Still, the classed, racialized sensibilities of the Scenes articulated with very real barriers to participation informed how *baianos* exercised their musical omnivorousness, with venues serving as sites of segregation and occasional and usually less visible transgressions of durable stereotypes.

The implications of venues for Salvador's musicians (and audiences for that matter) extend well beyond any individual club, theater, festival, or Carnaval parade, since the circuits can be productively understood as being based on loose agglomerations of these musical worksites. Genre, specifically the genres most strongly associated with each circuit and the venues comprising it, are of profound importance here and are inseparable from, among other things, issues of economic and cultural capital. As such the entangled meanings and politics of genre, circuit, and venue profoundly shape musicians' work conditions. They also inform and are informed by dominant thinking as well as debates about race, class, and music itself.

The Nonseasonal Circuit

On any given day, professional musicians are likely working somewhere in Salvador. Clubs, bars, restaurants, hotels, and theaters regularly feature live music. Rehearsals as well as performances at weddings, private parties, and music festivals large and small are common events. Recording sessions in facilities ranging from home project studios to state-of-the-art, commercial operations regularly produce label-backed albums, independent/vanity projects, demos, soundtracks, and jingles. Plenty of working musicians supplement their performing income by teaching locals and tourists, privately and through cultural organizations and schools. There are ebbs and flows in all of these jobs, and most musicians combine them in their own way to support themselves—few, if any, pay enough to be a sole means of support. A tactically cultivated aggregate provides a broad basis for potential employment throughout the year. Since two other more defined circuits of work opportunities are oriented around major seasonal celebrations, I consider this third, lower-profile but comparatively more constant collection of jobs a nonseasonal circuit of musical work.

Because the nonseasonal circuit is not organized around a specific occasion, it encompasses an especially broad range of musical practices and worksites, many of which are focal points for associated scenes. Many of the staple genres, for instance, MPB and jazz, tend to be highly valorized, rich in cultural capital both for audiences and the musicians who perform them. On the other hand, wages earned and career prospects for musicians who specialize in nonseasonal genres in Salvador are limited. Even so, owing to the constancy of such work and the associated cultural and social capital it can engender, it is important for musical careers—those of local jobbing musicians and a surprising number of performers who work/have worked with high-level acts regardless of genre.

MPB is by far the most prevalent nonseasonal genre, providing the fundamental repertoire for performers at private parties, bars, and restaurants. Strongly associated with the educated, urban, middle class and constitutive of middle-class identities, MPB was touted for its high quality by nearly every *baiano* I spoke with, regardless of social position and even if they said they did not actively listen to it—although very few musicians *said* they did not listen to or play it. Thus, MPB's cultural capital is rooted in its associations with the intellectual, financial, and cultural elite, very much in keeping with Bourdieu's formulation. However, its associated prestige and power to enhance position in the musical field in Salvador and, indeed, across Brazil, is inseparable from discourse and in particular the disciplined knowledge that it "is" good music, that those with good musical taste are *supposed* to like it, and that those who are "good musicians" are *supposed* to be able to perform it.

Another important aspect of MPB is that it and several other genres foundational to the nonseasonal circuit including samba and Brazilian pop/rock are mapped as national; the staples of both seasonal circuits, in contrast, are both considered "regional." This regional/national split emerging out of Rio samba's early twentieth-century nationalization (Vianna 1999) and the continued power of the Rio/São Paulo Axis limits the degree of success Bahia's musicians can achieve in national music without relocating southward. This was the path taken by luminaries of samba, bossa nova, MPB, and Brazilian rock such as Dorival Caymmi, João Gilberto, Gilberto Gil, Caetano Veloso, Gal Costa, Maria Bethânia, and Raul Seixas. By contrast, Daniela Mercury, Ivete Sangalo, Carlinhos Brown, and their peers gained their fame as performers of *Bahian* music. Locally, the independence from regional/seasonal festivals of genres such as MPB, samba, pop/rock, and an instrumental practice known as *chorinho,* solidifies their "universality" and suitability for year-round work as well as their esteem.[12] Ironically, these constructions also inform incorrect but still widely held assumptions that *baianos* cannot play non-Bahian (and for many, "quality") music. Farofa recounted that an audience member once told him that he played bossa nova too well to really be a *baiano.* Ostensibly rooted in geography, Bahia's Africanness along with Farofa's dark complexion and long dreadlocks suggest that racial conception underpinned this illogic. And, as it was in the past, Márcia Castro found it necessary to liberate herself from assumptions about Bahian musicians' skill at "quality music" and related career limitations by moving south to São Paulo to continue her upward trajectory as an MPB singer.

Several nonlocal popular musics other than MPB and samba also have strong presence in the nonseasonal circuits, providing work for local musicians and cultural capital for performers and listeners. These include salsa, reggae, blues, rock, and jazz. Each of these Afro-diasporic hybrids was widely embraced among musicians and middle-class audiences, with reggae also enjoying currency since the 1970s among poorer Afro-Bahians as an inspiration in the fight for racial justice (see Albuquerque 1997, Godi 2001, Pinho 2001) and more recently appealing to bourgeois, largely European-looking youth as party music. The former is exemplified by the ubiquity of Bob Marley images in locations such as Afro-centric NGOs; the latter is exemplified by the musical choices at a large gathering of students from a private university that I attended with Marcos. While the audience demographics and basis of appeal of these musics varied—for example, jazz was held up as a marker of good musicianship thanks to its harmonic complexity, especially among musicians, while reggae was praised by less musically educated people for its engaged lyrics[13]—all benefit from the cachet of being from an elsewhere.

In contrast to the preponderance of supralocal genres in the nonseasonal circuit, a few local practices have claimed some space there. In the early 2000s, *arrocha*, which was described to me as a sped-up version of *seresta* (romantic ballads) played against a bolero rhythm rendered by a sequencer, gained a primarily working-class following starting in the Bahian interior, then Subúrbio, and finally across the RMS. *Arrocha* never shed its *brega* mapping,[14] drew rabid criticism from members of the urban middle classes as well as many of Salvador's musicians, and seemed poised to vanish following its 2005 peak. However, it came back strongly in 2014. In its reemergence, the voice, keyboard, and saxophone trios that were the norm in working-class venues of the nonseasonal circuits were replaced by large bands performing for massive Carnaval audiences. Remaining the same were racy lyrics, unelaborated harmony, and pelvic gyrations that both contributed to its mass appeal and elicited damning critiques of the music, its performers, and its fans. Also holding firm were its associations with lower-class, less educated *baianos*, its disdain by the educated elite, its minimal cultural capital, and its potential to generate substantial revenue.

A second local genre to gain audibility in the nonseasonal circuit in the early part of the 2000s was *samba de roda*, a precursor to both national samba and Bahian *pagode*. Actively practiced in the interior since its genesis on sugar plantations, *samba de roda* was largely forgotten in urban settings until 2006, when it was recognized by UNESCO as a masterpiece of the oral and intangible heritage of humanity. This sparked new interest in the capital with a marked rise in performances by rural groups, the formation of urban-based *samba de roda* ensembles, and the incorporation of *samba de roda* songs into local performers' set lists. Among those drawing on this traditional practice were several artists who performed *pagode*,[15] which although most audible during Carnaval, is also somewhat audible throughout the year, especially in the poorer neighborhoods of the Cidade Baixa and Subúrbio. Indeed, between 2007 and 2010, I noticed that the attention attracted by *samba de roda* catalyzed increased space for all samba in Salvador.

The nonseasonal circuit sees subtle changes during seasonal circuit peaks and has its own activity surge at the end of the calendar year. Work in nonseasonal venues can slow or even cease during Carnaval, and to a lesser degree, São João. That which continues is often adapted to accommodate the music of the season. But at New Year's Eve plenty of well-paid work can be had performing anything from year-round staples such as MPB and pop/rock to Bahian Music.

Job possibilities in the nonseasonal circuit are extremely varied, and include everything from performances in neighborhood bars to massive outdoor festivals to recording sessions. Local musicians utilized particular language to delineate the various capacities and contexts in which they worked, with most performers moving rather fluidly between job types even if they were strongly associated with certain types. Commonly used terms such as "playing at night" or doing a "show" were more than just convenient shorthand. Rather, they conveyed information about pay, treatment, infrastructure, prestige, career implications, and the music "itself."

"PLAYING AT NIGHT"   The likely archetype of local musical labor, performing several sets of well-known songs in settings such as bars and restaurants is, in Salvador, referred to as "playing at night" (*tocar na noite*),[16] and the musicians who do this work are called *músicos da noite* (night musicians).[17] Some *músicos da noite* can garner devoted followings, but none that I encountered achieved star status or reverence for their artistry. Rather, most remained rather anonymous and were by and large treated as tradespeople, providers of entertainment, or even part of the atmosphere by audiences, employers, and at times, peers. Yet many of the same people who performed in obscurity "at night" also worked in the spotlight as side musicians for consecrated artists or as principal attractions themselves. Thus, while some performers come to be known primarily as *músicos da noite*, this identification is fluid, contingent, and at times misleading.[18]

Most musicians I heard in bars, restaurants, and at private events based their performances on the core genres of the nonseasonal circuit, especially MPB, with a focus on the most familiar hits. Singer Laís Nunes[19] called this repertory a "*kit de barzinho*" (bar [tool] kit), modifying it slightly to specify the foundational sambas for night work a "*kit de pagode.*"[20] Singers who accompany themselves on nylon-string acoustic guitar (*voz e violão*) or in some instances keyboard have been especially common over the years. This format provides several benefits, such as maximizing profit and control over repertoire and its manner of presentation. Thus, solo work provides tremendous flexibility in terms of possible work sites—many of which are restricted by space, budget, and volume limits—and nimbleness for adapting to emergent needs on the job.

Notably, I never saw a self-accompanied performance by a woman working as a night musician. This, despite the facts that bossa nova pioneer Nara Leão is often said to have made it acceptable for "nice girls" to sing and play guitar onstage, several female MPB stars regularly do so during their performances, and in my network, Márcia Castro began her musical training with *violão* lessons. In fact, at fifteen, she sang and played the instrument with an MPB trio on her first professional job in the Historic District. However, as she told me:

> I played [*violão*] a little. The guy who played with me then played better than I did, but I always played at shows. These days that is really rare. I prefer to just sing, grab a *violão* only at certain moments, and that's it. (Salvador, April 30, 2005)

Though I never saw Márcia play *violão* on any of the multiple performances I saw her deliver, her stated approach reflected a convention that I saw almost universally followed: female singers, especially those working at night, performed with male *violonistas* (or occasionally, keyboardists), sometimes with further backing from one to three more instrumentalists. Small ensembles were not solely the domain of women. Yet the vast majority of male singers I saw working at night accompanied themselves, augmenting what could have been a solo performance, usually with a percussionist. Since I met several women who were able to sing and accompany themselves, it is likely that men had more liberty to choose to work alone (and keep all the pay), adding additional musicians when they or the venue wanted fuller sound and when space and budget allowed. Perhaps focusing on singing and working with backing musicians was a matter of preference as Márcia suggested, but sediments of gendered proscriptions as well as issues of personal safety might well have informed such "preferences."

Though not as nimble as solo work, small ensembles are still fairly economical and organizationally efficient in terms of being performance ready. This is thanks to the musicians' competences catalyzed by reliance on the *kit de barzinho/pagode*, which helps cut overhead by streamlining rehearsals or eliminating them altogether for pick-up jobs that Bahian musicians call "gigs." A large body of common repertoire also facilitates the use of substitutes, which, for a number of reasons, was frequently necessary among my collaborators who worked in ongoing ensembles that played at night—flexibility that also came at the risk of providing evidence that few of them were irreplaceable and devaluing their labor.

On the other hand, the featuring of familiar repertoire also maximizes audiences' ability to sing along, a typical expectation that when met, can endear performers to their listeners and employers. Audience participation at the performances I saw was further catalyzed by the tendency of most *músicos da noite* to stay fairly close to the best-known versions of the songs they performed. Few of them, however, precisely replicated recordings, and none suggested that it was a goal unless they worked as "cover artists," which in Salvador is akin to doing a tribute act.[21] Audiences for *músicos da noite* never struck me as put off by a little variation either. Typically, then, the most popular rendition of a song, many of which had been recorded multiple times, provided a foundation upon which musicians based their performances, with small changes due to instrumentation, the gender of the singer, and individual proclivities, all of which were very much accepted by employers, peers, and patrons.

The importance placed on participation and the expectation that performers would invite it also point to an irony that was especially apparent in the context of playing at night: patrons at many upscale venues featuring "quality" music were not necessarily attentive, let alone active. I frequently saw them sing—and in so doing, clearly enjoy themselves while also demonstrating embodied cultural capital such as knowledge of the sophisticated poetry for which nonseasonal circuit staples are so esteemed. But I also saw them detach from performances almost entirely. Performances of music intended to move their minds became the backdrop for dining, drinking, and conversation with some frequency. On the other hand, I saw audiences in popular neighborhoods singing enthusiastically along with the very music that members of the middle classes and many musicians told me they did not want, or assumed they could not understand.[22]

For a variety of reasons, playing at night is a rather ambivalent proposition for working musicians. Pay varies greatly but is typically much lower than what is possible in the seasonal circuits. Treatment on the job can be poor as well, exemplified by silence after finishing a song or a night's worth of work and a general lack of respect. Musicians known for working as *músicos da noite* were rarely praised for their career achievements. On the other hand, bar and restaurant work is a fairly reliable, albeit nonlucrative, income stream for those with suitable skills and who do the legwork necessary to find it. Since the *kit de barzinho* leans heavily toward MPB and other esteemed music such as international pop and rock, night work can also provide evidence to peers and potential colleagues of competence performing music with sophisticated lyrics, harmonies, and arrangements—albeit as a worker or entertainer rather than as an Artist. Still, this somewhat attenuated cultural capital can be converted into economic capital in the form of other employment in similar contexts. And, on some occasions, demonstrations of respected skills for the right people can lead to better-paying jobs, better work conditions, and enhanced professional status. This was the case for Luciano Salvador Bahia, who got his start playing at night, doing so for many years before establishing himself as a musical director, song and sound track composer, and singer-songwriter—the work he does to this day.

At the time I was working in bars in Salvador that had music. I was living this way, playing in one, then another. Then I would meet someone who would call me to play somewhere else. It was only that . . . until now . . . I also began to get to know people who played at night who were not *only* playing at night. They also did theater shows. That way, I developed the qualities of being able to do shows in theaters too. In this regard, Dino Brasil, who was a singer here in Salvador, is really important. He took me a bit from playing in bars—I played a lot with him in bars—and he said, "I'm doing a show at Teatro ACBEU, and I want you to play." That is how I got to know about playing onstage for shows. The other thing that happened then that was really important for my career, was musical direction and composing sound tracks for theater. I was invited to compose a soundtrack for a play and from then on, I never stopped. (Salvador, September 29, 2005)

Whereas playing at night opened doors for Luciano to increase his economic and cultural capital—he now earns a middle-class income specializing in esteemed music —similar work experience also paved the way for others to find work in the seasonal circuits performing less esteemed music but for significantly more money. Leo, the singer from A Zorra mentioned that this was precisely his trajectory. For him, Luciano, and plenty of other musicians, the social capital they accumulated by playing at night—in many instances, a strong tie with one key person—catalyzed by the cultural capital of the *kit do barzinho* increased the value of their labor, especially but not only in a monetary sense. Finally, many musicians who leave comparatively lucrative jobs, for instance, with Carnaval circuit artists, can continue to live from music by working as *músicos da noite* provided they have the background and necessary contacts.

DANCE BAND WORK   Another common context for work in the nonseasonal circuit is the dance band. The dance bands I saw were usually quartets or quintets, though a few were larger. Smaller groups frequently utilized sequenced percussion or bass lines ("playback") to fill out their sound, prioritizing harmonic and lead melodic instruments. Most dance bands featured several singers in order to cover multiple genres over a long night of nearly continuous music. These ensembles work in a variety of venues ranging from private parties to some of the larger and more upscale clubs along the Orla. As such, dance band musicians can be understood as a type of *músico da noite*. However, unlike performers working in bars or restaurants, the primary objective of a dance band is to provide a suitable soundtrack for patrons to move rather than a backdrop for socializing, singing, or occasional close listening.

Most dance bands perform well-known songs often organized into discrete genre blocks. For example, several sambas might be followed by a sequence of pop/rock tunes, and then a series of danceable MPB hits. I also heard *axé*, *pagode*, and Forró favorites incorporated into the mix regularly and, depending on the band and the event, anything from rock 'n' roll oldies to disco to *brega* ballads or samba. Some bands distinguished themselves by emphasizing one of these genres more than others, but they nearly always included several kinds of music in their repertoire, both for variety and to avoid overly limiting their employment options. Whether they aimed for a more specialized profile or a more general one, the dance bands I heard stayed fairly close to the best-known versions of the songs they played while still allowing for some variation, much like other *músicos da noite*. Once again, the appropriateness and practicality of radically reworking repertoire was limited by the goal of inviting embodied participation, curtailed rehearsal time for increased profit, and the likelihood of musician substitutions and replacements.

Despite a prevalent tendency toward familiar arrangements of beloved songs, one type of radical reworking was common across the Scenes: adapting songs associated with one genre to another. This tactic was utilized by different performers in different contexts and in different ways, but it was especially practical for dance bands and other *músicos da noite*. Common practice was to perform regular repertoire over a different groove to satisfy requests, adapt to a room, fit with the season, or express a particular musical orientation. Examples of such *releituras* (rereadings) I heard include MPB songs played as *arrochas*, sambas played as *axé* (and vice versa), and even "Hotel California" played as salsa.[23]

Dance band work is hardly glamorous or lucrative. Yet several working pros cited its importance to their careers. For instance, bassist Son Melo cited the diversity of repertoire it required as key to his ability to live from music—he suggested that, owing to his background and preferences at the time, he might not have otherwise learned some of the genres or songs that were foundational to dance band performances. Others, especially *músicos da noite* who normally worked as solo singers, supplemented the income they earned working alone with dance band jobs. This brought an additional benefit of more work without overtaxing their voices since they shared vocal duties with other members. Several collaborators, including Patua drummer Pastel Reis and percussionist/drummer Junior Oliveira, turned to dance band jobs when their work with other employers slowed down or ended. And a few others worked with dance bands alongside their pursuit of more singular musical visions with projects geared toward doing "shows."

SHOWS When talking about his career trajectory from playing in bars to theater stages, Luciano Salvador Bahia specifically used the word "show." This was normal discourse in the Scenes when discussing presentations in theaters, certain kinds of clubs, and festivals such as Carnaval and São João that audiences attend to see, hear, and usually sing and dance along with a performance by a specific performer. In these contexts, the music is intended to be the focus of attention rather than background for other forms of socializing.[24] Work conditions and payment for shows vary in relation to setting within and across the three circuits, but all shows provide maximum space for acts to express their particular musical vision, their "*cara*" (face). Shows are also the most likely settings for working musicians to establish themselves beyond the local Scenes and gain elevated status and income. Thus, numerous musicians aspire to base their careers on doing this type of performance.

Since shows are so central to establishing a position as an Artist or star (rather than a workaday entertainer or craftsperson), I was initially surprised by the substantial amount of familiar repertoire I heard. Yet this was still another indication of the importance of engendering participation. The marked presence of familiar songs and their treatment were also audible clues that notions of creativity were different from what I experienced in other settings such as North American popular music scenes and discourse about Western art music (see chapter 5). Plenty of shows included *músicas inéditas* (original/unpublished songs), but very few eschewed all music popularized by well-known artists. This included shows by the biggest stars of Bahian music. And, very much in keeping with a long history of acclaimed *intérpretes* (interpreters) in Brazil—singers who primarily sing songs composed by others—many shows were comprised entirely of *releituras*.[25] From a repertoire standpoint, the principal difference between a show and a performance by *músicos da noite* or dance band was that, whereas restaurant, bar, and dance audiences accepted changes to familiar repertoire and musicians made them largely out of practicality, show audiences generally expected rearrangements and performers focused on presenting canonic songs with "*novas roupagens*" (new clothes), yet another term for reworking existing material composed and/or popularized by someone else.

Shows are also risky, especially for less prominent performers. Revenue is typically based on ticket sales, which can be unpredictable. Adding to that unpredictability and putting increased pressure on the musicians to promote themselves is that most show-suitable venues offer few attractions other than the music, such as food or even a regular clientele. Production costs can also be high and are borne by performers unless they have management support or sponsorship (see next chapter). While some musicians working in the nonseasonal circuit have such capital behind them, well-financed shows are much more common in the two seasonal circuits, especially the one oriented around Carnaval.

Carnaval: Its Music, Its Circuit, Its Meanings

Carnaval is the most audible, visible, and generally lucrative time for music in Salvador. Like the more famous festivities in Rio de Janeiro, it is a time when the city's population increases dramatically with an influx of tourists from other parts of the state, other Brazilian states, and other nation-states. In 2012, Salvador's municipal tourism agency predicted 500,000 tourists and related revenue of one billion Reis, with the organization's director affirming that "Carnaval is a matter of the city's survival" (quoted in Nucci 2012, my translation).[26] Part of the appeal is an emphasis on mass participation in public spaces, at least in theory.[27] Like claims of *democracia racial*, claims of democratic participation in Bahian Carnaval have rightly come under fire, at times during performances.[28] Regardless of any exaggeration of access equality, the popular music shows that animate parades on designated routes on city streets as well as numerous other stages across the RMS are attended by massive crowds that on the whole represent the diversity of identities in Bahia. Many businesses and year-round music venues close, though a few adapt to take advantage of increased tourist traffic and the fact that most residents are off work. From mid-morning until sunrise for the better part of a week, much of the city pulses with the frenetic energy of densely packed crowds singing and dancing along with performances, many of which can be accessed free of charge, and most of which feature Bahian music. This audibility coupled with the magnitude of the Carnaval circuit, which extends several months before and after the main event and that is driven by well-financed production companies and wealthy sponsors, drives the frequent characterization of the Scenes in and outside of Bahia: "Salvador is all/only *axé* and *pagode*."

AXÉ MUSIC Since its emergence in the 1980s, *axé* music has dominated the Bahian Carnaval soundscape and remains the genre most strongly identified with the event and Bahia itself. First used by a journalist as a slight for allegedly poor-quality popular music produced in Salvador,[29] the term gained traction for referencing a range of practices featured during pre-Lenten events and performed by several of Bahia's biggest stars. That *axé* never lost all of its negative connotations was apparent in the various debates I heard over which artists were and were not *axé*, and the many occasions that musicians at various levels of prominence distanced themselves from it or rejected it as a description of their music.

Despite disagreements and disavowals, I eventually found a kind of core discourse and set of practices that helped me better understand what music and which performers were most likely to be accepted as *axé*. *Baianos* generally use the term for high-energy dance music played for Carnaval and related events by relatively large ensembles. Typical *axé* bands include a male or female lead vocalist, one or more musicians playing electric guitar, an electric bassist,

FIGURE 1.1 Typical *axé* grooves for *repique* and *surdos*: A is played by one drummer with hands divided between the two drums; B is played by one drummer on *surdos* against the *repique* timeline played by another musician. Since each drummer now uses both hands on their respective instruments, embellishing fills are common and expected. *Examples by Edni Devay.*

a keyboardist, a kit drummer, and several percussionists. Ensembles commonly add horn sections, backup singers, and dancers as well. *Axé* music epitomizes the aesthetic of participation in its emphasis on catchy, repeated riffs and singable, playful lyrics that incite audiences to sing and dance individually but en masse often for hours.

Percussion is especially central in this regard. A conical hand drum called a *timbal* and especially a set of two or three *surdos* (horizontally mounted bass drums) are genre defining. These very Bahian instruments complement a standard drum set, conga pair, *repique* (tenor drum), and assorted other struck instruments. Together, they are the basis of grooves that animate huge audiences.

The manner in which the *surdo* set is played as well as the basic rhythms rendered are particular to *axé*. At the core is a rhythmic cell adapted from samba-reggae, the signature rhythm of the *blocos afro*. Whereas the drummers in groups such as Olodum and Ilê Aiyê each play one drum, *axé surdo* players utilize multiple instruments at once, in some cases incorporating a *repique*, to create a composite rhythm akin to what is normally played by several drummers.

There have been changes in percussionists' division of labor within *axé* ensembles, but the basic rhythmic cell has remained largely the same. In 2014, drummer Edni Deway told me that:

> [Now] the majority of the bands have one percussionist who plays only the *surdos*. Before, it was more common for a percussionist to play *surdo* and *repique* at the same time. This [change has happened] because the *surdo* is becoming valued more in music made here and is getting more attention. There are other reasons as well:
>
> It's better to play only *surdos* when the music is fast. When the percussionist only plays *surdos*, he can play more fills since he does not have to play *repique* at the same time . . . (Edni Devay, personal email communication 2014. My translation).

Whether the *surdos* and *repique* are played by one or two musicians, a majority of *axé* songs draw on this rhythmic base, combining it with elements and influences from numerous other musics including funk, pop, rock, salsa, *lambada*, and more.

The other characteristics common to *axé* and central to its ability to engender participation—its emphasis on repetition along with lyrical and harmonic simplicity—remain at the heart of the many critiques about it I have heard over the years. This exemplifies the Euro-mimetic sensibilities prevalent in the Scenes, especially the elevation of "mind music" over "body music," as well as the related cultural intimacy of too much African-ness in the mix. Indeed, *axé*'s historical and discursive ties to Blackness remain strong despite the more European-descended appearance of its biggest stars and a majority of the patrons who pay the largest fees to parade with them. Along with a genre-defining groove adapted from the *blocos afro*, several adaptations/appropriations of their songs were early *axé* hits and have become core repertoire during Carnaval (often played by bands performing for organizations that excluded dark-skinned *baianos*). Many such songs, and newly composed ones as well, refer to the pioneering Afro-centric groups, especially Olodum and Ilê Aiyê, by name. On a broader scale, and in many ways separate from the sonic and lyrical content of *axé*, Bahia's metonymic relationship with African-ness and "*axé*'s" frequent use as a synecdoche for Bahian music reinforces its entanglements with Blackness and characterization as "*mais afro*."

The way that *baianos* discussed *axé* (and other Bahian music) points to a less commonly explored but important aspect of Bourdieu's ideas: associations that can undermine a participant's position in a field. Notably, he closes his introduction to *Distinction* with a reference to such potential liabilities that are disavowed by those claiming elite taste, suggesting a kind of cultural anti-capital:

> The denial of lower, course, vulgar, venal, servile . . . implies an affirmation of the superiority of those who can be satisfied with the sublimated, refined, disinterested, gratuitous, distinguished pleasures forever closed to the profane. (1984, 7)

Similar to the kind of distancing Bourdieu describes, Bahian listeners from across racial and class categories consistently decried the quality of *axé* by telling me that it: "*não tem letra, não tem arranjo, e não tem harmonia*" (does not have [good] lyrics, arrangements, or harmonies). They also qualified any involvement with it as limited to parties and especially Carnaval, when everyday conventions of propriety are supposed to be relaxed and transgressed. Most, including those who paid large sums of money to sing and dance to it during Carnaval, further distanced from the event's prevalent music by asserting they would never buy it or listen to it at home. Regardless of negative evaluations of *axé*, it remains central to pre-Lenten celebration. Key, then, is the fact that Carnaval and related events emphasize the ludic relaxation of social norms, including so-called good taste. Participation can cost big money, and the city as well as many people who work in the Carnaval circuit, including musicians, can see dramatically higher earnings. References to temporal and conceptual containment as well as economics provided effective buffers from the intimacy of *axé*. Such distancing processes were also apparent when the topic of conversation turned to *pagode*, the other music featured in the Carnaval circuit.

BAHIAN PAGODE Not to be confused with small-ensemble, acoustic samba of the same name from Rio de Janeiro (see Galinsky 1996), Bahian *pagode* is a co-star of Carnaval, glossed as Bahian music, and a frequent target of disavowal and distancing by many *baianos*.[30] It became a sensation in Salvador and nationally in the 1990s, spearheaded by several of the same producers responsible for *axé*'s successes just prior.[31] Likely for this reason, along with its audibility in Carnaval circuit events, *pagode* is often conflated with *axé* outside of the state. Few *baianos*, however, would confuse the two.

Bahian *pagode* sounds more or less like an electrified version of its nationalized and much more esteemed namesake from Rio. This is largely due to its rhythmic structure, which emphasizes beat two (in 2/4) with a louder, longer note played on the lowest-pitched *surdo*. The Bahian variant stands apart with its heavier sound and feel provided by its extensive use not only of electric instruments but also horn sections and drum sets. Repetitive harmonies, usually cycling I – vi – ii – V – I chord progressions outlined in various patterns of sixteenth notes on the bass and/or *cavaquinho*, also help define Bahian *pagode*[32] with a groove that deviates radically from the *surdo*-synced bass lines and *cavaquinho* timelines common to Rio-style samba.

Harmonic simplicity and repetition were frequent targets of passionate critiques of Bahian *pagode*, which many *baianos* called "a corruption [of samba]." But its lyrical content, which ranges from playful to provocative and from risqué to misogynistic, drew even more ire. So too did *pagode* dancing, which features more exaggerated hip movements than "roots" sambas, at times following choreography described in song lyrics, demonstrated onstage, or both. As with *axé*, such efforts toward maximizing participation are successful and cited as key to *pagode*'s very audible and visible appeal. But they also elicit charges of banality and inferiority, which, in comparison to *axé*, were considerably more frequent and vitriolic.

Perhaps the fervor of *pagode*'s detractors has a basis in its musical content, which clearly deviates from "refined" (Euro-mimetic) musical sensibilities that prioritize contemplation. Its groove, repetition, and approachable lyrics that invite participation even at first listen are undeniably successful at moving the bodies of audiences. I never saw live *pagode* fail to inspire dancing and singing along, and I saw a group of young, dark-skinned women request *pagode* "so we can dance" when I sat in with a group performing "quality music" on a free to the public stage in the Historic District. In a memorable moment, the musicians dismissed their request, somewhat mockingly among themselves. Indeed, the dim view taken by *pagode*'s many critics is hard to disconnect from general attitudes toward its assumed audience, and references to *pagodeiros*' (*pagode* participants) "*baixa astral*," or "low vibe" were common. More than a generalized reference to an attitude or ethos, such condemnations were explicitly classed and often racialized.

Such problematic stereotypes are common and durable for several reasons, both past and present. *Pagode*'s history, as Brazilian ethnomusicologist Mônica Leme (2003) notes, rests with amateur musicians in Salvador's popular, and historically "Blacker" neighborhoods. In fact, Luciano Salvador Bahia specifically cited this "grassroots" history as what made *pagode* interesting to him. His perspective was unusual, however, and references to poorly executed, out-of-tune performances were much more common and offered as evidence of musical inferiority. A few collaborators found a kind of middle ground, noting that many of these infamous performances were the result of producers seeking to capitalize quickly on neighborhood popularity. In their eagerness to strike when the iron was hot, industry capitalists thrust amateur musicians into the professional spotlight lacking experience with the conditions of the new milieu, not the least of which was wide exposure to members of the middle classes whose tastes and investment in performing them was radically different from what they were accustomed to. Regardless of reason and even the veracity of the stories of these out-of-tune performances, the stigma of *pagode*'s past has proven hard to undo.

This is in part because *pagode* also continues to be very popular among the *povo*, including a large number of people of visible African descent. During Carnaval and related events, *pagode* bands typically perform for Carnaval *blocos*, many of which are very large but whose membership is less affluent and less European in appearance than those parading with *axé* artists.[33] And it is very audible in poorer parts of the city such as the Cidade Baixa and Upper City popular neighborhoods as a soundtrack for parties outside of Carnaval season.

Thus, *pagode*'s history and its sites of greatest audibility continue to inform negative attitudes toward it and its participants, especially among members of the middle and upper classes as well as numerous musicians not part of the *pagode* scene (and quite a few working in it). Assumptions that *pagode* musicians cannot play in tune persist despite the fact that several *pagode* ensembles are acknowledged for having honed their skills to a great degree and have provided work for well-respected musicians. Furthermore, despite clear evidence that *pagode* had gained some traction beyond the *povo* and outside of Afro-Bahian communities, I was also often told that it is music for "*pretos*," a pejorative term for Afro-Brazilians—once in the home of a middle-class, lightly pigmented family as their daughters demonstrated their favorite *pagode* dance moves for my wife and me. Another unforgettable discussion had a fair-skinned taxi driver describing *pagode* to me as "without culture" (*sem cultura*) and "Black people yelling" (*pretos gritando*).[34]

By most accounts, *pagode* is less popular than it was in the mid-1990s. Several musicians told me that pay for working with *pagode* ensembles had decreased—a former *cavaquinho* player with the elite-level band Terra Samba joked that he left the group because it was costing him money to work with them. *Pagode* is also less demonized in some circles; but it is still a lightning rod for performative complaints about musical quality and its participants' character, typically by musicians and members of the middle and upper classes. These associations severely limit its cultural capital, even in comparison to *axé*, which despite the criticism it receives, is more widely enjoyed by affluent (and fairer-skinned) audiences during the "safe period" prior to Lent and several exclusive, "safer" contexts therein. Chief among them are parading alongside *trios elétricos*, the mobile stages upon which prominent *axé* and *pagode* ensembles perform, providing what is for most people the definitive image and experience of Bahian Carnaval.

CARNAVAL AND ITS CIRCUIT'S MAIN STAGES: TRIOS ELÉTRICOS

The first *trio elétrico*, a "wired for sound" Model A Ford, was used in the mid-1950s to carry two musicians performing for an informal parade during Carnaval in Salvador. Since then, the trucks, like the bands and the crowds, have gotten bigger and more elaborate. Now most *trios* are tractor-trailer trucks outfitted with full stages, lights, and powerful PA systems capable of carrying the large ensembles that are the norm in Bahian music and immersing the massive audience, the *folia*, in chest-pounding sound.

Trio elétrico parade performances are the centerpieces of Carnaval in the Bahian capital, as well as a series of similarly organized celebrations, called *micaretas*, that take place after Ash Wednesday in other cities. Most well-established artists, regardless of genre, perform on *trios* affiliated with a *bloco*—a configuration called a *bloco do trio*. *Blocos* are clubs whose members purchase a shirt called an *abadá* that grants them access to an exclusive, roped-off area surrounding the truck. There within, *bloco* members walk, dance, and sing along the parade route separated from the mass of onlookers, many of whom cannot afford to parade with a *bloco*, protected by a human barricade of rope and the poorer, largely darker-skinned people who carry it.[35] For the main event in Salvador, there are two epicenters of such activity: one in the center of the Upper City and another along the Orla starting at the entrance to the bay.

The vast majority of *blocos de trio* feature *axé* or *pagode* performers. On all days during Carnaval and *micaretas*, they dominate prime time—usually from mid-afternoon to midnight on all days—and especially on the Monday and Tuesday before Ash Wednesday. Despite being the main stage for Bahian music and an emblem of Bahian Carnaval, many *blocos de trio* charge fees too high for a majority of *baianos* to afford.

In the capital, other types of Carnaval parade organizations feature *trio*-based performances as well. These include *blocos infantil*, which are similar to *blocos de trio* except that they cater to children,[36] and *blocos afro*, which use *trios* as a stage for singers and featured dancers who are accompanied by drummers and paying members in the street. *Blocos infantil* parade in the morning, after sunrise and until around 1:00 pm, when they are gradually superseded by *blocos de trio*. *Blocos afro* can be seen sporadically beginning in the early afternoon, but many are relegated to the hours after midnight—a continuing point of friction.[37]

Also appearing on the parade routes in between the various *blocos* and other types of organizations are *trios independentes* (independent *trios*). As the name suggests, *trios independentes* and the artists performing on them have no formal ties with a *bloco*. They are typically scheduled in the early afternoon before peak crowds of onlookers have amassed, or after midnight, when they have dissipated and media coverage has ceased. As Laurinha reminded me about her *trio* performance in 2005:

> I had a schedule that was really early when there was no one on the street. I left at 3:00 in the afternoon. At 7:30, Ivete Sangalo was still at the Farol da Barra in front of TVE (a local television station) . . . Nobody goes to the street at 3:00 or 4:00 in the afternoon. Carnaval da Bahia only starts after 5:00 or 5:30 when it starts to get dark because nobody can stand the heat . . . (Salvador, September 5, 2005).

She told me this in the context of describing her involvement with an attempt to form an association of independent artists to lobby for better working conditions during Carnaval (another point of contention was that independent artists were not permitted to stop to perform for or chat with media stationed along the parade routes). Nine years later, Laurinha's *trio* left the staging area after midnight, exemplifying the minimal success that this and other efforts to build labor solidarity among Salvador's working musicians have achieved. Nevertheless, independent *trios* continue to be important work sites for up-and-coming performers, artists whose prominence has decreased somewhat, and those who have avoided formal relationships with a large-scale production organization.

As might be expected, headliners working for elite *blocos* earn the highest wages, justified by their higher marginal revenue product—the artist performing is easily argued to (and often does) attract *bloco* members. Most musicians I spoke with were rather tight lipped about their own earnings, but stars' Carnaval pay was a fairly common topic of gossip. In 2005, members of *axé* star Ivete Sangalo's band were rumored to have earned over R$20,000 each for their Carnaval performances. By contrast, Laurinha was able to pay each member of her ten-piece band R$300 for four three-hour rehearsals and one three- to four-hour performance on her *trio independente* that same year.[38] Likely some independent artists pay better than Laurinha could, but many of the musicians working on *trios independentes* do it for less, for free, or at a loss. Laurinha told me she had gotten sponsorship from the state government (see below) worth R$15,000, from which she paid taxes, herself, her musicians, and all expenses other than the *trio*, which was provided by the city government. Many other artists are unsuccessful garnering even that level of funding. In the face of radical disparities of compensation and treatment, all shows on *trios elétricos*, with or without a *bloco*, require several hours of music performed in a manner that inspires the audience—whatever audience is present, that is—to sing and dance.

Stratification notwithstanding, *trio elétrico* jobs are generally higher profile and often better paying than most of the work done by local musicians in the nonseasonal circuit. Owing to comparatively larger and more enthusiastic crowds, they can also be quite fun for the musicians who work them. However, the danceable grooves and harmonic and lyrical simplicity that are so effective for engendering audience participation—and valued in *axé* and *pagode* scenes/subfields—do not provide a strong case for musical excellence within the Cartesian regime of cultural values that overarches the Scenes, the field of popular music practice, and Bahian (and Brazilian) society.

Though several musicians complained that this approach was to appease the *folia*, who they believed would not respond well to more elaborated, contemplative material, they also conceded that it made their performances possible. Indeed, typical work conditions make delivering polished performances of complex music difficult if not impossible, even if it were thought to be effective for engendering the party. As I suggested above, many artists have only limited time to rehearse their programs, which typically last more than three hours and can reach as many as six if their truck stops to play to large pockets of listeners or, in the case of bigger-name acts, TV cameras. In addition to the length of the shows and the expectation for continuous, familiar, participation engendering music, one of the most striking things about the *trios* I rode on was the degree to which the trucks bounced, jerked, and lurched. Equipment shifted, microphones fell, and the stage as a whole was anything but a stable platform that let the performers focus only on making music. Sometimes, just keeping instruments and bodies upright was a tall order. Such challenges were compounded by difficult hearing conditions due to ambient noise as well as blocked sight lines between players—extra people ride on trucks and musicians face outward and away from each other. On more than one occasion rain intruded on performances

I attended; but the presentations did not stop. Instead, crews wrestled canvas covers into place, awkwardly "dancing" with musicians to avoid collisions and keep the music playing. And the performers typically responded in kind, in many instances, managing to put enough of their own spin on the songs to express their project's *cara*.

OTHER MUSICAL WORK SITES DURING CARNAVAL By most accounts, an increasing number of people with adequate financial means participate in Carnaval from *camarotes*, box seats and temporary club venues that line the parade routes, rather than or in addition to parading with *blocos*. The growing presence of these exclusive spaces ("*camarotization*"), which provide a less physically intense way to enjoy Carnaval than parading, has been a contentious issue in the last several years. Like elite *blocos*, access to *camarotes* is also severely curtailed by high entry costs. Adding to the discontent is that the structures often impinge on sidewalk space along the parade routes, reducing the area in which anyone who wishes can, in fact, participate. This densely packed mass lining the streets is known as the "*pipoca*" (popcorn) for the way members energetically jump up and down as *trios* pass.[39] The *pipoca* exemplifies the democratized participation asserted in event PR. However, in addition to losing space to *camarotes*, it is also a site for petty theft and fights—I have seen several. Thus, many who have the means retreat to *camarotes*, putting an even greater distance between them and *pipoca* than a *bloco* while still providing a space for co-present participation in parades. Club-type *camarotes* also provide numerous amenities including seats, food, drinks, and separate entertainment, including live music. Many of the musicians they employ, further, perform the cultural capital-rich, "alternative" music typical of the nonseasonal circuit.

An array of music can also be heard further away from the parade routes. Venues that continue operating during Carnaval as well as the various plazas of the Historic District can be counted on to host a roster of artists more diverse, albeit usually less famous, than those performing on *trios*.[40] The city government also sponsors stages in neighborhoods across the Upper City, out through the beach areas to the north, and in the Lower City into Surbúrbio. The programming in these more remote locations is varied, including Bahian music as well as samba, pop/rock, and MPB. Performances range from that typical of *músicos da noite* or dance bands to full-blown shows. For alternative musicians who do not work in Bahian music and many performers who do, these venues provide a useful avenue for making the most of the Carnaval circuit's peak.

ROUNDING OUT THE CIRCUIT: OUT-OF-SEASON WORK Although Carnaval takes place in February or March, related activities begin long before and continue afterward, making it a year-round enterprise, at least for some. Elite *blocos* begin selling *abadás* for the coming year before the current event ends (and before wealthy visitors return home). Alliances between *blocos*, corporate sponsors, and headline artists continue throughout the year as well, as does promotion and planning. Established *axé* and *pagode* artists along with those working their way up industry ranks record new music and when possible, keep performing and promoting their work, during what is for most other local pros, an off season.

When Carnaval is over, *micaretas* in other cities extend the circuit, providing additional work for prominent *axé* and *pagode* performers and points of entry for newcomers with the proper connections. Typically lasting a weekend rather than a week, *micaretas* come complete with *trios elétricos*, corporate and government sponsorship, *blocos*, *camarotes*, and *pipoca*. Many Carnaval-oriented artists, primarily well-established ones, also perform at non-Carnaval-styled festivals, indoor shows, and corporate parties in cities other than Salvador, where, as Edni told me, *axé* is more marketable for more of the year.

For mid- and upper-tier *axé* and *pagode* artists as well as established *blocos*, Carnaval-related events in Salvador start as early as September. Though they are called *ensaios* (rehearsals), they are public shows complete with full production and admission charges. Yet they still provide a kind of dress-rehearsal function during which artists can hone their presentations in a setting that is more controlled than the main event. They also serve as a forum for potential *bloco* participants to audition the performers who might animate their Carnaval parade(s) before they spend considerably more money on an *abadá* and commit to a particular group. Perhaps most importantly, they provide audience members an opportunity to learn the words and practice singing the songs of the season. Coupled with any radio play and other forms of promotion,[41] *ensaios* also debut the artist's *carro chefe* (primary vehicle) or *música de trabalho* (work song), their featured song for the year.

Along with generating revenue and facilitating participation, *ensaios* provide several other career and commercial benefits for performers. Creating a buzz for the year's *carro chefe* increases the likelihood that other artists will perform it. This is more than a vanity exercise since local media tracks and gives awards for the most played new songs and the most animated *blocos*, further evidence of participation as a central aesthetic criterion. Success in these categories helps attract larg(er) audiences, justify high(er) fees, and generally elevates the status of artists and Carnaval entities. Songwriters are often credited too, so their work gains more currency among musicians, often leading to more work.

Whereas headline-level Bahian music artists and their supporting musicians and staff are, for all intents and purposes, engaged in Carnaval-related activity for much of the year, the work period for less prominent performers varies much more. A majority of independent musicians (re)turn to nonseasonal circuit work with some, especially side musicians, putting off their active search for Carnaval work until the event draws near. Bandleaders, however, often start their search for Carnaval circuit engagements and financial support (see next chapter) well in advance and alongside the more workaday performances they pursue. Even with advance planning, last-minute bookings and lineup changes are common. Laurinha's band for Carnaval 2005 included several musicians that I had not seen at rehearsals. Likewise, Farofa hired several backing musicians the day before his group's 2014 outing. That same year, Laurinha met the members of the band that would back her, save her regular bassist and keyboard player/ musical director, when she stepped onto the truck an hour before performance time. The centrality of familiar music during Carnaval performances again made such last-minute ensemble formation less problematic. But the labor devoted to developing this core repertoire competence and building relationships that lead to paid opportunities to put it to use rarely stops.

CARNAVAL POLITICS AND IMPLICATIONS FOR MUSICAL WORK AND WORKERS Thanks to its magnitude and expanding number of events, the Carnaval circuit provides Salvador-based musical workers plentiful job opportunities, the best possibilities for increased wages, and the most probable route to supralocal success. Still, reaping such possible rewards is hardly a given. Though several musicians told me in 2005 that Carnaval had enabled them to earn more than double their typical fees for comparable jobs at other times of the year, many also noted a downward trend in payment since the mid- to late 1990s. They pointed to different causes for the decline, ranging from increased competition to changing booking practices and finance policies that favored big-name acts. All expressed concerns about a widening gap between stars' wages and those of other performers, compounded by the cliquishness of the upper ranks of the Carnaval industries. As a result, work quantity and earnings for all but the most established musicians can vary greatly from year to year. I have seen close collaborators experience Carnaval seasons during which they performed only once or twice and others in which they worked multiple times, sometimes in the same day.

For many musicians I spoke with, the financial rewards and the pleasures of performing for large, enthusiastic crowds were also tempered by difficult performance conditions and local musical sensibilities that favored other music. As a result, the dominance of *axé* and *pagode* as the pathway toward high-level success and the best-known manifestations of Bahian music were frequent points of discontent among musicians. Long *trio* performances on unstable stages in unpredictable weather conditions combined with limited preparation time for many ensembles presented significant barriers to polished performances, a factor that several musicians linked with any genre-related dissatisfaction they expressed and perhaps the dim view taken by many in the general public. Especially for independent artists without a road crew, performance logistics are complicated to say the least. Large portions of main arteries are blocked off to form the parade routes and adjacent roads become congested with pedestrians. Getting equipment to and from the job is very labor intensive, and hiring help for the heavy lifting and transportation can be expensive.

Regardless of these discontents, it was also clear that many musicians—including those who complained about various aspects of Carnaval circuit work—placed a great deal of importance on it. Money certainly informed such sentiments. However, there were also plenty of smiles to be seen among ensemble members each time I attended an *ensaio* or rode on a Carnaval or *micareta trio*. And many musicians spoke to me and among themselves with pride about the jobs they had booked during Carnaval week as a sign of their professional (though not necessarily, musical) accomplishment and the value of their labor.

The June Seasonal Circuit

After Ash Wednesday, Salvador's soundscape shifts dramatically. Upper-tier Bahian music acts, along with lower-level projects trying to break into the upper strata of the Carnaval circuit, focus their performance schedules on other cities. Local musicians who are not involved in a full-time Bahian music project return to nonseasonal circuit venues where Bahian music goes largely silent in favor of national and international genres. This balance is somewhat short-lived since the post-Carnaval musical season change is marked by a gradual increase in the audibility of Forró. As the next large-scale seasonal celebrations, the *festas juninas*, approach, several variants of this accordion-based soundtrack for couples dancing progressively saturate the Bahian soundscape.

As their name suggests, the *festas juninas* take place in June, ostensibly commemorating the births of three Catholic saints: Santo Antônio (Saint Anthony) on June 13; São Pedro (Saint Peter) on June 29; and, most famously, São João (Saint John) on June 24, which is the biggest celebration of the season and a civic holiday (and likely the reason locals refer to the *festas juninas* in their entirety as São João). Like Carnaval, São João activities begin in advance of official celebrations and continue after them. Whereas the circuit of work oriented around Carnaval extends for several months before and after, the work related to the *festas juninas* is much more temporally constrained, usually starting to ramp up around April and for most Bahian musicians ending rather abruptly in July. But the June circuit is dense, with multiple São João-themed events large and small filling in between the official Saints' days throughout the state. The result is a brief, intense period of work opportunities, typically for seasonally increased wages.

In addition to paying homage to the saints, São João also commemorates the coinciding fall harvest. Thus, despite being rooted in Catholicism, most June celebrations I have attended fully embraced the secular. The season defined by these events brings with it numerous changes in behavior and ambiance that, while perhaps of a lesser magnitude than those during Carnaval, are still different from everyday life in Salvador. With the exception of June 24 and one or two days before and after, when those with adequate finances often travel to the interior of the state, most businesses in the capital continue to operate more or less as usual throughout the June season. However, the normal day to day is complemented by an increasing abundance of foods made from freshly reaped corn and assorted fruit liquors, all of which are sold in local stores, on the street, and at performances at shopping malls, restaurants, clubs, and festivals. At celebrations, many people, including those of visible African descent, enthusiastically don the "*caipira*" (hick) costume of the season, which includes overalls, straw hats, occasional blacked-out teeth, and painted-on freckles. The various aspects of commemorating the *festas juninas* mark a prominent move away from the African-ness that is so prevalent in the capital, and that largely defines the state for the rest of the year.

FORRÓ: NORTHEASTERN MUSIC AND DANCE Forró is an umbrella term for a number of related dance styles such as *baião, xote, xaxado*, and *arrasta-pe*. Most crucially, this music and dance is mapped as rural and *nordestino* (northeastern). Like so many Bahian artists who relocated to the Rio/São Paulo Axis to make their mark in nationally identified music, the dominant voice of Forró, Luiz Gonzaga, burst into the national spotlight following his move from the northeastern state of Pernambuco to Rio de Janeiro in the 1940s. His music, nevertheless retained its prior associations since, as noted by historian Bryan McCann (2004) and ethnomusicologist Larry Crook (2005, 2009), the words Gonzaga sang, the manner in which he presented them, and the image he cultivated all emphasized northeastern-ness. Although Forró ceded national interest to bossa nova in the 1950s, its practice continued apace in the Northeast and in the Southeast among northeastern migrants. In the 1990s, it experienced a new surge in popularity signaled by the successes of new artists, the emergence of new subgenres, and renewed national attention to the music of old stars such as Gonzaga. In Bahia, the seasonal embrace of various kinds of Forró and the *festas juninas* in general have been very apparent since my first June visit in 2003. Arguably, that embrace is growing tighter, as suggested by the growing number and size of São João events and the increasingly frequent comments of *baianos*, musicians and nonmusicians, who tell me that they prefer the June celebrations and the sounds of the season to Carnaval and Bahian music.

Along with the different dances that comprise the Forró complex, distinctions between three general stylistic approaches are recognized by performers and audiences. *Forró pé da serra* (foot of the hills) is generally considered to be the most traditional subgenre. Patterned very much after Gonzaga's oeuvre, it is played in a small ensemble usually consisting of a *sanfona* (accordion), a *zabumba* (a shallow bass drum), and a triangle. Although the core trio is considered essential, ensembles can be augmented with, for example, *violão* and bass. Musicians often dress in a *cangaçeiro*, or a northeastern hinterland bandit costume defined by a crescent-shaped leather cap as popularized by Gonzaga. Repertoire typically includes Gonzaga's tunes as well, along with classics by other artists such as Dominguinhos and Jackson do Pandeiro. Much of this music, as well as a good deal of newly composed *forró* in this style, emphasizes Northeastern themes, often with a nostalgic sensibility.

Slightly expanded ensembles are the norm for the approach pioneered by the musicians who repopularized Forró in São Paulo during the 1990s. Called *forró universitario* (university *forró*) in reference to the middle-class young adults at the core of this scene, ensembles tend to incorporate a *violão*, electric bass, keyboards, and a drum set with the basic trio. These ensembles typically write new music with a more pop rock sensibility. Along with instrumental augmentation/electrification and an emphasis on the *xote* rhythm, lyrical themes tend to step away from Northeastern nostalgia and toward the romantic. Gone too is the full *cangaçeiro* costume, which is usually replaced by jeans and t-shirts, giving the musicians and their music a more contemporary, urban sensibility. Even so, few *forrozeiros* would forget Forró's roots in the rural Northeast; and Gonzaga remains a point of reference, albeit perhaps a subtle one, even among the *universitário* crowd.

Around the same time that *forró universitário* was gaining popularity in the Southeast, electrified *forró* was becoming popular in the Northeast. This music, sometimes called *forró plástico* (plastic *forró*), less disparagingly *forró moderno* (modern *forró*), *forró eletrônico,* and in some circles, *forró estilizado* (stylized *forró*), has since the mid- to late-1990s had significant CD sales and high show attendance across Brazil. Bands that play this style have fully incorporated electric guitars, basses, and keyboards along with drum sets, additional percussion, and often, several lead singers into their lineups. The roles of the *sanfona, zabumba,* and triangle are less pronounced, and in some cases, eliminated. Also added to many performances are onstage dancers, usually couples, and elaborate scenic and light production. In comparison with *forró pé de serra* and *forró universitário*, more women take on lead singer duties, though they often alternate with male counterparts. Spandex and short skirts along with romantic and at times racy lyrics are very much the norm: one of the biggest bands of this style when I was living in Salvador was called Calcinha Preta (Black Panties). *Forró moderno* tends to carry more *brega* associations than either *pé de serra*, which is now often revered for its "roots authenticity," or *forró universitário*, which bears the marks of a gentrified version of a rural working class-mapped practice.[42]

Despite Forró's past and continued rural associations as well as any *brega* connotations it may carry, it has occupied a much less contested space in the Scenes in comparison to either *axé* or *pagode*. I have seen all Forró subgenres enjoyed without qualification by a wide variety of people, from very poor through solidly middle and upper class. *Forró moderno* tended to receive some criticism, usually from musicians or more educated elites. However, I never heard it or any type of Forró subjected to the force or volume of condemnation that I came to expect apropos of Bahian music, even when similar critiques of silly lyrics, exaggerated sexuality, unelaborated harmonies, simplistic arrangements, and in some instances, less than perfectly in tune performances could be made.

In other writing (e.g., Packman 2014), I have argued that this less severe judgment of Forró has much to do with race politics. To those arguments, I would add that Forró is given a wider berth in Bahia since it is less culturally intimate there than *axé* and *pagode*. As opposed to these genres, which are both explicitly linked to Bahia and deeply entangled historically, discursively, and performatively with Blackness, Forró is much more strongly linked with other places in Brazil and Indigenous/European hybridity. In the least, as argued by Jack Draper III (2010), it is more ambiguous in its racial mapping than many other Brazilian popular music practices.[43] In Bahia, Forró's audibility during a festival that mutes numerous otherwise ubiquitous aspects of Bahia's Afro-diasporic culture reinforces the sense that its sounds and movements are "less African" too — especially in comparison to Bahian music. The June festivals also lack the overt Afro-centric activism that is prominent during Bahian Carnaval. Thus, the celebration and its associated music portray a different kind of *mestiçagem* that expresses weaker ties to Brazil's African heritage, is less culturally intimate, and is more compliant with dominant narratives of racial harmony.

JUNE CIRCUIT MEANINGS AND WORK CONDITIONS Although the majority of the most nationally prominent Forró acts are from states further northeast than Bahia or national media centers in the Southeast, there is no shortage of Forró performed in Bahia by Bahian musicians. Like the most established *axé* and *pagode* artists, several of these locally based Forró ensembles are able to work throughout the year. That said, most of the musicians I met still tended to perform it on a seasonal basis, usually starting a month or so after the close of Carnaval and ending around the beginning of July.

Over the years I have watched as numerous musicians I know sought out, rejoined, and formed their own Forró groups to work for a few months of the year. In some instances, their June work meant strings of performances with the same group in multiple settings; others have mainly done Forró "gigs." And many others have combined the two approaches in ongoing efforts to capitalize on their flexibility, networks, and the genre-specific increased employment opportunities of the season.

Any discontent I have heard expressed about São João has concerned increasing similarities to Carnaval — and most complaints came from audiences rather than musicians. The most frequently lamented shift has been growing commercialization and spectacularization, which often go hand in hand with increased event admission prices. Corporate sponsorship is also prominent and many *forrós* are staged by production companies familiar from the Carnaval circuit. As part of this process, which was for a time referred to as the *carnivalização* ("carnivalization") of São João (see Packman 2013), prominent *axé* artists have come to host and headline events. Yet the importance of Forró as the soundtrack of the *festas juninas* is suggested by the fact that these stars augment their repertoire to include at least some of the most beloved songs of the June season. Also notable, most certainly related to carnivalization, and likely of the most consequence to working musicians, is a widening pay differential between headliners, both Bahian music stars and dedicated Forró artists, and local or new acts.

Alongside any emerging similarities to Carnaval, work conditions for musicians during São João are still considerably different. A key reason for this is that, in addition to the different genre conventions, *forrós* are organized as music festivals with a succession of performances on a fixed stage rather than as a series of parades. June season performers are thus spared the challenge of working on a platform that moves and shakes and instead are provided with a more controllable performance setting. Moreover, since preplanned sequences of showtimes on a single stage rather than completion of a parade route determine the duration of performances, stage time is limited to one or two hours rather than up to six. This allows for more precise set planning and for many, job multiplicity.[44]

Also significant for working musicians is the temporal and spatial span of the *festas juninas*. Unlike Carnaval, the June events typically touted as the biggest and/or most desirable for audiences and working musicians are held in rural locations—nearby cities and adjacent areas amenable to an outdoor festival and consistent with the season's country theme—rather than in the capital. These jobs are complemented by a seasonal increase in work for Forró performers at Salvador's bars, restaurants, and shopping malls as well as at the government-sponsored June festival held in the Historic District. As a result of the June circuit's temporal concentration and geographic spread, maximizing work and income often means frequent, and for busier acts, almost constant bus travel. While the Carnaval circuit also involves travel, *micaretas* are typically spaced out over sequential weekends for several months, allowing for a somewhat more relaxed pace once the frenzy of Carnaval week in Salvador is over. Likewise, preseasonal *ensaios* are weekly events (though they may be separated by dates in other cities). In contrast, several musicians I spoke with who worked with lower- to mid-level Forró acts noted that performing one- to two-hour sets in two and sometimes three different cities separated by several hours of driving on the same day was not unusual throughout the June season, especially around the São João holiday peak.

After the third of the June *festas*, São Pedro on June 29 (and Bahian Independence Day on July 2), Bahia undergoes another major shift in its cyclical soundscape. Many Forró bands go on hiatus; the genre's stars from other locales return home or to other work circuits; and the comparatively few headline-level Bahian Forró organizations see their live performance schedules slow considerably, at least in the capital. The long gap until the June circuit heats up again leaves time to undertake recording projects and pursue business relationships. Most Salvador-based musicians, regardless of their June circuit affiliations, seek out work in the nonseasonal circuit that will carry them forward, perhaps until the next São João, but more typically until the next peaks at New Years and Carnaval.

Although short and often intense, the June circuit provided many of the musicians I met with a period of increased pay without many of the genre-related dissatisfactions they associated with the Carnaval circuit and work in Bahian music. Some musicians, for instance, Patua drummer Pastel and Márcia Castro, expressed frustration with newer styles of northeastern music, but others including several who supported themselves primarily by working with *axé* bands, singled out Forró work as a welcome break from their normal routine. Key, however, was that as much as they enjoyed performing northeastern music, these musicians were well aware that their earning potential in it, much like nonseasonal, national, or international genres, was limited in comparison to what was possible performing Bahian music.

LAST NOTES

The circuits that form the basis of musical work in the Salvador Scenes are foundational for informing local musical participation, especially with respect to when, where, and how musicians work. But their implications only begin there. Their particulars are inseparable from the money working musicians earn, the conditions they face, and the sounds and meanings they make. These entanglements also inform and raise the stakes for the ways that working musicians make their ways through the Scenes trying to earn a living and often facing numerous contradictions along the way.

For instance, as I have argued, the genres, venues, and musical sensibilities central to each circuit are entangled with particular ideas about race and social class. Bahian musicians are frequently faced with the challenge of reconciling the prestige associated with working in "*boa música*" with their economic needs and the better wages available performing locally mapped music such as *axé* and *pagode* that both marked as more African and less good, except under certain circumstances when their nonconformity to dominant Euro-mimetic music sensibilities can be bracketed—for instance, during Carnaval.

In the Carnaval circuit, the visibility and demographics of the *pipoca* in terms of color and class, their promotion as the embodiment of the so-called Carnaval of Participation, and musical conventions that engender singing and dancing nevertheless provide fodder for vitriolic, cultural capital-diminishing critiques of Bahian music, audiences, and musicians that carry over beyond the period of alleged freedom from social norms. Yet, as I have argued, these conventions make the performances pleasurable and, in many instances, possible. Moreover, members of the elite classes also form a large part of the audience for such less esteemed music. However, their participation is more often than not sanctioned by the allowable transgressions of Carnaval and the restricted access to expensive *blocos* and *camarotes*.

In the June circuit, the prevalence of Forró along with temporal constraints and spatial organization create particular challenges, possibilities, and meanings for musicians and *baianos* in general. The expense of attending *forrós* in other cities lends a certain cachet to the music of the season even as it continues to carry some *brega* associations. More important is Forró's regional identification and racialization as northeastern and *caboclo,* or at least as not specifically Bahian and *mais afro.* While not providing the cultural capital of working in so-called quality music, performing with a *pé de serra trio,* a *forró universitário* ensemble, or even a *forró moderno* band during the June circuit does provide opportunities for enhanced income without the cultural intimacy of Bahian music or any of the potential stigma. However, this comes at the cost of intense travel, a short window of opportunity in comparison to the other circuits, and limited possibility for supraregional success for artists based in Bahia rather than in the far ("authentic") Northeast or the Rio/São Paulo Axis.

Likewise, the nonseasonal circuit provides limited career horizons for local musicians, even as it provides them with a work foundation and cultural capital. "*Boa música*" such as MPB, pop/rock, jazz, *choro*, and the like remains generally confined to smaller, more elite, and/or out of the way spaces, limiting the visibility of the many Bahian musicians who perform it and the many members of the *povo* who want it. As such, its upper-class associations remain strong. Moreover, large-scale production of national genres continues to be based in the Rio/São Paulo Axis. This in turn further limits its accessibility and economic viability in Salvador, where the commodification of African-ness dominates. These factors all conspire in the construction of music such as MPB as "artistic," further enhancing its cultural capital and evidencing its Euro-mimetic connotations. A byproduct of this complex of processes is the perpetuation of class and racial hierarchies and the continued marginalization of Bahia in relation to the more industrialized, affluent, and "European" south of Brazil.

Against this backdrop, Salvador's working musicians navigate their careers, moving tactically between circuits and, as I discuss in the next chapter, various formations for doing musical work within them. They range from powerful and well-capitalized organizations that dominate the Carnaval circuit and secondarily, the June circuit, to self-financed projects that are core to the nonseasonal circuit as well as the lower ranks of both seasonal circuits. As we will see, their tactical flexibility is what makes it possible for them to live from music in Salvador.

TWO

Musical Work Nexuses and
Working to Work

We're a nine-piece band with fifty-four f*@%in' pieces!
Trombonist Antoine Batiste (Wendell Pierce) from the television series Treme

Inseparable from the circuits of work that inform when, where, and what kind of music Salvador's musicians perform, are issues of with whom they do it and under what conditions. I had thought a great deal about band composition and dynamics, record label practices, and production company activities long before undertaking fieldwork. But time in the Scenes highlighted the variety and importance of different kinds of collaborative formations in which Bahian musicians do their jobs—some of which were nearly identical to contexts for musical work in other settings while others were quite particular to Salvador.

During Carnaval, it was hard to miss the stars of Bahian music performing on their *trios*, surrounded by *bloco* members clad in *abadás* adorned with corporate logos similar to those on the trucks, and supported by a team of engineers, technicians, and other staff who are easily identified by their t-shirts bearing the band's name and their role (e.g., *técnica*, technical, or *apoio*, support). Between headliners, it was abundantly clear that less established artists worked without such extensive backing in terms of personnel or sponsorship. But the necessity of collective labor was still plain to see, if for no other reason than the large size of the bands.

Similar patterns of collaborative work were evident during São João. Headliners at large-scale *forrós* were supported by extensive crews comprised partially of venue employees, as well as others whose attire and actions marked them as working directly with the band. The numerous opening acts that shared the stages typically had help from a scant few, if any, members of their own production team.

In the nonseasonal circuit, streamlined DIY formations were the majority and other issues related to group musical labor were also more readily seen. For example, the smaller scale of most performances and the circuit's more localized ambit made closer attention to band personnel easier. Attending multiple performances by the "same" ensemble showed that on a given night different musicians might be working. Over time I also noted how many of the same musicians worked with different ensembles.

These observations point to the numerous questions that arise related to the formations in and through which musical work is done. What kinds of relationships do the workers, including musicians, have with them? Who else is involved? Who leads the group? What does leadership entail? How do these formations find paid performances? How do they come into being and support themselves, especially before they are ready to perform in public? In considering such matters, this chapter builds on scholarship by ethnomusicologists (e.g., MacLeod 1993, Meintjes 2003, Cottrell 2004, Brinner 2009, Bates 2016) and sociologists (e.g., Peterson 1982, Becker 1982) who have explored the collective production of expressive culture.

This literature and my experiences in the Scenes leave little doubt that there is not a single answer to my initial questions or the myriad of others that derive from them. Yet prior scholarship and fieldwork also point to a number of dominant tendencies that I can address. I approach these tendencies through a discussion of musical work nexuses, variously organized collectives that serve as the bases of musicians' employment. The ways in which they operate as units and the ways participants operate within and between them are central tactics for making do with the instability of flexible employment practices in the music industries and making music under such conditions.[1] A central consideration is that, while tactics such as informal affiliations with multiple employers by nexuses and individual musicians alike can be pivotal for navigating prevalent industry conditions such as contractless employment, assumptions of high substitutability, and low pay, they can also further entrench them.

After introducing the nexus concept, I describe several prevalent approaches to nexus organization and administration, pointing to some of the benefits and challenges related to each. Focal concerns are musical and business leadership in relation to financial risks and rewards for different participants. The division of labor within the formations is also an important consideration. I next concentrate on business-related aspects of the numerous, frequently unseen activities that make performances and living from music possible—a complex of practices I call working to work. The chapter concludes with a discussion of how differently organized musical work nexuses find forms of financial support, including and beyond paid performances, in order to become going concerns that can help participants live from music.

MUSICAL WORK NEXUSES

The practices of *baianos* who live from music were in several ways very consistent with concerns addressed in the literature on creative production cited above;[2] but they also pointed to issues that have generally been overlooked. In particular, though myths of solitary creators and related understandings of expressive culture have been destabilized, the tactics used by working musicians leave little doubt that much more remains to be said about a fundamental aspect in creating (popular) music: the band. Benjamin Brinner's (2009) analysis of the "ethnic music scene" in Israel is a notable step toward querying this frequently taken-for-granted notion.[3] Drawing on network theory, he explores the effects of the multiple interactions and personnel shifts among three ensembles, resituating bands as not only actively constituted, but also effectively practiced into being. As Brinner's work portends, exploring the implications of relationships among participants in formations that might otherwise be glossed as bands working in the Salvador Scenes proved especially fruitful.

In comparison to the ensembles detailed by Brinner, many of the formations I encountered were even more fluidly composed, and most musicians were decidedly more multiple, flexible, and, often, mercenary. Farofa's activities during the 2005 June season exemplify this. Within a period of about one and a half months, he performed at several public festivals as a side musician with a six-piece Forró ensemble, and he led two or three different Forró *trios* working at shopping centers and private parties. During the same span he was also hired to back a series of "oratorios" for Santo Antônio at a Lower City church, and he taught percussion for a municipally funded São João-themed children's choir on the nearby island of Itaparica. All of these jobs were June peak additions to his ongoing work with an array of different artists and ensembles in the nonseasonal circuit; and they all tapered off after São João, with only some recurring in subsequent years.

Numerous studies, including Brinner's, build on foundational writing by sociologist Howard Becker, who coined the term "art world" in 1982 to account for the collective actions and cooperating actors that make art possible. Among Becker's many contributions is his recognition of people who play vital but often overlooked roles in creative production. Engineers, managers, and crew members participating in musical performances fit this characterization well; so too do musicians who back "solo artists" or who add extra voices to bands without being official members. Profoundly influential, Becker's work has also been rightly critiqued for an emphasis on consensus and product over process.[4]

These issues were especially evident in Salvador. As one example, members of Banda Patua found themselves embroiled in debate about adapting their repertoire for Carnaval 2005. All the musicians as well as Edmar, their *empresário* (producer/manager), agreed on the importance of adding hits from past celebrations as a matter of convention and as a way to engender crowd participation. They also unanimously rejected any *pagode*. However, they disagreed about how much *axé* to include and which songs. Despite earnest efforts to operate democratically, they never compiled a set list that pleased everyone. Other formations I encountered minimized such debates by reserving decisions for an explicitly defined leadership. The rest of the participants could "choose" to perform in a manner acceptable to ensemble leaders, or they could *seek* employment elsewhere.

Such circumstances point to additional issues related to creative collaborations. For one, the contributions of participants who leave a project might remain long after their departure. Temporary musicians might make repertoire or arrangement suggestions that end up on recordings or subsequent live presentations. Behind-the-scenes workers can have a lingering influence too. A manager might name a band and then leave. Yet the moniker can continue to affect branding—the way that remaining members present the group and its music to audiences and employers and how consumers identify and understand the band and its creations. Likewise, the business connections nurtured by former agents and managers can shape future bookings, work conditions, and earnings long beyond their tenure. Finally, the "core artist" (Becker 1982), the person fundamental to the project, might not be an artist at all, but instead a producer, an investor, or a team of them.

To account for these and other concerns arising from the organization and practices of professional ensembles that I saw working, I began to think about musical work as being done by people whose networks intersect to form what network theorists call a "node," and which, apropos of musical labor, I call a musical work nexus (see Nexus Overview, Figs. 2.1–2.5).[5] A nexus is a kind of node that comes together once, several times, or on an ongoing basis for making music and money. They might also be thought of as particular kinds of art worlds. For instance, it makes sense to describe the nexus that recorded a song or gave a performance, a formation that would include the musicians, engineer, crew, and producer as well as people working for the studio and the label (if there is one), and any other parties providing support of some kind including money. However, I see nexus as less defined by its product and more attentive to relationships of production across time, however brief or extended, and in relation to other similar formations. Beyond simply describing an isolated group, nexuses can be understood as clients, often one among many, with and for whom each of the participants work, often on different terms. As such, a nexus is a smaller, more tightly defined network of musicians, engineers, technicians, producers, investors, agents, and the like, within a broader web of professional acquaintances. Ensembles as well as "solo artists" who hire backing musicians are typical nexuses for working musicians.[6] So too are various enterprises such as bars, record labels, production companies, Carnaval *blocos*, studios, community organizations, schools, and individuals that employ them. And nearly all of this hiring is flexible—undertaken on an as-needed basis, with little guarantee of rehiring, and usually without any written agreement.

Such hiring flexibility permeates the Scenes, with nexuses typically having nexuses that hire them, and, perhaps, that they hire. A very abbreviated picture of Banda Patua drummer Pastel Reis' portfolio in 2004 and 2005 helps illustrate this concentric networked-ness. Before, during, and after the time he worked with Patua, Pastel frequently lent his services to a singer named Wilson Café. Thus, Patua and Café served as two of Pastel's multiple nexuses; and each of these formations, the leaders and their supporting membership, were, in turn, hired by clubs, promoters, agents, corporations, and individuals hosting parties, thereby serving as nexuses for the nexus leadership and, as such, the nexuses themselves.

This leads to another important point: nexuses are often organized around one person, a nexus principal, locally referred to as a "*dono*" (owner, master), or a team of them working as "*socios*" (partners). Furthermore, nexus principals are not necessarily musicians. They might be, but they might also be producers, managers, agents, club owners, investors, or party hosts. Alone or in combination, nexus principals provide the organizational, financial, and/or material foundations for professional music making. Those more on the business side of things do not necessarily determine creative direction, though my experience suggests that most have at least some influence; and some, especially principals of ensemble nexuses, have a great deal of creative power.

NEXUS OVERVIEW

Over time it became clear that some nexuses are quite durable while others are very fleeting, often existing for one job only. Even when a formation is short-lived, however, it can have long-term implications for participants. For instance, Farofa met percussionist/drummer Junior Oliveira when they were both hired to play percussion with an MPB singer in late 2004. The two hit it off, and Farofa subsequently introduced Junior to singer Laurinha, with whom he had worked sporadically over many years. Laurinha then hired both musicians for the project she initiated prior to Carnaval 2005, and both worked with her as needed and available for several years hence. As this illustrates, musical work with any nexus can shape relationships that can affect careers, even if the initial collaboration is one time only. Nexus collaborations can foster "bridging capital," access to previously distant people, groups, and resources, and it can also strengthen existing ties between those involved ("bonding capital"). On the other hand, both long-term and short-term collaborations can create strains that can damage careers. For example, disagreements or an unsatisfying performance can lead to a participant's firing or might prompt one to besmirch another's reputation.

FIGURE 2.1 A generic ensemble nexus: Four equal members (an "all principal band").

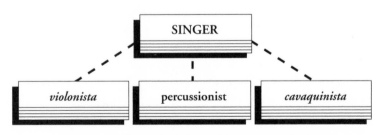

FIGURE 2.2A A more typical ensemble nexus organization:
One leader, a "nexus principal" who hires "lenders of services."

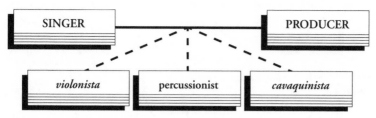

FIGURE 2.2B A similar common ensemble nexus organization:
Partner principals (*socios*) and lenders of services.

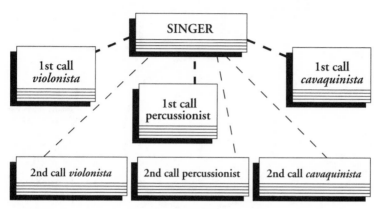

FIGURE 2.3 One of the most common nexus organizations: Nexus principal(s)
with multiple, substitutable lenders of services.

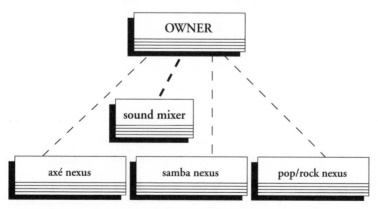

FIGURE 2.4 A common "enterprise" nexus: A bar that hires ensemble nexuses including "solo" performers as well as support staff (e.g., sound mixers). Production
companies, *blocos*, etc. are also enterprise nexuses.

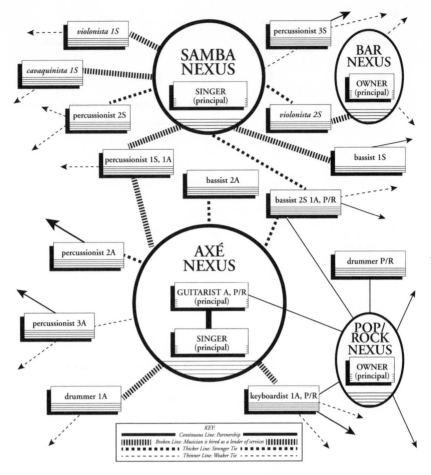

FIGURE 2.5 Nexuses in the Scenes: Most formations and individual
musicians work with many others.

Despite the necessity of collaboration, nexuses are not necessarily united by
shared musical sensibilities or motivations. Some musical workers might take a
job primarily as a way to earn money with minimal effort ("*matar um cache*")
while others might see the same job as the focus of their long-term career. Discrepant motivations can easily become contentious if, say, the group needs to
work at a reduced rate, which happens on occasion, or if scheduling conflicts
arise and some musicians prioritize other jobs. These kinds of differences are
further mediated by musical sensibilities, as was the case in Patua's repertoire

debates before Carnaval. Several musicians resisted Edmar's suggestion of including a significant amount of *axé*, which was intended to increase their marketability. While they all were equally invested in booking a Carnaval job and establishing the long-term viability of the project, the dissenters did not want to risk being heard performing so much Bahian music that the band or they as individuals would become too strongly associated with it. On the other hand, a few participants (who were slightly less committed to the project) were more receptive to Edmar's plan, provided it resulted in well-paid Carnaval employment. Such assessment and efforts to balance contradictory concerns, tactics, and understandings of implications were common. They figured prominently in nexus practices and individual musicians' career pathways.[7]

A final and very significant aspect of any formation that might be thought of as a nexus is that it does not have to be continuously active. Few ensembles work without pause and most venues refrain from hiring the same performers all the time. Moreover, the same nexus might use different musicians playing the same instrument on different nights. Yet any nexus can provide the possibility for work for those involved as long as core relationships remain intact to some degree. This is crucial for career longevity, owing to the waxing and waning of work in the seasonal circuits and the volatility of musical employment in general.

Pastel's reconnection in June 2005 with a Forró band from his past that had been inactive for several years exemplifies this scenario. Out of the blue, the group's producer called him, several musicians from prior iterations, and a couple of new performers and the reassembled lineup set about preparing for the coming season. They did a number of shows throughout the month and then halted activity shortly thereafter. While Pastel had maintained a fairly busy schedule in the nonseasonal circuit, this unexpected phone call gave him and the other participants a welcome June season income boost. Likewise, the fluid membership of the group over a *longue durée* enabled the producer, the lone principal, to assemble a performance-ready ensemble quickly and inexpensively.

Stability within Flexibility

A chief benefit of maintaining multiple nexuses is that, ironically, this flexible approach to working with employers can engender a degree of employment stability in the context of otherwise limited job security. Thus, it could be, and at times was, argued that musical workers willingly embrace flexible labor practices such as lack of contracts and working on a per-performance basis. On the other hand, the long-standing dominance of temporary hiring in music still seems very much the prerogative of employers—consider the variety of programming at a local bar or changing lineups at an annual music festival (at which the musicians are usually hired for one set only). At the same time, venue operators' and producers' ability to hire was often contingent as well, and variety rather than consistency of programming is, in many instances, key to an ongoing endeavor. Regardless of genesis, having many flexible work affiliations was the most common way performers and their employers created a modicum of reliable income in an unreliable market.

For both the individual musicians and nexuses I followed, employment was unpredictable and irregular in several ways. Periods of frantic activity morphed into stretches of little or no work with no warning; last-minute calls both offered jobs and canceled them; and pay varied widely. Furthermore, payment often arrived only after aggravating delays. Farofa told me that he would receive the fee for his group's Carnaval 2017 performance from the city government three months after the event. When I called another friend in April 2020 to see how she was faring during the Covid-19 crisis, she told me that payment for her New Year's Eve performance had not yet arrived. Payments from ensemble principals to lenders of services were not necessarily more timely, unless the venue paid cash on the spot, allowing the principal to do the same. As this suggests, payment rate, and especially delayed payment, trickles down. The same can be said about employment irregularity. Logically, an ensemble that has no work cannot provide jobs for its employees. When venues such as bars and restaurants struggle financially, music is often first to be cut. With so much uncertainty of employment and income, nearly all of the musicians whose careers I tracked, whether they worked as lenders of services, nexus principals, or both, aimed to create some stability through near-constant networking and maintaining several nexuses.

Singer/*violonista* Jorge Elaíde Gois exemplifies the latter tactic. When I accompanied his career most closely (from 2003 until about 2007), I saw him perform as a solo act and with several smaller ensembles that he led in a variety of bars and restaurants. While maintaining this schedule as a principal, during a several-month stretch from 2004 to 2005, he also lent services to a dance band two nights a week at yet another club. His multitasking was facilitated by careful scheduling, broad scene contacts, a degree of musical consistency in terms of repertoire across jobs, and a great deal of flexibility in how he performed those songs in each setting.

By all appearances, Jorge was able to create a fairly predictable work rhythm.

FIG. 2.6 Jorge Elaíde Gois lending services as a guitar player/vocalist to a dance band. *Photo by the author.*

This helped the musicians he hired schedule other work in ways that kept them available for his jobs while also providing them a base of regular employment. Such regularity also made it easier for Jorge's audience to find him. Consistent performances engendered by a fairly stable cast of backing musicians along with predictably good crowds certainly endeared him to the people who booked him and his ensembles. As a result, Jorge was able to keep working for many years at several venues that brought him back repeatedly for *temporadas*, weekly engagements for extended periods, usually a month. Such residencies were often followed by a month or two off to keep variety in the venue's programming. During these planned breaks, Jorge inked similar situations at different clubs and restaurants from his portfolio.

This predictable foundation also made it possible for him to slot in one-off jobs such as private parties, which typically paid better than club and restaurant work. Jorge's wide-ranging contacts also empowered him to refuse or leave problematic jobs if need be. I saw this in action when he quit a venue at which he had performed in various formations many times following a disagreement with the soundman, who was a fixed employee. Despite his disappointment, Jorge expressed little concern about lost income. He filled the gap quickly by booking a duo *temporada* at another club with a frequent collaborator who backed him on bass.

Musical Work Nexuses and Working to Work **87**

Ensemble Nexus Administration and Support

Thinking about musical work through the idea of nexuses also points to the inter-relationships between different and different kinds of formations, their specific roles within a broader network of activities, the importance of nonartists as core personnel, and the significance of financial arrangements in shaping most aspects of the formations' practices and productions. Against common (and romanticized) assumptions, business-related matters such as operational structure, leadership organization, participants' terms of employment, and general financial practices profoundly affected numerous aspects of formations that might otherwise be glossed as bands—including the sounds they created. Organizational structure and financial profile are also indicative of an act's level of commercial accomplishment and frequently a strong determinant of it. There are numerous variations, and changes happen too—for instance, as a project becomes more successful or loses stature one would expect a different financial picture, a different approach to managing affairs, and perhaps changes in musical direction. However, I also saw strong patterns among different kinds of music-making formations in the Scenes, especially around organizational practices and their relationship to their music, in a manner consistent with Peterson's (1982) "production of culture" perspective.

"SIGNED" NEXUSES John Williamson and Martin Cloonan's (2007) admonishment against equating "the music industry" with recording companies is especially relevant to Salvador, where other kinds of enterprises were much more central to business operations, the practices of many listeners, and the careers of musical workers. This is evident in a quote from Marcia Freire, a singer who fronted a headline *axé* band but failed to maintain the same level of success as a solo artist:

> Lack of a producer [*empresário*], a person of substance to invest in our careers ... I needed to have such a person, this makes the difference. Carla Visi [the singer who followed Freire in her band], who is an excellent singer and has a beautiful voice, was also unable to find such a person and ended up remaining by herself (quoted in Mello 2005, my translation).

Bahian sociologist Milton Moura (2001, 301) adds a layer to Freire's perspective in the context of the Carnaval industries, noting the necessity of an artist's association with a *bloco* organization to provide financial investment and business support in lieu of, in addition to, or akin to an *empresário*.

The activities that I saw and conversations that I had with working musicians were consistent with the pictures painted by Freire and Moura. Whereas artists in North America were (and in many instances, still are) discussed in terms of their recording label affiliation—signed versus unsigned or major versus indie—distinctions among Bahian artists often hinged on whether or not they had backing from an established business entity such as a production company or a *bloco*. While those that did not were explicitly called *independentes*, I never heard an antonym used. For that reason, I refer to nexuses that work through formally organized business enterprises as "signed."

In some ways, the ties between top signed artists and *blocos* and/or production companies reminded me of how North American and European artists work(ed) with major labels. But in Salvador, the relationships were often more integrated and akin to what have come to be known as 360-degree deals that underwrite and profit from recordings, live performances, and sales of merchandise. Many of these organizations, especially larger ones, also engage actively in multimedia promotion that can be fruitfully be understood as "branding . . . intended to link productions and services with resonant cultural meanings through the use of narratives and images" (Hearn 2008, 195).[8] At all levels, *empresários*, production companies, and *blocos* were, themselves or through a proxy, commonly principals in ensemble nexuses alongside or instead of musicians. They invested time, energy, and money in all aspects of a project, hiring performers and usually a cast of other workers to handle production, promotion, booking, merchandizing, and financial management. They also sought sponsors and relationships with record labels and distributors. The majority of the artists I met (with the exception of most *músicos da noite*) sought affiliation with *empresários* (and/or *blocos* if they were trying to work in the Carnaval circuit). Moreover, many acts, including star-level performers, were actually formed by an established entertainment or Carnaval enterprise.

Banda Patua was one such nexus, beginning in 2004 as an initiative of an official with Salvador's municipal tourism administration (EMTURSA) working in conjunction with Edmar's production company, Lua 23. Based on their prior work together, the EMTURSA official thought that singer Josehr Santos exemplified the image of Bahia she hoped to promote. The idea of a formally supported project that would showcase Bahian music and culture without featuring *axé* or *pagode* was also appealing to Josehr. A tall, elegant, dark-skinned man from a lower middle-class background, the singer's career had previously consisted of an eclectic mix of wedding accompaniment, choir performance, bands, jingle sessions, and coaching children's choirs. He also had a bachelor's degree in business administration and had worked in nonmusic industries.

With a government official and an *empresário* behind him, Josehr contacted Farofa, with whom he worked at the children's choir and on a prior Carnaval-oriented project, and the two began assembling the rest of the musicians needed for the group. Drawing on their close networks, soon they had bassist Son Melo, musical director and acoustic guitarist Luciano Caroso, drummer Pastel, and electric guitarist Ximbinha Mamede, as a foundation. They began rehearsals, augmented by a changing cast of keyboardists, background vocalists, additional percussionists, and occasionally wind players. Indicative of Edmar's hands-on approach to managing his investment, he attended a number of these initial practice sessions as well—but the EMTURSA official did not. At these gatherings it was clear that neither Josehr nor any of the other musicians were paying for the studio time. Nor was anyone paid for their work, that is, except for Mala, the roadie, who like the rest of Edmar's administrative and production staff, was a formal employee of Lua 23.

In contrast, none of the musicians involved in the band had contracts. Without performances booked, they all also continued working with their other nexuses in order to support themselves. This made it difficult to solidify the lineup beyond the core musicians, who out of interest in the project, belief in its potential, and established relationships with Josehr, Farofa, or both, continued to learn material and attend rehearsals for free. With the help of a paid session keyboardist, they recorded a demo CD that was underwritten by Edmar and the EMTURSA executive. Several remunerated performances followed, but jobs remained sporadic, resulting in an ongoing struggle to retain musicians. To fill out the ensemble for the two to four performances they did per month, they hired a revolving cast of side musicians, eventually giving up on using keyboards and winds due to high turnover and low availability. The core group continued with regular rehearsals once or twice a week.

Financial pressures increased over the next few months due to irregular bookings, limited bargaining power for fees, and ongoing production and rehearsal costs. As a solution, Josehr, Farofa, and Luciano were brought in as *socios*, each agreeing (as far as I know, orally) to exchange guaranteed payment for each performance for a percentage of net earnings. The move ensured higher wages

FIGURE 2.7 Banda Patua. From left: Katia, Son, Farofa, Josehr. *Photo by the author.*

for the others, who, despite demonstrating a fair degree of commitment to the project, were more likely to leave without a direct payment incentive. They all still worked for less than they earned with most of their other nexuses.

Despite several promising performances, including the city's Réveillon 2004 concert at the Farol da Barra, things started to unravel in the lead up to Carnaval 2005. Efforts to book either an independent *trio* performance or a job in a *camarote* failed, an outcome several of the musicians speculated was because of the entrance of a new municipal government just prior to the event and the related exit of their EMTURSA contact. Regardless of whether this was the cause, the loss of their powerfully positioned patron, the inability to become self-sustaining before her exit, and an absence from Carnaval amounted to a death blow for Patua. This confluence of failures signaled to all concerned, most importantly, Edmar who controlled the finances, that the project was not going to become commercially viable.

Patua's story illustrates how formalized, top-down ensemble organizations can impact the careers of working musicians. Projects such as this can provide lenders of services paid work at minimal expense, occasionally create partnership opportunities (albeit with attendant risks), and engender/strengthen professional and personal relationships, including some that continue after the project ends. Nearly all of Patua's musicians and the EMTURSA official are still in touch and occasionally work together. The group's formation and denouement also point to the centrality of economic and social capital, at times in the hands of just a few people, in shaping the success or failure of a musical project.

In most ways, though, Patua was an exception among signed projects. Unlike typical organizationally formed or backed projects, its genre orientation restricted its activity primarily to nonseasonal circuit work. By contrast, the magnitude of the Carnaval circuit and its rootedness in Bahian music and culture mean that *axé* and *pagode* acts—those that play music that is *mais afro*—are the focus for the majority of Bahia's most powerful music industry enterprises, which capitalize on the commodifiability of Bahia's African-ness. Forró performers attract *empresários* too, but all indications suggest that they remain secondary to Carnaval-oriented projects in winning attention from the major players because, I would argue, of Forró's nonlocal associations and the fact that it does not exemplify the Afro-Bahian-ness on which Bahian industries of cultural production rely so heavily.

Thanks to Edni Devay, who played drums with an up-and-coming *axé* band called A Zorra for many years, I got a close look at work with a signed Carnival circuit ensemble. A Zorra was put together by one of the largest production companies in Salvador, Central do Carnaval, with support from several major stars of *axé*, one of whom "discovered" the singer, Leo. Leo joined forces with the percussion-playing sons of the founding drummer from legendary *axé* band Chiclete com Banana (then a cash cow for Central do Carnaval). The three of them were made *socios* and, along with their producers, handpicked the rest of the ensemble. With a massive organization behind them, all of A Zorra's musicians were treated well, paid for their work in a timely manner, and compensated better than the majority of the other Bahian musicians I have known. Their *empresários* forged strategic relationships with other organizations, including a *bloco*, Acadêmicos, for which A Zorra performed when I rode with them on their Carnaval 2005 *trio*. They also contracted with other *blocos*, event producers, product distributors, and sponsors, thus keeping the group working and earning from several different sources.

A key benefit for A Zorra's lenders of services, in addition to regular work and income, was that none of them were expected to tend to business-related affairs. Nor did they go out of pocket for band-related expenses other than their

FIGURE 2.8 Banda A Zorra during Carnaval 2005. Note the two crew
members in the foreground wearing dark t-shirts. Edni is at lower right;
Leo is at center left. *Photo by the author.*

instruments.[9] Rather, their obligations were to be present at rehearsals, shows,
recording sessions, and promotional events and to make music. This can be
said about most nexuses organized around principal(s) and lenders of services,
but in the case of signed acts, the division of labor is generally quite clear and
rather strictly maintained.

For all the benefits of lending services to a signed act in Salvador, there are
also downsides. The seasonal circuit focus of most production companies meant
that a large number of the musicians I met who worked with them expressed
dissatisfaction over the music that they played most often. High expectations of
availability for frequent work resulted in limited ability to perform in contexts
they said were more musically satisfying—though most musicians I spoke with
who worked in signed seasonal acts still tried. Their employment conditions
also made it difficult to build and maintain a portfolio of nexuses to buffer
unexpected job loss despite the fact that lenders of services are not typically
bound by contracts and thus "free" to do so. Indeed, as informally hired workers in a flexible workforce, it is in their best interest to keep other options open.
Raising the stakes for their employment precarity is that being fired from an

elite ensemble not only results in a significant loss of income, but it can also be visible and potentially stigmatizing. Finally, extended periods away from home that is the norm at this level can take a significant toll on workers' families and other relationships—something I saw happen on a couple of occasions and heard about on others apropos of men and women of varying ages and financial backgrounds.[10]

Musicians who are *socios* in a signed project are spared some of the concerns faced by lenders of services, and they stand to benefit in ways not available to their supporting musicians. Of course, their roles and attendant perks come with certain liabilities as well. *Socios'* jobs are more secure, but this comes at the cost of even less flexibility, added responsibilities, and more risk. Edmar expected his musician-principals to be musically monogamous since he sees them as the "faces" of the band. He also required their participation in promotional activities such as TV and radio appearances, interviews with journalists, and meet-and-greets with fans; and to varying degrees he involved them in business negotiations and planning. Unlike lenders of services, *socios* do not get paid if a performance does not generate a profit. They are, however, entitled to a prenegotiated share of the net earnings and rewards of any large-scale success that side musicians rarely see.[11]

While production companies are likely the most powerful enterprises supporting professional music making in the Scenes, Carnaval *blocos* are the most visible. Ostensibly, they are clubs for parading. However, in practice, the more prominent ones produce parades and *ensaios* for which they secure equipment, supplies, venues when necessary, and personnel including performers. Not just casual party clubs, many *blocos* are large-scale, formally operated, multifaceted businesses.

Not all of them begin that way, however. Many start off as little more than a gathering of friends, albeit usually well-capitalized ones. To take their party to the street, they pool resources and sell memberships. Some secure government funding or commercial sponsorships, sometimes prior to ever appearing on a parade route. With or without initial outside support, those that manage to attract enough members to survive more than one outing usually seek out and formalize ties with sponsors, both private and public, and a production company. In other instances, production companies, established *blocos*, and stars of Bahian music form new *blocos*. Despite their less humble beginnings, these *blocos* then follow trajectories similar to more ground-up organizations, seeking paying members, building new business partnerships, and forming musical alliances.

Blocos also establish and administer their relationships with musicians in different but related ways. Some hire performers in a manner similar to a club or restaurant. At times they enter into long-term relationships like a production company. Others form, invest in, and manage their own bands.

This was the case with Bloco Cheiro de Amor following two years of well-populated parades in the mid-1980s animated by hired musicians. Riding on their success, the *donos* of the club auditioned and hired a number of local musicians including Laurinha, and set about building an ensemble that, along with its namesake *bloco*, would eventually rise to the ranks of Bahian music's elite.[12] From the outset, the band and its integrated supporting enterprise served as a signed nexus for its lenders of services.[13]

This kind of corporate approach is also important in the June circuit. Several production companies from the Carnaval circuit have become quite active during São João, and smaller operations such as Edmar's Lua 23 work more exclusively with Forró projects. Like his Carnaval-circuit counterparts, Edmar, through his company, has supported himself primarily by managing and occasionally forming ensembles. At June shows I attended involving one of his bands, it was clear that he employed a support staff that was considerably smaller than A Zorra's (but larger than Patua's). Edmar also told me that most of the musicians in his employ were lenders of services.

With *axé*, *pagode*, and Forró ensconced as primary foci for the best-capitalized production organizations in Salvador, I encountered only a few acts working primarily or exclusively in the nonseasonal circuit that were signed with a well-capitalized organization. A majority were dance bands (see chapter 1) rather than projects aiming to create more singular artistic statements—Patua, the *arrocha* projects that drew the attention of producers in the early 2000s, and a couple of other nexuses I encountered over the years were the exceptions. Regardless of musical orientation, signed nonseasonal acts typically involved a producer-principal, who, with or without musician *socios*, hired and managed an ensemble composed primarily of lenders of services. As evidenced by a formally managed samba-dance band that Farofa worked with and a salsa group to which Junior lent services, musician membership was especially fluid and support staff was very limited. Most nonseasonal artists as well as a majority of new acts hoping to break into the seasonal circuits begin and continue to work with even less backing.

INDEPENDENTS The Salvador Scenes are home to a seemingly infinite number of projects that are initiated and pursued with few resources beyond those of the musicians involved. With the right combination of commercial success, active networking, and a bit of luck, *some* independent projects, usually *axé*, *pagode*, or secondarily, Forró acts, sign with an *empresário*, *a bloco*, or perhaps a label or distributor. Getting to that point is contingent on the investment of energy, time, and money by entrepreneurial musicians.

Like signed acts, independents are not of a single kind; rather, there are varied degrees and approaches to independence shaped by issues that all principals must address. How much control, musical and business, are they willing to cede to an outside party? How much of any profit are they willing to share? How willing are they to devote time and energy to finding jobs instead of making music? Another factor informing a project's independence is resources. Do the principals have economic capital to pay for rehearsals? Promotional material and activities? Do they and their lenders of services have the means to support themselves until the project becomes profitable? How will they balance other necessary work with that of their project? Social capital is also an issue. Do principals have a network of musicians willing to risk participating in a new project? Do they have contacts in the scenes that can help them book work or raise money? Do they have an audience? Such questions are entangled with the basic organization of the nexus. Is it led by one or a small number of principals who hire lenders of services? Or is it a band of principals who try to share duties, investment, and success more or less equally?

Against any inclination to view "grassroots" endeavors as somehow more autonomous or authentic than "top-down" projects, it is important to emphasize that most independent musicians I spoke with actively worked to make their projects profitable, and most eventually sought outside affiliation to support that endeavor at the cost of some independence. Still, a desire for a degree of insulation from market concerns and related matters of genre was motivation for the occasional independent project. So too was the fun of making music with friends. Yet owing to the frenetic pace inherent to living from music, such situations often took a back seat to those that promised capital return more quickly.

One example of a project that prioritized fun and independence over profit was a short-lived band called Som Ki Lufa pursued by Farofa, Son, Luciano Caroso, and a busy local saxophonist, Kiko Souza. The four musicians acted together as principals and invested more or less equally in a slick demo of instrumental music, effectively as a break from their routines, but with a fleeting hope that it might help them find enough jobs to continue the project. Their recording featured heady arrangements and improvisation, and thus seemed well poised to earn plenty of musical esteem. Yet between the limited market for such music, their busy schedules, and a lack of someone to do their legwork, they were unable to book paid jobs, and all involved moved on to more lucrative pursuits.

Indeed, on top of honing their music, musicians leading independent projects are saddled with numerous mundane but crucial logistical, production, and business duties. Against common assertions that such work increased as a result of the rise of digital distribution platforms (e.g., Hracs 2016, Mühbach and Arora 2020), local musicians, those who have not achieved "artist" status by virtue of industry support, and thus the vast majority of my collaborators in Salvador, have always devoted a significant amount of time to such non-sound-producing activities (i.e., working to work). Behind the laments over the "new order" of musical labor, though, is another assumption that holds more water: that most musicians would rather be making music than looking for ways to support, sell, and promote the music they make. In order to minimize what are for many the distractions and displeasures of working to work, most independent musicians I spoke with sought to increase their project's organizational infrastructure. Not all would sacrifice their independence entirely, but many pursued external management and investment well aware that some loss of autonomy was the likely price.

Pop/rock band Funk 'n' Roll, a project that Junior spearheaded parallel to his multifaceted work as a lender of services, provides another example of an independent, start-up ensemble organized as an all-principal nexus that followed this path. Like Som Ki Lufa, their work was tailored primarily for the nonseasonal circuit. However, they differed in that they worked to work extensively, brought in others to help, and experienced some success for their efforts.

The band was conceived of and organized by Junior, his vocalist cousin Thiago, and several of their musical colleague-friends as a way to play music they loved (as the name suggests, Brazilian pop/rock, MPB, and English-language rock, mostly with a funky edge). From the outset, they agreed to share creative input and benefit equally from any monetary returns. Accordingly, all members were expected to assume comparable risk by investing time and money. They divided costs such as rehearsal studios, recording time, promotion, and on occasion roadies. They held frequent meetings at which everything from scheduling to repertoire to finances was discussed and decided by vote.

Together, they also drew on, and sought to expand, their networks of venue operators, *empresários*, local business owners, and other contacts who might connect them with potential investors and employers. Junior emphasized to me that giving up even a large percentage of receipts to agents and managers was

FIGURE 2.9 Funk 'n' Roll. From left: Marquinhos, Eugênio, Thiago, Junior, and Rafa. *Photo by the author.*

justifiable if it freed him and the other musicians to focus on making music. They were not, however, willing to cede much creative control. Accordingly, they brought in the first of two managers early on. Neither she nor her successor invested money; only time and labor in exchange for a percentage of earnings. She offered suggestions, sometimes strongly, about business choices, but rarely did I see her comment on musical direction. Even with managerial support, Junior, Thiago, and guitarist Eugênio continued to consult and at times assist with band business, especially booking and production.

The core trio's continued involvement in business-related activities marked a progressive shift away from the initial collective vision of the group. Along the way, various fissures and evidence of instability became more apparent. They eliminated the turntableist who was a founding member. A few months later, after what seemed to me a crowded, well-performed, and enthusiastically received show, the bassist gleefully told me about another alternative music project he was starting. Making this all the more surprising was that the group had managed to secure a succession of sponsorship agreements with local businesses. In spite of indications that they were headed toward becoming self-sustaining and perhaps signing with a more formalized enterprise, they never crossed either threshold and finally disbanded.

In contrast to Funk 'n' Roll's initial band approach, Márcia Castro was working as an independent "solo" artist when we met in 2004. As might be expected from a well-educated member of Brazil's middle classes, she specialized in MPB and accordingly aimed her work toward the nonseasonal circuit. As the only principal, she hired backing musicians to accompany her on various jobs. She was the creative focus of her projects, bore all of the costs, and earned the greatest rewards of any successes.

Still, such independence was not her long-term objective. Owing to her focus on MPB and the preference of Bahian *empresários* for seasonal genres, she eventually relocated to São Paulo, where she had a better chance of signing with a well-capitalized organization and breaking out of the local (MPB) scene. Even with her genre specialization, Márcia described her premove work as divided between "the Márcia Castro who wants to be a star" and "the Márcia Castro that wants to make a living as a singer" (Salvador, April 30, 2005).

Working as a lone principal facilitated this dual approach. In pursuit of becoming a star, she made recordings and did shows for which she assumed all costs. She hired musicians and crew as needed, serving as a nexus for them and occasionally earning a profit for herself. Her socioeconomic background likely gave her a financial cushion—one not available to many others pursing similar pathways—but much of the funding for her "star" project came from working in bars, restaurants, and private parties. In addition to the fees she earned in contexts that paid for services rendered, this work helped make Márcia audible, provided performance experience, and enabled her to establish a reliable network of supporting musicians.

Mundane as it may have been, the local work Márcia did in Salvador was crucial for her eventual national success from São Paulo. Her performance experience and seasoned nexus participants propelled her to a win in a music competition, the prize for which was resources for a label-quality CD. With a polished product in hand, her continued working to work landed a song from the CD on a national *telenovela*. This notoriety coupled with relocation made it possible for her to build a more formal infrastructure including a producer and affiliation with Sony Brazil.

That Márcia's career has been this fruitful does not mean that being a solo artist or lone principal in a nexus is a more surefire route to stardom than pursuing a project with a band of principals or working as a lender of services. Yet independent solo projects can afford more freedom of choice with respect to repertoire, image, promotion, ensemble type, rehearsal, and logistics. Performers such as Márcia can also accept and reject jobs with less accountability to others such as lenders of services or partners. On the other hand, leading a nexus alone is expensive and time intensive.

In contrast to the other examples discussed, Patua guitarist Ximbinha Mamede

FIGURE 2.10 Márcia Castro earning a living as a singer, backed by Farofa on percussion and Son on bass. *Photo by the author.*

FIGURE 2.11 Márcia Castro working to become a star, with Luciano Salvador Bahia on *violão* seated at far left. *Photo by the author.*

and his wife, singer Thais, pursued a partner-led project, Makueto, aimed solidly toward the most lucrative sector of the Bahian music industries, *axé*. They told me they were not necessarily fans of *axé*; rather their genre choice was informed by the desire to lead a profitable project. Their decision was further fueled by awareness of the typical interests of *empresários* and their need for one in order to accomplish their financial objectives.

Also contrary to Márcia Castro and even Funk 'n' Roll, Ximbinha saw securing outside support as fundamental to the *genesis* of the project rather than a long-term goal. He explained to me that he and Thais prioritized finding an *empresário* ahead of booking performances, an approach very different from his past projects:

> In our case, we started like this: first, let's record a disk, find an *empresário* with the material already ready, and from there, do shows. The majority of the bands I have been part of did show after show, then after years, recorded a disc, (did more) shows, and after that sought an *empresário*. We wanted to skip these steps to expedite the process. (Salvador, April 27, 2005)

While he was working with Patua and several other nexuses, Ximbinha and Thais assembled and arranged repertoire. They enlisted supporting musicians, and at their own expense held ten rehearsals to learn twenty-six songs. They paid to record a promotional demo containing eighteen of what Ximbinha called "the most commercial" tracks, and they put MP3s of two of them on free internet sites. Shortly thereafter, and before they had booked a job, they were contacted by an *empresário*, who, not coincidentally, had worked previously with their bassist. He subsequently took over booking and promotion duties in exchange for a share of future profit.

Like Junior, Ximbinha also noted that having someone who could allow him and Thais to focus primarily on matters of musical sound and performance was well worth the cost. He added that the value of an *empresário* went beyond relieving the principals from less appealing labor. In particular, he noted that his *empresário* had business contacts in multiple cities, that is, significant social capital.

XM: Each city has a person who might be considered an intermediary in the negotiations between city governments, private shows. For example: I'm going to do a show in Rio de Janeiro, there is a person there who belongs to a group. If I want to book a show with the city government, I can't go straight to them. I have to go through this guy.

JP: Seriously? Is it always like that?

XM: A majority of the time. If I book directly, I'll probably only do one show. I won't [be able to] return. Our *empresário* knows lots of these people in Brazil . . . and he passes our material to this type of person, who takes it to sell our product to city governments, clubs. You can't skip these intermediaries.

Ximbinha added that his *empresário* also had the economic resources to travel to each locale and the cultural capital to court the intermediaries appropriately.

Much as Márcia Castro's example might give the false impression that working as a solo artist is a more direct route to success, Makueto's story belies the difficulty most artists have securing outside support while also illustrating the importance of getting it. Ximbinha, Thais, and all of the other independent artists I saw working also made it clear that until they signed with a large-scale operation, their work with *empresários* and agents usually led to *shared* responsibilities for booking, promotion, and production arrangements. Furthermore, only on occasion did independent artists mention receiving direct payments from the people who attended to their business affairs. Most continued to bear the costs of their projects themselves.

Despite the fact that nexus multiplicity by all participants in independent projects made many of them possible at all, this necessity also invariably led to problems. Farofa lamented numerous times that, despite working with performers he considered to be first rate in ensembles specializing in esteemed genres such as MPB, many failed to live up to their potential. He attributed this largely to the frequency with which musicians were substituted because they had better-paying work elsewhere. Despite the extreme flexibility I saw in a majority of the musicians I met, I cannot help but think that divided attention also contributed to this situation. In any case, the implication is that plenty of performances of so-called *boa música* done by "good" performers were not as good as they could be.

Funk 'n' Roll's initial band ethos was informed by a desire to avoid this pitfall. Yet their commitment to work only with a fixed lineup of musicians logically restricted their availability, since a schedule conflict for one of the musicians meant that the entire band could not work. Thus, coordinating performances, rehearsals, and other necessary work that did not impinge on members' ability to make a living invariably led to tough choices. For example, Junior turned down better-paying work that conflicted with Funk 'n' Roll shows. Likewise, a fixed-member approach can restrict some ensembles' employment options since many bars, clubs, and restaurants lack the money, structure, or will to support performances by large groups.

In contrast, principals working with lenders of services are at liberty to pare down their formations as needed, albeit often at the cost of ensemble cohesion. Still, this was the path taken by most projects, both independent and signed, and was exemplified by Márcia Castro, Laurinha, and Jorge Elaíde Gois. Arguably, for signed acts, working primarily with lenders of services is a matter of retaining creative control and maximizing principals' profit. Such issues are of concern among independents too, but matters such as limited start-up funds, scheduling, and ability to work are likely even more pressing. The predominance of organizations in which one or a small number of principals hire lenders of services is also inseparable from most musicians' need for composite income to survive. With livelihoods at stake, most working musicians I met were unwilling to commit to a single project, invest a significant amount of time and money in one organized as a band of principals, or participate in just any speculative endeavor. Over time I noticed that many independent bands that did not involve lenders of services and/or those comprised of musicians who did not work with other ensembles were frequently made up of people who were not reliant on music as their primary source of income.

Clearly, independent musicians (and those in signed acts too) approach their careers differently. However, they all face job instability and the related demand of near-constant working to work—challenges that increase the more independent they are, be it by choice or by circumstance. More often than not, a tenable approach to flexible employment was central to success of any kind, from cobbling together a living locally to finding work with a signed project and to signing with a production company. Thus, musicians who invested their labor time in projects hoping for future returns usually counterbalanced such speculative work with more immediately remunerated jobs, even if they were less musically satisfying. Many worked in seasonal circuit nexuses during the appropriate peak—and some joined signed acts if given the chance. Finally, most of the musicians I met, regardless of their position in the Scenes or highest plateau of career achievement, had worked as *músico da noite* at some point in their lives, and many did so on an ongoing basis.

This is because performing in local restaurants, bars, clubs, and private parties is arguably the most reliable source of income for musicians unless, until, and often after they are hired by or become a headline artist. The labor done by *músi-*

cos da noite is not glamorous or well paid, and all too often disrespected (despite the fact that it often entails performing esteemed music and many musicians from headline acts take "night" jobs too). The artists who do it are also unlikely to sign with a production company or any other well-capitalized organization unless their project is a dance band. However, as numerous examples including Márcia Castro, Luciano Salvador Bahia, the members of A Zorra, and even stars such as Daniela Mercury demonstrate, providing background music for socializing and dancing can create conditions of possibility for career growth in other pathways. In addition to being plentiful enough to provide an income, such work is flexible enough for those with the proper competences, motivation, and connections to pursue other projects, including those aimed at stardom or that have signed work in the seasonal circuits. Even if such high-level success does not follow, working as a *músico da noite* allows flexible local musicians to fill out their nexus portfolios to the degree that many can continue to support themselves as musicians for years.

Nexuses and Economic Capital

All of the ensembles, solo artists, and individual musicians discussed above earned the bulk of their income making musical sounds in real time before co-present audiences whether or not they were signed or very independent. Across the Scenes, the vast majority of musical workers at recording sessions, in theaters and restaurants, on Carnaval *trios* and São João stages, and at shopping malls and private parties earned a flat sum for the job, a share of the entry fees, or a combination of the two (no one ever mentioned receiving part of the bar take or food sales in a restaurant or club venue; only composers mentioned royalties, and those instances were rare).[14] No matter how grass roots or top-down a project was, and irrespective of their level of success, artists, including independents, commonly seek out sources of revenue beyond performances, and in the case of start-ups, to make possible foundational income from performances.

BUSINESS SPONSORSHIP   Backing from non-music-business *patrocínios* (sponsors) has long been a much sought-after way for principals to cover expenses associated with starting a musical project and to secure additional revenue streams if they find paid work and make commercial commodities. In most instances that I saw, sponsorship entailed payment(s) in exchange for advertising banners, signs, and logos on Carnaval *trios, bloco abadás,* and *camarote* paraphernalia as well as on June *forró* stages. Nonseasonal circuit venue stages also feature *patrocínios'* logos on occasion, as do CD covers, artists' websites, and band wardrobe (usually matching shirts) regardless of circuit focus.

Unsurprisingly, there is a marked gap between the kinds of investors and the level of support available for stars and less prominent performers. It is the norm to see national corporations such as beer companies and department store chains sponsoring Carnaval and São João headliners, while independent acts, if they have a sponsor at all, typically work with local businesses regardless of circuit. Upward mobility is possible, but the appeal of affiliation with a star is a significant hurdle for new projects, as is the magnitude of the seasonal circuits for all alternative musicians.

According to Son, conditions were not always so dire for independent artists working at Carnaval, but a change in booking procedures made securing sponsorship significantly more difficult. Until the early 1990s, *trio* and stage assignments were overseen by the Sindicato dos Músicos, the Musicians' Union, based on auditions and, in the case of returning artists, evaluations of past performances. Regardless of any politics involved, Son's recollection was that "the best bands were given the best stages, the best performance times, and the best *trios*; and the other bands were . . . put on the rest of the stages . . . [and that] . . . the money was good." (Salvador, January 25, 2004). With the assurance of a visible performance, even performers without *blocos* were able to secure financial support beyond the sum received from the city's budget. Son also told me that this patronage included national companies, not just local ones. When Carnaval scheduling was brought under the exclusive control of the city government, corporate patrons continued sponsoring well-established artists, *blocos*, and *camarotes* as they had always done but refrained from investing in independents. Instead, they channeled any money earmarked for less well-known acts entirely toward the municipal fund, to be dispersed at EMTURSA's discretion. This adjustment enabled donors to maintain the visibility provided by sponsoring a star while also securing the goodwill of local politicians. It also buys them a breadth of ad spaces with their independent artist money rather than limiting their coverage to one recipient whose performance might not be seen by many people.

Whereas the previous system minimized this risk, it became quite real under the new process. Compounding problems related to the desystemization of booking, EMTURSA made scheduling independent acts a low priority. Programs printed in newspapers and posted online immediately before Carnaval week list the names of *blocos* and their accompanying artists interspersed with the generic *trio independente* without any performer specified. The years that I rode with Laurinha on her *trio*, and every year that I have asked her about her Carnaval performances, it has been clear that she too gets performance details at the last minute. Understandably, sponsors seeking to maximize visibility balk at such uncertainty, especially since many *trios independentes* end up slated to perform at less-than-favorable times. No performer or their representative is precluded from approaching sponsors as they did in the past. However, everything I saw and was told suggests that headline artists and prominent Carnaval organizations are by far the most likely to secure sponsorship.[15]

The role and impact of *patrocínios* is most evident in the Carnaval circuit, but they are also crucial for the *festas juninas*. With increasing involvement from the major players in Bahian music, both artists and producers, insignias familiar from *blocos* and *camarotes* are also visible at *forrós*. It is possible that such carnivalization (see previous chapter) limits the space and money available for new, independent, and local acts; but those that do secure jobs at São João events can actually benefit from headliners' resources in a manner not possible during Carnaval. Since June festival performances typically take place on a common stage rather than on discrete *trios*, performers frequently share equipment, sound reinforcement, lights, and other resources that have been bankrolled by sponsors. Not all artists have equal access, but a degree of democratizing is all but inevitable.

In comparison to both the June and Carnaval circuits, the nonseasonal circuit is markedly less entangled with *patrocínio* investment, but it is still a factor. Funk 'n' Roll was a case in point. Although limited, the support they secured in exchange for flying company banners at shows was certainly beneficial. One early *patrocínio* even paid the members a small stipend. Their relationship was short-lived, and subsequent agreements only provided enough money to help with production expenses. Not insignificantly, though, the band was able to rent better sound systems and occasionally ease their non-music-making labor by hiring roadies. As fragile and limited as sponsorship relationships proved to be, their importance is suggested by the fact that Junior, Tiago, and Eugênio remained active in their pursuit until the end of Funk 'n' Roll.

Since the small crowds typical of the nonseasonal circuit limit return on investment by commercial sponsors, social capital is especially crucial for securing patronage support. No doubt, seasonal circuit notables leverage their "QI" to gain access to major corporations, but the promise of mass visibility through advertisements on star-studded *trios* and headliners' stages is a powerful lure for investors even in the absence of more personal connections. At the more local level, strong ties can be even more crucial for making sponsorship deals happen—this was the case with at least one of Funk 'n' Roll's sponsors, a gym where Thiago regularly worked out. Leaders from other independent projects in my network also sought out and received informal gifts and donations, both monetary and material, from friends, family, and acquaintances. Farofa's long-term friendship with the owners of a sound-reinforcement company has availed him of high-quality PA equipment for private party jobs he booked and more recently, for Samba de Farofa performances, in exchange for running occasional errands. Somewhat surprisingly, only one pair of artists in my network has utilized online crowd funding, something they did to support CD projects in 2016 and 2018 and as a way to secure donations for local musicians left unemployed during venue closures during the Covid-19 pandemic of 2020.

GOVERNMENT SUPPORT In addition to producing public events and operating several performance spaces, city and state government agencies also provide support for local musicians. One notable example is contribution to the funding pool supporting *trios independentes*. More indirectly, programs such as Faz Cultura (Make Culture) offer tax incentives to businesses that contribute to expressive culture projects including music, often prioritizing alternative genres and especially events that feature them. Quite a few individual artists have been successful at securing Faz Cultura support, as evidenced by the frequent appearance of its logo on CD jackets, promotional materials, and stage banners. Once again, personal connections were crucial for access to businesses willing to participate in the program, and, according to several musicians I spoke with, for getting applications approved at the governmental level.

Both the city and state governments also provide a degree of direct support for a few principals who submit successful proposals for their projects, which might include anything from Carnaval performances to recordings. Such funding is limited, competitive, and often linked to QI; but it has been vital for several local artists including Laurinha, who has received monetary support from Bahia's secretary of agriculture for many years. Combining this money with the city's independent *trio* fund, she has been able to pay herself, her musicians, and her production costs for Carnaval performances, and, in some cases, those that followed in the nonseasonal circuit. In 2005, though, she noted that her state funding had been steadily decreasing. This was painfully evident during Carnaval

FIGURE 2.12 Laurinha's Carnaval 2005 *trio independente* performance. She is at left with microphone. Son is bottom center. *Photo by the author.*

2014, when I attended her unrehearsed and shared *trio elétrico* performance—her grant was not enough to cover rehearsal studio costs, fees for her whole band, or a *trio* of her own. Laurinha has nevertheless continued to pursue and receive government support for her projects.

Despite being difficult to secure, backing from government programs and private *patrocínios* can be extremely beneficial for Salvador's musicians. As a result, most of my collaborators who lead projects have remained on the lookout for new sources of support and contacts with people who might provide the QI necessary to open doors and wallets. As their examples suggest, such working to work is a necessary complement to their ongoing efforts to exchange musical labor for wages.

WORKING TO SELL NEXUSES' WORK

With live performance as the foundation of musical work, booking and promoting it was at the fore of working to work activities among most nexus principals

I met.[16] This was the case even for those whose projects were successful enough to be sought out by employers and sponsors. Edmar, for example, told me that he was frequently approached by investors, agents, and event producers seeking to work with one or more of his artists (or his company). However, it was also clear that he did a significant amount of his own legwork in the effort to secure paid appearances for his artists. To do this, he, like other nexus principals, utilized multipronged approaches involving various combinations of promotional materials and personal contacts.

Promotional Material

Musicians in Salvador, like their counterparts in other locations, have long produced recordings for sale and for publicity. Even with wider use of the internet, a surprising number have continued to create physical products, usually CDs, for the nexuses they lead.[17] Over the years, I have seen and received them from principals and participants in everything from MPB solo projects to dance bands to heavy-metal outfits to *axé* acts.

The production quality of the promotional recordings that I have encountered has varied widely. Some are one-off discs that sounded as if they were tracked on a boom box. Others are virtually indistinguishable from major label releases — aside from containing no acknowledgment of copyright approval and perhaps bearing the words "*venda prohibida*" (sale prohibited). Likewise, the few promotional DVDs that I saw were professional- or near professional-quality productions. Video clips, both self-produced and shot by audience members, have also become increasingly common on artist websites as well as YouTube, Instagram, and Facebook.

Regardless of production quality most recordings by local musicians, including those aiming to do shows, contained a large quantity of well-known songs owing to the importance and expectation of participation in live performances. Familiar music outnumbered *músicas indeditas* (original/unpublished compositions) on nearly all the recordings used for booking purposes that I encountered, regardless of the circuit for which they were geared. Within that corpus, however, demos by projects such as Banda Patua seeking to express particular and highly individulalized *caras* took more liberties with arrangements than, for example, dance bands, which tended to keep closer to the best-known versions of the songs they recorded.

Because inclusion of well-known songs on recordings is the norm, producing them for legal sale can be cost prohibitive, especially for independent projects. Many vendors, disk manufacturers, and recording studios demand proof that all copyrights have been paid before undertaking any work. Especially prior to the proliferation of affordable home studios and online music sales, most productions were relegated to being used as demos or for sale on the "pirate" market—a trend that seems to have continued. A few unsigned artists in my network such as Márcia Castro produced full-length, legally sellable CDs comprised of their own compositions and/or songs for which permissions had been secured. But low financial return even for many label recordings and a related prevalent attitude that a CD is typically little more than a *"cartão de visita"* (calling card) suggests that nearly all recordings by local artists are, in a sense, demos. Even so, many go to great trouble and expense to produce them for sale at shows, as giveaways to potential employers, or to be streamed or downloaded for free. Regardless of the likelihood of financial loss, most interlocutors noted that a high-quality recording, most often in the form of CD, was an important mark of legitimacy and career accomplishment that enhanced their ability to secure live work.

In addition to recordings, several, but certainly not a majority of the projects in my network, had at the ready some form of printed material to support their booking and promotion efforts. I saw occasional packages of photos and band member bios to be given to agents, contractors, and potential investors, usually by principals or official representatives of the project. I also came across and was given general promotional items such as photocopied flyers and adhesive stickers that were passed out on the street or left on venue tables. Logo-emblazoned clothing, including *abadás*, are more common among elite acts, as are advertising billboards that line main thoroughfares, both promoting performances and occasionally recordings and also marking the changes of Salvador's musical seasons.

In comparison to the material media used for booking and promotion, use of the internet has been decidedly less uniform among my collaborators. When I began fieldwork, many of Salvador's top-tier performers and production organizations were using websites for promotion, and most, including A Zorra, also made it possible for contractors to contact their management about booking. Among less established projects, however, internet use was more limited. Makueto and Funk 'n' Roll were among the few projects in my immediate network that had significant online presence in the early years of my research. Only pianist/musical director Kadija Teles told me that she booked work, mostly her wedding accompaniment jobs, online. Project promotion, not booking, via Facebook and Instagram has subsequently become more common, largely replacing performance notices that in the past I received via printed media, telephone, text messages, and email. Often on these sites, the personal and professional are mixed, lending support for assertions by scholars such as Gregg (2011) who note how online forums have further blurred the lines between recreation and leisure in numerous labor sectors. Yet this line has always been blurry in contexts such as professional music making that have been entrenched in flexible labor practices — and whose focal activities are recreation for many people — long before it became a widespread concern. Likewise, the increase in personal web pages for projects and individual musicians, though mainly those who lead projects, in my network might suggest increased attention to working to work or at least a shift in how it is done. However, as I have argued, non-sound-producing labor has long been vital to the labor done by working musicians, and within my network at least, material and in-person approaches to promotion and especially booking remain the norm, albeit now supported more by digital resources.

Showing Up to Close the Deal

The travels of Makueto's *empresário* and Edmar's constant pavement pounding on behalf of Patua and his other artists suggest the importance of personal contact between nexus principals or representatives and potential employers. Fierce competition in a saturated market means that only a select few of the most elite acts can expect to be contacted for bookings without active job seeking. For the elite few, strong presence in the media can act in lieu of representatives on the street. Independent and smaller-scale projects, on the other hand, often relied on in-person visits to hand off promotional materials and to initiate booking arrangements.

Músicos da noite were especially dependent on often extensive face-to-face interaction. Carol, a young singer I met in 2004 performing in a duo with her father on keyboards and backup vocals, told me that making a demo recording available, even delivering it to venues, was rarely enough to secure a job. Rather, to book her project, she and the musicians who backed her typically needed to audition. Her assertion was confirmed by Dona Conçeição, the owner-operator of a venerable seaside restaurant and live-music venue, who told me that she hired performers based *exclusively* on live auditions, citing a distrust of recordings, which she felt were too easily manipulated. Accordingly, our (brief) mid-afternoon interview was interrupted several times by phone calls from performers hoping to schedule a try out.

In numerous other settings that hosted *músicos da noite*, I saw performers present a single set of music for an early, usually small, crowd before giving up the stage to another artist. It is possible that some of these early performances were done by paid opening acts. However, venue employees and musicians that I asked about such situations confirmed they were most likely nonpaid auditions.

Although (because) auditions led to paid work and could be pleasurable, some venue operators exploited them as a way of extracting free labor. Upon arriving early one night at a popular restaurant/club in Barra that regularly hosted live music, I saw a band of very young musicians onstage passionately delivering their set of pop/rock.[18] I asked a waiter about the booking policy, and he confirmed that the group was auditioning. I then asked if at some point that evening he would introduce me to the person who made hiring decisions. The server gave me the booker's office phone number and told me that he was not at the club that night.

I can only speculate about the circumstances surrounding this audition/free performance—it is possible that the staff gave the booker a report on the performance—but Márcia Castro was involved in a clear instance of exploitation in the guise of an audition. In collaboration with an upscale restaurant, an event producer organized a weekly series of performances that were promoted as a kind of musical tournament. The winner, they claimed, would earn a booking and expense-paid travel to perform at a large street festival in Italy. Over the course of several weeks, elimination rounds were held during which three artists each presented an hour-long set for a panel of judges. The winner each night advanced to the next round and the entire process repeated until one victor remained. As incentive for performers to promote their appearances, an audience poll figured into the judges' decisions.

In preparation, Márcia, and presumably the other competitors, assembled their bands, rehearsed their material at their own expense, and invited fans to each show. Their publicity efforts were effective—crowds on the nights I attended were much larger than I had seen on other visits to this venue (admission charges were higher than normal too). In the end, Márcia won the competition; but she was never sent to Italy.

Her project's eventual success suggests that it was not adversely affected in the long run by the competition facade. Perhaps her efforts to become a star might have even benefitted her to some degree, since there was local media coverage following the deception—I never got the chance to discuss it with her. And while this was an example that was extreme enough to attract press coverage, no one in my network seemed especially surprised, suggesting that such exploitation was hardly novel.

CAPITAL, NETWORKS, AND NETWORKING

As all of the examples discussed illustrate, musical projects became profitable only after the investment of capital, the accumulation and utilization of which usually fell primarily to nexus principals. Regardless of a project's genre, which informed its cultural capital, economic capital was essential for getting it up and running and hired. Places to rehearse cost money, as do promotional materials and, often, getting them to potential employers. People with hiring power are not necessarily readily accessible, thus pointing to the importance of social capital. Over time and with success, projects can accumulate economic, social, and cultural capital, but money and contacts are especially vital early on, both for building a portfolio of venues and, often, for assembling the musicians necessary to collaborate in the music-making process.

While they still require it, *músicos da noite* are somewhat less dependent on significant start-up money than principals of projects aimed at headline spots on Carnaval, São João, or theater stages. The reliance on familiar repertoire, conventional arrangements, and all too often, inattentive audiences in bars and restaurants means less pressure to rehearse, which significantly reduces monetary investment. Yet cultural capital, in the form of embodied knowledge of the *kit de barzinho/pagode*, underpins night musicians' ability to work, and social capital is often crucial for access to jobs and the competences they require. Still, the comparatively enhanced possibility of a quick transition from inception to profitability was a common motivation for many musicians to build or accept offers to work with nexuses that "played at night."

Endeavors such as Patua and Márcia Castro's star project are much more demanding of all types of capital. Patua required significant funding for rehearsals, demo recordings, and publicity. Despite any large-scale success that might befall such projects, profit in general is often slow in coming. And as was the case with Patua, most such projects never generate significant returns on investments. Márcia Castro's trajectory, however, shows the potential payoffs for embracing enhanced risk, which is often made possible through increased capital early on. Her musical knowledge and preferred genre were certainly appealing to potential side musicians and the nexus principals from whom she sought work. However, much of the work she did was done at a loss—theater bookings and recording sessions were costly and did not guarantee financial returns. Yet her willingness and ability to invest provided paid work for lenders of service, significantly strengthened existing ties, and facilitated new ones with backing musicians, industry personnel, and audiences.

Thus, other artists I met followed Márcia's dual pathway, but most were unable to accomplish what she did. While a number of factors likely inform the discrepant outcomes, Márcia's situation also says something about her particular social capital. Without taking anything away from the work she had done to cultivate her music and her following, her solidly middle-class background meant that she had grown up around and nurtured relationships with people with disposable income and an affinity for her preferred genre, MPB. Thus, she had numerous contacts who were willing and able to attend her performances, even at pricey venues. Márcia's social capital, and I would speculate assumptions about it based on her self-presentation (her comportment and color), likely enhanced her appeal to venue owners looking to maximize attendance by attracting people willing to spend enthusiastically on food and drinks.

Lack of this kind of "enhanced" social capital (or the ability to suggest having it) can create challenges. In contrast to Márcia, members of Farofa's family and most people in their immediate circles were unable to come to many of his performances because of the cost—something he mentioned on several occasions. This meant that projects that he led in spaces where payment was contingent on audience turnout were especially risky. Moreover, awareness or even the assumption on the part of a venue booker that a leader might have a limited following can inhibit booking power. I suspect that this placed workaday musicians, and especially those who mapped as more African, at a disadvantage when compared to, for instance, part-time musicians who supported themselves at white-collar jobs. To be sure, I saw many such musicians who were highly skilled performers with polished projects and who often hired full-time musicians. Yet I noted frequently—for instance at performances by a samba/dance band to which Farofa lent services led by a physician and an attorney—that their audiences were often quite large and bore many trappings of affluence (and often mapped as more European).[19] Farofa's most recent project, Samba de Farofa, demonstrates that over time, projects comprised entirely of local pros can build followings, which in turn endear them to venue operators and increase revenues. However, this is far from guaranteed and is more often than not the result of significant investment of personal money and, especially, labor time working to work.

In the face of such challenges, a strong tie with a well-placed person in the Scenes can make the difference between booking a particular job and failing. Recommendations or demonstrating a shared contact can open doors and much more.[20] Sometimes jobs are given as a favor to a mutual friend or as a way to curry favor with a more distant power broker who knows the job seeker.

In either instance, QI also serves as a kind of disciplining technology. Several performers I spoke with indicated that vouching for another musician is a risk since their failure on the job can be read as the recommender's lack of musical knowledge, a point noted by Kingsbury (1988) in a conservatory. Among professionals, Cottrell (2004) notes that an unsatisfactory performance by an endorsed musician, in this case, one sent as a substitute, can damage existing working relationships between the recommending musician and their employer. On the other hand, such surveillance might motivate venue operators to think twice before mistreating well-connected performers or those with whom they shared mutual contacts.[21] At the same time, QI also enables and fortifies cliques, referred to locally as "mafias," and illustrated by Ximbinha's comments about his *empresário* and the risks of circumventing the established system of intermediaries.

Along with formal routes to booking, an informal but no less QI-entangled practice is an effective means by which musicians get work for their projects, promote them, and generally network: "*canjas*,"[22] or sitting in on performances by others. Accordingly, I have seen numerous *canjas* over the years and in various contexts by a single guest artist, several musicians representing an ensemble, or in some instances, the entire band. In many instances, such appearances involved friends of the performers booked on a given night and many were planned and promoted in advance. Following Carnaval 2005 and with her sights set on getting her project work in the year-round circuit, Laurinha told me of both her intention to do multiple *canjas* and the willingness of several of her colleagues to allow them. *Canjas* are also frequently planned and promoted on publicity materials for shows, usually with the language of *convidados* (invited guests).

In addition to preplanned *canjas*, many are spontaneous. However, they are no less entangled with QI. Most unplanned instances of sitting in that I saw were predicated on some familiarity or acquaintance shared between the hosting musicians and the guest(s). I have also been at performances during which a stranger asked to sit in; and I have seen resistance to granting such requests. *Violonista*-singer Roberval Santos specifically told me that he refused to allow *canjas* from strangers. Some venues have policies against sitting in, but the

FIGURE 2.13 Josehr and Luciano from Banda Patua doing a *canja*. *Photo by the author.*

frequency with which I saw them happen suggests that prohibitions are rarely enforced, though they do provide a convenient rationale for refusal.

Canjas are thus underpinned by a complex politics. On the surface, they appear to be friendly supportive gestures, acts of showmanship, and even performances of community. They are; but there are other layers. For instance, I noticed Funk 'n' Roll earned several paid *temporadas* after sitting in during performances by friends. Subsequently, I saw them make space during their shows for other performers—including those who had allowed them to sit in—suggesting an economy of reciprocity. On the other hand, allowing a *canja* risks marring a performance if the guest's work is not received favorably, or it can place the host at risk of being upstaged. Thus, sitting in encapsulates social capital, knowing and being known by others in the Scenes, in many ways. Both are political, performative, and frequently exclusive; and both are also crucial for how working musicians find jobs, establish reputations, and, at times, protect both.

LAST NOTES

Examination of the formations in which musical labor is done brings to the fore several challenges faced by professional musicians and some of the ways they make do with and even overcome them. Flexible and informal employment practices result in near-constant competition alongside the cooperation necessary to make and live from music. Musicians and ensembles vie for many of the same positions and resources including jobs, *empresários, patrocínios,* and audiences. Recommendations from peers are often the best way to gain access. The extreme imbalance between musical labor supply and demand compounded with the vagaries of musicians' marginal revenue product impede wage growth for all but a select few who become less substitutable and reach the upper strata of the industries. This fortifies the need for most musicians to maintain multiple nexuses in order to survive. Yet this common tactic can undermine the quality of performances and fuel conditions for schedule conflicts, incongruent goals within formations, and turf protection that exacerbate instability. At the same time, musicians who successfully maintain diverse nexus portfolios for themselves and the projects they lead can and do create some stability. Likewise, fluidity within any one formation allows it to continue in the face of losing lenders of services. Such concerns and many others are constantly negotiated as nexuses of various types are formed and work toward becoming profitable music-making enterprises. Against numerous challenges, musicians such as Farofa, Laurinha, Jorge Elaíde Gois, Márcia Castro, and many others do just that and on occasion, much more.

THREE

Tactical Affiliations and Performances
of Musicians' Selves

> In acting and speaking, men show who they are, reveal actively
> their unique personal identities and thus make their appearance in the
> human world, while their physical identities appear without any activity
> of their own in the unique shape of the body and sound of the voice.
> This disclosure of "who" in contradistinction to "what" somebody is—
> his qualities, gifts, talents, and shortcomings, which he may display
> or hide—is implicit in everything somebody says and does.
>
> *Hannah Arendt,* The Human Condition *(1958)*

In September 2010 I was invited to speak about my research with ethnomusicologists at the Federal University of Bahia's (UFBA) school of music. Farofa came with me, and he added plenty of insightful details about the Scenes while also generally enlivening the conversation. His main point was that living from music in Salvador hinged on two questions that all working musicians are asked regularly: "What do you play? and with whom?" His assessment resonated with most present, the majority of whom had likely participated in countless conversations on these very topics as active or former musicians and ethnographers.

Although Farofa's "career questions" sound like a relatively obvious way to frame any musician's pathway, they are actually multivalent, interrelated, and entangled with numerous other concerns. For instance, as I discussed in the last chapter when describing nexuses, what and with whom professional musicians play is hardly straightforward. Rather, since working musicians actively pursue careers in a changing field, such "facts" are not givens, but are instead produced as they negotiate impediments and opportunities in relation to their own resources, tastes, predilections, and competences—that is, through their practices. Nexus principals and lenders of services alike make decisions about which jobs to seek, whether or not to accept those that are offered, and when it might be time to end an employment relationship. Whether acting on their own behalf or as a representative of a project, working musicians affiliate selectively, generally with a portfolio of nexuses in relation to what is possible at the time, but usually with an eye toward the future as well. Finally, most professionals I met worked in different music and musical roles at various points in their careers, and often simultaneously, in order to better their position or make do and survive. Their moves were informed by and informed Scenes sensibilities, the value and meanings of different forms of capital, and the sounds of music.

Listening to and participating in many conversations that broached Farofa's questions before and after performances and rehearsals as well as on the street left me with no doubt that the work musicians do to *represent* what and with whom they play is as important as what they actually do with instruments in hand.[1] Shop talk about past jobs and commentary about work in process was common, as were discussions about colleagues' activities and evaluations of performances and recordings by everyone from local musicians to international stars. Much of it seemed innocuous enough, at least on the surface. But on several instances it was apparent that colleague-competitors, employees, and employers were not so subtly jockeying for positions as they traded stories. Even if posturing were not the objective, this type of banter still affected the ways that the participants in the exchanges came to know each other and themselves, with implications for any number of issues ranging from performance details to future work possibilities to broadly held notions about music and music participants. Put another way, discussions among musicians practicing in a field about what and with whom they play are, like demonstrations of taste, evaluative, entangled with power, and constitutive of capital. They are also negotiations through which (net)working musicians use their capital (usually cultural and social), with consequences for musical careers, sounds, and meanings.

This chapter moves inward from my prior descriptions of musicians working in an array of nexuses, genres, and roles to further explore their career pathways, their representations of them, and the implications of both. Immediately at issue are the ways performers maintain and protect their possibilities of earning livings making music. These processes and outcomes are inseparable from broader discourses about music, the people who participate in it, and attendant cultural politics. After relating the work musicians accept—what and with whom—to positions in the Scenes and notions of self, I discuss the affiliation decisions of several musicians I met that illustrate common career tactics, the limits of professional flexibility, and the challenges, benefits, and potential risks of how those limits are broached. I then illustrate the importance of how working musicians represent their musical participation as a means to emphasize perceived strengths and mitigate liabilities in terms of their work histories and musical selves. Following these discussions, which focus on how musicians work to work, I move to an examination of how several I met positioned themselves on jobs they had already secured, in part in an effort to influence the work being done. The chapter closes with a consideration of stasis and change in the performative practices among Bahian musicians. At stake in their performances, both sonic and discursive, are numerous issues including authority on a given job, professional identities, future employment options and pay (i.e., the value of their labor), and Scenes sensibilities.

MUSICIANS' SELVES IN THE SALVADOR SCENES

The importance the musicians I saw working to work placed on what and with whom they and their peers perform pointed strongly to an underlying politics of musical participation conceived through the racialized and classed genre associations discussed in chapter 1. Notable too was that when such matters were discussed, participants in the conversation mentioned music and music participants they disliked and avoided—most commonly *axé*, *pagode*, and *arrocha*—almost as much as they spoke about those they embraced. As was the case among listeners, and as Faulkner (1971) notes about studio musicians in Hollywood, predictable patterns of participation, disavowal, and rationale for each emerged rather quickly despite the multiplicity and flexibility that was the norm. Whereas Faulkner's interview subjects' patterns of self-positioning varied in relation to their imaginings of musical success apropos of their specific instruments,[2] their past work in relation to genre (e.g., jazz vs "classical"), and the trade-offs they made for the money and relative stability of studio work, comparable tactics among musicians I met were more uniform across instruments and were more clearly entangled with racial conception even as the art/commerce binary loomed large.

Indeed, working musicians' distancing, literal and discursive, from Bahian music despite its economic potential and audibility strikes me as a particular and a particularly Bahian tactic for dealing with the musical stuff of Bahia's cultural intimacy—the emphasis on (local) African-ness that sets it outside of the national ideal of musical *mestiçagem* exemplified in "*música de qualidade*," MPB, and marketable as Bahian. Position takings around musical participation and avoidance, both through pathways and discourse, were so conscientiously pursued by so many people, musicians and listeners, that I came to see them as embodied "technologies of the self," (Foucault 1988) that informed who they "were" in relation to who they wanted to be, and for working musicians, how they felt they needed to be known in the Scenes in order to succeed in their careers. Their presentations of selves were deployed in relation to specific situations, meaning they could be strategic and exercised by someone in a relatively empowered position or, more commonly, tactical, and utilized by flexible and often precarious workers in a volatile industry as they sought a leg up or a way in. Regardless of the relative relationships between participants, their negotiations of power and position were never separate from wider disciplining forces, especially racial conception and Euro-mimetic musical sensibilities. An important caveat is that even as musicians' tactics could be quite effective making do with and even challenging dominant strategies, unintended and often disempowering consequences were always close at hand. For example, practices and discourse of professional musicians that provided an advantage in a given situation could simultaneously reinforce the cultural capital of hegemonic genres and associated participants and/or contribute to the vilification of their "others." Crucially, these othered musics were often the ones most central to local musicians' livelihoods, the basis of local industries of cultural production, and mappings of Bahia.

Another manifestation of unintended consequences deriving from common tactics is that misunderstandings about *baianos'* and musicians' work ethics are often reinforced by their visibility while working to work in what appear to be purely social situations backstage, in clubs, and on the street. Gregg (2011) rightly notes that although the encroachment of work time into leisure time is increasingly the norm across labor sectors and enabled by the fact that much of the work being done is similar to recreational pastimes (e.g., using social media), career rewards such as remuneration for extra labor are inequitably distributed. Rather than making work more fun and profitable for everyone, she argues, the normalization of labor during off hours reinforces existing, and often gendered, hierarchies, allows for employee surveillance, and paves the way for the exploitation of increasingly precarious workers. Yet I would argue that for the office and knowledge-economy workers that are Gregg's focus, such nonstop labor is still generally seen as productive, as part of their job, even though it is easily appropriated by their employers to nefarious ends. In contrast, musicians, *baianos*, and Bahian musicians have been and continue to be denied recognition for the almost continuous work, however pleasurable, they must do. This is thanks to lingering idealizations of music's autonomy from economics, hackneyed racialized and classed stereotypes that still hold strong in Bahia, and limited understandings and misrecognition of multiple facets of working to work and musical labor in general.

Among the musicians I met, however, the near-constant labor necessary to live from music was not misrecognized or underestimated in its importance. On the contrary, many aspects of the substance, discipline, and especially constructive power of their discursive practices as they work to work and on the job resonated strongly with anthropologist Dorinne Kondo's (1990) writing on labor as a central vector of identity formation. Her detailed analysis of an interaction with a male artisan in a Tokyo factory, for example, strikes a very familiar chord with many exchanges I saw in Salvador. In an effort to assert his empowered position over her and as a reflexive act of identity construction, Kondo argues, the factory employee she spoke with narrated a "selective account of selfhood, which he centered exclusively around work as a way of claiming for himself certain culturally celebrated ideals of craftsmanship" (1990, 257). I too saw musicians narrate musical work selves to me, to each other, and to themselves by claiming certain celebrated notions of musicianship, most often based on their participation in and knowledge of esteemed genres, but also through assertions of their affiliation with notable performers. Such presentations also commonly involved creating discursive buffers between themselves and less valorized musics—the latter all the more if they performed Bahian music with any frequency. Such narrations as particular kinds of position takings in the field were crucial for creating opportunities to make musical sounds and creating value for their labor.[3]

Beyond material implications for working musicians, performances of musical work selves also helped reify longstanding assumptions about what it is to be a good musician and what constitutes good music. While we did not address the topic at the UFBA roundtable, it was apparent in numerous conversations that many *baianos*, musicians and nonmusicians alike, took it as almost axiomatic that people who played "good" music were "good" musicians and that those who played "bad" music were "bad" musicians. A conversation with a young bassist who, among his various endeavors, worked with various *pagode* bands, is illustrative:

JP: Is there prejudice against . . .

VANDO: . . . Musicians who play *pagode*? The majority of the musicians who play *pagode* only play *pagode*, understand? They only know how to play it and generally . . . their *cavaquinhos* are always out of tune. *Pagode* musicians only want to play it. This is why they are discriminated against so much. They aren't musically educated. (Salvador, March 2, 2005)

In addition to illustrating a widely accepted but problematic homology, Vando's comments also illustrate that versatility is not only an economic necessity for most working musicians, but it is also valuable, for instance as a means for mitigating associations with less esteemed music. On the other hand, specialization in music with high cultural capital was, in keeping with ideologies of autonomous art, embraced as a virtue since, more often than not, it came at the cost of income and as such signaled sacrifice and an idealized notion of artistic integrity. And, musicians who could play so-called good music were frequently given the benefit of the doubt in their ability to play less esteemed ones, which were (wrongly) assumed to be easier, natural, and in *baianos'* blood.

Commentary similar to Vando's about *pagode* as well as *arrocha* and *axé* music and performers was very much the norm, though *axé* musicians were somewhat less frequently in the crosshairs of fervent detractors. Nevertheless, I still heard multiple discussions that conflated the perceived poor quality of Bahian music—again, usually based in its lack of lyrical, harmonic, and arrangement complexity—with the purported failings of those who created it. Musicians who played "bad music" were condemned for doing so and in doing so "badly," making it "bad." Such players were also commonly assumed to be and condemned for being incapable of performing other, "better," music, which often closed off possibilities to do so and demonstrate otherwise. The way out, as I saw on multiple occasions, was to take a variety of very active steps to perform musical selves that countered such assumptions.

Understandably, most musicians I saw working sought to maximize opportunities to be seen, heard, and thus known as a *bom músico* (a good musician), importantly, according to dominant Euro-mimetic notions of musical "goodness."[4] In keeping with the notion that disavowing the "inferior" can be a crucial tactic for doing this, they also avoided situations that might reflect negatively on them when possible. As professionals, their efforts were overlaid by any number of other factors, not the least of which was economics. Plenty of good musicians performed denigrated music, especially during Carnaval and São

João, thus undermining at least one common illogic for condemnation. Still, negative impressions of the music and dominant criteria of evaluation were reinforced when those who did perform less respected music tried to mitigate their association with it to avoid negative repercussions of association. And their efforts frequently hinged on verbally asserting their ability and preference for performing esteemed music with respected musicians, coupled with references to the money.

Thus, on the one hand, I saw a fair bit of variety in the kinds of work musicians accepted and rejected. On the other hand, within this range of pathways, there were clear patterns of association, avoidance, and discursive buffering. Predictably, Bahian music was the target of most distancing while more seemingly contemplative and cosmopolitan genres as well as several "authentic" traditional practices were claimed actively and with great frequency by musicians known and aiming to be known as good.

CAREER PATHWAYS AND PATTERNS
OF AFFILIATION AND AVOIDANCE

Another consequence of the volatility of the music industries and the related instability of most musicians' jobs is that career pathways are often nonlinear. One job does not necessarily lead to another, let alone a better one, though most musicians indicated that it was easier to get hired if they were already working, and that a badly received performance could hinder future opportunities. Among my collaborators, I saw periods of frequent work turn to employment droughts quickly and without warning. Most worked with the knowledge that projects, even established ones, could fail at any time; dismissals from existing nexuses were rarely out of the question; and that many of their peers left lucrative jobs never again to enjoy a comparable level of economic success (or notoriety or prestige) in music. As Jorge Elaíde Gois's example from the previous chapter illustrated, contacts and a reputation for being a good musician were crucial for ensuring, or at least bettering chances, for career sustainability. Accumulated social and cultural capital were also vital for advancing careers, providing building blocks for a potentially more linear progression up through the ranks. Finally, social capital in the form of a support network proved invaluable for the many musicians who lacked savings accounts that could see them through tough times.

Yet accumulation of such capital is complex, contradictory, and hardly automatic. According to nearly all of the musicians I spoke with, the work that would allow them to spotlight their competence in esteemed music, the skills widely embraced to constitute good musicianship, paid less than jobs in genres providing less cultural capital. Owing to the organization of the circuits, most cultural capital-rich labor continues to be done in smaller, less well-publicized venues than less respected genres. This shapes the ways most musicians are seen and heard by potential employers in particular, and not necessarily favorable ways. Moreover, subsequent employers might lack the ability or will to increase pay or improve work conditions from prior work situations. Finally, future support or even cooperation on the job are not guaranteed since agendas, personalities, authority, and musical preferences and abilities can and do clash and are negotiated on the bandstand and in the studio. As a result, no simple or single pathway to success, however defined, existed for my collaborators, nor did the resumes of successful musicians demonstrate much consistent logic. Perhaps the one thing they shared was evidence of tactical navigation of dominant tendencies and sensibilities that helped them balance their work activities in ways that allowed them to create selves as musicians capable of performing certain kinds of music with certain people.

Thus a first step in considering this aspect of working to work is taking Farofa's career questions at face value, and discussing what, and with whom, several musicians I met played. Notable is that in spite of the flexibility that I have argued is central to their livelihoods, a majority of the working musicians I encountered had limits to the jobs, nexus affiliations, and roles they would accept. These "self-imposed" constraints were not hard and fast and could change in relation to opportunity and need. But on the whole, the musicians I followed were well considered in their multimusicality. Most often, they refused certain employment opportunities, even well-paid ones, if they thought they might typecast them in ways they did not see as beneficial to their careers in the long run.

Farofa, for example, has received several invitations to work with *pagode* bands, including some that were signed with powerful production companies. Yet concerns about possible career-ending stigmatization made him think twice about doing so. He has never been shy about stating his dislike for *pagode* and his conviction that its sexualized lyrics and performance conventions reinforce negative stereotypes about *baianos*. But as he told me, his refusal of lucrative job offers was also out of concern for how his future job prospects might be negatively affected owing to common stereotypes surrounding *pagodeiros'* lack of musical competence. His stance has shifted somewhat, perhaps as a result of performing blocks of *pagode* tunes with a busy, (Rio-style) samba-focused dance band with an abundant and affluent following. Playing music that he would have otherwise avoided while being paid well, treated respectfully, and received enthusiastically in venues filled to capacity enhanced his understanding of why some musicians, including those capable of performing "better" music, might opt for a job in Bahian music. But he has nevertheless remained steadfast in his refusal to become part of a *pagode* band of any kind lest he be marked as a *pagodeiro*.

Jorge Elaíde Gois, similarly, drew a line when he feared the risk of becoming strongly identified with another genre of Bahian music was too great. In contrast to Farofa, whose generic multiplicity has been facilitated by his instrument, percussion, and his role as lender of services in most settings, Jorge was somewhat more restricted in the genres he performed since he was a singer and usually, a nexus principal. Such visibility onstage and in his booking practices has led him to focus primarily on MPB and pop/rock—a certain degree of consistency was necessary to build an audience and his portfolio of employers. Still, new job opportunities, the need for some variety, and especially audience requests were often met with inclusion of other genres beyond his usual *praia*.

Always the consummate professional, Jorge rarely let on if he had any reservations about taking such excursions if the situation demanded it. Moreover, he expressed his willingness to perform *axé* if it would lead to a higher level of income and overall career achievement. Indeed, his frustration was apparent as he told me about the mafias that he believed had conspired to keep him from getting a well-paid job with an *axé* ensemble. Yet despite his clear, albeit contextually informed openness to multiple genres, he eventually found his limit when he received, and declined, an offer from a producer to record an *arrocha* CD.

Given *arrocha*'s popularity at the time (c. 2004–2005), this fully funded project would likely have provided Jorge with a substantial income boost and an opportunity to work in significantly bigger venues, possibly under star-like conditions. The rationale behind his refusal of the recording contract was clear even if it seemed contradictory given his history. I had seen him play *arrocha* on prior jobs with dance bands and in voice and *violão* work when requested by the audience—though in the latter case, he typically met requests by playing an MPB song to an *arrocha* groove. The durability of a recording, the plan for it to be a solo project in his name, and the publicity efforts that would have followed the CD release, however, all but ensured Jorge's definitive identification as an *arrocha* performer. He would lose the anonymity of being a backing player in a large ensemble, the buffer of performing it tactically (i.e., as an adapted MPB song), and the ephemerality of doing either in a passing moment in front of a relatively limited audience. By recording a "solo" CD of "real" *arrocha* and promoting it on a large scale, he would surrender the distance he had previously managed to maintain from a music that he found objectionable and that he and most of his peers thought would be a short-lived fad. Regardless of any quickly realized economic benefit or showbiz perks, the proposed project asked him to flex beyond the limits of how he knew himself as a musician and the pathway that he believed would enable him to sustain and enjoy his career into the future.

Whereas neither Farofa nor Jorge ever participated in a project that was dedicated to Bahian music, the long-standing audibility of *axé*, and *pagode* in the seasonal circuits and *arrocha*'s two popularity surges leave no doubt than numerous musicians in Salvador do accept jobs performing these genres almost exclusively. Furthermore, a number of musicians I met who based their careers primarily in other, "alternative" contexts had worked with Bahian music artists at one or more points in their careers. Their histories push against the widespread assumptions in the Scenes that performers of Bahian music could not play "quality" music and that musicians known for playing Bahian music were unable to support themselves if they left jobs with *axé*, *pagode*, or *arrocha* artists—a belief rooted in acceptance of the first assumption. Yet the pathways of musicians with sustained careers also illustrate that these beliefs and the actual challenges of career viability for performers of Bahian music were ongoing concerns.

To illustrate, one of Junior's first musical jobs was as a percussionist with a prominent early (and long disbanded) *axé* ensemble, Banda Reflexus. Although he told me on several occasions that he had nothing against *axé* or *pagode*, in 2005 he nevertheless declined an opportunity to work with an *axé* band of comparable, if not slightly higher status than A Zorra. This indicated to me, and Junior implied, that he saw accepting this job as a poor long-term career choice despite the promise of more money than he was earning with his varied MPB work, Funk 'n' Roll, and his main nexus, a well-regarded local salsa band, Salsalitro. Perhaps a return to frequent travel away from home was a deterrent. He was married and had a young son at the time. But at no point since I have known him has he accepted any job dedicated to performing Bahian music.

On the other hand, the flexibility and comparative anonymity of most backing musicians such as Junior also raises the stakes for their tactics of affiliation. Since they are not usually definitive of their nexuses in the way that, say, a singer is, they are more substitutable and thus, more precarious (unless they are *socios*). Moreover, almost by definition, multitasking side musicians' work selves are more strongly linked to them as "real" people rather than a "musical persona" (Auslander 2006) let alone a brand constructed onstage, via recordings, and through promotional material. Any persona they enact is generally secondary to that of the front people or the project itself. Moreover, it must be malleable enough to mesh without distraction from their employer(s)' personas if they aim to work in multiple nexuses. Their employment is more typically in the hands of other musicians, too. For that reason, their self as a musician and coworker—good, bad, easy to work with, dependable, etc.—takes a particular primacy. This all puts pressure on working musicians' efforts to maintain their work affiliations in ways that allow them to earn enough income and demonstrate skills appropriate to their intended pathway.

Pathway Challenges and Related Navigational Tactics

In spite of best efforts, success at achieving an optimum mix of projects that balances economic, cultural, and social capital can be limited by a number of factors, not the least of which is financial need. Complete avoidance of Bahian music can be difficult in Bahia, especially if a musician wishes to make the most of the economic opportunities available during Carnaval. Opportunities for backing musicians also vary depending on the specific instrument they play and several other factors beyond their control. For instance, the dearth of women working in roles other than singer suggests a durable barrier to them being accepted as, say, a good guitarist or drummer. Yet the importance of enacting a musical work self that was not overly rooted in less esteemed genres was evident in most lenders of services' practices of participation, avoidance, and narration of their careers regardless of their (gender, class, color, sexual) identity or instrument.

Understandably, the musicians I met, however flexible, tended to prioritize their most lucrative nexuses, even if their stated musical preferences and/or career ambitions lay elsewhere. As exemplified by Edni's experiences with A Zorra, performers who worked with mid- and especially upper-level organizations tended to be less available for side work, especially around Carnaval and São João, owing to busy schedules and frequent travel. Despite limited free time and less financial need, I nevertheless saw him and a number of other musicians with similar employment circumstances performing different, usually more valorized music, in less lucrative, lower-profile situations, when their primary nexus's schedule permitted, especially during the off-seasons.[5]

Without financial pressure or the lure of higher payment, it is reasonable to infer that other issues were at stake for the side work taken by musicians employed by signed acts. Self-protection against job loss certainly figured in, and awareness of the perils of mafias was especially high among *axé* performers. The pleasure of variety, new musical challenges, or performing with friends was also a frequently cited motivation, as exemplified by Kiko's involvement with Som Ki Lufa and even Junior's work with Funk 'n' Roll. An added benefit was that tactical side work could pave the way toward leaving or losing a primary affiliation with a better-prepared road to career longevity.

Owing to their schedules and nexus prioritizing, much of the side work done by musicians lending services to higher-profile organizations involved one-off performances and sporadic dates with ongoing nexuses. This was the case with Márcio Dhiniz, whom I met when he lent services to an MPB singer on a local show that fell during a break from his primary job playing drums for Margareth Menezes. Over the next year or so I attended several other performances and rehearsals by the same singer. Most involved a consistent cast of backing players, but Márcio missed several because of commitments to Margareth's band. When he was in Salvador, however, he not only worked with this nexus, but he also very deliberately targeted and worked with others that featured him performing a range of esteemed genres including MPB, samba, pop/rock, and jazz. Although they paid significantly less than his work with Margareth — and diminished his ability to rest when coming off the road — these jobs provided avenues for Márcio to demonstrate a wider range of (valued) musical competences than he could showcase in his main job.

Márcio's tactics were successful. For instance, the MPB singer I saw him backing commented that unlike so many musicians in Salvador, he could "really play Brazilian music" (as opposed to "just" Bahian music). Her opinion was, apparently, widely shared across the Scenes: when he lost his job with Margareth, I never heard speculation that it was due to lack of ability. On the contrary, several people asserted he was the victim of mafia conspiring. By avoiding being typecast as "merely" a performer of Bahian music with targeted side jobs while backing a Bahian music star, Márcio was able to secure increased work in nonseasonal venues performing a range of genres with multiple artists shortly after a prominent and lucrative nexus affiliation ended.

During this same period, roughly 2004–2005, I saw several other musicians with primary jobs in Bahian music doing dates with other artists in other, more respected genres. Margareth's bassist backed Márcia Castro at a private event celebrating the release of her first (MPB) CD. Likewise, Edni did Forró jobs with other ensembles during the June season in 2005, and I saw him play MPB and pop/rock in small clubs on several occasions during his tenure with the group and after it. I also went with him during a slow period for A Zorra to see several of his bandmates do an MPB and pop/rock performance at an upscale restaurant/bar with their bassist's brother, whose main job was playing percussion for Daniela Mercury.

This last performance was an eye-opening example of how lenders of services to signed acts working in a less esteemed genre can exercise their social capital and use that association to create standing as good musicians. The event was sonically indistinguishable from countless other presentations I had heard by *músicos da noite*. Yet on this night the venue was not only more crowded than other times I had been there, but it was also peppered with numerous prominent local musicians and industry personnel. Among them were people I knew or was told to be linked to A Zorra, their management company, Chiclete com Banana (which shared management with A Zorra), and Daniela Mercury's band. As a result, an otherwise rather mundane job provided an effective (and pleasurable) means for musicians known primarily for performing *axé* to demonstrate their competence at esteemed music for peers and other influential people in the Scenes.

In addition to the musicians who lent their services to more than one nexus—the majority—several that I met who supported themselves working with a high-profile signed act were also simultaneously principals in other, albeit lower-level endeavors, that they called their *"projectos paralelos"* (parallel projects). Elpidio Bastos, the bassist and musical director for Olodum, was an especially notable example of this tactic. Like several others I met in similar situations, for instance, Edni and Márcio, Elpidio's primary job was lucrative enough to support him. In all likelihood, his roles in the group also provided a degree of job security greater than other members, especially the drummers, who are much more substitutable owing to their abundance and the narrower range of skills they demonstrate in their jobs. Nevertheless, the group's genre mapping still created liabilities for him.

In particular, ex-Olodum members were frequently cited as the examples par excellence of the perils of working in Bahian music. I first saw this in 2003 when a prominent Bahian historian gave a lecture to a group of U.S. university students at a language school I was attending. The speaker told us that he had recently seen a former drummer from the group working as a parking valet. His not-so-subtle point, which was part of a larger critique of the seductive power of show business and its ill effects on local youth, was that this musician lacked the (musical) knowledge to continue a musical (or another "respectable") career despite the fame, money, and travel he had enjoyed while working with the group. Subsequently, I heard other working musicians tell similar stories about former Olodum drummers who were unable to find musical work following dismissal from the group. It is impossible to know if these musicians had the capacity to perform other music (or if they were the same person). However, given the assumptions about musicians who perform Bahian music, and similar stories about other *axé* and *pagode* performers who suffered the same fate, it is likely that their reported inability to maintain careers after leaving Olodum resulted from a failure to make any of the more far-ranging and more respected competences they might have had known to people who could have subsequently employed them. In a sense, they failed to confirm the value of their labor in any other musical context.

Elpidio's tactics of affiliation provided him with a very visible challenge to this prevalent narrative. As Olodum's musical director, it is safe to assume that his level of musicianship was less in question than the other performers in the group and those who were the subject of cautionary tales. Still, his targeted work as the singer, *violonista*, and composer of an MPB project left little doubt about his ability to perform "good" music well, thus bolstering his identification as a *bom músico*.

Elpidio also made tactical use of the social capital he generated through affiliation with one of Bahian music's most prominent representatives to promote his parallel project and himself. I saw him do this by inviting several Olodum drummers to do a *canja* at a show in an upscale club. Their appearance was warmly welcomed by the crowd; and since the show was promoted in advance, the featured guest performers likely helped attract a larger and likely different demographic than might normally have attended such an event. The increased and enthusiastic crowd enhanced the potential appeal of his project to industry personnel and, as was the case with Edni's colleagues from A Zorra and Daniela Mercury's band, it allowed Elpidio to demonstrate another, more esteemed side of his musical self to a segment of listeners who might otherwise never have heard it.

In contrast to the route taken by Elpidio during the time I followed his career, I am also aware of musicians known for working in more esteemed contexts who accept jobs with signed performers of Bahian music. In several instances, those providing the account stressed that their associations with respected music and musicians paved the way for the jobs. In a sense, these musicians' work history effectively increased the value of their labor since the moves marked significant pay raises. That they were finally earning a decent wage figured prominently in many discussions, and I never heard the musician in question criticized for "selling out." Instead, the circumstances leading to their change of direction were lamented and cited as evidence that the *povo* did not want good music and the general difficulty of earning a living wage playing it. With solid reputations as good musicians, these performers were much freer to work in a range of contexts with less chance of collateral damage.

Indeed, with the financial limitations of performing alternative genres well known across the Scenes, working musicians seemed to give a fairly wide berth to colleagues who accepted work performing music that did not highlight their "chops" or musical good taste—that is, provided they had sufficiently demonstrated them in other contexts. Several years before Farofa ever performed a *pagode* tune on a job and admitted enjoying it, he conceded that "it's no wonder so many people take jobs playing *axé* and *pagode*," suggesting some empathy for "good" musicians who "chose" to play "bad" music." Not coincidentally, Farofa's concession happened after we had battled crosstown for hours in the hot sun in order to work an unpaid, promotional instrumental music show. Further evidence that financial reward can provide an effective means of distancing from less esteemed music was provided by the numerous musicians who rubbed their thumb and forefinger together, the money gesture, when discussing their job with an *axé* or *pagode* artist, often just before talking about their parallel project in a more esteemed genre.

Another important consideration for many professional musicians is how they understand their musician selves in relation to particular genres, including the most prestigious ones, and how this knowledge informs their pathways. Such decisions are often both a matter of reputation and allocation of effort. For example, Israel, a busy bassist that I met backing an MPB singer in 2004, told me that he avoided taking jazz work despite the respect it engendered. In 2014 Edni characterized this same period in the Scenes as a time that most musicians believed that "you had to play jazz to be a *bom músico*," and several mentioned jazz jam sessions to me on various trips to Bahia as places to hear "good" musicians.[6] Despite this orthodoxy, Israel's rationale was that jazz work would not allow him to present his abilities well without significant preparation on his part. Since his professional identity was already strongly established through his work in MPB, pop/rock, and samba, he felt he had little to gain with such an effort, despite jazz's tremendous cultural capital and the connections it could provide via working with other respected musicians.

Since the musicians I met took so many different approaches to the work they did and did not accept, the ways that they framed their pathways were equally if not more important, especially in terms of how they were known in the Scenes. In this discursive aspect of their working to work, they were also selective and tactical. And there was some variety, much as there was with their actual affiliations. However, in their presentations of musician selves I saw even greater consistency in their efforts to distance from Bahian music and claim knowledge of esteemed music and musicians.

DISCURSIVE PERFORMANCES
OF MUSICAL WORK SELVES

Even if they were not frequently visible performing esteemed music, numerous musicians, including several stars of Bahian music, made various overtures and discursive moves to emphasize their connection to them, and to varying degrees, to subtly distance themselves from the music that was their bread and butter. An illustrative instance of this took place during the Margareth Menezes show that I attended during my first trip to Salvador. Although I had understood Margareth to be exemplary of *axé* based on the literature I had read prior to coming and the recordings I had listened to, she was introduced to the Rock 'n' Rio crowd as an MPB singer. In one sense, *axé* is a form of MPB. It *is* Brazilian popular music. Yet Margareth's band that night comprised an archetypal *axé* ensemble in terms of its instrumentation and in their heavy use of samba-reggae-related grooves performing Carnaval (that is, *axé*) hits. While not a misrepresentation of her work, her dis-identification with *axé* in favor of a cultural capital-rich national genre is illuminating and a position I have seen taken repeatedly since then.

Within my network, Laurinha also utilized several tactics of self-positioning that limited her association with *axé*. Although she achieved arguably her greatest notoriety as the singer for Pimenta de Cheiro, which was the first band formed by the venerable Carnaval *bloco* Cheiro de Amor, Laurinha has long positioned herself in her promotional materials as a "precursor to *axé* music" rather than an *axé* singer per se. This manner of self-presentation has helped support a long career following her departure from the group through the creation of what anthropologist Carol Laderman (1993) might call an "aesthetic distance." Key to Laderman's conceptualization and Laurinha's tactic is proximity to a threatening situation — in Laurinha's case, the cultural intimacy of Bahian music — that is close enough to engender personal transformation but remote enough to prevent harm. Like wealthy *baianos* who participate in Carnaval from expensive *blocos* or *camarotes*, Laurinha has discursively created a safe space for her involvement with a potentially stigmatizing music. More than that, though, by presenting herself as a precursor to this music, and the first woman to animate a *bloco do trio* parade, she is able to safely emphasize a significant rather than tangential role in the history of what would become Bahia's most lucrative musical product rather than its present.

This kind of tactical positioning was evident in the project she initiated prior to Carnaval 2005. The project she was developing was called Pop Azeitado ("oiled pop"), which in many parts of Brazil could be taken as a reference to enhanced or hot pop music. However, Laurinha's use of "*azeitado*" was more specific—it was an overt reference to *dende* oil, a staple of Afro-Bahian cuisine, and thus, Bahian-ness. Her website stated as much: "*a fusão do pop brasileiro com a per-cussão baiana é igual ao* Pop Azeitado" ("Pop Azeitado is the fusion of Brazilian pop with Bahian percussion").[7] Our conversations and especially her set list also made clear that the "pop" in question was MPB. Pop Azeitado's performances consisted of classic songs by the likes of Chico Buarque, Jorge Benjor, and Dorival Caymmi adapted to include local (Afro-Bahian) rhythms, including some that were very *axé*-like (e.g., samba-reggae), played by a drummer and several per-cussionists playing instruments heard in a typical *axé* ensemble—the *surdo* set, *repique* played with two flexible plastic sticks, and *timbal*. In a manner resonant with Freyreian notions of *mestiçagem*, Laurinha's project aimed to combine the "best" aspects of MPB with the "best" features of Bahian music. Contextualizing Pop Azeitado with an awareness of Bahian cultural politics and musical sensi-bilities as well as Laurinha's own views on music, something we discussed on multiple occasions, helps underscore her project as a concerted effort to localize beloved and cultural capital-rich music and make it more suitable for dancing and large-scale parties without sacrificing its cultural capital-producing lyrical and harmonic interest. For many *baianos*, neither Laurinha's approach nor the descriptive language for the project needed explanation—a point confirmed for me by Son, who played bass on the project and acted as its musical director for a time. Laurinha's various distancing tactics have thus allowed her to claim and capitalize on her history with Bahian music rather than potentially suffer from it. She presented a convincing argument that she is authentically Bahian, but just Bahian enough, and not "merely" an *axé* singer.

Elpidio too has utilized particular representational strategies to frame his in-volvement with Bahian music. In our interview, he corrected me when I referred to Olodum as an *axé* band.[8] Instead, he described their music as "Afro-Pop," aligning it with a more cosmopolitan, and thus less intimately Black, genre.[9] This familiar pattern of positioning has continued. Elpidio's music was more recently described on his management company's website as "MPB Brazilian Folk." The text stresses (in English) that "he walks in the samba, salsa, funk, and his own style" (http://www.odarasprod.com/artists, accessed October 6, 2017). Olodum is mentioned (as is his role as musical director), but much more text is devoted to his collaborations with star performers, only one of whom, Daniela Mercury, would not invite debate at being categorized as an *axé* performer.[10] Likewise, the other names mentioned in Elpidio's bio are lauded representatives of MPB and international musics including jazz and British reggae. Nowhere on the site is mention made of *axé* music, and the diverse roster of prominent leaders with whom he has worked strongly affirms his skill and versatility as a backing musician who is not limited to Bahian music or even his own "*boa música*." Thus, Elpidio is presented as a highly versatile musician capable of making valuable contributions to projects in a wide range of genres—that is, it is a message that he is capable of playing "everything."

In my everyday interactions with musicians in the Scenes, I noted similar tactics of discursive distancing and alignment. After his performance at an A Zorra *ensaio*, Edni introduced me to a percussionist from a storied *axé* ensemble, Banda Beijo. After Edni told me with whom his friend worked, we briefly chatted about what his group was up to. The percussionist told me that Beijo were working on a video, part of which involved filming performances at a soccer stadium. I acknowledged this as very exciting, but despite my enthusiasm for his band and their latest endeavor, he quickly changed the subject to his *projeto paralelo*—a *maracatu* fusion project.[11]

As might be expected, *pagode* was also a frequent target of tactical discursive distancing by musicians involved with it. On my second trip to Salvador, before I had even heard much about *pagode*, I spoke with young man who was standing outside the school at which I was studying Portuguese. He was waiting for a bus holding a *cavaquinho* case. Since I was interested in taking *cavaquinho* lessons and also hoping to make contacts for my then nascent research, I asked him about his music. He told me that he played with a *pagode* band. As he did so, he made a sour face and rubbed his thumb and forefinger together. He quickly followed up, adding that he was a music student at UFBA who specialized in *choro*.

A similar instance of distancing from *pagode* in favor of a more Euro-mimetically esteemed music occurred the first time I went with Farofa to the house of his older brother, Porco Olho.[12] When I arrived, the brothers introduced me to a family friend, André, who was also over for a visit. André and I struck up a conversation in the living room while our hosts adjourned to the kitchen to fetch beer and cobble together a quick meal. As we talked, I learned that he was a singer for a band called Raça Pura that played what he specifically called "samba." This piqued my interest. Aware of the difficulty of living from performing samba, as opposed to *pagode*, in Salvador, I asked André if Raça Pura played Rio-style samba—to which he replied, "a version of it." At that moment, Farofa shouted from the kitchen that I needed to interview his friend to get "the other side of the story," adding that he was, in fact, the vocalist for a *pagode* band.

Excited by this revelation, I continued my chat with André. With my prompting, he told me that Raça Pura had organizational backing from one of the more prominent *pagode* producers in Salvador at the time. He added that they had travelled nationally to perform but that their schedule had gotten slower in the last few years. That was it. Before I could ask more about Raça Pura and *pagode*, André changed the subject and told me that he had a *temporada* every Friday at a nearby neighborhood bar where he performed MPB on *voz* and *violão*. Although he worked with a notable *pagode* band, André was much more interested in discussing his much-lower-profile work in "quality" music, regardless of the interest I expressed in hearing about his primary job.

Despite the importance of performing musical work selves rooted in a very particular politics of musical quality and competence—and the traction of the understandings underpinning them—I also have little doubt that when the musicians I heard at work made music, they were striving to give the best performances they could. Akin to the studio musicians Faulkner (1971) interviewed who lamented "going commercial," most musicians I met who performed less esteemed music were at least craftsman-like in their enthusiasm for a job well done. Moreover, they (rightly) did not automatically see themselves as less skilled performers, a few I met challenged critiques of the kind of music they played, and most acknowledged that performing for enthusiastically participatory audiences was not only the purpose of the music, but also a source of pleasure and even positive feelings toward it. Yet I found a majority of them to be rather reluctant advocates, using language such as *"nada contra"* (nothing against it) or, in a manner akin to the men who told me *pagode* was alright for Carnaval, a party, drinking, and watching women dance, expressing any fondness for the music in a very relativistic, situation-specific way. This type of qualified praise was exemplified in my conversation with Vando when I asked him if he liked playing *pagode*:

To be sincere, I like to play *pagode*. But . . . I like *pagode* when I am onstage. But if I weren't playing, I wouldn't like it much. I don't like it, I don't enjoy it. I don't listen to it at home. I don't spend time in the street playing (it) because I don't like it. I only like it when I am there onstage and even rehearsing . . . (Salvador, March 2, 2005)

Moreover, regardless of the opinion they expressed to me about the music they performed and their musicianship, like Vando, many of the musicians I met who worked in Bahian music were acutely aware of the widespread sentiment against the music, often then inspiring various tactics of distancing.

JP: There are lots of people who say that *pagode* especially is bad music.
VANDO: Bad, yeah.
JP: What do you say to them?
VANDO: Man (laughs). Me too! *Pagode* doesn't have decent lyrics . . . the only
    pagode band that I consider, that people who like music consider, is Har-
    monia do Samba. They are a band with good lyrics . . . *Pagode* is only good
    for a big party, really. (Salvador, March 2, 2005)

As I have written elsewhere (Packman 2011), my own identity as a North American music scholar likely informed comments such as Vando's. Aware of this, I often pushed back against condemnations or mentioned that I liked Bahian music — something for which I was teased on occasion. In such instances, some concessions were offered, but usually couched in a distancing qualification — "it's okay for a party" or "it serves its purpose well at Carnaval," and often followed by something to the effect of, "music with too much information just would not work." Moreover, indictments and derision of *axé*, *arrocha*, and *pagode* were normal parts of backstage and on-the-street conversations between musicians in which I was nothing more than a bystander and whose careers I had no capacity to affect. It was also prevalent in printed media such as interviews with prominent musicians. For example, noted Bahian bandleader, composer, and music researcher Fred Dantas, who himself worked with several foundational *axé* stars in the past but who now focuses on instrumental music, told an interviewer in 2012 that:

The musical growth of *axé* . . . was diluted by producers. An idea began . . . but it didn't advance at all because the *povo* only likes simple things. This prevailed to the point that *axé* arrangements became imbecilic (quoted in Serravale 2012, my translation).

There is much to be gleaned from Dantas's statement, including his disdain for commercialism, perceptions of public taste, and nostalgia for *axé*'s past. But the thrust and basis of his critique and his discursive step away from (recent) Bahian music are clear. Moreover, as a musical authority, it is not hard to see how such discourse informs dominant musical sensibilities. Finally, and most importantly, whereas Dantas's career is well established—the article about him was a celebration of his accomplishments—his statement can still be seen as a presentation of a particular kind of musical self. Even if it was not an active job-seeking move, it helped him affirm his position as a good musician. Similar narrations that created distance from "bad," meaning Bahian, music were equally if not more common in moments when not only reputations but also future jobs were thought to be at stake.

On the other hand, and despite prevalent patterns in the ways musicians presented their musical work selves in terms of what they play, with whom, and how they feel about it, there was also evidence that they adapted what they expressed according to immediate circumstances. In contrast to Dantas, who risked very little with his very public critique, musicians working with *axé* or *pagode* bands understandably refrained from distancing discourse and generally assumed a more positive stance when in the company of their ensemble's leaders, management, or fans. Hardly disingenuous, however, most were able to find positive aspects of each job they did. They just gave voice to them when it served them. In contrast, when they were with musicians not affiliated with the group, close confidants in the ensemble, and with me, conversations about parallel projects in esteemed genres, distaste for less valorized music, and on a few occasions, assertions of lack of fluency in those styles were the norm. Thus, the power of dominant sensibilities rarely faded from view, and few musicians hesitated to claim affiliations with so-called quality music or, when it was safe (or potentially expedient), to distance themselves from its others.

Care in presenting musical selves and career pathways apropos of issues other than what musicians played or with whom they were working—for example, whether they were working at all—were also central to working to work. Drummer Ivan Torres told me that networking musicians seeking employment had to be careful about how open they were about needing work even as they were actively job hunting. He therefore made it a point not to let it be widely known if his performance schedule was slow for fear that he would be marked as inferior.[13] According to him, many in the Scenes assumed that a good musician should always be working—this, despite the fact that the difficulty of doing so and the challenges of living from music were both widely known and frequently commented on. To avoid being stigmatized as unskilled or otherwise undesirable as a collaborative performer, Ivan confided that he only spoke candidly about his employment status to his closest friends and colleagues. To other participants in the Scenes, he had to represent himself as available . . . but not *too* available.[14]

Son agreed with Ivan's assessment, but he utilized a slightly different tactic to the conundrum of not being able to ask for work when he most needed it: he made it a point to always be working on something. Whether or not what he worked on was profitable was, for him, secondary—at least in terms of self-presentation—to being able to say truthfully that he was actively making music in some type of project, again usually one involving an esteemed genre. Between his portfolio of nexuses, a teaching method that he was developing at the time and supporting with clinic appearances, and working in his home project studio, Son was, in fact, nearly always musically occupied. At the same time, he was also free to casually mention that he was not too busy to take on another job if he suspected an interesting opportunity emerging.

This was an important caveat in his positioning since seeming too busy or too successful could actually limit offers for jobs. Following a rehearsal, Farofa received a call from a bandleader who had called him several times over the previous year or so hoping to hire him. On each instance including this one Farofa had to decline because of prior commitments. Eventually, the bandleader quit calling, expressing his frustration that Farofa was never available. Farofa did wish to work with this leader—but he actually lost desirable work because he seemed too successful.

In Farofa's situation, his presumed over-successfulness was related to availability, but issues of payment and its representation were also of concern in terms of how musicians presented themselves and how they were perceived. Save for a few close collaborators, many interlocutors were reticent to talk about their income beyond telling me they took jobs in Bahian music "for the money"—perhaps another indication of the stakes for self-presentation. Common too were complaints about decreasing wages across the Scenes, which were at times chalked up to "amateurs" or other musicians who undercut wages. Several who spoke to this issue, including Jorge Elaíde Gois, suggested that, with awareness of the availability of cheaper labor, employers assumed they would not perform for the wage they offered and refrained from even making an offer. These conversations were with musicians who worked, and were known for working, extensively in the nonseasonal circuit. While no one mentioned it, I suspect that the challenges faced by veterans of upper-level Bahian music acts when trying to book local jobs could also be related to assumptions about their payment expectations—that is, unless they had paved the way to show their willingness to do such work.

Conversely, a reputation for working too cheaply could also undermine efforts toward a viable career. Among all of the musicians I spoke with, Farofa was the most forthcoming about this, especially when it became a pressing concern for him and a cultural capital-rich ensemble to which he regularly lent services. In 2005, the group leader, a highly regarded flamenco-fusion guitarist, accepted a *temporada* at a small venue with a reputation for booking *boa música*, MPB, but also bossa nova, samba, and various types of instrumental music. For each weekly show, the group was to be paid a portion of the cover charge. Despite the venue's status, its prime location along the Orla, and the notoriety of the group and especially its leader, the club crowd was disappointingly small on several occasions. On these instances, the three musicians earned between R$20–30 each for a full night's work—significantly less than Farofa earned at much less prestigious jobs, including shopping centers, let alone typical pay for seasonal circuit work performing Bahian music or Forró. Despite the fact that Farofa had cited working with this guitarist as a point of pride—and that such mentions enhanced his status—after one show, he candidly expressed to me his concern that if too many people were to find out that he was working for such a low wage, it could undermine his efforts to charge more for other jobs. By the same token, he felt strongly that the leader's choice to work under these conditions risked undermining his own status, despite his otherwise advantaged position as a virtuosic performer who was able to find work at a prestigious venue known for its discriminating booking policy.

Despite working musicians' various approaches to building and maintaining profiles as good, busy enough, and appropriately paid musicians, many aspects of their efforts and certainly the results still remain beyond their control. No performers are at their best all of the time, financial need or personal obligations lead plenty of musicians to accept jobs they might otherwise turn down, and numerous aspects of any performance are unpredictable. Likewise, musicians' actions, abilities, and selves are interpreted differently by different people in the Scenes. All of this raises the stakes for aspects of their practices over which they have some rein, such as their job selection and self-representation, but also other discursive practices that reflect indirectly on them as well.

For instance, another side of QI, the importance of being recommended for a job, is the impact *making* recommendations has on positions in the Scenes.[15] As an example, on the way to a Patua rehearsal, Farofa seemed especially troubled about events following his recommendation of the studio owner to substitute for him on an unrehearsed MPB gig. This musician, while an able percussionist, was young and had more experience performing *axé* and *pagode* than MPB. For whatever reason—perhaps because of the musical work self he had established at the time—his performance was not acceptable to the bandleader, who then complained to Farofa. This may have been no more than a way to advise him not to send the same musician on another date with his group. However, the larger implication was that Farofa was responsible for the unsatisfactory performance of a person he had endorsed. Frustrated by this reminder of his accountability for other people's performances, Farofa expressed his desire to quit recommending anyone for any jobs.

Although such a move might have seemed a reasonable solution, it is not especially practical. Perhaps it might be possible to avoid recommending musicians to colleagues in general, say for a new project. However, consistent with London's classical music scene detailed by Cottrell, the Hollywood studio scene in the 1970s discussed by Faulkner, and professional music making in eighteenth-century Britain as described by historian Cyril Ehrlich (1985), frequent schedule conflicts resulted from most Bahian working musicians' efforts to cobble together a living working in multiple settings. As a result, substitutes were frequently needed, and finding one's own was a common aspect of nexus affiliation. While principals typically have a stable of players able to fill the various roles in the group, lenders of services were often asked to do so. What might seem to be a burden and a potential source of tension, however, could actually provide lenders of services a degree of control over a potentially risky situation and a means to protect their relationship with their employer and their job.

The catch is that, as is the case with allowing *canjas*, choosing substitutes can be a difficult path to traverse. There is a risk that the principals will prefer the work of the fill-in musician over that of the first-call performer and will call him or her in the future (see Cottrell 2004, 63–64). Or, recommending a musician that does not meet with the approval of the bandleader can create tensions and threaten broad repercussions, including loss of credibility and damaged reputation—the likely gist of Farofa's concern above. On the other hand, tactical selection of substitutes can solidify a musicians' place in an ensemble and the Scenes by creating goodwill with the leader and other musicians.

In light of the potential risks involved in choosing a substitute, I saw several musicians opt to only call close friends to work in their place. This approach, however, is not always possible, nor is it necessarily the most useful approach to networking. Seeming too protective can also create liabilities. Critiques of mafias and untrustworthiness have enough power that, if a musician is widely perceived as being too "*mafioso*" (too devoted to their clique), or if s/he has a reputation for being devious or unreliable, they can go from being in demand to being on the margins of the workforce. Furthermore, as a mobilization of Granovetter's theory of weak ties, which asserts the importance of distant acquaintances for finding employment, recommendations beyond a musician's immediate circle can be an effective way of building alliances with a broader range of contacts who might provide bridges to other opportunities. While reciprocity is not a given in such situations, it is far from rare and did open doors for various collaborators on a number of occasions, very much in keeping with the "sense of honour-bound reciprocal obligation" Cottrell (2004, 73) notes in London's classical scene.

The ways working musicians represented seemingly objective facts such as what and with whom they play, and how much they earned while doing so, as well more subjective aspects of their musical selves such as what they like to play and who they approve of as colleagues, actively shaped these very aspects of their pathways and selves. Though not without long-term liabilities and short-term risks, carefully deployed tactics at least provided avenues of self-protection. At best, they helped networking professionals better their positions, as well as get and keep jobs. These performances of musician selves can also influence sonic outcomes once jobs have been booked.

PERFORMING "MUSICIAN" ON THE JOB

Performances and interpretations of musical work selves are not only important for securing jobs, but they also inform conditions on the job and the sounds produced once employment has been secured. I saw this play out in a number of different contexts and in a number of different ways. However, the underpinning sensibilities and uses of capital—what was embraced or disavowed and why—were rather consistent across work settings in studios, at performances, and even before and after them.

A multifaceted negotiation involving various claims of valued notions of music and musicianship took place during a recording session I attended with Farofa. The session was for a CD project by an MPB singer who was, based on the tracks that I heard that day, borrowing liberally from multiple musical genres ranging from Forró to Indian classical music. Farofa had been hired by her producer, Angelo, with whom he had worked as a musical advisor for a play at the Teatro Castro Alves, the major theatrical venue in town. Angelo was also well regarded as a choral conductor, and was, at the time, completing a doctoral degree in music at UFBA. This is all to say that his musical credentials, both professional and academic, were quite impressive. His self as a *bom músico* figured prominently in an event that transpired at the session, which was held at a small studio owned by the engineer, who also worked locally as a bassist.

By most measures, the job was like many others I had watched collaborators do. But the way that the engineer spoke about what and with whom he played is a clear example of the kinds of position-taking, narrative presentations of musical selves that I saw with some frequency. Also notable in this example is how the other participants at the session, both Farofa and Angelo, navigated an ongoing process of jockeying for position.

Prior to doing any recording or even talking about the work to be done, the studio owner/engineer began speaking at length about his parallel project, an instrumental fusion ensemble that he named after Schoenberg's *Pierrot Lunaire*. He also not so subtly clarified the reference. He went on to assert repeatedly how he and all musicians working with him in the project and who he hired for sessions were accomplished readers, a fairly scarce competence in Bahia, a clear marker of musical education, and owing to the costs of formal training, an oblique indication of class position. His rather extended narration struck me as a thinly veiled effort to impress his clients and perhaps to establish a degree of authority over the session he would be engineering, but not producing.

More negotiations of positions ensued once the session was underway. For the first tune, Farofa played *zabumba*—the genre-defining drum in Forró—to prerecorded scratch vocals, sparse, keyboard "harmonium" and *violão* pads, and a click track. The slow and unforgiving tempo set by the click, the loose time feel of the backing tracks, and the rhythm Angelo asked Farofa to play were all markedly different from the conditions of the more conventional Forró settings in which he would normally play this drum. As a result, a fair bit of experimentation and more time than originally planned were necessary to get a clean take.

Over the course of multiple run-throughs and punch-ins,[16] Angelo and Farofa became progressively more serious and focused; but neither let any frustration they might have felt show. When they had what everyone thought to be an error-free, good-feeling track, Farofa returned to the control room for a final listen. As he sat down next to me, he joked very quietly in my ear that we should "send up fireworks," both a nod to his belief that what they had accomplished would work and also a subtle hint of his relief that he had succeeded. He kept any acknowledgment of the difficulty he had very much between us, out of the engineer's and Angelo's hearing range.

On the ride to the studio, Farofa had mentioned to me that he hoped that this session would lead to more work with Angelo. It was not an especially well-paid or high-profile job, so the primary benefit was in the social capital it promised. Since he and Angelo already shared some history, I also suspect that the engineer's posturing prior to tracking also weighed on Farofa's mind during tracking—he is primarily self-taught and does not read music. While superficially simple sounding, the tune was challenging since he had to learn its form, a new groove (which meant re-coordinating his hands), and a number of breaks on the spot, orally, and with "tape" rolling.[17] Farofa's guarded behavior about his limitations and struggles both during the tracking and at the final listen thus spoke loudly.

In contrast, Angelo, who occupied a relatively more empowered position, took a more active approach in the negotiation with the engineer, especially after the keeper track was recorded. As we sat in the control room listening to the take, he was visibly pleased by the result despite the time and effort required. While he could have simply said "keep it" and "let's move on," he instead made it a point to state out loud while gesturing toward the engineer that Farofa's professionalism and grace under pressure enabled him to rise to the occasion. He affirmed that the need for multiple takes and punch-ins (which were actually quite common on most sessions I attended) was a matter of the difficulty of the music and the pressure of recording for his exacting ear, either of which, he said, would likely have gotten the better of a lesser musician.

Angelo's reframing of the situation as a testament to Farofa's abilities (and more subtly, his own) was strategic in many ways. He effectively defended Farofa's reputation as a *bom músico* and his own as a producer able to choose his session musicians wisely. With no way to control how the engineer might recount the events at the session to others in the Scenes, Angelo at least planted the seeds for a positive report. More immediately, his affirmation helped keep the session from going off the rails by restoring confidence and trust, especially Farofa's. He also maintained his situational authority, making it clear to the engineer in particular that he had everything well in hand. This paved the way for results that could reflect well on all involved.

Farofa was a more active participant in another exemplary instance of musicians and technical staff negotiating positions on the job; but this time their position taking was even more explicitly entangled with dominant sensibilities in the Scenes as related to genre politics. It took place at a multiday music festival in the popular neighborhood of Liberdade in the Lower City. Prior to the evening's performances. Farofa, several of the other musicians from a reggae ensemble to which he was lending services, and various members of the crew working the event hung out near the mixing table engaging in typical shop talk. In the midst of a flurry of fast-paced banter, the head engineer volunteered how glad he was to learn that this group was not a *pagode* band. He added that he had "suffered" through several sets of *pagode* the previous day and was reaching the limits of his tolerance. I was familiar with most of the other musicians in the band and knew that they worked frequently in the nonseasonal circuits performing a range of music from pop/rock to MPB and samba. Thus, I was not surprised to see the entire group join together in their disapproval of the programming. Within the chorus of grimaces, groans, rolling eyes, and shaking heads, Farofa offered his condolences in words—"*sinto muito*" (I'm so sorry)—as if he were speaking to someone who had suffered a tragedy. His response seemed to punctuate the general sentiment with an exclamation mark or perhaps a rim shot, since it was followed by a hearty laugh from the others.

Despite the apparent lightness of tone, the gestures, comments, and laughter did serious work. They visibly and audibly established the foundational musical sensibility to be shared among various parties who would soon be working together, some for the first time. Through this collective performance, all were able to position themselves as musically like-minded, or at least united in their aversion to *pagode*. Perhaps some in the group did not share the exact same views, but any dissenting voices were silenced. Regardless of whether the exchanges marked an expression of a unanimous and "genuine" sentiment or a coercive moment in which dissenters went along with the crowd, the outcome was a collaborative performance of musical work selves that set the stage for the on-stage work to follow. The comments, gestures, and laughs also framed the general parameters of musical quality and taste for the event through expressions of disavowal. The moment also served strategic ends for the engineer, who was able to enact a position of some authority based on those sensibilities, while also opening the door for Farofa's more tactical positioning that provided him both short-term and long-term benefits for his musical credibility.

In its emphasis on distancing and humor, this interaction stands apart from the negotiations in the studio, which were more serious and rooted exclusively in the claiming of cultural capital. But similar, albeit humorous claims followed. As I had seen him do on many occasions—though notably not at the recording session—Farofa also affirmatively positioned himself as the conversation continued by telling funny stories about working with noted performers of genres such as samba, bossa nova, and MPB. His comedic stance typically endeared him to his coworkers while the content of his narrations further affirmed his musical sensibilities and positioned him as capable of performing quality music with the approval of experts—a self-narrativizing that differed from that of the engineer in tone, subtlety, and ultimately, success. By invoking his social and cultural capital in this way, Farofa was able to claim a degree of authority and influence over several aspects of this and other performances, including stage configuration and set pacing, as well as the front of house and monitor mixes.[18]

Farofa's reticence at the recording session with Angelo, his outspokenness prior to the reggae performance, and the possible silencing of dissenting voices during that conversation illustrate how musicians actively deploy their capitals in situation-specific ways—they are tactically flexible. Another implication is that having cultural, social, and even economic capital is not enough. Rather, like the financial elite, capitalists par excellence so frequently lauded for their investment savvy, a nuanced understanding of how and when to use amassed capital, whatever "it" is in a given situation, is crucial in the everyday for musical laborers. That Farofa's performances have provided him with a degree of influence on various jobs he has done indicates that his references were generally intelligible to coworkers and that his humor did not alienate them. In contrast, I suspect that the recording engineer's claims at Angelo's session did not necessarily impress the producer (though they may have put pressure on Farofa), and that his manner of delivery was transparent enough to limit their efficacy.

The importance of measured deployments of social and cultural capital and the perils of poorly judged self-positioning were evident in a variety of other contexts. I never saw working musicians bite the hand that feeds by denigrating a musical project in front of nexus principals—though, depending on the situation, they did have the power to offer constructive critique. I also saw several musicians other than Farofa speak about high-level jobs in the context of a disarmingly funny story—Pastel, Son, and Laurinha all did this with some frequency. On the other hand, unfounded arrogance was a common point of criticism in backstage banter, and it was easily enough debunked owing to the entangled nature of the Scenes. On one occasion, the overstepping of a less established player became the basis of an ongoing joke. Several times I saw Pastel reenact a moment when this musician naively claimed his place among a group of much-higher-status performers when a visitor complemented the band with which he was rehearsing: "*So tem musico fera aqui . . . Eu . . .*" (There are only monsters, that is, excellent musicians here . . . Me! . . . (and . . .). The mocking quote nearly always elicited cackles from those who heard it, whether or not they knew the backstory. Pastel's schtick suggests that awareness of the consequences of making overblown or false claims adds an additional layer of surveillance that can discipline how, when, and to whom some musicians present their musician selves.

Professional musicians' success on the job and in the Scenes at large thus depends on making tactical choices, not only about what they represent about their pathways and musical work selves but how and when. Knowledge of "good music" and QI are powerful forms of capital, but they must be deployed with a critical awareness of self and audience in order to be most effective. Lack of reflexivity can not only squander opportunities but it can also damage reputations and hamper careers if news of missteps travels too far and fast in the Scenes via shop talk or gossip. Even with any shifts in musical sensibilities and general conditions of musical work, such tactical and occasionally strategic awareness remains foundational to living from music.

STASIS AND CHANGE IN MUSICAL DISCOURSE AND PERFORMANCES OF "MUSICIAN"

Although the importance of performing particular kinds of musical work selves and the terms by which good music and musicianship are defined have held fairly firm over the years, I have also noticed some shifts. For example, several years after I began going to Salvador, I noted the emergence of the assumption that the top acts of Bahian music hire the "best" musicians. However, remaining the same is that many of these "best" musicians earned their status by performing other more respected genres. Further, many if not most have continued to do so through sporadic nonseasonal circuit dates and parallel projects, as exemplified by Edni, Márcio Dhiniz, and Elpidio Bastos. Even Farofa eventually conceded that he had come to think of *axé* as "bad music that is well played." Despite this and the positive experiences he had with a few renderings of *pagode* tunes with the samba/dance band, it is unlikely that he will be accepting full-time work in Bahian music anytime soon, in part owing to his ongoing ability to support himself playing alternative musics, but especially because of his lingering musical sensibilities. On a broader scale, similarly, the predominance of Euro-mimetic musical sensibilities as they apply to genre associations remains, despite any shifts in the affiliation practices and discourse of a number of respected musicians and audience members who are now more likely to say "*nada contra*" about Bahian music before shifting the conversation to a more esteemed genre.

Within this broad context, Laurinha negotiated an interesting and informative repositioning starting in 2013. When combing the internet I noted, much to my surprise, that the singer had begun a project called MemoriAxé (Axé Memory). During MemoriAxé shows, she sang a full night of Bahian Carnaval hits from the 1980s and 1990s. Included were some of the very tunes she spent years avoiding and that, when all but mandated to perform them during Carnaval, I saw her cede to other vocalists on her *trio* in 2005.

Through repertoire, the title of the project, and frequent guest appearances by important names in the history of *axé* such as Marcia Freire, Gilmelandia, and Carla Visi, Laurinha performed a musical persona much closer to *axé* than she ever did after leaving Banda Pimenta de Cheiro. However, I noted that she did so from an aesthetic distance, underpinned by a rationale not that far removed from that which guided her approach to Pop Azeitado in 2005, or her ongoing self-positioning as a precursor to *axé*. She made this clear to me in 2014, when I asked about MemoriAxé and the change of heart it suggested. Laurinha answered me with a question: "Have you heard the new music they are playing? It's SO much worse!"

Despite the evident nostalgia and discursive distancing, as our conversation continued Laurinha also made it clear to me that there was more to the story and more at stake for MemoriAxé. For instance, she reiterated her belief that Carnaval was no longer for Bahians but instead, for "gringos." This critique was not necessarily new—several *baianos* have said similar things over the years. But it did seem to me that Carnaval 2014 included significantly more non-Bahian artists and more non-Bahian music than I had seen before. While this might suggest that the prayers of the many *baianos* who have condemned *axé* and *pagode* from the beginning had been answered, it also marks a loss of what has, for good and for bad, been mapped as a very Bahian space. Coupled with the much-talked-about presence of *arrocha* during the 2014 celebration, concerns over the future of what had been the definitive musics of Bahian Carnaval were more apparent, even among people who in that past would not have expressed support for *axé* or *pagode*.

MemoriAxé, then, offered Laurinha (and other participants in her shows) the possibility of countering these losses from the aesthetic distance of the past, which allowed for direct but safe association with music she had previously sought to avoid performing as much as possible. Her tactical reclaiming of "classic" *axé* also created greater distance from the musical trends of the day that she saw as even more objectionable.

Though I followed MemoriAxé primarily from afar, it appeared to have brought several benefits to Laurinha. She continued to work during Carnaval and maintain a performance agenda outside of the main event as well (nonseasonal circuit work would have been more difficult with a project geared toward current *axé*). Surfing the internet also showed Laurinha and several peers whose careers had declined following their moment in the Carnaval spotlight to be receiving increased recognition via various interviews and short articles. In June 2019 when I visited Salvador to work on a new project, Laurinha also told me she had recently embarked on an acting career. I cannot say with any certainty that MemoriAxé opened that door, though it is quite possible. I can say, however that on that same trip I saw her greeted as a celebrity and implored to perform at a public jam session that we attended with the intention of just hanging out — she told me beforehand that she did not want to sing.

LAST NOTES

Though a relative surprise, Laurinha's turn to acting was not out of the blue. As far back as 2014 she was talking about retiring — she was especially frustrated by the late-night, shared *trio* performance to which she was relegated and the last-minute notice she (once again) received about the performance. However, she subsequently continued MemoriAxé, morphing it into Club Axé and Axévivo Acustico (Axé Live Acoustic). And although she told me that she was enjoying acting more than singing, her rather extended *canja* at the jam session suggested that music was still fun for her. Equally notable was that the audience that greeted her performance so enthusiastically was comprised of middle-aged people from the middle classes who, exactly as I would have expected, had been enjoying performances of MPB, bossa nova, samba, and the occasional classic Forró tune before Laurinha took the microphone at their insistence. She did sing several

MPB songs too; but the crowd requested, and Laurinha performed, one of the classic Carnaval hits she had featured in MemoriAxé—the theme song of the *bloco* Cheiro de Amor.

Other shifts in attitudes toward Bahian music have been evident on other fronts as well. In 2016 there was a very visible push to reclaim Carnaval for the Bahian *povo*. Some elite *baianos* turned their backs to that message, which was given voice during a massive, cord-free *trio elétrico* performance by a particularly controversial *pagode* performer—for example, a middle-class Bahian woman living in Toronto commented that it was "all people from the ghetto." However, the debates the singer and the many people who paraded with him sparked further suggest that at least some were giving music they once dismissed another chance.

Despite some changes over the years, I nevertheless continue to see that among musicians and audiences, especially middle-class ones, musical validation generally remains strongly tied to practices that allow performers to demonstrate mastery of harmonic, formal, and textual complexity and refinement rather than their ability to get people, often thousands of them at once, singing and dancing—the central aesthetic of Bahian music. The hegemony of middle-class musical taste remains strong, and MPB has not been displaced as the epitome of "good music." Bahian music, *axé* and especially *pagode* and *arrocha*, continues to invoke the scorn and derision of many, including those who perform it, dance to it, or watch others dance to it, albeit often in sanctioned spaces. The sediments of these attitudes and related cultural politics continue to have important consequences for working musicians. Even as people such as Laurinha and Farofa might be thinking and acting differently about certain kinds of local music production, Euro-mimetic values never seem far behind, emerging through rationalizations and other subtle distancing tactics that frequently punctuate moments that otherwise suggest a shift.

Something that also continues for all of my collaborators is that, as professional performers managing musical careers in Salvador, they must continually adjust their tactics according to the conditions of possibility and constraint they encounter. Importantly, these conditions are different from person to person and (sub)scene to (sub)scene. Further, they are ever changing, often as a result of the ways that Scenes participants make do with the situations they face at any juncture. Mafias remain an ongoing concern too—especially for those unable to penetrate them—and even well-established musicians who have their own close network remain aware that they might fall victim to such exclusionary "simplexes" (see Peterson and White 1979). Thus, Farofa evinced a rather sanguine attitude when he told me that he knew his (lucrative) tenure with the samba/ dance band was likely finite. And it did come to an end shortly after that very conversation, which followed a clandestine rehearsal at which a new musician was being tried out to replace another lender of services to the group. Yet his calm in the face of precarity was tempered by the knowledge that he has established a well-regarded self as a musician, an extensive network of active and potential collaborators, and a large portfolio of ongoing work nexuses. Other musicians in Salvador are not so well positioned, lacking cultural, social, and/or economic capital to maintain their pathway in the face of a significant loss. Still, over the long term, nearly all the musicians I have followed have recalculated their career directions in some way. In many instances what made such changes possible were the relationships, reputations, and cultural and social capital they had established both as musicians and as members of their communities.

Thus, networking tactics and other processes of flexible work have long been and will likely remain necessary parts of economic survival, career building, and job longevity for people living from music in Salvador. As I have suggested, however, these same tactics can collaterally reify the very conditions that made them (seem) necessary or effective to begin with: low pay, job instability, Euromimetic cultural values, and the like.

One aspect of local working musicians' flexible musical work practices that is less susceptible to creating unintended consequences and shifts in Scenes sensibilities is performing musical sounds in ways that, in their context, are embraced as good by other musicians, audiences, and industry personnel. It is this all-important aspect of musical labor to which I turn in the chapters that follow.

FOUR

Performance Preparation and Behind-the-Scenes Performances

Young person with a violin, apparently lost in New York City:
"Excuse me, how do you get to Carnegie Hall?"
New Yorker: "Practice kid, practice."

Suingue, suingue pra você e pra mim
E sinta no corpo a razão de existir
Swing, swing for you and for me
And feel in your body the reason to [be]

"Liberar Geral," words and music by Reinaldo Silva Nascimento and Ed Binho,
recorded by Terra Samba

Several aspects of professional performers' practices are more obviously laborious and musical than the more socially oriented activities they undertake to create conditions of possibility to live from music. Even "playing" onstage belies the work involved. In contrast, it is hard to deny that learning songs and polishing shows takes effort, however pleasurable and musical. Abundant scholarly attention (e.g., Faulkner 1971, Meintjes 2004, Scales 2012, Hitchens 2014, Bates 2016) coupled with popular media also leave little doubt that recording sessions are meaning rich, often creative, and frequently well-paid moments of musical labor. Perhaps less widely known about, but no less worklike, musically oriented, and deserving of analysis are processes glossed as "sound check," during which musicians, often in collaboration with sound engineers, adjust their instruments and the sound of the ensemble prior to public presentation.

As plainly worklike and musical as these practices are, they are not necessarily income earning, and they are generally obscured from the views of everyone but the workers involved, a curtain this chapter aims to breach. Magazine articles, music documentaries, and perhaps early arrival to a venue can provide glimpses at such behind-the-scenes sonic work, but these instances of visibility are rare and usually brief compared to the vast amount of time professional musicians spend in individual and ensemble rehearsal, recording sessions, and sound checks that are by and large private affairs. The frequency of this work and its frequently restricted access, however, suggest its importance.

In this chapter I discuss the several aspects of the largely unseen musical work undertaken by professional musicians as they prepare their music and themselves for public airing, live and on recording. I first sketch several approaches to rehearsing as they relate to differently organized nexuses getting ready for various kinds of presentations. Though the literature on rehearsing is vast, much of it has a pedagogical bent. Among scholars who have written about musical labor, Bennett (1980) stands out for dedicating an entire chapter to rehearsal. Like the rock bands he discusses, a central concern among professional nexuses in Salvador was the relationship between rehearsal processes and quantity, available time, and desired outcomes. Whereas the rock musicians in Bennett's study devoted extensive practice to learning music from recordings in an exacting way, the expectations and economics of the New York club date scene detailed by MacLeod (1993) inform a conspicuous lack of ensemble rehearsal. In Salvador, I saw everything from frequent meticulous sessions to none at all. However, the primacy of economizing money and time coupled with minimal concern with fidelity to recordings meant that many if not most performances were readied with very few rehearsals, nearly always the minimum thought necessary to achieve the desired or required ends of the performance in terms of aesthetics and profit on investment.

Material conditions at the rehearsal site(s) also held important implications for the ensembles and the individual musicians comprising them. Of particular interest here are how musicians interact with the instruments they use and the spaces in which they do so in relation to how they come to know the music, each other, and themselves. This chapter situates such matters of musical-social knowledge in relation to the work of scholars (e.g., Bennett 2010) who are grappling with human and nonhuman interactions, entanglements that I suggest inform habitus and thus practice in the Scenes as a field.[1]

Other issues emerge in rehearsal as well, for instance the ontology of a popular music song in Bahia. As suggested above, rehearsing and preparing a piece of music for performance was rarely a matter of learning The Song as defined by a preexisting text, be it a recording or a notated score. Rather, the process involved various negotiations of memory, influence, and conditions of production by which a song, be it newly composed or more typically, a well-known piece of music, was for all intents and purposes (re)composed through collective acts of remembering and performance. As I discuss in the next chapter, the sonic results can fruitfully be interpreted through Henry Louis Gates's (1988) description of Signifyin(g) or creative variation in Afro-diasporic expressive practice in combination with different degrees of weight given to the authority of "originals." More at issue now, however, is gaining a sense of where and what the "music" "is" and the processes by which "it" is made audible and ready for audiences.

In comparison to their rehearsal room counterparts, musical work practices and sonic outcomes in recording studios are woven into an even more elaborate network of people, things, and especially electronic technology, as detailed by Meintjes (2003) and Bates (2016). While local professional musicians in Salvador need not be skilled operators of multitrack recording—though many are—they must have enough understanding of it to adjust their performances when using it. This kind of competence points to the importance of an electronically informed habitus, embodied and put into action through, to borrow from literary theorist Katherine Hayles (1994, 4), "the distributed cognition of the posthuman." Hayles's larger argument is that posthuman subjectivity "complicates agency," a politics evident in the ways that participants in recording sessions negotiate (or not) control over the processes and to a degree, the products of their labor. At stake are the eventual durable public representations of the project, which in some instances generate income through exchange, and more commonly, affect opportunities for earning through live performance.

Sound checks are the last step in preparation for the live presentations that are the bedrock of Salvador's music industries and musicians' earning power. Several aspects of the negotiations of power-knowledge and "posthuman" habitus that take place immediately prior to live events resonate with those typical of recording sessions. However, time is usually more compressed, and electronic as well as material conditions vary more widely. This makes achieving control over sonic representations all the more challenging, with many of the problems that result unfixable. Rather, they are destined to be audible in the moment of rendering with no chance for multitrack-enabled editing or overdubbing. Since live performances are so central to musical work in Salvador, the sound checks prior to them are where nearly all musical workers will participate most often in what I believe to be the highest-stakes negotiations of musical preferences, performance needs, and musical technological understanding. They are crucial opportunities for working musicians to establish the conditions for their most typical and arguably most audible presentations of their musical selves, with implications for the value of their labor and wider musical sensibilities. I also want to suggest that making visible the ways in which they do this also has the potential to push back against racialized assumptions about Bahian musicians' "natural, uncultivated musicality" and Bahia's "backwardness."

REHEARSALS

Rehearsal processes varied significantly depending on the type of nexus involved and the kind of performance being prepared. Unrehearsed "gigs" were very much the norm for *músicos da noite* and many recordings were done with little or no prior rehearsal as well.[2] So too were a surprising number of shows in high-visibility situations such as Carnaval parades and São João *forrós*—especially when a last-minute substitution precluded preshow preparation with the group. At the far other end of the spectrum, some ensembles, especially newly formed ones, rehearsed extensively before working in public. The majority operated somewhere between these extremes.

That so much music seems to be performed without a hitch in spite of minimal or no dedicated rehearsal belies the fact that such successes are only possible thanks to competences developed through extensive work beforehand. These include knowledge of genre conventions, the ability to sense the need for improvised adjustments in the heat of performance, and the technical facility to execute them. As guitarist Ximbinha told me, the busiest musicians in the Scenes were those who were the most "*actualizado*" (actualized) with relevant knowledge for a broad range of jobs, musical sensibilities that engendered appropriate choices for each context, and the ability to learn new material and adapt to immediate demands quickly when working with other musicians. Hence the importance of rehearsal.

Although they take place in what might seem to be relatively lower-pressure contexts, rehearsals also make demands similar to those encountered in public performances and in recording studios. There was a fairly relaxed atmosphere at the many rehearsals I attended, but this vibe disguised the fact that evaluations of musicianship and positions were still frequently negotiated among participants. Before, during, and after rehearsals I saw musicians engage in the kinds of performances of musical selves discussed in the previous chapter. For instance, during load in or out, encounters with incoming or outgoing peers allowed musicians to frame their association with whomever they were rehearsing: "I've worked with her for many years;" or if they were working with a less well-reputed performer: "he's an old friend," "I'm filling in for my colleague," "I'm getting paid a lot," or "tomorrow I am working with _____." Such qualifications provided all-important context and promised to mitigate negative associations that might have otherwise been assumed; or they could reinforce positive assumptions.

Even if overt jockeying for position did not take place, rehearsals were nearly always negotiations of money, time, and materiality. Limited time to prepare for performances as well as financial outlay for studio rental were the norm and common points of tension. Schedule coordination was also a frequent problem since committing to an unpaid rehearsal session posed the risk of conflicting with a paid performance. As such, preparatory work can reasonably be seen as a speculative investment of time, energy, and often money that ideally, but not always, leads to income, actualized ensembles and musicians, fortified social and cultural capital among participants, and hopefully, satisfying performances.

Nexuses and Rehearsals

Despite the fact that several *baianos* spoke enviously to me about their impressions of North American and European musicians' refined, no-nonsense rehearsal processes, nearly all of the sessions I attended were remarkably focused — more so than many in which I participated in the U.S. Though details varied in relation to the specifics of the nexus and the job at hand, time in rehearsal studios was, as might be expected, typically devoted to learning repertoire, polishing arrangements, and honing patterns of interaction. Notably, I never saw a complete show rehearsed. Rather, once the songs were learned well enough for the job, the sessions ceased. In most instances, economy-minded efficiency was a central concern, with work rationalized in relation to various conditions including the amount of time before the performance and the cost of rehearsing. Also crucial were the organization and circumstances of the nexus — was it an ongoing project? Did it have (paid) performances lined up or financial backing?

Was it an all-principal band or an ensemble populated primarily by lenders of services? How were the various participants positioned in the Scenes and in the nexus? Finally, the type of job was a primary consideration for determining how finely tuned the presentation needed to be, and thus the importance of multiple rehearsals. For instance, the music for many theater shows by ongoing projects was extensively rehearsed even if profit was not guaranteed—Márcia Castro told me that she usually aimed for ten rehearsals. In contrast, one-time-only performances in venues known for less than attentive audiences often left much more to chance even if they paid relatively well. Such variables and related tactics informed what transpired in the sessions as song arrangements were finalized, individual musicians fleshed out their parts and sized up their coworkers, and the group honed its collective feel for the music.

ORGANIZATION AND AUTHORITY With efficiency toward achieving a de-fined goal a priority, the chain of command at most rehearsals I attended was fairly well, albeit variably, defined and adhered to. Nexus type was a central informing factor, with short-term projects, solo acts, and ensembles in which a musician-principal had secured some form of backing typically having the most clarity about who was in charge. All-principal nexuses such as Funk 'n' Roll, conversely, typically aimed for a more democratic approach. Within the various organizational schemes, authority was nevertheless negotiated to varying degrees with implications for the sound of the resulting performance(s) and the efficiency with which a performance-ready presentation was achieved.

Although Funk 'n' Roll was formed with the intention of equity in invest-ment, return, and creative input, final decisions still had to be made, especially as performances approached. Between jobs, efficiency and fixity of presentation content were secondary to developing a group sound and the pleasure of playing together. Thus, there was plenty of time for experimentation and discussion of things such as repertoire, arrangement, and individual parts. However, those priorities shifted when a show date neared and repertoire needed to be firmed up. Over the course of several repetitions of this process, Junior, Thiago, and Eugênio emerged as the more authoritative voices, in part owing to their greater investment in business-related issues, but also because of Junior's position as an in-demand percussionist with several well-respected affiliations, Eugênio's musi-cal knowledge and related big-picture perspective on the ensemble, and Thiago's role as front person. Even as the chain of command emerged, however, I never saw contributions from the others quashed, though the bassist, keyboardist, and while he was with the group, the turntableist were noticeably less vocal.

In contrast to bands like Funk 'n' Roll, principal/lender-of-services nexuses such as A Zorra, Laurinha's Pop Azeitado, Márcia Castro's various pursuits, and numerous others were unambiguously led in all rehearsals by musician-principals and, usually, a named musical director. It was notable to me, further, that despite any potential for gendered assumptions of musical knowledge or patriarchal tendencies in Bahian society, I never saw the authority of female principals, or in Kadija's case, a female musical director, challenged by their lenders of services, who were nearly always men. This is not to say there were never disagreements, but during rehearsals I attended by ensembles led or co-led by five different women, their directives, whether mediated by a musical director or not, were followed without any pushback or posturing. Márcia and I discussed gender relations in the rehearsal room:

> JP: How is it for you as a woman working with all these men? Do they show you respect?
>
> MC: Yes, yes they do. It is cool. I am very playful. I don't demand this formality that exists in a lot of cases. There is a fear among a lot of musicians, especially of singers, stars who treat their musicians like inferiors. There is resistance, a lot of time for not knowing. Never (in my bands). The musicians are as important as I am. I am a musician. (Salvador, April 30, 2005)

It is certainly possible that, once again, my identity informed Márcia's response and Laurinha's similar one when we broached the same topic. Nevertheless, their comments were very much supported each time I watched them in the studio, backstage, and onstage. It is also notable that both of these women did, in fact, joke around, at times in rather ribald ways, with their band members. They generally acted as just another musician, as Márcia stated, and often as "one of the boys"—though Laurinha's musicians often referred to her as "*mamãe*" (mommy), suggesting another dynamic. Whether fraternal, maternal, or "all business," as was the case at rehearsals I attended led by other women, when they indicated that it was time for serious work, the "boys" fell in line.

Patua, on the other hand, was somewhat exceptional in their openness to discussion and debate in the rehearsal studio. Even so, Luciano was brought on as a designated musical director before the first full practice session was held. Thus, although input from all participants never ceased to be welcomed, there was rarely any doubt who had final say—though Luciano's decisions could be, and occasionally were, revisited later. Moreover, like Funk 'n' Roll, when Patua needed to be ready for a coming performance, little time was spent negotiating and, instead, Luciano made definitive choices that were normally adhered to closely. Likewise, in nearly all instances, musicians lending services adhered to the defined chain of command and were often quite deferential when leaders' reputations, and demonstrated ability on the job, left little doubt about their work selves as good musicians.

This very directed, streamlined rehearsal approach was by far the most common that I saw, likely because most ensembles involved a majority of lenders of services working for a small number of principals, because of the cost of the studio, and also because so many nexuses rehearsed only when there was a performance booked. Jamming "just for fun" in rehearsal settings was rare—*canjas* and organized jam sessions in public venues more typically satisfied that role for working pros—and most speculative projects that did not book work soon after gathering to rehearse disbanded. Regardless of their rehearsal rhythm—regular or primarily before jobs—most principal/lender-of-services nexuses left limited room for musicians other than the musical director and principal(s) to exert influence over matters beyond their individual parts. Furthermore, in several instances in such organizations and in Patua too, the parts side musicians played were strongly shaped by the defined leaders. I did notice that lenders of services with higher profiles in the Scenes were able to exert somewhat more independence of role and general influence than less established musicians—that is if they wished to. However, they, like most other side musicians I saw working, frequently followed the ensemble's musical power structure, if for no other reason than to streamline the preparation process.

The degree to which even well-established musicians who in theory might have been able to exert stronger influence actually tried to guide rehearsals also depended on their relative position and investment in each ensemble in which they were involved. For instance, in contrast to his leadership role in Funk 'n' Roll, Junior was much less vocal and more compliant with the musical director's instructions when he worked as a lender of services in Pop Azeitado and Salsalitro. Even Farofa, who could command a fair bit of authority on most jobs, occasionally assumed a very passive position. The recording session I discussed in the previous chapter was one such instance, but I also saw him quietly do his job at rehearsals with the samba/dance band and several other one-time bookings.

Though I attended numerous rehearsals with many different nexuses over the course of many years, I only saw a musical director's authority overtly challenged once. On that unique instance, a very established musician who was hired as a *violonista* (he also worked as a bassist and musical director himself) repeatedly questioned and visibly expressed his disapproval of numerous directives given by the musician hired to direct a large ensemble for a performance underwritten by the city government. While he did not lose the job as far as I know, his behavior was commented on negatively during the car ride home by several others involved in the rehearsal. In most instances, any resistance to musical direction was expressed through subtle changes to the parts that were dictated—so long as they were not noticed—and occasional complaining out of ear shot of the group's leadership.

Rehearsal Frequency, Timing, and Preparation

Another indication of the importance of efficiency in rehearsal can be found in the way that frequency correlated with nexus type and the status of their job roster at a given time. As I suggested above apropos of Funk 'n' Roll, ensembles comprised entirely of principals could be expected to rehearse most often, whether or not they had work on the books, owing to their stronger commitment among members and shared contribution to covering costs. Projects with financial backing, or a well-capitalized principal, could in theory rehearse more frequently as well, as was the case with Patua. However, even when groups could maintain regular schedules of paid performances with a stable membership and had the financial means, many, such as A Zorra, eschewed rehearsals unless a particularly important milestone lay ahead. With few exceptions, fluidly comprised nexuses gravitated toward one or a handful of rehearsals immediately prior to an engagement as a way to conserve the resources they had, both financial and human.

Laurinha, as an independent artist-principal with limited financial backing, exemplifies this efficiency-minded, individual-performance-targeted approach even as she aimed toward establishing Pop Azeitado as an ongoing project. The number of rehearsals she could call was informed in large measure by the fact that she alone had to pay for studio space. For Carnaval, that meant drawing on whatever funds she got from the Secretary of Agriculture and, once that pool was dried up, her own pocket. Since hers was an entrepreneurial venture, these expenses would ideally be reimbursed from show revenues (or bankrolled in advance against expected earnings) while also leaving enough to yield a net profit; but that was never guaranteed. Laurinha's rehearsal plans were also shaped by the knowledge that less committed lenders of services commonly ask for higher

per-performance fees or balk altogether at involvement with projects that involve extensive rehearsal that might cut into their ability to do paid work. Thus
Laurinha, like other similarly positioned principals, had to repeatedly analyze
and address several entangled implications of her approach to performance
preparation. In effect, the musicians were hired at an expense within the project's
budget and the projected returns in payment and exposure from each public
performance—and this is to say nothing about the impact on relationships within
the nexus or musical/professional satisfaction. The fact that Laurinha had paid
work, including Carnaval, incentivized income-seeking musicians to commit to
her rehearsals. Nevertheless, she still had to deal with last-minute absences and
a high rate of turnover over time as multitasking lenders of services inevitably
had schedule conflicts or chose to devote their energies to other projects. At
the same time, Laurinha has cultivated long-term working relationships with a
number of musicians.

The influence of economics and proximity of performance on rehearsal type
and frequency was further mitigated by the annual cycle of work and the specifics of the circuits. For example, during the several years that I followed them
closely, A Zorra did most of their rehearsing during the off-season despite various
resources such as capital backing that could have facilitated greater frequency.
However, their time, energy, and money were tactically invested in regular rehearsal when paid work was less plentiful. This rhythm helped keep the band
performance-ready and allowed them to compose new original material during
slow periods. Though this seems entirely logical since full performance schedules leave little time for other activities, the fact that audiences expect to hear
the emerging hits of the current season means that working ensembles must
find ways to learn them even as common-sense economics say they should be
performing and earning, not rehearsing and paying. The solution, according to
Edni, was to add new songs immediately before shows, for instance during sound
check, or during the performance itself in a manner akin to a gig by *músicos da
noite*. In such instances, A Zorra's on-the-fly arrangement was facilitated by their
shared musical knowledge, including some familiarity with the newly released
recording, and ability to give and follow cues—chemistry developed onstage to
be sure, but also through in-studio rehearsals.

When time permitted, A Zorra pursued rehearsals much like other ensembles, especially when developing authorial material. Their rational approach
to this work was evident when their performance schedule slowed during the
depth of the low season following the 2005 June *festas*. Rather than launch

into full-blown, studio-based practice sessions involving the entire group for the preproduction of their next CD, they maximized efficiency and minimized expense. They first gathered in smaller configurations referred to as harmony rehearsals led by the singer and the group's musical director/keyboardist. More often than not, the harmony rehearsals I attended for various projects were held in musicians' homes, and were, thus, essentially free. At these gatherings, songs were composed and arranged, with those present defining and working through everything from keys to song forms to individual parts. Though not the norm among the many nexuses I saw develop new material, A Zorra utilized sequenced recordings of the newly composed songs that could be used by the rest of the band to begin learning their parts on their own. Whether or not such recordings were used, ensembles typically gathered in full force at rehearsal studios only once a fair bit of material had been fleshed out.

Thus, although A Zorra was somewhat singular in their use of sequenced tracks and their comparative focus on their own material, many other nexuses did distribute recordings of material by other performers that they would reread. As useful as recordings were—most musicians I met had used them to learn new songs—the cues, reminders, and instructions rehearsal participants gave each other were even more important.[3] Indicative of the approach to inscribed compositions dominant in the Scenes, Farofa told me that while he did devote individual study to learning songs from the recordings, he and his peers rarely learned the music note for note before performing with the ensemble. He explained this saying it was common knowledge that many features would likely be changed as they worked through them in a process that can be aptly described as flexible, collective remembering (see below).

In slight contrast, Márcia Castro's sessions prior to each performance utilized recordings of *her* versions of the songs to be learned. Since hers was an ongoing and already established project, she expected her musicians to replicate her rereadings rather closely, especially in terms of form and arrangement-defining breaks, grooves, and riffs. More fidelity to a recording was also the norm in the seasonal circuits, especially when learning new releases for which there was only one recorded version in short order—A Zorra's example above is a case in point. In similar fashion, as new rereadings by most ensembles I saw rehearsing coalesced, their expectations for fidelity to a recording, be it a studio demo, a commercial CD, or a cassette made on a portable device also increased. Successful substitutes for such nexuses were those whose past experiences and prerehearsal rehearsals provided them with enough knowledge of the group's versions of the songs to replicate them quickly and the ability to listen for any modifications, follow cues, and adapt accordingly in the course of performance.

With or without their own recordings, the ability of most nexuses to get ready for a coming performance while minimizing investment of time and money was dependent on tactical preproduction and certain requisite competences among the musicians. This was the case for Laurinha and her lenders of services prior to the Carnaval debut of Pop Azeitado. Before entering a rehearsal facility with the ensemble she assembled only weeks before the event, the singer worked out the project's concept and the basic framework of the show with her musical director and another long-term collaborator during in-home harmony rehearsals. Their extended networks helped them bring together a core group of seasoned musicians, many of whom were acquainted with each other and all of whom were quite familiar with at least one version of most of the songs in the planned repertoire. Since the project was predicated on significant rereadings of every song, however, what the participants knew from past experience was necessarily flexed in rehearsal. Yet their familiarity with the music in a general sense and, to varying degrees, their knowledge of each other, enabled them to remember the music together and mount the show when they finally gathered as a whole for a few sessions just before Carnaval week.

Similar scenarios of relying on preproduction, shared general repertoire knowledge, and flexible collective remembering were common in all three circuits. Pastel's 2005 June season reunion with his previously on hiatus Forró nexus required past members to reacquaint themselves with each other, new members, and old material. No recording was ever mentioned or played at the rehearsals I attended. What I did see, however, was each member of the group remembering the songs as well as they could, reminding each other about various details, and collaboratively rearranging the music, including newly released Forró hits, under the guidance of their musical director. In the nonseasonal circuit, Funk 'n' Roll's more regular rehearsals relied more heavily on circulated recordings, but a comparable collaborative recall process was still central to every rehearsal of theirs that I attended. Indeed, they rarely referred to the recordings except in rare moments of great uncertainty or unresolvable disagreement. This was the case at the majority of rehearsals I saw, regardless of the ensemble and despite the presence of the necessary equipment to do so at most rehearsal sites.

Rehearsal Sites

The prevalence of in-home harmony sessions as stepping stones toward full group rehearsals in commercial studios suggests that location might be an important consideration for readying public performances. Economics are certainly central in choosing to begin at home versus in a rented space; efficiency of process is a clear benefit as well, even as the process places certain demands for specific competences on the musicians. Such issues are, further, variously entangled with the materialities of popular music practice in Bahia and the rehearsal facilities themselves.

It likely goes without saying that the norms of practice for many types of popular music mean that not just any room will serve for hosting full-scale rehearsals. In Bahia, genre-defining percussion instruments are loud by nature, necessitating powerful amplifiers for guitars, bases, keyboards, and voices lest they be entirely drowned out. I frequently heard large-venue sound systems pushed past the point of distortion and, at times, beyond the threshold of pain. Indeed, loudness was often an expected part of live popular music participation, making rehearsals that aimed to approach performance conditions equipment-heavy affairs that required significant space and a fair bit of isolation, if not insulation. Since most professional musicians I met preferred rehearsing during the day so that their nights were free for paid work, their practice sessions were unwelcome in many parts of the city where more conventional labor was done. Day or night, full ensemble rehearsals were largely incompatible with densely populated and, especially, more affluent residential areas as well.

As a result, the vast majority of full ensemble rehearsals I attended were held in specialized studios that were configured to limit sound leakage (but were hardly soundproof) and located in moderately traveled commercial zones and especially semi-industrial areas. This was in part because the requisite space in ritzier parts of town was cost prohibitive. But their typical localization also helped operators avoid drawing the ire of neighbors or attention from police, who over the years have become more attentive to "noise" violations.

In addition to providing some sound buffering from the outside world, Salvador's commercial rehearsal spaces typically came equipped with a full drum set, a basic Bahian music percussion outfit (two to three *surdos*, *repique*, *timbal*, and congas), as well as guitar and bass amplifiers and, most crucially, a PA system for vocals, keyboards, and acoustic guitars. Most had some kind of accommodation for musicians and guests to hang out before and after practice sessions, thus facilitating networking and word-of-mouth promotion. Several studios were owned or staffed by working musicians, including Edni, providing extra income, additional networking opportunities, and an accessible location for them and their projects to rehearse. Without a discount-enabling connection to the owners, principal(s) typically rented rehearsal studios in three-hour blocks costing anywhere from R$35–50.

Beyond simply housing practice sessions and providing opportunities for networking, the materialities of rehearsal studios can also have important implications that provide further justification of costs. Fully equipped studios reduced setup time, enabling musicians to maximize the practice they got for their rental payment. They also minimized the need to carry around heavy equipment, reducing wear and tear on musicians' bodies and the personal gear they owned. Surprisingly, a large number of very busy guitarists, bassists, and keyboardists did not have their own amps; and though drummers and percussionists were more likely to purchase equipment, most welcomed the chance to use whatever was already at the studios.

The trade-off for these conveniences is that they constantly had to adjust to unfamiliar gear. Drummers and percussionists often prepared for performances on configurations far different from what they were accustomed to and dissimilar to ones that would be used on the actual job. Some differences were minimal, for example, slightly different-sized drums that required small adjustments in body position when played. Others were more drastic; sometimes certain instruments were entirely absent, forcing the performers to completely change how they performed the music. Guitarists, bassists, keyboardists, and vocalists faced similar challenges when trying to tailor the sound of multiple, communally used amplification systems that were often in less-than-ideal shape. Despite similarities of instrument types and translatability of most playing skills, most musicians I have spoken with acknowledge that a comfortable, good-sounding one makes performing more pleasurable and easier—comments supported by the care that many take when choosing and setting up their equipment and grousing (or worse) when gear does not feel right or behave as expected.

In the context of rehearsals, then, unfamiliar or problematic equipment substituted one source of possible stress for another. Time saved by not having to load and assemble personal equipment was lost if musicians struggled to dial in acceptable sounds. While a relatively minor issue for established ensembles and among musicians familiar with each other, the stakes were higher for musicians working in new contexts where equipment-related failures to sound good could contribute to less-than-favorable impressions and diminishing authority and cultural capital. With seasoned ensembles, struggles to achieve the desired sounds could inhibit the preparation process if musicians found themselves unable perform as they envisioned, or if musical details could not be heard well enough to be addressed.

Perhaps ironically, equipment-related challenges in rehearsal studios can also provide certain benefits as working musicians ready themselves for public performances. Many venues I attended, from clubs to *trios elétricos* to festival stages, provided backline gear such as amplifiers, drums, and PA systems, much like rehearsal studios. The quality and condition of the equipment varied greatly and often left a great deal to be desired. But by constantly using variable-quality and unfamiliar rehearsal studio gear, musicians in effect practiced adaptability and honed their ability to get the most out of whatever instruments were available. This translated directly to their public labors with similar gear conditions and higher stakes for making do as well as increased pressure to make adjustments quickly. Moreover, by learning what was essential for delivering an acceptable performance, working musicians could invest in their own equipment tactically. Thus, most focused on instruments that would come into tactile contact with their bodies—guitars, basses, keyboards, and bass drum pedals, for example, and gear that would help them get their sound regardless of what the venue provided. This included digital effects that facilitate getting specific sounds with nearly any amplifier, as well as snare drums for drummers.

Numerous aspects of the ways different nexuses approached rehearsals, including their organization of authority as well as their tactical use of resources such as money, time, and materials, point to an overarching ethos of rehearsal in the Scenes: sufficient and efficient preparation. Perhaps most central was that rehearsal sessions were concentrated on honing skills and processes necessary for performing—knowledge and comfort with the music, musicians, and use of equipment—rather than the performance itself. This focus was especially evident once the doors to the practice room were shut, sounds were dialed in, and members of the ensemble began to perform the music.

Nexuses Rehearsing

Apparent at most rehearsals I attended was an emphasis on using resources efficiently to create competences and conditions of possibility for successful performances. Across an array of different types of ensembles preparing different kinds of presentations under varied circumstances, I noted several shared tactics for making do with commonly held concerns such as available rehearsal time, variations in musicians' level of actualization, and local ontologies of songs. Chief among them was placing an emphasis on learning how to collectively perform the music rather than perfecting The Show or replicating The Song.

Perhaps most notable is that, regardless of nexus type or the type of job being prepared for, I never saw what I would call a "dress rehearsal" of a performance under simulated stage conditions. Rather, the rehearsals I attended were conducted in ways that took the ensemble to the point of being ready for such a presentation; but once all of the music was arranged and learned to everyone's (or the musical director and principals') satisfaction, the next step was generally the stage. Perhaps an ensemble might go as far as running down the complete set in order, if possible without stopping. But one notable difference from the presentation to follow was that at every rehearsal I attended, the musicians nearly always stood, or more commonly sat, in an inward facing "circle" along the studio walls rather than face forward, usually standing up, as they would onstage.[4] Part of this was likely habit and a matter of space constraint. Large rooms were expensive, and most ensembles chose facilities just large enough to accommodate them as a way to economize rehearsal expenditures. But by positioning themselves facing each other, participants facilitated interaction as they worked through the material (and sitting conserved their energy too). This all suggests that the emphasis in rehearsal was on learning the process of playing songs together rather than perfecting a finished product.

Entangled with this approach is the fact that many successful popular music performers in Salvador are self-taught and had (and have) minimal or no ability to read Western notation (*partitura*). This, combined with minimal demands for fidelity to the recording (and varied degrees of familiarity with any one version of a song), informed the attitudes and practices of musical directors.[5] For instance, Luciano told me that his work as musical director for Banda Patua required him to be very flexible and patient about how he worked with band members and guided them toward the results he sought. These traits were evident when I watched him and several other MDs do their jobs leading rehearsals.

Such patience was especially important at Salsalitro rehearsals, which compared to most other ensembles I saw rehearse, required a considerable amount of very active teaching. This was because the group performed intricate arrangements that were precisely executed (even as they maintained an infectious groove that kept their crowds dancing). This helped Salsalitro work frequently, but their genre orientation meant that they usually earned less money than similarly prominent Bahian music or even Forró acts. Although the group was viewed by many local musicians as a kind of proving ground for "good" musicians, frequent but low-paid work meant that membership was fairly fluid. Salsalitro's musicians generally needed and were able to find other work to fill out their incomes; and many moved on to better-paying jobs, often in Bahian music, arguably empowered by their association with the salsa outfit.

Membership fluidity, complex arrangements, and plenty of work necessitated frequent rehearsals. Singer-principal Jorge Zarath (who was also the composer of several *axé* hits) told me it was simply not possible for a new participant in the group, be it a new lender of services or a substitute, to learn the material for a show in one or two practice sessions let alone during a performance. And while several of the musicians in the band I saw rehearsing could read *partitura*, and despite the fact that Salsalitro's musical director, Nogueira, wrote out detailed charts and provided recordings of all new music, much of the group's time in the studio was dedicated to the patient teaching of parts.

In a manner akin to most other show-oriented, principal/lender-of-services nexuses that I saw rehearse, the side musicians offered occasional input, often based in any presession preparation they had done. But in contrast, it was also apparent that most of the preplanned details were unlikely to change: like Márcia Castro, Salsalitro's circulated material was the band's arrangement, not a preexisting text by another artist. Yet even with all of this advance material and, I assume, an understanding that much of what was on the circulated texts was to be adhered to, Nogueira still sang or played the lines he wanted. And he did so for the readers (primarily the horn players) just as he did for all of the other, nonreading ensemble members. The recordings and charts mainly supported what was by and large an (inter)active, oral process of rehearsing the music, itself comprised of varying modes of composition, arranging, remembering, memorizing, and to varying degrees, teaching, that was foundational to the rehearsals of all ensembles I saw working.[6]

Furthermore, repeated listening to recordings—be they of the band's original arrangement or of a well-known version of a song—were not the norm once ensembles, including Salsalitro, reached the studio. Rather, if recordings were played at all, they were given one or two cursory listens and then put away, usually permanently. Thus, an essential skill for an actualized player was the ability to hear and learn songs quickly and in the presence of other musicians doing the same thing, especially if they had not done so prior to coming to the session. If a recording was used, musicians typically had little opportunity to repeat sections, experiment, or even hear themselves as everyone scrambled to lift their parts at the same time as others in the room. Individualized teaching and working out parts were no less challenging, since they were spotlighted interactions between side player and musical director, which only added to the pressure to learn quickly and, thus, demonstrate competence for the colleagues and employers looking on.

Since this public learning was so common, most musicians had developed a technique for doing it effectively. Some used Western notation or a type of shorthand that they understood and that allowed them to reproduce the salient characteristics of the music using what they called a "*pesca*," slang for a cheat sheet. Others rarely used any form of written information and instead relied on their ears, memory, and ability to adapt on the fly. And between the extremes was a seemingly infinite variety of ways to keep track of the music. Son and Ivan laughingly told me of a drummer they knew (whom they both described as amazing) who had developed an onomatopoetic system for notating his parts—it was indecipherable for anyone else, but remarkably effective for him. Son carried Western notation, sketches of song forms, and/or textual reminders. In contrast, bassist Israel was notable for not writing anything. To compensate for his self-described weakness as a reader, he told me, he watched the fretting hand of the guitarist and drew on his own knowledge of the guitar's fret board, his ears, and his experience to guide him through songs. Jorge Elaíde Gois wrote out lyrics, but no harmony or melody information; Laurinha had lyric *pescas* for Carnaval, when her repertoire increased, but relied primarily on her memory for shows; and Farofa jotted textual descriptions of grooves and the main instrument(s) to be used on his set lists, that is, if he wrote out anything at all.

Whether or not a musician used some form of written reminder or not, those who seemed unable to learn and reproduce songs quickly and accurately enough were not viewed well. I saw Farofa, who normally has a great deal of patience, became visibly frustrated with a drummer who struggled to remember the intricacies of a band's repertoire during a rehearsal. Likewise, following a session with Patua, he expressed his disappointment with a keyboard player who had been unable to read chord charts. His contention was that each musician should develop the necessary skills to do his/her job quickly and efficiently, be it through memory or notation. He and several others also stipulated that reading was not always the ideal solution. While musical literacy was often viewed favorably, in part because of the level of education it suggests, several musicians asserted that readers often played with a rigid time feel, lacking in what they called *suingue* (see below). Finally, Luciano suggested that overreliance on the written page all too often came at the expense of internalizing the music.

Complicating the efforts of many professional musicians to learn repertoire was the fact that most must do so for several nexuses at once. Not only did that mean that they were responsible for a large number of songs, but also several different versions of the "same" ones (see next chapter). Potentially muddying things further was that many of these same songs, especially from the MBP and samba repertories, had been recorded multiple times. All of this meant that musicians frequently worked from several referents, recorded, experience based, and, occasionally, notated.

Epitomizing efficiency and economization, albeit with trade-offs including increased moments of stress, sloppiness, or on occasion, an "*arguidá*" (slang for a major musical mishap), so-called gigs called the openness and multiplicity of repertoire into question in rather extreme ways by requiring everyone to "just play" based on prior knowledge of the material, in-the-moment interaction and improvisation, and whatever mnemonic devices they had handy. But with efficiency also at a premium in rehearsals, the teaching and learning that took place in private usually unfolded in a manner not terribly distant. Underpinning performances in both contexts was a process akin to a kind of collective remembering and often, recomposition, rooted in musical familiarity and realized through acts and discussions of making musical sounds.

FAMILIARITY, COLLECTIVE REMEMBERING, AND PROCESSUAL (RE) COMPOSITION Viewed cynically, the prevalence of beloved music at highly commercialized events such as Carnaval and São João *forrós* and in lower-key, but no less economically driven contexts such as clubs, might invite a Marxian "Culture Industry critique" (e.g., Horkheimer and Adorno [1944] 1999) in which familiarity from incessant repetition breeds uncritical consumption and profitable commodification at the expense of artist creativity and audience agency. On a few instances musicians expressed their frustration with being expected to play songs that they did not like because they knew the audience expected to hear them. Yet a passive-audience argument falls short in the Scenes since these same musicians recognized that they would be evaluated for their ability to rework material in ways that enhanced or at least did not impoverish it within a given context. Even the precise choice of material bore scrutiny, as suggested by Laurinha and Patua's careful attention to repertoire. The importance of song selection was also evident in comments made by Pablo, a vocalist/*violonista*/ composer who criticized the performance of another, better-known composer for his overly generic repertoire while he was working in a small club as a *músico da noite*. Emerging as an ideal was emphasizing familiarity but not falling back into the cliché, a balance that suggests a creative tension between Signifyin(g) as theorized by Gates and reverence for canonic composers and their creations more akin to Western notions of authority/authorship. This hybrid sensibility of interpretation is an important factor informing the musical work processes I saw unfold in Bahia.

Perhaps most significant from the perspective of musical labor is that the primacy of familiar music in most performances reduces the need for many nexuses to engage in extensive rehearsals before they are ready to perform. Though some musicians I spoke with saw this as a limitation on the quality and interest of some performances, they also recognized that familiarity made multiplicity of nexuses possible, thereby facilitating achievement of, at least, their economic goals. A genuine affinity for at least some of the music they performed, coupled with musical sensibilities that recognize creativity in repetition with a difference, that is, Signifyin(g), often made working within the parameters of the aesthetic of participation pleasurable. Finally, since multiple recordings of most canonic songs exist and listeners including musicians encounter countless interpretations of them in live performance, signally different versions of The Song do not lose identification with "it."

This marks a step away from an understanding of the musical Work that gives primacy to the composer's original intent, *Werktreue* (cf. Goehr 1992). Instead, predominant in the Scenes is a tendency toward "an unlimited number of ontologically equivalent instantiations [of a song], all existing on the same 'horizontal' plane," to borrow from musicologist Nicholas Cook (2001, 17). Cook notes that certain instantiations accrue more authority and influence, and this is certainly the case in Salvador, where, for instance, parade performances of Carnaval hits tend to hew closely to the initial recording, especially in the debut year. This is in part a matter of practicality—they must be learned fast. But speed of learning that effaces certain inscribed details, differences in instrumentation and voices, and as Edni mentioned, varying degrees of efforts to express a *cara*, yield performances that can deviate somewhat from the "original" without inviting critique for infidelity. Further along the spectrum of acceptable variation is MPB, which, as Luciano Salvador Bahia asserted, gets part of its "charm" specifically from multiplicity in interpretation (the "quality arrangements" for which Bahian music is attacked for lacking). Regardless of genre, at least some liberty to shape of the sound of any performance of any song underpins negotiations of how songs are and should be performed. These negotiations often begin in the rehearsal studio.

As "collective remembering" implies, during the rehearsals I attended, participants' varying knowledge of "the same" music was brought together and negotiated to create the versions of the songs they would perform together. Whether or not they listened to a recording first, the typical way to begin preparing a song was to have a short discussion about groove, tempo, key, etc., and then to just begin playing together. Most often, they played until a significant enough problem arose to make them stop to make a correction. Minor problems were frequently ignored until after the song was completed, mimicking the process of adding a new song in performance, doing an unrehearsed gig, or dealing with errors onstage regardless of prior rehearsal. A run-through was typically followed with a postmortem to address any issues musicians noted and start finalizing the arrangement. Decisions about starting and stopping the run throughs were typically made by the musical director or principal; but other musicians waved off the band if they felt things got too far off track.

At these stopping points, the organization of the nexus informed how the problem would be addressed — a group decision, a recommendation from one of the members, or most often, according to the musical director or principal's instructions. I also saw several occasions in which either a musician struggling with a part or the MD working with such a player asked to move on to the next song, leaving the problem section to be learned at home. In a few instances, including Patua rehearsals, after an arrangement was fleshed out, the musical director recorded it for future reference.

As I saw on repeated occasions, the techniques utilized in rehearsals provided an efficient means for musicians working with an ensemble to establish a basis for their coming performances. Thus, the competences developed by rehearsal participants with one nexus were also generally transferrable to others. Transferrable too was their knowledge of commonly performed songs, although adaptations of key, form, rhythmic breaks, and even genre were the norm. Less specifically addressed than these textualizable elements of a song, but arguably equally crucial to its performance, were issues of its time feel, which was, nevertheless, honed collectively in rehearsal studios as the musicians learned to play the music together. Along with song details they learned, memorized, and at times notated, feel was also a focus of several collaborators' individual preparation, and an embodied marker of musical competence.

Practicing Feel/Embodying Cultural Capital

Most of the time and energy during the rehearsals I attended was devoted to learning chords, melodies, rhythms, words, and song forms. Demonstrated mastery of them was also the most common basis of claiming authority both within a given nexus and across the Scenes. However, a less tangible but frequently discussed aspect of performances and performers' competence was "feel," or in local terminology, "*suingue*" (swing).[7] Terms such as "*duro*" (hard) and "*enquadrado*" (square) were common criticisms of individual musicians, ensembles, renderings of a single song, and entire performances. On the other hand, in most contexts it was high praise for a musician or a performance to be called "*suingado*" or "*balancado*" (swinging).

Recognizing the importance and particularity of rhythmic feel in Bahia, ethnomusicologist Christianne Gerischer (2006) conducted a measurement study of percussion grooves in *samba de roda*, samba-reggae, and *samba de caboclo* (a Candomblé rhythm). She found similar patterns of microrhythmic variation across the genres, suggesting a kind of Bahian "accent" (locally, *sotaque*). While her argument is convincing, listening to working musicians talking about their peers' performances also suggested that they were also attentive to specific *differences* in the rhythmic feels of genres, including local ones. Their discussions also left me with little doubt that many of them felt not all musicians played all *sotaques* with equal fluency. The underlying implication is that the ability to play "everything" depended on having enough flexibility to capture the proper *suingue* of the specific music being played in a given moment, with the ensemble at hand, and for the specific audience (including coperformers). Crucially, even as "good music" and "good musicians" were defined by contemplative (and notatable) features—harmony, arrangement, poetry—a stiff performance of any music could undermine claims and ascriptions of musical skill, even if the player rendered chords, lyrics, and formal features in a manner that was correct on paper. As in language, while a speaker might have a good technical understanding of vocabulary and grammar, an improper accent betrays a lack of mastery that is easily detected by the more enculturated. One could argue further that the stakes for *sotaque* are even higher in music not valorized for its ability to move the mind, since its assumed simplicity belies the challenges of striking a groove that will be effective for making audiences dance.

In this way, rhythmic feel, like a spoken accent or effortless mastery of social etiquette, serves as a marker of habitus, which Bourdieu has famously glossed as a "*feel* for the game." Performing harmonically, lyrically, and formally complex music with the right *suingue* served as an especially powerful confirmation of embodied cultural capital, which, owing to the existing hierarchy of musical sensibilities, was effective across the Scenes. On the other hand, playing less valued genres such as *axé* and *pagode* with proper *sotaques* also provided cultural capital. However, its efficacy for asserting positions was more limited to their particular subfields.

Although issues of *suingue* and *sotaque* are paramount for drummers and percussionists—they do not work with harmony or melody and poor ensemble *suingue* was frequently blamed on them—most scholars and, I believe, musicians, recognize that the time feel of an ensemble ultimately boils down to interaction between all of the members, rather than being the domain of just the so-called timekeepers. Moreover, when any instrument is played in a solo context, the performer's *sotaque* is fully exposed. Thus, Roberval Santos placed tremendous importance on his *suingue* as a key component of his *violão* playing. He told me that he spent a fair bit of his individual rehearsal time refining his right-hand (finger-picking) technique and developing numerous subtle variations, sensitivity to feel, and control over his execution. He contrasted his focus on this aspect of the music with the many "gringos" he teaches to play samba, bossa nova, and MPB who can usually master the chords and right-hand *patterns* he teaches them—and which they come to him seeking to learn—but who regularly struggle with the subtleties of *suingue* that are crucial for a convincing performance. My own *violão* teacher, Henrique, responded to my rendering of an MPB standard with a sour face and an emphatic (but kind) "*isso foi muito ruim*, Jeff" (that was very bad, Jeff). I had gotten the chords right and executed the basic right-hand patterns correctly. My *sotaque*, however, was all wrong, although I could not tell. As an enculturated listener, however, Henrique was immediately uncomfortable with my stilted, gringo groove.

Again, a linguistic analogy is somewhat appropriate. Honing a musical *sotaque* can be productively likened to learning a new language, at least how I have experienced it. Much as I generally knew when I played a chord wrong, I am painfully aware when I stumble for vocabulary when speaking Portuguese. In those instances when the words seem to flow, I can imagine myself sounding passably Bahian. Yet puzzled looks from native speakers suggest otherwise (listening to myself on a recording quickly undoes any delusion of native fluency). In a similar way, actualized coperformers and enculturated audiences could detect problems in feel that were unbeknownst to the performers. This was evident in Henrique's critique of my playing, the many discussions of hard or square time feels in shop talk among musicians, job failures such as that of Farofa's substitute, and the occasional performance I saw when, for no reason I could detect, audiences did not dance (or sing) to songs that had been crowd-pleasers in other instances. Yet, in music anyway, this analogy only goes so far, and its shortcomings are important for how working musicians approached their preparation.

For lenders of services whose careers depend on moving seamlessly between different ensembles in different circuits in order to support themselves—in other words, a majority of them—sensitivity to the subtleties and specificities of feel was a crucial skill. I noted that on several occasions musicians, usually those who were both quite busy and widely recognized as good players, did have a fairly strong sense of whether or not what they were playing did, in fact, feel right. For instance, several times during his *zabumba* session discussed in the previous chapter, Farofa asked to redo sections that had, to my ears, seemed to be error free in order to capture a better time feel. Moreover, it was also evident that actualized musicians (Farofa and Roberval among them) took seriously the idea that to be able to work frequently, they needed to do more than just deliver correct harmonies, forms, and breaks regardless of how simple the music seemed or was reputed to be. Indeed, Son pointed out that when he worked with one *pagode* ensemble, the other musicians were quick to correct his feel.

The importance of proper *suingue* for specific genres thus impacted Farofa's individual practice when Patua, then Pop Azeitado, and finally the samba/dance band demanded he perform significantly more Bahian music than he had in the past. Prior to Patua, he had played *axé* plenty of times during Carnaval; but he typically shared duties with several other percussionists who were more comfortable with the groove patterns, and especially their feel, than he. In Patua, however, he was both the primary percussionist and, on most jobs, one of only two. This meant that he could no longer lean on the other members of the percussion section by playing a less prominent instrument such as a secondary *repique* or *timbal*. Rather, he was responsible for the genre-defining composite *surdo* and *repique* part.

Thanks to past experiences and voracious listening, Farofa knew that a serviceable *axé* groove was within reach provided he did the necessary work—a clear challenge to assumptions of Bahian music's purported lack of cultivation. To ready himself for the demands of the emerging project, he set about rehearsing basic patterns and fills on his own. His initial barometer for success was how comfortable, automatic, and unshakable a groove he could strike. Yet he was very aware that convincing performances required more than "just" a technically correct rendering of the rhythms. So, when possible, he played along with *axé* recordings to associate his body's movements with the sounds and feels captured by prominent performers of the music. And such work continued at group rehearsals where his more *axé*-fluent bandmates such as Ximbinha and Pastel provided feedback and in-performance guidance that helped Farofa embody a participation-engendering, properly *suingado axé sotaque*.

As these examples suggest, working musicians' competences, often as rearticulated through *suingue*, were spotlighted as they moved between nexuses, genres, and rehearsal contexts and as they worked in private to prepare for varied types of public performances. Time and money made efficiency a primary concern while particular, flexible notions of songs and an ethos that emphasized process over product informed the (tactical) practices of multitasking musicians. On the line were the relative success or failure of each performance, the trajectory of the project, and over time, the careers of the participating musicians.

These concerns are further intensified during behind-the-scenes activities in nonrehearsal settings such as recording studios and sound checks for public performances. This is attributable to several factors. Among them are competences necessitated by the addition of several layers of electronic mediation that help make the music publicly audible and that inform its sound, feel, and the embodied actions that produce them.

PERFORMANCES IN RECORDING STUDIOS

Recording technology has, to say the least, had a profound impact on music practices, sounds, and meanings.[8] It is often utilized in very specialized contexts, less private than rehearsals, less public than live performances, and crucial for shaping the public presentation of musicians and their projects. For that reason alone, recording sessions are often high-stakes endeavors. Upping the ante are the costs borne by project principals. Well-equipped recording studios frequently charge a premium for use, as do experienced studio engineers and musicians, and although equipment is increasingly more affordable, it is still cost prohibitive for many musicians. Also adding intensity to recording sessions is that working in a studio, be it as an engineer, singer, or instrumentalist, requires skills and knowledge related to, but nevertheless distinct from, "normal" modes of performing in rehearsal or onstage. Recordings are also durable evidence of a musician's competence that often exceeds their control, both in process and after completion. Like they did in rehearsals, the musicians I saw working in the studio balanced issues of efficiency and cost effectiveness against the outcome they deemed necessary for the intended use of the resulting product.

Recording Conditions and Competences

One of the most important ways that the recording sessions I attended in Salvador differed from rehearsals and live presentations was that *none* of them involved the entire ensemble playing simultaneously. Though there are infinite variations of the recording process, the songs I saw recorded in Bahian studios were produced in multiple steps with performances by individual musicians or subgroups of the ensemble and then assembled (mixed) after the fact. Most aspects of the process, further, were tightly controlled by the project leaders via the work of the engineer(s).

For most projects, drum tracks were recorded first, with other parts subsequently layered on (overdubbed) until the full ensemble was on tape or more commonly, a digital hard drive. The first musicians to work in the studio, regardless of instrument, commonly played along to preprepared guide tracks made in a harmony rehearsal that outlined the form of the tune with sequenced or simply recorded chords, perhaps a bass line, and nearly always an electronically generated "click track" (metronome) to set the tempo. In the absence of prerecorded guide tracks, the click track was typically programmed on a drum machine at the session to provide a tempo reference for the first tracks to be recorded at the studio. Little or none of this reference material was kept; it was usually replaced by better performances or the part eliminated altogether as the process progressed. When drummers recorded first, other musicians occasionally played along to guide his or her performance instead of, or in addition to, any preprepared guide tracks. The accompanying live performances were commonly recorded too, but usually as "scratch tracks" to orient subsequent takes. On occasion a scratch track—most often the bass—was kept for the finished product, though doing so usually necessitated "punch-ins" to correct errors. Ideally, such tactical recording of bass and drums, and on occasion other rhythm section members, saved time and money by consolidating labor—assuming that together, they could produce clean takes faster than when working alone. Many musicians, producers, and engineers also believe that tracking at least bass and drums together creates a better, less mechanical or technologized, and more human time feel.

Whether subgroups were used or each musician recorded individually, the process of playing along with existing tracks to add new ones was more or less repeated until the leaders of the project had all the components of the song they thought necessary and "clean" (error free, grooving) enough to be usable for the final product. With all the parts in place, the discrete tracks were then mixed to yield the public-facing version of the song. Importantly, these final mixes were often prepared without input from or even the presence of many and, on occasion, any of the musicians who performed the music.

This selective inclusion during mixing was due to a number of factors. Paid session musicians were not typically hired to do anything more than play their parts. Most delivered their tracks and left, often to do other jobs. Musicians who lent services to nexuses in an ongoing way, for example, Laurinha's musicians and members, behaved in much the same way at the sessions I attended, though they were generally not paid for their work—Edni told me he received a *cachê simbolico* (symbolic fee) in the form of reimbursed gas money for the CD sessions I saw him do for A Zorra. For him and others with similar relationships to a nexus, any monetary reward would come from the live work generated by the recording. Thus, their participation was a speculative investment of their labor time rather than an exchange with well-defined parameters, as was more often the case for hired session players.[9] Studio size also factored in. Most were limited operations with facilities too small to accommodate more than a few people. The process was, however, generally the same for sessions I attended at large commercial studios including WR Discos, the fabled birthplace of *axé* music. Whether by design or happenstance, normal studio procedures usually supported the nexus's existing chain of command, with principals calling most of the shots, albeit now mediated by the engineer.

Recording sessions were thus guided by material, economic, and aesthetic concerns via a tightly controlled, rationalized production process reliant on multitrack recording. Various techniques to isolate the recorded performance of each musician, especially sequential tracking, maximized the power of this technology while also limiting it to those with sufficient knowledge and authority to use it. Once recorded adequately, the various tracks could be used as project leadership saw fit—errors could be repaired (or not); the performances could be altered with equalization and effects or segmented and spliced; and each discrete track could be mixed more loudly, more softly, or omitted completely from the final product. This organization of authority has numerous implications for the musicians who do behind-the-scenes recording labor.

Studio Performance and the Challenge of Listening

Numerous aspects of the multitrack recording process dramatically affect how musicians make musical sounds. First and foremost is that practices of production control and efficiency mean that much of what appears on a finished recording is audible evidence of a performance that never "really" happened. Since musicians do not necessarily play together and most parts are edited for errors or compiled from multiple takes, interactions are necessarily affected. Much of this impact hinges on the ways they see and especially hear each other and themselves while performing.

On most sessions, the musicians were separated physically if they were not isolated temporally. Guitarists and keyboardists, as well as most bassists and several singers, typically worked in the control room alongside the engineer, regardless of when in the recording sequence they performed, whether or not they were tracking a keeper part or guide track, and whether or not they did so alone or with other musicians. The larger tracking rooms were separated by sound-insulated walls and double-pane glass, and they were typically reserved for the loudest instruments, especially drums and percussion, as well as the occasional bassist who preferred to record in close proximity to the drummer (several singers also worked in the tracking room when recording the final track, but all scratch vocals I saw done were performed in the control room). No matter where the musicians were positioned physically, all electronic instruments and microphones were plugged directly into the mixing board or into amps isolated in other rooms and miked straight to the console. This kept all of the tracks entirely separate and inaudible from any live mics in the main tracking room. This maximized control and flexibility of editing and mixing.

Despite the sonic advantages and comfort this arrangement afforded for some, it also created very specific performance conditions for all of the musicians to contend with. First, those working in the control room did not listen to the music as they normally would. Rather than hear themselves and their coperformers acoustically or through individual amplifiers as is the norm at rehearsals and *some* live performances (see below), they (we) all listened through studio monitors, the speakers in the control room ostensibly for the mixer and producer's reference. Though the musicians could usually specify their preferences and needs, the engineer was ultimately in control of what was heard. Further, with speakers set up to create a listening field that prioritizes those sitting at the mixing table, others in the room had to make do with what was dialed in from that perspective. Or, if there was more room for adjustment, everyone still had to agree on a single mix that might be far from optimal for their specific needs. Individually tailored sound was not an option unless extra steps were taken (see below). This made it difficult, for me anyway, to pick out individual parts, since everything effectively emanated from the same place rather than differently located amplifiers and drums. While seasoned studio musicians must become fluent at working like this, it seemed to me a further disconnect from the visceral experience of live performing, during which sounds can often be located spatially, making it easier for each musician to distinguish the various parts being played, including their own.

On the other side of the glass, drummers and anyone else working in the live room were partially cut off from much of what took place in the control room. The window between provided them with a view of the mixing-table area, but nothing to either side of it, where the other musicians typically positioned themselves. At the least, these blind spots inhibited cues developed in practice and live performance. Moreover, between takes, conversations in the control room were inaudible to those in the tracking room unless the engineer deliberately turned on a "talk back" mic. In contrast, the instrument mics in the tracking room picked up conversations or snippets of them. The result of all of this for those in the tracking room, as noted by Bates (2016), can be an eerie sense of isolation and surveillance.

Finally, and most significantly, in order to keep unwanted sounds, especially other instruments, from being picked up while recording, anyone working in the tracking room has to listen to the performance through headphones. Depending on the studio, headphone mixes can be customized to a great degree. However, their use nevertheless puts layers of mediation between what the musicians play and what they hear, adding to the list of studio-specific competences needed by recording musicians that I saw put to use at the sessions I saw in Salvador.

A Zorra in the Recording Studio

A recording session I attended for an A Zorra CD project helps spotlight a number of studio competences and various other issues related to the recording process, especially the implications of technology. I highlight Edni's work at this session owing to the particular challenges that drummers face in the studio. These include their reliance on headphones, the difficulty of editing errors, their prominent role in establishing the groove (however problematic that assumption may be), and the irony of the importance of technology and technological know-how in the context of playing "primitive" instruments to create a danceable *axé* groove—what many assume to be the most body-centric aspect of a music valued primarily for its capacity to animate the body (and, relatedly, flows of economic capital). Many of the issues are nevertheless resonant with those entangled with recording other instruments. And, owing to the racial mappings of Bahian music as well as its media prominence as a representation of Bahia and *baianos*, so too are the underlying politics, implications, and ironies.

Following São João 2005, A Zorra embarked in earnest on their third CD project, a follow up to their BMG-distributed release that had driven the success they had been enjoying at the time. Despite their upward momentum, distribution for the new recording was as yet uncertain. Since they had not broken into the ranks of Bahian music's elite, this project was in some ways a make-it-or-break-it affair. Although they were still signed with Central do Carnaval, they were nevertheless under pressure to produce the CD efficiently and economically. Their production schedule called for Edni to complete twelve drums tracks in one day—a tremendous challenge by any measure.

In keeping with typical recording practices, Edni recorded first. The arrangements he would play had been fleshed out in preproduction rehearsals, but no prerecorded guide tracks had been made. Therefore, the guitarist, musical director/keyboardist, and bassist all played scratch tracks from the control room. Leo, the singer, sang bits of the songs to orient the group, and several of the bass tracks were repaired and kept for the final mix. Everyone else replaced or overdubbed their final parts later. To facilitate this, a click track was used. The group's live engineer, Marcelo, mixed the session, and several other A Zorra musicians filtered in and out over the course of the day to lend their support.

After unloading his equipment, Edni and the studio crew spent about an hour adjusting drum and mic placement in an effort to both capture the sounds properly and allow him to play in an unrestricted way. Once that was done, Marcelo adjusted the signal from each mic on each component of the kit one by one. Finally, he recorded Edni playing a few grooves to fine-tune the drum sound, primarily for balance and equalization.

At the same time, the other musicians present plugged their instruments into the mixing board. With drum levels set, Marcelo quickly adjusted their sound in the studio monitors, and with the group jamming, arrived at a rough but passable control-room mix. Since drum tracks were the focus of the session, slightly more time was spent fine-tuning Edni's (separate) headphone mix. Conversing with the drummer via the talkback mic, Marcelo adjusted the volume of each instrument, and importantly, the click track, until Edni was comfortable. The process was quick, and everyone was ready to go in short order.

The first few songs went down rather easily using basically the same process. They played each tune together with the goal of capturing a good-feeling groove and marking the form. If need be, Edni alone recorded one or two subsequent takes until he came up with one that everyone agreed was good enough for the CD.

For the most part, Edni played what had been worked out in preproduction and live shows. However, there were several instances in which he, along with Leo and the musical director, reworked a groove or a fill thought to risk clashing with a part yet to be recorded, especially percussion. On at least one of these instances, the bassist recut his part in relation to the change.

Several hours and several completed drum (and a few bass) tracks into the session, things got more difficult. When they started working on a song called "Doi Amor," they struggled to settle into a solid groove. Despite still fitting comfortably within the conventions of *axé* like all of the prior tunes, "Doi Amor" was slower and called for a swung sixteenth-note groove. Maintaining *suingue* at this slower tempo, which was unforgivingly controlled by the click pounding out quarter notes, proved challenging and time consuming.

After multiple failed attempts interspersed with discussions about changing the drum part and increasing the volume of the click to make it easier to follow, Edni offered a different and seemingly counterintuitive solution—why not double its tempo? Rather than play along to the quarter-note pulse they had programmed with the intention of providing space in the groove for the other percussion parts and to create a proper *axé sotaque*, his idea was that a tighter time grid would help him better secure his part, thereby enabling him to create the *suingue* they wanted despite the rigid and uncomfortably slow tempo.

Edni's idea worked. They captured the next take and moved on to the next tune without losing any more time. Ironically, by decreasing the space in the electronic groove and creating more points of constraint, they left more space in the overall groove, allowing it to feel looser and more relaxed. Another way to think about what happened is that doubling the click filled in timeline gaps that would, in the future, be occupied by other instruments. Despite being electronic and lacking the microrhythmic variations Gerisher links with the *suingue baiano* (and scholars such as Paul Theberge [1997] have associated with human-ness), the density of click pulses made it comfortable for Edni and the other rhythm section players to "just play" as usual. It was not necessary for them to concentrate on either maintaining space in the track in service to *suingue* or staying locked with the metronome in order to facilitate multitrack techniques. In effect, their habitus took over. This was possible because Edni had a sense of what he wanted to hear in his headphones and his mind's ear, as well as the willingness to reconsider any preconceived ideas, and the flexibility to implement tactical changes. As a result, the CD was completed on time, on budget, and judging from the fact that A Zorra has continued long after its release, with an *axé*-appropriate, *suingue baiano* that kept Carnaval circuit fans interested in singing, dancing to, and purchasing their music—thanks to the thoughtful, creative, and (economically) efficient use of studio technology.

SOUNDING OUT LIVE PERFORMANCES

A third type of largely unseen, but decidedly musical, working to work is sound check (*passagem de som*). Not unlike the process prior to Edni's recording session or what takes place before a rehearsal, sound check before a live performance involves a varied complex of activities during which musicians, sound engineers, or both, adjust the equipment that will amplify the performance, making it audible to a wide public. Unlike those other settings, sound checks for performances, be they in a small *barzinho*, on a massive concert stage, or in any venue in-between, are not protected by the privacy of studio walls or the ability to change the results after the musicians have played. Rather, the mix established before the performances informs the sound that will be heard during its final airing by both musicians and their audience at the same time—although, as I discuss, they do not necessarily hear the same things. As unseen labor that supports the "product" audiences pay for, and for which, in theory, the musicians are paid (their time onstage), participants tend to aim for efficient sound checks that provide suitable sound in short order—a goal that becomes more pressing since access to venues before performances can also be limited. For this reason, and owing to the different roles involved, sound checks also demand particular negotiations of musical memory and sensibilities, as well as specific competences for interacting with musical coworkers via mediating technology. As I saw many times, this involved more than a conventionally assumed (Bahian) musical habitus based on "just playing music" and instead demanded various trade-offs, and often, comfort with electronically distributed processes of (post-human) cognition that drew on and informed a particular, context-specific sense of human embodiment to create the desired *suingue*.

Mixing Sounds, Bodies, and Technology

As suggested by the differences between rehearsal and recording studio conditions, working musicians must be able to do their jobs under tremendously variable circumstances. This variability is greatly multiplied when live performance is figured in. A typical week for a *músico da noite* might include a duo gig in a small, windowless bar on a stage tucked away in a corner of the room on one night; a dance-band job on an elevated, outdoor stage the next; and, on the evening after that, a solo presentation at Dona Conceição's restaurant, where the foot-high stage is enclosed in a three-walled room with the fourth side open to an outdoor patio where most of the audience sits. Add in private party jobs on condo patios and hotel banquet rooms, shopping mall presentations, and shows in theaters, the Historic District plazas, June circuit *forrós*, and Carnaval circuit parades, and the variety of spaces in which local professionals work seems nearly infinite.

The radically varied physical configurations in each of these venues informed a wide variety of "meta-instruments" (Blesser and Salter 2009), the acoustic spaces that shape the listening experience for all within them: is the performance inside or outdoors? Are the surfaces hard and resonant or sound absorbing? Is the stage elevated? Where is it positioned in relation to the audience? Optimizing sound in light of these variables was further complicated for my collaborators because they used different amplification systems in each venue. Only the most elite artists had their own sound systems, and they still must be fine-tuned for each performance space.

Then there is the issue of who operates the sound systems. Signed acts frequently had an engineer as part of the nexus, while independent artists and *músicos da noite* typically worked with whomever had been hired by the venue or producer for the job. On a few instances I saw Jorge Elaíde Gois mix himself when he worked solo in small venues. Yet any work of adjusting the volume, equalization, and effects such as reverb on his voice, *violão*, and drum machine was complicated by the fact that few restaurant or party spaces were built with live music in mind. Sound quality in clubs designed for music also varied greatly.

Although most venues had their own sound system and engineer, the musicians did not always benefit from the established linkages between operator, equipment, and space that might point toward a facilitated mixing process. House engineers were not necessarily familiar with, or even interested in the music and preferences of the revolving cast of musicians they worked with from night to night. While relationships and familiarity can and did develop over time, working musicians had much to gain from having enough understanding of sound reinforcement to explain their desired mix to the people with their hands on the faders, help them achieve it (provided they were willing), and understand the limitations of the situation at hand should they struggle to dial in their ideal sound. Even with this expertise, and personalities notwithstanding, material conditions often meant that mixes were at best acceptable rather than perfect, and almost always arrived at through a series of negotiations and compromises.

In smaller venues, this was because amplification systems were usually quite limited and configured in a way so that the audience and each performer all listened to the same mix. The simplicity of this setup can be overshadowed by the problem that the musicians' hearing needs can be at odds with those of the audience. Performers nearly always must situate themselves in relation to sound-system speakers (and their own amplifiers) in ways that minimize the chance of feedback—the painful squeal that results when a microphone or instrument picks up its own amplified signal—while trying to give the audience the most complete and best-sounding mix possible. Even if feedback was not a concern—it almost always was—uniform sound for the entire audience was difficult because patrons sitting next to, for instance, a guitar amp on one side of the stage might get a much louder dose of guitar than those sitting near the bass amp on the other side. These types of conditions similarly made it difficult for some musicians to hear their bandmates or themselves. More often than not, the resultant mix in a small venue with a simple sound system was a functional compromise that provided the best possible sound to the audience while allowing the musicians to hear just well enough to do their jobs. This often took a fair bit of skill on the part of the mixer, who in some cases was a member of the ensemble, and collaborative spirit among all of the workers—neither of which was a given. Even under ideal human conditions, workable mixes could be elusive due to time and material constraints. In such instances, performers had to make do with a difficult hearing and therefore, playing, setting.

Larger music venues, in contrast, often employed more elaborate sound systems designed to accommodate the many challenges of live sound reinforcement. A fundamental step for reconciling the clashing needs of differently positioned and involved live listeners was, as in the case of the studio, isolation of ensemble voices. Ideally, nearly every sound source onstage—each vocalist, acoustic instrument, and electric instrument amplifier—would be outfitted with a microphone or set up with a direct plug-in so that the signals could be fed into *two* related but discrete amplification systems. This separation allows performers and audience members to hear the best possible mixes under their circumstances. The musicians listen to what is called a monitor mix ("*playback*" in Salvador), and it is akin to what is heard in studio headphones. Depending on how elaborate the system, several monitor mixes are possible, allowing subgroups or even individual musicians to customize what they hear onstage very precisely. Even when only one monitor mix is available, however, it still eliminates the need to compromise stage sound with audience sound. The main constraints, then, are the sophistication of the system, the skill of its operators, and as is always the case when microphones are near the amplifiers to which they are connected, feedback. The sound heard by the audience, called the front of house, or just house mix, is akin to the final version of a recording. All of the previously isolated sounds are combined in a way to provide a finely tuned and consistent sonic experience across the audience area, independent of what the musicians hear. This type of system requires a great deal of equipment and knowledgeable users, including, at times, separate engineers for monitors and the house. Thus, it is expensive. However, the quality and control of sound it offers cannot be rivaled by smaller, single-mix systems.

The spatial techniques used by engineers to optimize control and volume while minimizing the likelihood of feedback make performers especially dependent on their monitors. For instance, the speakers for the house mix are typically positioned in front of performers so that stage microphones will not pick up the sounds they emit. Stage amplifiers are usually set at fairly low volumes so that vocal and drum microphones will not pick up the sound they produce. To maximize this sonic separation and create room onstage, guitar and bass amplifiers are typically set at the back. While effective for sound isolation and space, amp placement at the rear of the stage nevertheless can hinder musicians' ability to hear them, and thus, themselves and their coperformers. Without a monitor, proximity to the percussion section or the drum set can exacerbate the situation owing to their acoustic volume, which might be louder than the reduced stage volume of guitar and bass amps. On the other hand, odd as it may seem, the wash of sound from the multiple sound sources including the audience can obscure the sound of even the loudest voices onstage. Imagine not being able to hear the drum set you are playing or standing next to.

In the radically variable, fragmented soundscape typical of large and outdoor venues (including Carnaval *trios*), each musician I saw working was typically provided with a speaker or headphones through which they listened to themselves and the other musicians in the ensemble in a mix that, ideally, they helped adjust.[10] Predictably, a good monitor mix makes performing much easier and more pleasurable, while monitor problems make doing the job more difficult. Thus, monitor mixes and the engineers who controlled them were a fairly frequent point of after-show conversation, especially if they were bad. Performers rarely if ever commented on the front-of-house mix since, in most instances, they never heard it.

At most sound checks I attended, musicians surrendered control over house mixes to the engineer and instead devoted most of their attention to their monitors.[11] Not only were they the aspect of the sound system over which the performers had some authority—assuming that a sound check slot was, in fact, available before downbeat—but the monitor mix, be it shared with other musicians or theirs alone, was the sound source that most directly shaped their performance experience. Generally unable to hear the house mix or even the direct sound of their own instruments and voices, musicians were availed of a vital live listening lifeline in their monitors; that is, provided they had sufficient knowledge of working with them and the capacity to get their listening needs met.

The Politics of Sound Check

In 1980 composer R. Murray Schafer coined the term "sound imperialism" to suggest that the ability to control the sound in a space provided power over that space, and, implicitly, the people within it. As this idea implies, although sound mixers are employees of the venue, sound company, or band, and are ostensibly hired to collaborate with the performers onstage, they nevertheless hold a great deal of power over them, as operators of the sound system are the final arbiters of what all participants will hear. As specialists, they tend to have the strongest sense of the mixing possibilities with the system and space used for the performance. And as musicians in their own right, they usually had their own aesthetic sensibilities, and often memories of how the songs being performed should sound. On various occasions, such as Jorge Elaíde's clash with the house sound man (see chapter 2), these understandings did not necessarily align with the preferences and needs of the performers (or audiences or venue operators). Here lies the kernel of tension that often needed to be worked out in sound check.

As a result, various deployments of cultural, social, and economic capital helped define a chain of authority. Reminders of who held the purse strings provided a fair bit of influence over mixes. More commonly, subtle demonstrations of knowledge (of people, music, and technology) engendered respect and cooperation (as was the case at the Liberdade reggae show discussed in chapter 3).[12] Sometimes this influence was enhanced by the networking agenda of the mixer. For instance, Farofa's references to noted musicians with whom he worked rarely failed to garner support from engineers looking to earn his favor. Perceptions of position also worked the other way. Vando, the young bassist from the Subúrbio Ferroviário, recounted instances when house engineers blatantly dismissed his *partido alto* band when they found out where they were from. Since *partido alto* is typically an esteemed genre, one can only imagine the potential disregard for non-star-level *pagode*, *axé*, and *arrocha* artists (especially if they were associated with an economically challenged part of the city or visibly of African decent).

Another common complaint indicative of the importance of perceived position was that engineers at multiact shows such as Réveillon typically lavished attention on headliners while remaining indifferent to opening acts. While perhaps a matter of practicality, the organization of sound check highlights this and contributes to the perception. The headliner (usually the last to perform) generally sound checks first. After the stage and mix is configured to their satisfaction, the other acts follow in reverse order. Because name artists are commonly given as much time as they feel they need to sound check, the remaining performers made do with whatever time was left over. Depending on their place in the order, however, this could mean that opening acts got no preperformance sound check whatsoever. On the whole, and despite a fair amount of shop talk about bad mixes and power struggles over sound, most interactions I saw between engineers and performers suggested that everyone involved was invested in doing a good job, with most squabbles related to differing opinions about how to achieve it.

Patua Sound Check, Posthuman Listening, Bahian Suingue

The processes, politics, and stakes of sound check are exemplified by a rather typical sequence of events that I watched before Patua's performance on Réveillon 2004. As was often the case, drums were again central to the negotiations of position, musical sensibilities, and technological knowledge that took place behind the scenes, with profound implications for the public presentation to follow. In particular, drummer Pastel's collaboration with the engineer as they adjusted his monitor and, to a lesser degree, the house mix, before the show point clearly to the complexities of mediated listening under conditions evocative of distributed, and per Hayles, "posthuman" cognition. This type of listening is fundamental to many professional musicians' habitus when working with technology onstage and in the studio. Indeed, in some ways, the circumstances of Pastel's sound check were similar to those during Edni's recording. However, Pastel's interests were primarily with how he heard himself, and how that would affect the feel of a performance with human coperformers. In contrast, Edni, after his own studio sound check, turned his attention to solving a problem related primarily to how he heard and performed with others, including live musicians, performers who had not yet played, and a drum machine. Neither of these scenarios are exclusive to one context or the other. However, Pastel's work during this live sound check both points to several particularities of the preshow process and nicely illustrates how mediated listening informs embodiment and ultimately the experiences of those participating in the music.

As the opening performers for a multiact show, Patua was required to work with a crew that was hired by the event producers, possibly at the request of the headliners. Thus the sound technicians were not knowledgeable about Patua's intended sound or mix preferences. Thankfully, though, the mixer was willing to work closely with the band to optimize their sonic representation. He spent a considerable amount of time working with Pastel to adjust the sounds and relative volumes of the various parts of the drum kit so that they could be heard in an ideal way by all participants. This was possible since, as is the norm for a show of this scale, each piece of the kit was outfitted with a different microphone and fed into a different channel of the PA system, making rather precise control possible.

The kind of technologized volume control the engineer and Pastel were after is not artificial—the sounds themselves are another matter. Adjusting the relative loudness of different drums enhances electronically what many skilled drummers do normally—they commonly "mix themselves" by playing the different kit components—especially their bass drum, snare drum, and hi-hat—more loudly or quietly. Still, when using sound reinforcement, each of these components is also equalized separately, perhaps modified by outboard effects such as reverb, and further raised or lowered in volume independent of what the drummer does. As a result, the components of a groove and what is ultimately heard of the drum set onstage and in the audience are shaped both by the force and manner of the drummer's strokes *and* by faders and knobs as adjusted by the engineer.

Knowing this, and because of the limited time he had as a member of an opening act, Pastel focused most of his attention on his snare drum. He was concerned about the engineer's use of a noise gate in both the monitor and house mixes—he noticed it almost immediately in his monitor when he first played. Since a noise gate is used to cut off signals below a certain volume threshold to minimize the presence of unintended sounds in the mix, Pastel worried that the subtleties of his snare drum work, in particular, his "ghost notes"—very quiet taps played between accented snare strikes to smooth out and add motion to his time playing—would be silenced. If this were to happen, he felt that an important feature of his feel that was central to its *suingue* would be lost. Thus, he wanted his listeners (audience members and bandmates) to hear these snare drum strikes at their proper volume level so they would experience his performance as he idealized it. For the same reasons, he was convinced that *he* needed to hear the ghost notes as well.

Thus, Pastel went to great lengths to make sure that even his softly played snare strikes were present in his monitor mix; but only *barely so*. He told me that if he could not hear the ghost notes, he would be unable to play them precisely and would likely compensate by hitting harder. Aware of the discreteness of the monitor and house mixes, Pastel worried that ghost notes he played more forcefully for his own benefit might appear too prominently to the audience, obscuring intended accents and yielding a cluttered, awkward groove. He also told me that if he were to hear the ghost notes too loudly, he would likely pull back or stop playing them altogether in response to hearing the cluttered groove.

Not unlike Edni in the recording session described above and Farofa in his preparation for work with Patua, Pastel was concerned with achieving a particular sense of rhythmic flow that was his yardstick for a proper-sounding and -feeling groove. His ability to do this was directly shaped by the fact that the way he heard himself was entangled with several stages of technological mediation. Since much of this would be under the control of someone else, he needed to ensure that what he heard would not misguide how he used his body in performance, despite doing things that, in principle, he had done countless times before.

Without miking, amplification, and monitors, the many adjustments a drummer, or any other musician, makes in the course of performance are regulated via a rather simple information loop, since sounds are heard more directly. With sound reinforcement and monitor systems, however, the loop becomes integrated with electronic circuitry, digital processors, loudspeakers, and the perception and judgment of other people. What emerges is an almost seamless merging of humans and machines made possible by the ephemerality of musical sound and the conversion of soundwaves into electric impulses and back again. At the New Year's Eve show in Salvador, all of this fluidity and flux was given materiality in Pastel's body as he created his grooves, and in the bodies of other listeners as they listened, played, sang, and danced along with him.

Such blurred boundaries—between the organic and the cybernetic and the embodied and the ephemeral—are also of concern to Hayles in her writing about the posthuman cognition and embodiment. A key part of her query hinges on a critique of the ways that discourses about technology have come to suggest an absence of the body on one hand and a universalizing of it on the other. Her assertion is that a critical engagement with the idea of posthuman-ness compels us to consider how our senses of being human are particularly informed and embodied rather than flattened or erased by interactions with technology.

Pastel's sound check exemplifies this. His actions show that he knew he would respond physically and musically according to what he heard in his monitors, and that without careful attention, what he heard might not correspond with what he would otherwise expect from the groove-producing movements of his hands and feet. As they worked to find a mix, drummer and engineer effectively endeavored to reunite the electronically fragmented sonic results of Pastel's bodily motion, configuring anew sounding gestures that were otherwise deeply embedded in his habitus. Thus, it was vital that Pastel account for the technologically rede-fined limits of his sense of embodiment. Being able to do this, and to effectively communicate how, were key steps toward maintaining better control of his body and his music in relation to his feel for the "game" and the *suingue* of the music.

Yet Pastel's music-making experience (and Edni's too, for that matter) was also informed by the knowledge that the most public aspect of the performance would be mediated in ways that put much of it beyond his control. The stakes for this could not have been higher since, in numerous conversations, audience members conflated mix quality with the quality of performances and perform-ers. More accurately, good mixes were rarely remarked on and bad ones were commonly read as musicians playing badly. In a very real sense, whether or not a performance can help bolster an ensemble's or an individual musicians' repu-tation is in the hands of the sound mixer and a web of circuitry and speakers.

Moreover, owing to Pauta's focus on performing (their particular take on) Bahian music Pastel's effort to make his ghost notes sound and feel right was very much about making his musical production Bahian. It was also a basis by which his performance, and that of his band, would be judged as good or not by a large audience, most of whom would not have otherwise heard them had they not been drawn in by one of the more prominent headliners or the accessibility of the city-sponsored, free event. Pastel's ability to create suitable grooves also affected his bandmates' ability to do so—or at least the perception of it. Though Patua's feel had been defined through extensive rehearsal and numerous shows together, a critical variable informing their sense of *suingue* was how their inter-actions could be communicated between them via whatever system for listening to each other was in use. And, regardless of the collective nature of group feel, not to mention the profound impact of the engineer, much of the responsibility for establishing the groove—for good or for bad—would likely be placed with the person behind the drum kit.

Beyond evaluations of Pastel's performance or that of his band, his use of technology flies in the face of frequently voiced stereotypes of Bahia's back-wardness, many of which are supported by images of drums and Black bodies and references to natural rhythm in media and popular representations that convey an image of nontechnological, primitive, and at various times in history, even less-than-human *baianos*. Notably, a central part of Hayles's engagement with posthuman-ness involves problematizing how and to what effects *human-ness* has been constructed. With such questions in mind, it is vital to note that sound-reinforcement techniques and other entanglements with technology are hardly new to music making in Bahia or anywhere else. Perhaps, then, as Hayles suggests, "we have always been posthuman" (1999, 291), or at least we have been human in ways less widely assumed. As musicians such as Pastel, Edni, and numerous others I saw working in Salvador illustrate, post-human interactions with technology are vital to making music, making it audible, and making it groove in a distinctly Bahian, and indeed, human way.

LAST NOTES

While no musicians I met would say that the most important aspect of their career was anything but their public presentations on recordings and stage, few would discount the importance of the various types of working to work they do to make those performances possible. As crucial and musical as the behind-the-scenes labor I have discussed may be, however, it is typically an investment of time, knowledge, and at times, money, rather than a source of income. Thus, it was done tactically to make do with the various conditions informing it and oriented toward achieving an outcome appropriate for the job being prepared, rather than for perfection.

Even when rehearsals were possible—they were not always—they were not necessarily the most sensible option given the economic and musical constraints of a given job. Similarly, in most instances, only enough sessions were under-taken to prepare the performance, or more precisely, to optimize the process and underpinning competences necessary to do the performance. Broadly shared knowledge of repertoire and musical conventions combined with flexible understandings of The Song, a clearly defined chain of command, patience, and experience-engendered adaptability to changing material conditions facilitated efficacy. Yet subtle negotiations of authority and control also informed rehearsal practices, becoming not so subtle from time to time.

Recording sessions often followed similar logics, but with higher stakes complicated by extensive technological entanglement and higher costs. While the economic payoff of most recordings was minimal, the durability of the recorded product led session workers to take the work very seriously. Interestingly, unless the project was well financed and bound for wide distribution, the hired labor, the musicians, often fared better than the capitalists investing in the project—at least initially. Studio expenses took time to recoup, but since lenders of services did not pay, they could quickly turn a profit with guaranteed payment for the live work facilitated by the recording, while principals started from a debt position. Still, recordings were vigorously pursued by many nexus leaders, and most lenders of services approached studio work with a willingness to bend in terms of their time and earnings. Indeed, most evidenced a genuine interest in capturing their best possible performances even if the money was or was likely to be minimal. Effective recording work was always dependent on an understanding of the particularities of studio performance, not the least of which was interacting with technology in the effort to create swinging, non-mechanical-sounding grooves.

Finally, several aspects of such recording session sensibilities parallel the aims and necessities of live sound checks, where the finer points of live sound-reinforcement technology and the vagaries of sonic preferences must be communicated and negotiated toward creating a successful performance. Again, mediated listening and its implications for embodied music making were central concerns, complicated by potentially clashing aesthetics and needs among participants as well as highly varied material conditions and for most, time constraints. Making the process more intense was the immediacy of live performance and its centrality to musicians' livelihoods.

With rehearsals, recording sessions, and sound checks carried out, the most crucial and public aspects of musical labor could follow—public presentations of musical sounds. These performances and various manifestations and understandings of the music therein are the topics of the chapter that follows.

FIVE

Staging and Sounding Live Performances

A banda que toca dobrado chegou
chegou pra tocar, chegou pra tocar.
E o povo satisfeito cantou
The band that plays *dobrado* (a Brazilian genre similar to *frevo*) arrived
Arrived to play
And the satisfied people sang

"Avisa a Vizinha (Vixe Maria)," composed by Gilson Babilonia,
performed by Banda Ara Ketu

On a Sunday afternoon in May 2004, my wife and I went with Farofa to see a
group called Bagagem de Mão (Carry-on Luggage) perform samba at one of the
Historic District's plazas. He had several friends on the job including a drummer named Papa Mel, who was a frequent lender of services to this group and
several ensembles around town, including the reggae band Farofa worked with
in Liberdade (discussed in chapter 3). Exemplifying the ensemble fluidity and
situational adaptability that I saw so often, the group was also working with an
extra *violonista*, who was subbing for their first-call bassist who had a family
emergency. Apparently, confronted with his last-minute absence, the principals
were unable to find another bass player on short notice.

The group's show was comprised mostly of classic sambas, but they also included a few instrumental *choros* featuring their *bandolinista* and one or two
tunes set to the rhythm of *ijexá*. These repertoire choices set them apart from
other samba-oriented groups. With Ash Wednesday behind us and São João fast

approaching, they also performed a block of Forró, but without an accordion or *zabumba*, as well as a *"pout-pourri axé"*—a medley of Carnaval favorites. Like the Forró sequence, songs such as "Maimbe Dande" by Daniela Mercury, "Festa" by Ivete Sangalo, and "Dandalunda" by Margareth Menezes were adapted to suit the ensemble and the specifics of the job. But now the changes went well beyond instrumentation. Rather, trademark tunes by some of Bahian music's biggest stars were played as sambas rather than anything that could be taken for *axé*. Even with the different groove—or perhaps because of it—the crowd flooded the dance floor at the sounding of the first recognizable notes of the first song of the medley. They sang at full volume and moved energetically throughout the song sequence, much as would have been the case a few months earlier on a parade route; but samba steps replaced the vertical jumping typical of pre-Lenten revelers.

Although unremarkable at first glance, that afternoon in the Historic District encapsulates numerous issues I have been discussing throughout the book, including socio-professional networks, multiple nexus affiliation, genre politics, circuits of musical work, and the importance of the aesthetic of participation. A more critical querying of the events raises several specific and related questions: how did Bagagem da Mão prepare for the show involving a rather dramatic change in personnel and instrumentation with such minimal advance notice? How did they conceal from the audience any stress related to their bassist's absence and deliver a performance that was, by all indications, satisfying for participants on and off stage? In their dancing and singing, did the audience even think about what had taken place immediately before the performance? Few if any of us were around when equipment was carried across the crowded, hilly, cobblestone streets of the Historic District, and on this afternoon, the gates to the plaza were locked until showtime, meaning none of us saw setup or sound check.[1] More broadly, what, if any, are the implications if the audience is privy to such labor? What, if anything, do musicians do to mitigate them?

The circumstances and questions surrounding Bagagem da Mão's show as well as the centrality of live performance to the Bahian music industries and the careers of Bahian musicians suggests that public presentations are a culmination of numerous issues navigated by musicians in their day-to-day work activities (e.g., networking, presentations of selves, nexus affiliation, rehearsal processes, etc.) and also vital sites for further negotiation. Whereas prior position-takings as part of working to work are for the most part private and done for free or at a cost, onstage they become public, (usually) for payment, and at a cost to someone else. Even if money were not on the line, and arguably all the more so because it so often is, public performances are open for wide scrutiny with no opportunities for "do overs." The outcomes, ephemeral as they may be, subsequently (re)inform sensibilities and strategies in the Scenes along with related practices of living from music.

This chapter focuses on the live performances that Salvador's working musicians do as the most audible, visible, (usually) remunerated, and, therefore, risky aspects of their labor. Building from my previous discussion of comparatively hidden work, I first detail the interrelationships between the material and temporal conditions in several main types of worksites and the ways that working musicians present themselves, their music, and their attendant practices therein. Different settings afford different opportunities to show and also conceal aspects of musical work in ways that inform musicians' treatment on the job and their positions in the Scenes. Next, I move to the performances themselves, considering how musicians organize and present their time onstage in front of audiences, how they do or do not adapt to the immediacies of the context, and the implications of their tactics. Finally, I focus on the content of the performances, the songs, considering an overarching concern of this and the prior chapter: tactical balancing of participation-engendering familiarity and expressive difference in the context of working musicians' multiple nexus affiliations. At issue is a local, hybrid understanding of creativity that features various types of mixing filtered through reverence for authors and their creations on one hand, and Signifyin(g) practices, that is, making changes to those creations, on the other. In a sense, this analysis illustrates the sound of musical flexibility in relation to prevalent sensibilities, strategies, and tactics in the Scenes. The sonic results inform treatment on a given job and the trajectories of musical careers. Yet, as I have suggested, however effective these audible manifestations of tactics may be in localized moments, they also risk reifying existing Euro-mimetic politics of musical quality and competence across the Scenes that cost Bahian music and the musicians who play it respect even as they are the prime drivers of local music industries.

FRAMING PERFORMANCES/PERFORMING THE "FRONT STAGE" FRAME

After accompanying collaborators through the multiple steps leading to paid public performances, both over the long term and on the day of the job, I noted a striking if not necessarily surprising variety of means and degrees to which everyday musical labors were separated from the work of playing the music. There is a certain irony here since, as I have argued, so much working to work does not look like labor (or music), and this appearance informs problematic stereotypes of musicians and *baianos*. A glimpse backstage might offer a possible way to challenge assumptions about lacking work ethics and push back against "function creep," the unrecognized, unremunerated, technologically accelerated encroachment of work time into leisure time that Gregg (2011) notes has, in the knowledge economy, exacerbated worker precarity and fortified power structures established during prior iterations of capitalism. Yet beliefs that music is not, and ideally should not be work remain, inhibiting such an intervention. Overtly labor-like activities immediately prior to and necessary for music performance continue to be bracketed when possible, lest the musicians' status (and career possibilities) be diminished. And since more remote working to work remains unrecognized—"'they' are socializing when they should be working"—misperceptions of musical labor continue. Indeed, the mystique-enabling myth persists that even when musicians *are* working, they are "playing."

Often, preperformance labor was separated from performing music through particular uses of materials and space as well as various practices of organizing on-stage behavior, itself in dialogue with material conditions and employer and audience expectations. On numerous occasions I saw musicians seemingly flick a switch with the first notes of a performance, regardless of prejob stressors such as taxing load ins, difficult or nonexistent sound checks, traffic jams[2] or long stretches of highway en route to the venue, last-minute substitutes, and limited time to prepare. Signs of tiredness, frustration, and nerves seemed to turn magically into smiles and effortless music making, further occluding the notion that music is work. If navigated successfully, though, the result was usually an appropriately engaged (or detached) audience, pleased employers, and ideally, but not always, satisfied musicians.

The posture switch undertaken by performers at the moment their presentation began marked a threshold between distinct but entangled settings for their labor: what sociologist Erving Goffman (1959) might call the publicly accessible "front region" of a work site and the "back region,"[3] which is typically only visible to a small group of insiders, usually the workers themselves. Numerous aspects of how the performances I attended in Salvador were presented and received suggested the importance of such separation. While nearly all musical performances, both backstage and onstage, obscured the labor of "playing" music from the public to some degree,[4] different venues enhanced or inhibited musicians' efforts to distinguish front and back regions and to conceal their "less musical" work. The type and degree of distinction often informed whether a performance was regarded as something special or mundane, art or atmosphere, with implications for how musicians were treated by audiences, employers, and coworkers in the short and long terms—that is, whether they were viewed as artists, stars, or even professionals worthy of respect and remuneration.

Below, I discuss the contents of performance, the musical sounds. However, what, how, and to what effects those sounds are performed, as I have been arguing, are directly informed by the setting. Fundamental here are the material conditions of the various venues in which musicians work and the type of performance involved.

MATERIAL AND TEMPORAL FRAMES

Throughout the book I have emphasized genres and circuits as organizing structures for professional musicians' practices. Entangled with them are distinctions between job types, specifically, doing shows and "playing at night," and the related implications. As discussed in chapter 1, shows are intended to present a more singular musical vision, while playing at night is more generic; shows are typically presented as the focus of audiences' attention, while playing at night is typically attendant to other activities; doing shows is both more risky and a more likely path to stardom and wealth than playing at night, which offers limited potential for celebrity or windfall financial gain, but is more attainable as a way to live from music; and performers who do shows are often cast as Artists and in some instances, celebrities, while *músicos da noite* are typically seen as service personnel. Finally, the most direct pathway to large-scale success is doing shows in Bahian music; but the genres' limited cultural capital makes this route less likely to earn performers accolades for their artistry, though the trappings of showbiz stardom are more common. While these distinctions and attendant hierarchies are directly related to matters of repertoire and its treatment (see below and chapter 2), as well as the cultural intimacy of Bahia's African-ness, the material conditions of typical performance contexts and the ways participants enact the separation of front- and back-region labor also figure prominently.

Shows, especially those in theaters, tended to enforce the division between audience and performer and between special event and everyday activity most strongly through their use of physical space and materials. In this regard, they in many ways exemplify what ethnomusicologist Thomas Turino has discussed as "the *frame* for presentational performance" (2008, 52; emphasis in original), which, through the use of stages, lighting, etc., as well as particular modes of planning and executing the music, construct it as "an art object" (Turino, 54). I would add that even if the performer is not regarded as an Artist and their music as Art, they still benefit from the creation of a star mystique that is more readily commodifiable than mundane performances (and many "artistic" ones). At theater shows in Salvador, stages were clearly delineated from spectator areas; and they were also separate from backstage regions, allowing performers to stay out of sight until showtime. Load in, setup, and sound check typically happened behind closed doors as well, with audiences only admitted once the stage, mix, and performers were ready to go. This helped support the impression that those onstage were Artists. In the least, it helped cast them as not audience members or everyday folks. In smaller venues for shows, such physical and temporal distinctions could be harder to maintain, but the organization of onstage time via repertoire, arrangement, and set presentation nevertheless helped enact a separation from the everyday.

At festivals with multiple acts, the kinds of physical and temporal separation possible in theaters was not always possible, at least not equally for all perform-ers. The norm at these events was for all acts to use a common stage. Once the gates were open, the crowd was more or less in place, so transitions between presentations were very visible. Obscuring the back-region work by headliners, thus, took priority—and it was usually successful—thereby reinforcing their elevated status. Typically, top-tier performers were given priority for setting up and sound checking. They went first and were usually given ample time to arrange the stage and set the mixes to their liking, in many instances before the gates opened. Acts lower on the bill worked with whatever space and time was left over, which could mean a cramped performance area, rushed setup and sound check, and in some cases, carrying out the latter two operations in front of the audience. The likelihood of backstage work having to be done in public was even higher during São João, when many local and regional artists stacked up performances in several venues in short succession to maximize the earning potential of the seasonal peak. As a result, they often arrived just prior to their performance time, negating any possibility for obscured back-region work. In contrast, most headliners earned enough money to schedule one performance per day, allowing them to set up and sound check, or more likely, have their crew do such labor, as if it were a theater show.

This holds tremendous implications for framing the performance and the performers. Whereas headliners who set up and sound check in advance all but ensure the best possible conditions for their performance, those with inadequate sound-check time frequently needed to adjust their mixes (house and monitor) during their first few songs, and sometimes beyond. Less than ideal mixes, feedback that might result as sounds were dialed in, communication between engineers and performers, and performance errors resulting from poor monitor mixes further diminished the presentation's polish and audience perception of the performers as skilled professionals. When back-region work was impossible to hide, crew members moving gear contributed to a more star- or artist-like image for the musicians (in addition to lessening their physical and mental burdens) — that is, if the performers could afford them. Otherwise, it was incumbent on the musicians to make do with the circumstances, carrying out their visible "backstage labor" while appearing as unphased as possible. Yet for all performers, once the show was underway, proscenium stages and the norms of performance in these contexts nevertheless reinforced the notion that audience attention was to be focused on them and that they were not "human jukeboxes."

Carnaval and *micareta* performances on *trios elétricos* present their own set of challenges and possibilities in terms of framing performances. Like stages at most theater shows and large festivals, the performance area on the trucks are elevated, clearly defined, very separate spaces. Yet efforts to obscure back-region labor are more difficult. Every Carnaval I have attended has been marked by sound checks audible for miles and *trios* staging on side streets adjacent to the main party that were traversed by crowds on their way to and from the festivities. For the most part, though, the messier aspects of framing a Carnaval parade show, including *trio* setup and striking, sound check, and the gathering of the *bloco* within the *trio*-surrounding cords, were out of most onlookers' field of attention since few people lingered in staging areas or paid close attention to activity there. Complete, theater-like separation was never possible, but most spectators had been habituated to position themselves in the designated "front" regions of the event, in a sense participating in the illusion of separation. Media coverage, further, focused on the official parade routes. Ideally, the turn from the staging street onto the parade route served as a rising curtain, allowing at least some spectators to bracket off backstage labor from front-stage play.

Yet any such bracketing was often muddied, especially for independent *trios*, where performers not ready to make the turn had less power to hold up the "curtain" than signed artists. Typically, the driver of a signed act's truck was an employee of their nexus principals. Laurinha confirmed that stars were allowed by event organizers to start and stop, thus insulating them from any repercussions should scheduling be disrupted somewhat. Independent *trios*, on the other hand, were hired by the city and their crews were, in effect, city employees. With a different source of payment and authority, they were, Laurinha told me, prohibited from stopping at the request of the (typically lower-status) performers they carried. Rather, the *trios independentes* I saw started moving as close to schedule as possible and tended to keep moving in an effort to stay on the schedule defined by their employers—that is, unless a star ahead of them in line stopped. As a result, several independent *trios* that I saw, including those I rode on with Laurinha, had to continue adjusting sound for several blocks after they made the opening turn. They also emerged without a *bloco* and thus lacking an audience that stood out as being specifically theirs. With less than auspicious, but still quite visible, entries onto the parade route, their positions as nonstars were reinforced at least until they got their sounds adjusted and assembled a crowd, that is, if they ever did.

As challenging as it may be for nonheadline acts at Carnaval or multiact festivals to separate their front- and backstage labor, it was even more difficult for *músicos da noite*. Though there were exceptions, the conditions of performance at a majority of restaurants, hotels, bars, shopping malls, and private parties were such that the performers had to load in themselves and sound check in front of whatever patrons happened to be present at the time. Except for a few dance clubs that I visited, the option of holding the doors until after sound check did not exist. Further, the physical layout of most venues in which *músicos da noite* worked was not conducive to framing their presentation as Artistic or even especially distinct from the mundane. Stages, if there was one, were often small, and I rarely saw separate dressing rooms or backstage areas. More often than not, performers began their presentations after walking through the audience, plugging in their instruments, publicly adjusting the sound as well as they could, and starting with little ado. In fact, many simply slid into their performance while others politely greeted the crowd before an equally gentle beginning. I never heard a grand introduction or the start of a performance by a *músico da noite* welcomed with much applause.

Although this lack of framing devices to enact separation did little to help *músicos da noite* command a more artistic or star-like persona, it did seem to invite audience participation. Though I rarely saw much hesitation to dance and sing at shows by stars or performers regarded as Artists, proximity and the sense of accessibility it fostered arguably helped club and restaurant patrons feel especially comfortable joining in with the performance as they wished, while also allowing them to tune out quite easily—an option less available at a theater show, let alone Carnaval or a big *forró*. A significant disadvantage of such accessibility is that, unlike show audiences, restaurant and club crowds often took their access a step further, speaking to musicians during songs, making requests (demands), offering unsolicited advice or criticism, and asking to sit in. It also enabled indifference. Such conditions thus did significant work to frame *músicos da noite* as there to serve rather than as Artists empowered with creative autonomy or celebrities commanding a high wage or meriting star treatment.

The performance conditions working musicians encountered doing different types of live work combined with the limited tactics available to make do with them affected how and what music they presented in those settings and, as might be expected, their musical selves and careers. More under their control, but still subject to various constraints, were the ways they were asked to and did organize the music they presented in relation to these conditions, and several more mercurial human factors at performances.

ONSTAGE PLANS, PLANNING, AND PRESENTATIONS

Although access to back-region and front-region activity through staging and variably obscured preperformance labor had consequences for how musicians were received by audiences, the way they presented their music and themselves during the performance proper was, understandably, more crucial. Thus, I saw a range of approaches to performance planning and execution that, by and large, corresponded to the particular work setting. Multiple entangled variables such as the physical layout of the front-stage area, the expected length, organization, and content of onstage labor time, and conditions of audience interaction shaped how and to what degree performances were planned to unfold and how they actually did. A primary informing factor was whether the performances were in contexts for "playing at night" such as a restaurant or bar, or whether they were shows, which were themselves organized differently depending on the specific venue type (e.g., a theater or a *trio elétrico*). The sounds of the performances and the experiences of participants were affected, but also, and once again, so too were the ways the performers were read by their audience and positioned in the Scenes.

Shows on Stages

In addition to the separation between audience and performer enacted by various aspects of the presentational frame utilized at theater and festival shows, the conventions of presentation planning and execution in these settings also bolstered musicians' positions as Artists, celebrities, and/or professionals. In addition to the norm of theater shows comprised of combinations of extensively reworked beloved songs and authorial material, these performances were usually presented in one, perhaps two carefully planned sets. Onstage formations were fairly standard and thus familiar and comfortable for performers and audiences alike, yielding a tableau easily recognized as a concert. Between-song banter was usually improvised, but some performers had certain phrases that I heard in multiple shows. Spur-of-the moment insertions of unplanned material happened on occasion as well, and encores were fairly common. But too much spontaneity could prove problematic, for instance, if the bill featured several performers scheduled at specific times. Lone acts doing theater shows adhered to this approach too—perhaps to comply with venue working hours and, in some spaces such as the prestigious Concha Acústica in the center of town, to comply with noise regulations.

Strictly planned and controlled stage time, regardless of reason, coupled with the liberty to include less familiar musical material maximized conditions that enabled show performers to present their music and themselves in a manner very much in keeping with their intended *cara*. While engineers and venue operators had the final say on mixes, I never heard musicians working in theaters told to turn the volume down once the show had started—a common event in more humble surrounds. Likewise, unlike more everyday and accessibly framed settings, I rarely saw show performers obliged to respond to audience song requests. Even though the aesthetic of participation meant that at least some familiar (enough) music was generally expected and frequently included during a show, regardless of type, most aspects of the organization of musicians' front-region time on theater and festival stages helped set them apart from workaday musicians, entertainers, or amateurs.

Shows on Trios Elétricos

Trio elétrico performances share much with theater shows in the sense that the performers were typically the focus of audience attention, their efforts were aimed at establishing a distinct musical *cara*, and aspects of the presentational frame were employed to create separation from audiences. However, conventions of the Carnaval circuit parade nevertheless also pushed performers toward roles more akin to workaday musicians. In addition to the increased access to the back-region activity that was possible during Carnaval and *micaretas*, difficult and unpredictable physical conditions made meticulously planned sets difficult and impractical to render. Rather, *trio* shows demanded significantly more flexibility than those on theater and festival stages, even when done by the same performers. Moreover, the vast majority of *trio* presentations I heard were especially full of music readily associated with other artists. Indeed, another American I met at a restaurant performance expressed his disdain for Carnaval saying, "they all play the same songs."

Regardless of this convention for sameness and familiarity during Carnaval parades, *trio* performances were still marked by the unexpected, demanding near-constant on-the-fly adaptation. Since the stage is a moving truck, it jostles constantly—all the more so if the parade route includes a tight turn, as does the Circuito Osmar at the intersection of the Avenida Sete de Setembro and Avenida Carlos Gomes, just below the ascent to the Historic District. On each instance I rode on a *trio*, bodies shifted, instruments on stands wobbled, and microphones fell as the floor beneath us shifted, lurched, and bounced up and down. Hearing was always a challenge thanks to ambient noise, including performances from other *trios*. Communicating with sound engineers was difficult too, as a result of poor visibility and the need to keep the music coming without interruptions to fix anything but the biggest of problems. Complicating things further is that all performers, except the forward-facing drummer, stand around the perimeter of the stage looking outward toward the audience on both sides. This means that sight lines that might enable awareness of problems and otherwise facilitate cueing are impaired.

Other more dramatic challenges are common too. Downpours intruded on several parades I attended, including Samba de Farofa's 2014 outing. Each time the clouds burst—the rain started and stopped several times—the crew scrambled to cover the back of the truck with a tarp to prevent equipment damage and soggy musicians, technicians, and guests. When the downpour stopped, they pulled the marginally effective cover back, usually partially, for the sake of appearance and to give those of us onboard some fresh air. Each placement and removal required the musicians to continue performing while trying to stay clear of crew members wrestling with a heavy, awkward, and after the first

FIGURE 5.1 Samba de Farofa at Carnaval 2014. The sun had started to shine, but the tarp was left partially in place in case the rain returned. It did. *Photo by the author.*

squall, wet canvas. Similar evasive tactics were also needed when I rode on A Zorra's *trio* during the 2005 *micareta* in Feira de Santana. Telephone and power lines crisscrossed the parade route, requiring all of us to duck as the truck approached them. More than once the cables were so low that crew members had to lift them over the musicians, who continued playing, seemingly unfettered.

Adding to the challenge of working on a *trio* during a Carnaval circuit parade is the long and variable duration of performances. Parades last anywhere from two hours to more than six, and performances thus require multiple adjustments depending on whether the truck cruises the route with few or no stops—typical for *trios independentes*, especially during off hours when stars are not ahead of them in line—or if it starts and stops frequently, which is the norm for signed acts and the *trios independentes* immediately behind them. When appropriate, performers insert certain songs and otherwise attend to especially animated pockets of the *pipoca*, play to a favored *camarote*, and, in the case of stars, interact with television commentators. More predictable is that audiences for any *trio* performance expect high-energy music for the duration of the parade, with a minimum of pauses except when singers address them to rally even more excitement.

Well aware of the importance of continuity, familiarity, and flexibility, the acts I accompanied on their *trios* had several preplanned blocks of songs at the ready, many of which had rehearsed segues and/or were stylistic medleys. Such preplanned sequences allowed the bands to provide nearly nonstop music for extended periods of time, minimizing pauses to call tunes or even count them off, which owing to blocked sight lines and ambient noise, could be difficult. At the same time, it was also clear that leaders such as Laurinha and Leo from A Zorra read their audiences and adapted their performances, choosing songs and song sequences from repertoire lists taped to the *trio* stage floor.

As a way to better manage A Zorra's extensive repertoire, Leo's song lists were organized into tempo and genre categories as well as several *pout pourris* (marked "P. P._____": see figure 5.2). This helped him keep track of possibilities and respond in a way that, based on his read of the audience, was likely to engender enthusiastic participation, maintain continuity, or conversely, provide a change of pace. Owing to their long history of working together, the rest of the group was able to respond in kind, minimizing pauses between songs even when they did not play presequenced blocks or made an abrupt change of trajectory. Unless cued otherwise, the percussion section maintained their groove and tempo and Leo signaled the next song, often by playing the first few chords on his guitar. The process remained the same when the band had stopped, as Edni confirmed in a 2018 email:

> In A Zorra, the repertoire was very big and there were various ways in which we were advised what would be the next song. The singer sometimes began to play his guitar alone, after which the band would begin to play. Lots of songs were played together and the band didn't stop playing. The singer took advantage of the similar groove to sing a different song over the same rhythm (November 22, 2018, my translation)

On other occasions, Leo and the other leaders I saw working announced tunes out loud to the audience. In those instances, after picking up the audible cue, one of the musicians, say a guitar player or often the drummer, would either count off the song or simply start playing, establishing a groove for the rest of the ensemble to join.

Such improvised song starts were but one rather unique feature of typical Carnaval *trio* performance practices. Also unlike performances in most other settings, the *trio* acts I accompanied for the length of their performances played some songs several times on a single day/night. Frequently repeated tunes in-

FIGURE 5.2 A Zorra's repertoire list for Carnaval 2005. Titles in bold are the group's authorial songs. "P.P." refers to *pout-pourri*, a medley of songs in a genre with which the group did not strongly identify but was at the ready to perform. *Photo by the author.*

cluded venerable Carnaval classics, emerging hits of the current year, and audience and band favorites from their project-defining repertoire. Each rendering of a hit nearly always elicited frenzied responses from audiences, and tactical repetition allowed performers to showcase the material that helped define their *cara*.

Thus, despite similarities between *trio* performances such as an abundance of very familiar Carnaval songs performed by most acts, there were also variations that were planned and of consequence. For instance, Laurinha's Pop Azeitado featured their MPB rereadings, while more prominent artists plugged their current authorial releases, and especially their *carro chefe*. Several signed acts also featured rereadings of music by other performers that they saw as positioning them in particular ways. A Zorra, for instance, included a samba-reggae version of "Hotel California," which Edni told me was not a common song among other *axé* bands—though he was surprised to hear that Salsalitro and Funk 'n' Roll both played it. In 2005 I also heard a recording of *axé*'s then rising stars, Babado Novo, performing Led Zeppelin's "D'yer Maker." Perhaps more unique to A Zorra than classic Anglo rock (which carried tremendous cultural capital nonetheless) was the inclusion of a number of *galopes* in their set. *Galope* is a fast rhythm considered by those I spoke with as part of the Forró complex; but it has a long history specifically in Bahian music, dating back to Dodo and Osmar and later, Chiclete com Banana. By including *galopes*, A Zorra was able to audibly perform their connections to treasured Bahian Carnaval history and one of its most elite acts, with whom they had family and business ties (see chapter 2).

In selecting which songs to play and when, leaders such as Leo and Laurinha had to balance crowd-pleasing familiarity with efforts to publicize their more unique, *cara*-defining music, all in relation to their own threshold for redundancy and their perceived sense of their audience's (which did not necessarily align). Making this more complicated was the fact that artists on *trios* with *blocos* effectively had two audiences with distinct perspectives. Since *bloco* members parade alongside the band, on the *carro de apoio* (the trailing support truck), or, in the case of a few, on the *trio* itself, they hear every repetition of every song. In contrast, stationary listeners in the *pipoca*, *camarotes*, and viewing on television via fixed cameras along the parade route likely do not know if a song had been played earlier. In either case, performers who catered too much to perceived audience demand by playing other artists' hits at multiple stages of the procession risked limiting their time to present material that they wished to showcase, while overemphasis on more unique material risked their disengagement.

Although song selection for acts on independent *trios* was in some ways simpler since they were less accountable to distinct audiences (no *bloco*), it was more challenging in other ways. Chiefly, if they were a new project or their performance was put together just before Carnaval, as many independent projects including Pop Azeitado were, they understandably had only a limited amount of well-prepared repertoire. Thus, they were even more reliant on their musicians' ability to render songs without rehearsals, as if on a gig (and in the manner A Zorra did when confronted with adding songs that were rapidly gaining popularity without time for studio rehearsals). Even with such competences, the independent *trios* I rode on repeated material out of necessity; but they nevertheless did so with attention to their sense of the audience. For instance, songs were generally not repeated in close proximity. They also made choices in the course of performance whether or not to showcase their *cara*-defining material or try to animate the audience with a hit.

Whether a *trio* performance was by a star or an independent artist and independent of the length of time on the parade route, the show's "curtain" closed at the designated end point just after the final stretch of *camarotes*. There were no encores, and once across the end line, the trucks sped up markedly to head to a destaging area. From there, musicians and crew scurried to strike the stage, cover any gear that would remain on the *trio*, and unload personal equipment to take to the next destination, which in some instances was another job. Other musicians stashed their gear as needed and headed to the street to join the party in a different way; and more than a few headed home to rest up for the next day's work.

"At Night" Performances

Compared to performers doing shows, musicians who worked as *músicos da noite* were under a greater expectation to prioritize audience and venue operator preferences over individualistic expression. As a result, they were generally not in a position to organize their presentations in ways that cast them as Artists or stars. However, like *trio elétrico* performers—and in contrast to their stage-performing counterparts doing shows—*músicos da noite* were nevertheless asked to demonstrate tremendous flexibility in their performances. While this generally inhibited their capacity to perform highly distinct musical *caras*, such seemingly servile flexibility could and often did help fortify their ability to live from music. Ironically, by being substitutable in context—that is, by not standing too far apart from other acts working in the same venue—they could limit their own substitutability by setting themselves apart from performers who were less adaptable or otherwise less able to fit with the venue's format.

Both material conditions and performance conventions faced by musicians who played at night limited or closed off opportunities to perform selves as Artists that were more available in show settings. In many venues where *músicos da noite* worked, they were tucked into a corner and asked to set up in whatever configuration could accommodate them. This could impact their orientation to the audience and each other, making them a sidebar rather than the center of attention and changing avenues for hearing and conveying visual cues. Since working at night, with the exception of dance-band performances, typically involved small venues, volume was also a common point of tension. Sound levels conducive to socializing rather than focused listening could be less than gratifying and even difficult for performers, especially if drums and percussion were involved. Thus, while the sound levels I heard in different venues varied, patrons commonly complained when they felt the music was too loud. In one instance, a group of people who had chosen to dine on the patio of a restaurant with an *arrocha* duo performing inside slammed shutters on the connecting window to insulate themselves from the music. On other occasions I noticed musicians jockeying less theatrically with audiences and employers over sound levels— most commonly with verbal exchanges between and occasionally during songs.

Even more important than volume in the contexts where *músicos da noite* performed were expectations for repertoire and its treatment. The convention in most restaurant, bar, and dance venues was for performances of familiar music rendered in familiar ways. The patrons I encountered in these venues that seemed most satisfied were those who were able to sing along if and when they wished, while also being able to slide effortlessly in and out of their conversations. Without a primary goal of capturing and keeping audiences' undivided attention through loud music, elaborate staging, or most of all, a high degree of musical novelty, most *músicos da noite* relied heavily on their *kits do barzinho* or *pagode*.

Although largely dictated by convention, expectations, and venue booking policy, reliance on familiar repertoire and arrangements was also a matter of practicality. *Músicos da noite* were usually hired to perform multiple sets of music over the course of a night, but the fees they earned did not generally justify much or any rehearsal to work up a large repertoire. Further, since substitutes were often necessary owing to busy schedules and related conflicts, short notice combined with low pay further incentivized rehearsal studio avoidance.

Still, many musicians who worked regularly at night, including Jorge Elaíde Gois, found subtle ways to put their own stamp on their performances lest they either lose interest in the work or be viewed as too bland to stand apart (enough) from their abundant competition. Jorge managed to do this without precluding enthusiastic audience participation, thus helping him build a following, a good reputation, and a reliable portfolio of venue nexuses. As was the case in most contexts, finding a proper balance between familiarity and difference made all the difference in his ability to sustain a career over time. In the bars, restaurants, and dance clubs that were his primary milieu, however, the balance strongly favored the familiar.

Jorge, like other busy *músicos da noite*, could also chalk up his successes to the ability to read audiences and adapt accordingly in process. Most venues specified very little about repertoire other than genre orientation, and clientele shifted, so finding the ideal proportion of musical novelty and sameness was an ongoing negotiation. And while several sets of music were the norm—Márcia Castro mentioned that four, forty-five-minute sets with fifteen-minute breaks in between was fairly standard—I saw several collaborators working in situations where the operators simply provided general start and stop times rather than fixed set lengths and numbers. On multiple occasions, time onstage was flexed according to crowd size and energy, at least to a point. Dona Conceição, who was known for exercising a strong hand when it came to managing her establishment, expressed her trust in the professionalism and responsibility of the musicians she hired to remain onstage and off for suitable periods of time without her intervention. I would imagine, however, that she would not hesitate to hustle performers back if she perceived them to be milking a break.

Within the parameters established ahead of time, *músicos da noite* structured their presentations in a rather improvisational manner. When I watched him work alone or in a duo, Jorge drew from an enormous reservoir of material, suggested by the size of his binder of lyrics (to which I rarely saw him refer). He nevertheless repeated his favorite songs and those that he saw as somewhat defining of his *cara* with some frequency from venue to venue; "Sultans of Swing" by Dire Straits and "Amor e Sexo" by Rita Lee were two that I heard a lot. However, most of his song choices varied according to what he knew to work well for crowds typical of each venue based on past experience. He also had little problem trying new directions if asked or if he sensed it was necessary based on audience response, which he called "*o movimento*" (the movement).

When working with dance bands, Jorge's work was slightly more regimented and less under his control. His groups and others like them typically relied on preplanned stylistic blocks that helped keep patrons on the dance floor with long stretches of songs that did not require them to alter their dancing. Even then, interactions with the audience suggested that they were always able and often willing to adapt to requests for songs, genres, and more time to keep the dancers satisfied.

Whether in a restaurant, bar, or dance club, Jorge and all musicians working as *músicos da noite* that I heard performed the songs in a manner akin to, but not exactly like, the best-known versions. Liberties were taken in instrumentation, key, and in many instances, length. Such minor deviations were rarely commented on either positively or negatively. The most radical changes I saw made with any frequency—and which were also generally embraced—were adaptations across genres to suit the venue, the artists' tastes, the season, or all of the above. Thus, I heard anything from samba versions of *axé* songs to MPB classics performed over an *arrocha* groove—a tactic Jorge embraced to satisfy need without having to sing lyrics he did not care for. Further, adaptations across genres are also entangled with the politics of musical sensibilities in Salvador, as informed by racial conception articulated with lingering Eurocentrism.

Since he worked so frequently at private parties, Roberval Santos was even more flexible than Jorge about how he planned and presented his (mostly) solo and small-ensemble performances. I never saw Roberval work with a written set list or any notated references at all. Instead, he loosely planned his performances ahead of time according to whatever information he could glean from the host, venue operator, or based on his knowledge of the work site. Then, he told me, he visually surveyed the crowd before starting his set(s), making intermediate plans as he thought necessary based on what he saw. For instance, he said that he oriented his presentations toward more pop/rock for younger crowds or more bossa nova for older ones. But on numerous occasions at parties, restaurants, and in shopping malls,[5] Roberval, like Jorge, nimbly made midperformance adjustments based on the crowd's *movimento* and his own mood.

Even as Roberval, Jorge, and other performers who worked in similar contexts emphasized their choice in performance planning and adjustment, I also saw multiple instances in which they fielded barrages of song requests passed along on napkins dropped off in front of them or verbally, sometimes in the middle of a song. Requests could be anything from "*Parabens pra Voce*" ("Congratulations to You [on your birthday]" sung to the melody of "Happy Birthday" but in 2/4) to favorite songs usually consistent with the general genre orientation of the performance setting. At times, though, requests ventured far beyond the general thrust of the presentation and the performers' preferences, as exemplified by the requests for *arrocha* Jorge received during its initial wave of popularity.

The liberty most audiences felt to make requests of *músicos da noite* was hard to separate from a general perception of them as service personnel. Rendering familiar repertoire rather than deviating from the norm contributed to this, as did the various physical and temporal conditions of most work settings, which left them very accessible to audiences. They lacked the insulating power of celebrity or the ability to cast themselves as (autonomous) Artists in part because they did both their front- and backstage labor in close proximity to their audience. The fact that their labor was, in fact, (skilled) labor was also obscured by the perception that they were doing what so many others in Bahia do casually and in comparable ways for fun at home, at parties, and at other social gatherings. Against this backdrop, willingness to please by granting requests compounded this sense of accessibility, empowering audiences to make demands, sometimes excessive ones. An ex-*músico da noite* I met at a dinner party cited this as his main reason for demurring from such work: "they (patrons) try to control you," he lamented.

While the willingness of musicians such as Jorge to significantly adapt their performances in relation to the demands of a particular job, rather than resisting in an effort to maintain their "artistic integrity," might be interpreted as servility or selling out, it can also be seen as a useful professional tactic. Though they were generally not able to showcase themselves in ways that would lead to stardom or artistic consecration, *músicos da noite* were able to earn economic, social, and even cultural capital. Along with payment for services rendered, their typical work settings often allowed them to demonstrate their competence at esteemed music often before middle-class audiences. The ability to grant wide-ranging requests provided an audience-pleasing opportunity to perform a musical self with extensive musical knowledge and long sets chock full of crowd favorites (*"boa música"* or not) rendered at an appropriate volume, and with the right balance of familiarity and difference also created goodwill with patrons and venue operators. That this helped pave the way for future employment is suggested by the multiple return engagements done by Roberval and Jorge and the fact that I saw them book new jobs while on the bandstand. Their social capital and the resultant steady work also endeared them with the musicians they hired, creating conditions of possibility for reciprocity and still more work. Thus, seemingly subservient behavior helped support the perception and indeed a self as a professional with a good work ethic, esteemed musical skills, and the ability to entertain, who could parlay those competences into living from music.

The various ways a musician who works as a *músico da noite* adapts to the specificity of each job he or she does translates to a broader picture of how working musicians in general make do with the conditions of performance. As I have been arguing, few if any professional musicians work with a single ensemble, and even if they do, they can be expected to encounter varied material conditions at different performance sites. A Zorra was a case in point. In 2004 and 2005 they held *ensaios* under theater show-like conditions during the lead up to Carnaval and the *micaretas* that followed, when they shifted to primarily *trio elétrico* performances. Then, they changed the focus of their work again after São João, returning to stages at corporate parties, theater shows, and music festivals. The individual members, like so many other working musicians in Salvador, took other work under still different circumstances, including those encountered regularly by artists who work primarily as *músicos da noite*. Likewise, a musician working "at night" in a small, out-of-the-way restaurant one night might headline a theater show the next; and that same musician might be a member of a group such as A Zorra or even a higher-level outfit. Such are the pathways of working musicians.

Even with this kind of flexibility, a chameleon-like ability to adapt to the different settings in which they worked, most working musicians nevertheless became more strongly identified with certain types of work and indeed, musical work selves. While the framing of front-stage performances, backstage negotiations, and all aspects of working to work informed their positions in the Scenes, the ways they were viewed by peers, fans, and themselves, their most important position-takings and technologies of self, were the sounds they made public, most often while working onstage.

SHARING SONGS/SOUNDING FLEXIBILITY

Much as the working musicians I met moved between performance spaces, nexuses, circuits, and genres, so too did many of the songs they perform. Likewise, just as there are economic and political entanglements and implications for musicians' flexibility, the same can be said for the flexibility of this music. On one hand, the sounds, meanings, and associations of different songs are central to informing how musicians work. On the other hand, the effects of their various work processes are audible in the music they make along with its meanings and associations, which then inform other aspects of musicians' careers. And the cycle continues.

Any number of factors including nexus multiplicity, limitations on rehearsal time, and the importance of familiarity for engendering audience participation underpinned the tendency toward the sharing of repertoire between nexuses and circuits. As I discussed above, presentation type (e.g., show or "gig at night") also informed the degree to which performers reworked familiar material, with genre serving as a primary point of reference. This is much as might be expected—*trio elétrico* shows during Carnaval typically featured *axé* or *pagode* songs while gigs at *barzinhos* tended to feature MPB or perhaps samba (especially on Sundays). However, more striking is that I also saw and heard numerous instances in which songs from far-flung genres were reworked to fit the expected genre for the context of the performance at hand. Indeed, adaptations of core repertoire both within and across genres, scenes, and circuits were a key and very common tactic for facilitating work multiplicity and pleasing listeners. The practice provided familiar melodies and lyrics for audience singing wrapped in worksite-appropriate genre markers for dancing or more contemplative listening while giving musicians a large pool of mutually shared and beloved music to draw from and to varying degrees, personalize. Their song flexing, further, like their other practices of career navigation, was tactical in relation to the overarching strategies of the Scenes, not the least of which was the tension between economic capital possible through the extensive commodifying and commodifiability of Afro-Bahian music and the cultural capital of more Euro-mimetic, deliberately contemplative genres.

The repeated albeit flexible use of beloved songs regardless of genre by different performers in multiple contexts in combination with the implications of such circulation also points to particular, hybrid understandings of creativity, authorship, and ontology of The Song that overarched the Scenes. Evident within these conceptualizations were traces of reverence for Artist-Authors (composers and lyricists) and their Works (likely attributable to European influence and capitalist entanglements, i.e., copyright laws) coupled with valorization of variation and difference in performance resonant with Gates's notion of Signifyin(g) as an Afro-diasporic practice.

Though I encountered everything from what sounded like deliberate efforts to reproduce the sound of a recording to those that only vaguely referred to a prior version, most renderings fit somewhere between the extremes. Regardless of context, and in keeping with Gates's ideas, the approach to rereading I heard most often in Bahia called attention to the performance and performers themselves more than the text being signified on or its author.[6] Instrumentation, rhythms, melodic details, and arrangements were regularly altered. Sometimes changes resulted from very careful and deliberate reworking. Other times they emerged more or less "organically," due to circumstances such as the composition of the ensemble hired for the job or drift over time, "allowed" by a relative lack of concern for strict fidelity to an authoritative original. In most cases some degree of variation was expected and embraced by audiences. It was also a primary means by which performers defined their projects. Thus, the personal touches they added were frequent points of evaluation for their work.

As important as the performance at hand was in shaping the sound of single pieces, entire performances, and musical careers, rarely if ever did presentations eliminate prior traces of a song as a text or its author(s). Instead, overt references to composers or well-known performers of the piece, as well as sedimented memories of either or both, further shaped how the performance and the performers were received. The openness of songs was evident in the fact that I never saw raised eyebrows or expressions of surprise or discontent if, for instance, a man sang a song associated with a female singer or vice versa. Likewise, when adaptations intended to facilitate dancing were appropriate to a given context—

such as MPB songs performed as *arrochas* or over samba-reggae grooves, or *axé* tunes performed as sambas—they typically resulted in packed dance floors and enthusiastic singing along.[7] Less immediately visible than satisfied audiences but no less important for musical careers was that such adaptations enabled the performers to position themselves sonically within their field. For instance, in keeping with the cultural politics that stood as dominant strategies in the Scenes, musicians could showcase their knowledge of music high in cultural capital and effectively create distance from those that were less esteemed, much as they did through the tactical narrative and nexus-affiliation position-taking I discussed in earlier chapters.

An important consideration, especially for the musicians who were responsible for performing these flexible and circulating songs, was that with repeated versioning, both live and on recordings, the identity and related authority of any one "original" text could and often did become more distant, obscured by multiplicity and varied awareness of prior iterations. For instance, when I commented on Jorge Elaíde Gois's performance of a voice and *violão* version of Simon and Garfunkle's "The Boxer," his wife Iza responded by smiling and saying "Limão com Mel" in reference to the *forró eletrônico* stalwarts who had released a *versão* of the song several years prior.[8] Even in the context of one ensemble, the members might have differing points of reference. In conceptual terms, this meant that a rendering of a piece of music might simultaneously signify on one, several, or no other performances for differently aware listeners. Yet the frequency with which performers introduced their songs with a mention of its composer or one or more interpreters countered this diffusion of reference, pulling it back to *an* author. Different memories and associations with songs in tension with occasional, but still common references to specific versions provided leeway for different levels of fidelity to potentially authoritative versions of a song, but always in relation to context. In addition to awareness of the limits of variation, the potentially vast pool of referential texts for local musicians' performances coupled with the varied demands of the different jobs they did meant that active knowledge of many songs, and multiple versions of each, was a core competence for many if not most working musicians.

Multiple Knowledges of the Song

The expectation that local musicians will have multiple versions of songs at the ready or be able to render a new version on the spot is rooted in how the identities of songs are understood in the Scenes, local, Signifyin(g)-informed understandings of authorship and creativity, and the prominence of flexible employment practices and ensemble formation. Most obviously, different ensemble nexuses performed different arrangements of many of the "same" songs. However, even in the context of a single band, new versions might be required for a variety of reasons, for instance, if a member (or their function in the group) was different or missing.

Although changes in ensemble membership involving anyone other than a lead singer were rarely remarked upon by audiences, they could be quite significant for the musicians involved. For instance, I heard several instances of musicians transposing songs they already "knew" when working with a different singer because of a *canja* or a substitution. The implications of transposition in terms of knowledge is suggested by MacLeod's statement apropos of the professionals working the New York club date scene, where "knowing the song in the wrong key signature became tantamount to not knowing the song" (1993, 47). According to MacLeod, original charts and recordings became the basis for stock arrangements that defined the "right" key. As I suggested above, however, such centralized points of reference were not the norm in Bahia. Thus, akin to jazz musicians (cf. Faulkner and Becker 2009), knowledge of songs in multiple "right" keys is a very useful, albeit not universal, competence that facilitates career sustainability, allowing them to work with multiple nexuses with different vocalists with different ranges.

Changes involving other members of an ensemble or general instrumentation can also necessitate the adaptation of parts. This was exemplified by Bagagem da Mão's use of a second *violonista* in place of an absent bassist. Faced with his nontypical role, the substitute emphasized melodic runs in lower registers to suggest bass lines rather than providing chordal support, as he likely did on the majority of his other jobs. For the other musicians, the parts nevertheless sounded in a different register and with timbre different from the electric bass they were used to, even as the *violonista* endeavored to approximate its function. In ensembles with several harmonic instruments, two or more *violões* or a keyboardist for instance, one of the musicians might emphasize single-line melodies as a way to create space, add interest, and avoid voicing clashes. Analogous accommodations were also necessary in the percussion section. Adaptations might be worked out ahead of time, or they might be implemented on the spot at a gig or in the case of a last-minute line-up change. In the moment, pressure increases with less preparation owing to reduced opportunities for the exchange of preferences and an unchanged expectation for the capacity to adapt. I got a good sense of this on the ride home from a blues job with Farofa as he expressed his frustration with the drummer, who, in his estimation, played as if he were working alone, leaving little room for any other percussive voices, cluttering the groove, and making the show a chore. His lack of actualization stands in stark contrast to how Edni tailored his drum groove during the A Zorra CD session discussed in the previous chapter, through his use of the click track and his imagining of percussion parts yet to be tracked.

These kinds of adjustments were very much the norm both in the context of any one nexus and especially for the many musicians who worked with multiple formations. Day-to-day demands meant that such flexible musical workers played many of the same songs with different singers and different backing musicians, making it their job to be able to perform them in different ways. On one memorable night, Junior played "Hotel California" on congas as a salsa tune with Salsalitro, followed a few hours later by a rock version on a drum set that more closely approximated the Eagles' 1976 studio release.

Important and expected as such flexible knowledge was—and as evident as it was among the musicians in my network—I also heard in speech and example that it was not a given and instead varied considerably. My *violão* teacher, Henrique—the person who first mentioned this competence to me—noted that many *violonistas* in Salvador simply played the chords of songs in the only positions that they knew them. He added that more experienced musicians were quite aware of who could (or would) not adjust. As suggested by Henrique's perspective, Farofa's aggravation with the overly busy blues drummer, and the importance Ximbinha placed on being "actualized" for maintaining a busy work schedule, situation-appropriate flexibility was a criterion by which local musicians judged musicianship, at times independent of genre association. Remember, though, that the dominant assumption in the Scenes was that musicians able to play "good" music were better able to adapt to and competently perform other music than those who "merely" played Bahian music.

Signifyin(g) on Songs

Though the ability to know and perform music with different people in different ways is at a premium for working musicians in the Salvador Scenes, it is not unique to them. Again, jazz immediately comes to mind—and it is also a practice overarched by Signifyin(g) as an informing sensibility and frame for analysis, evaluation, and meaning making (see Murphy 1990, Monson 1996, Walser 1993). Likewise, the reworking of songs across genres and scenes in Brazil was widespread, including within the oeuvre of the nation's best-known popular music composers and performers. It is easy to find more than one version of Tom Jobim or João Gilberto performing music they composed in different settings, with different ensemble configurations, and in different arrangements. Brazilian popular music also enjoys a long history of singers who have built very successful careers rereading "other people's" music. MPB legends Elis Regina, Gal Costa, and Marisa Monte are three, but there are many more. That this is a common, accepted, and indeed very valued practice is suggested by the fact that these musicians are designated specifically as *intérpretes* (interpreters). Still, traces of gendered notions of authorship and related power remain, evidenced by the fact that by and large most *intérpretes* have been women while most singer-songwriters (and composers) — the names most commonly invoked when *releituras* were performed — have been men.[9]

In the Scenes, the conventions of interpretation have numerous implications. The dominant gendering of roles — composer versus *intérprete* — informs who has access to and even who aspires to certain kinds of work, and thus sources of income and recognition. Among those who perform for a living, the need for and expectation of interpretation in combination with aesthetic of participation overarches the negotiation of tensions between familiarity to invite dancing and singing along and difference as a means to express a particular *cara*. Tactical reworking of familiar songs also allows performers to position themselves as particular kinds of players in relation to genre, ability level, and status — e.g., *músico da noite*, artist, or star. The flexible practices of musicians help maintain ontologies of songs in the manner I suggested in the previous chapter. Each instantiation potentially contributes to what The Song is known to be and what playing "it" entails. Finally, the multiplicity of reference and rendition creates multiple and potentially conflicting understandings of a song and any performance of it, a result central to Signifyin(g).

At the same time, the frequency with which performers mentioned composers and prior performers sets Signifyin(g) in Salvador somewhat apart from how it has been exemplified in the literature on Afro-diasporic practices. In writing on jazz and rap (e.g., Rose 1990), for instance, the emphasis is on the immediacy of the performance and performers at hand. While more a matter of degree than kind, most scholars who have written about musical Signifyin(g) tend to cast it primarily if not exclusively as a means of defying existing power, including that of composers, inscribed works, and originating artists. However, in Salvador, prior authors were not necessarily overshadowed, nor was the *concept* of authorship rendered irrelevant. Rather, authorial presence was acknowledged repeatedly not only from the stage, but also among listeners and critics, for example, in newspaper write-ups. In most instances of favorable reception, the (often markedly different) rearrangements were understood as a compliment to the prior authors' accomplishments even as the performers were appreciated for their own creative, indeed, authorial contributions. On the other hand, terms such as "corruption" were used to critique revisions deemed inappropriate or poorly done.

THE SOUNDS AND SKILLS OF FLEXIBILITY

Among the numerous songs I heard performed in multiple contexts a few stand out for illustrating the hybrid, multifaceted processes of flexible musical knowing in Salvador. "Hotel California was one, but a Dorival Caymmi *canção praieira* (beach song) titled "Pescaria (Canoeiro)" (Fishing [Boatman]) was especially notable since it is a song composed by a Bahian musician and because it was reread several times within Farofa's immediate network. A much-beloved but not ubiquitously performed song by the venerable Caymmi, "Pescaria" featured prominently in the repertoires of both Banda Patua and Pop Azeitado. As members of both nexuses, Son and Farofa played it in at least two different ways during rehearsals and performances that overlapped temporally, circa Carnaval 2005. I also heard Farofa perform it prior to that period with an MPB singer in a third distinct arrangement. Since each ensemble also involved several different musicians, who also managed different nexus portfolios involving varied repertoires and genres, "Pescaria" helps illustrate how the circulation of musicians and music between nexuses informs musical sounds and is entangled with racialized musical sensibilities in the Scenes.

Though "Pescaria" has been recorded by several nationally known MPB artists including Leila Pinheiro and Gal Costa, it was penned in the 1940s and recorded first by Trio de Ouro (1944) before the term MPB came into wide use and the genre it describes had coalesced. Caymmi recorded it at least twice himself and included it on several releases between 1954 and 1985 (Silveira 2017).[10] Both Laurinha and Josehr, who addressed the audience for Patua shows, typically

FIGURE 5.3 Basic *violão* pattern for "Pescaria."

introduced it as a Caymmi song. On one recording from a Pop Azeitado show that I have, Laurinha simply says "Dorival Caymmi" as the band sets up the vamp at the beginning of their rereading. Despite its strong association with the composer, however, several people including Patua musical director Luciano, told me Costa's recording was likely the most widely known version.[11]

In what follows, I treat Caymmi's ([1959] 2004) recording as a primary reference since his presence looms so large, though not as singularly authoritative, across the multiple versions. Figures 5.3, 5.4, and 5.5 are my transcriptions of Caymmi's recording. A comparison of his arrangement to that of Patua situated in relation to Pinheiro and Costa's recordings follows in this subsection, with similar treatment of Pop Azeitado's in the next. A summary of Caymmi's, Patua's, and Pop Azeitado's arrangements is shown in table 5.1.

Caymmi's "Pescaria" is a relatively sparse arrangement for voice and *violão*. The accompaniment is built on a bass line that alternates between the root and fifth of each chord. Caymmi, who played the part on the 1959 recording, plucks the treble strings with his fingers between each bass note that he plays with his thumb. To this basic pattern he adds the occasional rhythmic embellishment in the upper voices.

Note that Caymmi tuned his guitar down a whole step to accommodate his vocal range, facilitating this pattern, which is played from the A "cowboy chord" shape.[12] As sounded, this pattern is not possible on a normally tuned six-string guitar, for which the lowest note is E.

The A section of the AABA' song form is shown in figure 5.4, and consists of four phrases.

A G chord played in the manner discussed above underlies the first, second, and fourth phrases of the A section. In the second bar of the first phrase, Caymmi moves to a C triad for the full measure, before moving back to the G chord, thereby further suggesting G as a tonal center. The third phrase of the section is also played over a C chord, but instead of moving (as might be expected in G) to

FIGURE 5.4 The A section melody of "Pescaria."

FIGURE 5.5 The B section ("Prayer Interlude") from "Pescaria."

D, giving us a V chord to end the phrase, Caymmi instead moves to F, (analyzable as IV/IV or ♭ VII). This moment is also marked with a melodic peak on the highest note of the vocal melody, a. This climax occurs on an upbeat sixteenth note and is held through the first beat of the next bar for greater emphasis.

The B section shown in figure 5.5 is what I call the "prayer interlude," signaled by a pause in Caymmi's alternating bass line.

This section is also distinguished by the lyrics, "*louvado seja Deus, o meu pai*" (Praise be to God, my Father), sung in two phrases and characterized by longer note durations and rubato tempo. The relaxed time feel and the inclusion of full arpeggios reinforce the section's prayer-like quality. The interlude begins with the slow unfolding of a G9 chord, which is sustained throughout the first melodic phrase. The second phrase begins on a C chord, which moves to D and resolves to G, setting up the return to the final A section.

In contrast to Caymmi's recording of the song, which begins with his driving *violão* pattern, Banda Patua's arrangement begins with a rubato duet of voice and *violão*. This is conceptually reminiscent of Leila Pinheiro's somewhat more obscure recording, which begins with a harmonically elaborated version of the prayer interlude. Notably, a recording of Pinheiro's version was circulated among the band members as they prepared their arrangement. Despite this shared reference, the group opted to omit the prayer section entirely and instead introduces "Pescaria" with one verse of another Caymmi song, "Suite do Pescador." Thus, the presence of composer Caymmi is reinforced despite deviating from his composition, as reflected on his own widely circulated recording and the rereadings of other interpreters. His presence also affirms Patua's *cara* — Bahian music other than *axé* and *pagode* — against the non-Bahian references in their arrangement.

This is important because, by virtue of instrumentation alone, Patua's arrangement using electric guitar, bass, *violão*, percussion, drum set, flute, and on their demo recording, accordion, presents a marked contrast to Caymmi's and arguably, the imagery of Bahia he expressed. For example, where Caymmi's voice and *violão* rendition conjures the work and the simple sea-oriented life of a fisherman, Pauta's rereading is rich with intermusical references and sonic imagery that counters the lyrics' seafaring theme and sonic simplicity — that is, to listeners who recognize the Signifyin(g). The accordion, in combination with the hand-percussion rhythms, strongly references a *baião* (from the Forró complex) and as such, the arid northeastern hinterlands. So too does Pinheiro's version, which, while introduced by a rubato prayer interlude rendered on voice and *violão*, is based primarily on a piano, *pandeiro*, triangle, and bass accompaniment that hints at *baião* as well.

Patua takes the northeastern reference further, not only with the accordion, the signature instrument of Forró, but also with the drum pattern. This took on even greater significance after the group recorded the song for their demo, since they never worked live with an accordionist and eventually ceased working with a keyboardist, who could have approximated the accordion part fairly well.

Pastel's groove suggests *baião*, but he plays the defining rhythm every other

FIGURES 5.6a AND 5.6b Typical *baião* rhythms.

FIGURE 5.7 Pastel's drum set pattern from Pauta's "Pescaria."
The final measure contains the *maracatu* reference.

(2/4) bar rather than in the more consistent repetition every two beats, as is
normally played on *zabumba* in traditional contexts and on the bass drum when
a drum set is part of the ensemble (figures 5.6a and b).

This more open groove hints at Pinheiro's recording, on which the piano
acknowledges the rhythm every other bar, with the *pandeiro* making the figure
much more sporadically. But Pastel adds a snare drum back beat on beat two
of the second measure of each four-bar phrase, further setting it apart from the
other versions. This lends a half-time feel to the song and also offers a kind of
"call" to another intermusical reference to the northeast: drum and floor tom
accents on the first two sixteenth notes of both beats in every fourth measure
(figure 5.7). These hits mimic the rhythm of an *alfaia*, which is the bass drum
used in *maracatu*, an Afro-Brazilian Carnaval music and dance from Pernambuco farther to the north and east of Bahia.

As a feature of another region's pre-Lenten celebration, *maracatu* is not especially common in Salvador. However, most of the musicians I spoke with
were familiar with it, and more than a few spoke of it in rather reverent terms.
It was typically cited as either an "authentic folk" practice or as a foundation
for "quality" popular music, in particular, that created by Chico Science and
Nação Zumbi, an outfit from Pernambuco who were the pioneers of the 1990s
sensation, Mangue Beat. This short-lived movement, which garnered national
popular and critical acclaim (Galinsky 2002), was roughly coincidental with the
national heyday of *axé* and *pagode*. Its cultural capital remains, as exemplified
by the *axé* percussionist whose distancing tactic from Bahian music involved

mentioning his *maracatu*-fusion parallel project (see chapter 3).[13] Thus, Patua's rereading of a classic Caymmi tune provides the Bahian reference so important to their musical *cara*, further "enhancing" it with references to an esteemed music from an elsewhere. In one brush, their version conjures the cultural capital of Caymmi's music, manages proximity to the intimacy of Bahian Blackness, and packages it all in a danceable and properly balanced mix of local and cosmopolitan, mind and body.

Beyond this politicized interpretation of a sonic object, however, Patua's use of *maracatu* in the Caymmi tune is inseparable from the career pathways of the group's members. Based on Pastel's longtime history lending services to the northeastern-styled music ensembles led by singer Wilson Café as well as several Forró nexuses, I had initially thought that the *maracatu* reference was his idea. However, musical director Luciano clarified that a prior percussionist, who was especially fond of northeastern music and *maracatu*, had actually made the suggestion. He was long gone, but his arrangement contribution remained, thus pointing to the lasting impact of past members in a nexus. Pastel's breadth of work experiences and related actualization meant that he was not only receptive to Patua's scheme, but also more than capable of implementing it quickly and convincingly.

In addition to the influence of nexus members past and present, and several musical genres—Caymmi's *canção praieira*, Forró, *maracatu*, Pinheiro's MPB— the webs of intermusicality in Patua's version of "Pescaria" also extend to Costa's recording. While the references to Caymmi's version and northeastern rhythms are the most easily gleaned, Patua's use of *maracatu* adds yet another dimension, making their Signifyin(g) even more of an insider's game with respect to the "best known version of the song." This is because the bass line on Costa's recording is clearly based on the *maracatu* bell pattern, as shown in figures 5.8a and 5.8b.

Patua's harmonic approach to "Pescaria" also shares more in common with Costa's arrangement than Caymmi's, but it draws especially hard on Pinheiro's. For example, Patua, Costa, and Pinheiro all move through the IV chord in the

FIGURES 5.8a AND 5.8b
Comparison of bass line from
Gal Costa's arrangement of
"Pescaria" (5.8a) with *maracatu*
gongue (bell) rhythm (5.8b).

third phrase to a V chord under the melodic peak before resolving back to the I chord in the fourth phrase. Like Pinheiro, Patua modulates up a half-step on each of three repetitions of the A section, while Caymmi (and Costa) stay in the same key throughout the song.

Despite the numerous features in Patua's arrangement that can be found in other versions of the song, their particular combination of diverse influences from varied locations and musical traditions is unique. Moreover, they draw/ Signify on notable features of esteemed genres and recordings in a manner resonant with idealized notions of *mestiçagem*, combining the "best" elements of different peoples and cultures.

To their *cara*-identifying mix, Patua's version adds touches not found in the other performers' renditions, further suggesting the importance of adding "signal difference" as part of their project. Most significant among them is their treatment of the melodic accent in the third phrase. On every successive repetition of the A section, they increase the length of the held note and the break in the groove. First one bar, then three, and finally six full measures of rest are inserted, along with a flute cadenza. By contrast, Pinheiro, Costa, and Caymmi each treat this event differently from each other, but basically the same way each time. To further punctuate this break and establish Patua's vision for the song, bassist Son remains on the root of the IV chord while the other harmonic instruments move to V. This calls greater attention to the break through the use of an unexpected chord voicing.

Patua's arrangement of "Pescaria" thus incorporates elements from several different versions of the song as found on recordings and in members' memories and experiences. In so doing, the members can be understood to have Signified on each or any of the earlier arrangements of the song and on esteemed musical practices from a variety of places and eras while acknowledging beloved musical authors (composers and *intérpretes*) all the while. The influence of past nexus participants merged with the experiences and musical visions of current performers as well, further shaping the final arrangement and allowing them to produce a unique reading of well-known music that expressed their musical *cara* and tactically managed the cultural intimacy of Bahia's African-ness.

The "Same" Song Differently

Whereas Patua played "Pescaria" as a *maracatu*-inflected *baião*, Pop Azeitado, in keeping with Laurinha's vision of combining classic Brazilian popular music with

TABLE 5.1

Artist	Form	Comments
Dorival Caymmi	AABA'	Voice and *violão*
Banda Patua	CAA'A" C section is excerpt from another song, A section modulates up a half-step on each repetition *Baião-Maracatu* groove	Full band arrangement
Laurinha and Pop Azeitado	BBAASA'BB B section played in 6/8 A Section played as samba-reggae Includes guitar solo (S)	Full band arrangement

Bahian rhythms, set the song to a groove that she described as samba-reggae. The singer also told me that she did not base her rereading on any particular version of the song and that she did not consult either Costa's or Pinheiro's recordings (though it is likely that she had heard them). Rather, she kept to her Pop Azeitado formula and used a slightly modified but decidedly Bahian groove to support beloved and respected lyrics, melodies, and harmonies borrowed and adapted from (Bahian composer) Caymmi. However, since Son and especially Farofa contributed to Pop Azeitado's arrangement—and Farofa suggested it in the first place—Laurinha's rereading is not separate from the web of intermusicality I discussed above. Nor is it outside of local cultural politics.

What is more, it further highlights different perspectives on the same music within the same ensemble. For Laurinha, her rereading Signifies on *axé* music as well as the Caymmi tune. She also affirmed Caymmi's authorship with her introduction of the song at most performances. Yet her rereading also inverts

Caymmi's song form by beginning and ending with the prayer interlude. Despite her assertion of not basing her rereading on other versions, beginning with the interlude is a feature of Pinheiro's recording that was certainly familiar to Son and Farofa and possibly other musicians involved in creating Pop Azeitado's arrangement.

In a marked departure from any version of "Pescaria" that I had heard before, however, Laurinha sings the prayer lyrics over a variation of a common Afro-Cuban 6/8 groove played on congas, drums, and guitar. While this seems a clear step away from MPB, *axé*, and even Bahian-ness, inclusion of this rhythm can also be understood as performing a diasporic link in a manner consistent with the racial politics of the *blocos afro* and their discursive and sonic connections to other Black Atlantic music cultures, including Jamaican reggae (see Crook 1993, Godi 2001) and, in the case of Olodum, Cuba. The group's first musical director, Neguinho do Samba, who is widely credited for inventing samba-reggae, used timbales when directing the group. This link is brought full circle by the influence of *bloco afro* music on *axé*. The Cuba reference also conjures the cultural capital of cosmopolitanism via sounding/Signifyin(g) on the music of an elsewhere. For Farofa, who exerted a strong hand in creating this arrangement, use of congas in the introduction also allowed him to showcase his knowledge of esteemed, cosmopolitan, Afro-diasporic music. Along with Caymmi's text and stature, this rhythmic framing helps to mitigate the intimacy of *axé*, which maintains a strong presence via the samba-reggae groove, however modified, and the electric instruments used in the rest of the song.

Pop Azeitado's harmonic approach to "Pescaria" is also distinct from the other versions I have heard with respect to their treatment of the third phrase's melodic peak. Most notably, the band remains on the IV chord for the rhythmic accent that follows Laurinha's vocal climax. Only the bass moves to the V for one beat, creating a sudden and unexpected dissonance. Indicative of input from individual musicians in the ensemble, bassist Son's line is reminiscent of how he approached this same moment in Patua's arrangement. By playing unexpected notes at this climactic moment in the songs, Son both creates a unique sound for each group and spotlights his own distinctive style in different contexts while playing what might be seen as the same song.

In creating their parts for "Pescaria," Son and Farofa made tactical use of the Scenes' customary, and for all intents and purposes, required practice of reworking other artists' songs. While working with groups drawing on beloved material as a way to appease audience demand for participation-engendering fa-

FIGURE 5.9 Son's bass line as played with Pop Azeitado.

miliarity, both musicians used knowledge they had already developed with other ensembles as a way to facilitate their musical multitasking. They contributed to the creation of distinct enough versions of the song to distinguish each ensemble that performed it. Their parts also helped distinguish them as players, making the work potentially beneficial for their reputations, while also adding additional layers of pleasure through creation and performance. And despite playing music that could be heard as *axé*, their Signifyin(g) helped all of the musicians in Pop Azeitado (and Patua, for that matter) create a buffering, aesthetic distance from the intimacy of Bahian music.

LAST NOTES

Malleable notions of music can create challenges and frustrations for professional popular musicians in Salvador. In the context of revolving casts of musicians, different versions of familiar songs both intended and circumstantial are all but inevitable and necessary as matters of practicality. But they are also very much in keeping with local music sensibilities. The premium audiences place on familiar sounds, however, can constrain performers' ability to stand out from the crowd, limiting prospects for artists and ensembles that wish to compose new music rather than rework existing material. I was often told that there is a minimal audience in Salvador for newly composed music, especially by new and unknown artists and/or those working in alternative genres. As a result, most local performers find it difficult to legally produce and sell CDs that have the potential to attract large audiences and earn substantial sums of money because they cannot afford to pay the copyright fees on the beloved material that they are often obliged to include. As a result, many skilled musicians are relegated to selling their recordings of rearranged favorites on the pirate market or giving away their CDs in hopes of gaining the attention of a booking agent, label, *empresário, patrocínio,* or *bloco.*

Moreover, while the differentiated repetition of beloved music by canonic composers can keep that repertoire fresh, it may do more than just that. Frequent sounding and expressions of appreciation for these core compositions and affirmations of the presence of their authors can reinforce, and by all indications has reinforced the centrality of a handful of consecrated artists and the musical sensibilities they represent—including the maleness of composers and the purported superiority of music for the mind over music for the body. In addition to limiting space for new faces and sounds, this contributes to discourse that has long pushed Bahian music to the side in favor of contemplative and/or cosmopolitan genres, since so much of the core repertoire comes from artists based in the Rio/São Paulo axis or beyond.

Further reifying the status quo of Bahian music and musicians are the conditions of many of their performances and indeed, the pathways many must follow in order to make do. Work settings that are foundational for musicians' income do not necessarily frame them as Artists or even workers to be respected. Occasional opportunities for lower-tier artists to share stages with better-known acts can provide exposure, but they can also highlight status differentials; and headline performances that feature local artists in venues such as theaters that can present them in the best possible frame are often financially risky. As the music business has shifted globally, new opportunities have emerged for some local musicians. But the career trajectories of the majority of my collaborators suggest that live work is still the foundation of living from music in Salvador even as opportunities and pay for doing so ebb and flow and are, by several accounts, decreasing.

In spite of these many obstacles, Salvador's musicians do make inroads and livings in a crowded field. Each year, new faces and sounds emerge and there is no shortage of musicians such as Farofa, Jorge Elaíde Gois, Roberval, and Laurinha who manage to sustain careers over very long periods of time. Their flexibility and tactical use of beloved material certainly makes this possible and often pleasurable, allowing them to perform music they enjoy, often infused with their personal touches, in several guises and with different coperformers. As a career tactic it allows for their musical multitasking and in some cases creates avenues to showcase their musical knowledge, adaptability, and musicality. Even the less pleasurable and more overtly labor-like aspects of their jobs can create opportunities. Ride sharing to performances can create bonds between musicians and social capital, and something as mundane as hiring a roadie can serve as a way to provide some income to friends who need work. For instance, drummer Papa Mel and later Farofa hired a young man from Papa Mel's neighborhood for that very purpose. His work with them led to other jobs with Funk 'n' Roll—a bridge created when Farofa and Junior worked together—and eventually ongoing employment with a fairly prominent *axé* artist.

In a similar way, the flexibility that allows music makers to make the most of a given moment in their career path also is central to sustaining those careers over the long term. As I will discuss in the concluding chapter, few if any of the musicians I have known over the years are doing exactly what they did when we met. Most have seen numerous ups and downs in their careers, too. But quite a few of them have utilized their flexible musical competences as well as the economic, social, and cultural capital they have earned over the years to continue to live from music in some form or fashion.

Livings, Living from Music, Music for a Lifetime

The remaining repositories of "work" within the wage-labor system are, despite the ruthless transformation of virtually all of its products and producers into commodities, the diminishing instances of petty craft production (occupations that are frequently suffused with the uncertainties connected with self-employment), art, and the products of the relatively small proportion of those who produce knowledge.

Stanley Aronowitz and William DiFazio, The Jobless Future

The above epigraph, taken from the conclusion of Aronowitz and DiFazio's ominously titled 1994 study, held on to a glimmer of hope for the employment prospects of craftspeople, artists, and intellectuals. Yet just a few pages later, they walk back their qualified optimism, conceding that such "creative labor" had, like manufacturing and most conventional employment sectors, also been threatened by "late capitalism," though perhaps not to the same degree. Their position was (and, as is evident in their book's second, 2014 edition,[1] remains) that continued rationalization of industry along with post-Fordist techniques including flexible hiring practices drove the radical restructuring of most workforces—and not in positive ways.[2] Against Marx's mid-nineteenth-century warnings about alienated laborers, Aronowitz and DiFazio suggest that throughout the better part of the twentieth century, many (U.S.) workers had been able to find satisfaction, social connection, and personal fulfillment in their jobs in addition to earning a livable wage.[3] Yet they also make clear their conviction that by century's end,

Marx's dire assessment of laborers sacrificing their individuality for a wage had come to be the norm and that, worse still, the wages for which they exchanged so much were rapidly becoming scarce commodities themselves.

As I have discussed throughout the book, the experiences of people living from music in Salvador exemplify several aspects of Aronowitz and DiFazio's "jobless future" — though not joblessness itself. The many flexible musical workers I met, like numerous other musicians worldwide, work and have worked in gig economies for years; their jobs have been repeatedly altered and sometimes eliminated by technological developments,[4] and their ability to support themselves has long been complicated by flexible hiring practices compounded by their substitutability and the problems of valuing their labor time and the resultant production.

Hewing more closely to the notion of joblessness, musicians' career futures have rarely been assured and wages for many are in decline. Some performers parlay their multiple nexuses into career advancement, but for many others, their labor is only as valuable as their last job; and as I suggested in chapter 3, many musical workers see career turmoil following a prominent affiliation, in some cases, as a result of it.

Yet a majority of the professional musicians I have met, in Salvador and Los Angeles (and Texas before that), were anything but alienated from the products and processes of their labor. They *did* derive meaning from their work, and they *did* nurture meaningful relationships with peers, colleagues, audiences, and even employers and competitors. And, despite often struggling, sometimes failing, and nearly always experiencing ups and downs, many have managed to make at least enough money to support themselves and their families by making music over an extended period of time.

While not a jobless career path, job success and sustainability in music are thus ongoing challenges. This is especially but certainly not uniquely the case in popular music, where trends often favor youth. In Bahian popular music, youthful vigor if not youth itself is crucial since work conditions place extreme demands on bodies, exemplified by Carnaval performances under a hot sun for multiple hours nonstop. In most avenues of professional music making, frequent and/or extended periods of travel, late nights, and endemic financial uncertainty place further strains on musicians and their families as well.

Faced with these conditions, the performers I encountered who achieved some degree of career fulfillment and longevity often did so through their tactical practices of flexibility. Their ability to perform different kinds of music with different people was a foundational competence protecting them from the precariousness caused by lack of contracts, fierce competition, weak to nonexistent support from organized labor, and employers whose own conditions were often precarious. Owing to the importance of embodied participation in most work contexts, skill at performing the "same" music in different settings was especially important. Musicians actualized in this way were better able to move between nexuses, genres, and circuits according to the demands of the present and the opportunities with which they were presented, as nurtured through past activities and resources. When the best-paying jobs provided less musical satisfaction and cultural capital than other options, as was often the case, musical multiplicity kept their interest up and helped stave off alienation from music itself. Performing "good music" also helped do reputation work that could enable future employment possibilities.

Entangled with this contradictory relationship between money and musical prestige is the racial conception that permeates nearly all aspects of life in Salvador. Cultural and economic capital are at odds in numerous musical scenes. Common too in other settings for musical work are job precarity, function creep, exclusive cliques, and particular constructions of musical competence and quality. However, the ideas about phenotype and the racialization of cultural difference and social position that underpin local habitus, musical and social sensibilities, genre politics, and interactions in spaces where music is made and consumed are more particular, though not entirely unique to Bahia. Racial conception was thus an always already strategy navigated by working musicians and, as such, an ever-present reference for their tactics. Selective and varied self-positioning in relation to Bahian music was perhaps the most palpable evidence of this, providing evidence of the cultural intimacy of African-ness in Bahia's racial-cultural mix as well as the stakes for managing it. Often effective for performing cultural capital and building social capital in the moment, some of these tactics also had the unintended effects of reifying extant power relations and hegemonic (Euro-mimetic) musical sensibilities in a setting marked by frequent and prideful references to *mestiçagem*, racial democracy, and Afro-diasporic heritage as central to local identities. Perhaps more unsettling is the 2016 election of a president who unapologetically traffics in racial stereotypes about lazy Black people (see the Introduction). While Freyrean notions of *mestiçagem* and *democracia racial* have been rightly critiqued for their strategic utility for obfuscating systematic and entrenched racial hierarchies, exclusion, and violence, overt racism at the highest levels of government and a majority's willingness to look the other way or perhaps worse, follow suit, is a bone-chilling development. On the other hand,

I have seen some evidence that recent events served as a call to action against complacency engendered by long-standing constructions of Brazilian-ness and Bahian-ness. The extent to which any such contestations will continue and their outcomes remain to be seen, but needless to say, their stakes are especially high in and for the capital of Afro-Brazil.

MUSICAL JOBS IN THE RECENT PAST
AND NEAR FUTURE

Along with ongoing scholarly attention to issues of race, music, and race and music in Brazil, and parallel to increasing concerns expressed among research-ers and the public about the changing nature of work in late capitalism, there is no shortage of academic and journalistic commentary on the sea changes seen in music industries worldwide over the last twenty or so years. Issues of inter-est to scholars and journalists such as the rise of the internet and the breakup/ consolidation of major recording labels have, without a doubt, had dramatic implications for music participants of all kinds. And professional musicians as well as those who aspire to become professionals certainly count among them. Largely gone are the days when album sales and other forms of royalties could generate enough income to ease pressures for constant or near-constant live performance as a means of earning for those not among the absolute elite of the industries. While such residual income has always been reserved for a select few, the few has become significantly fewer, with artists once in the position of touring to support record sales now touring to survive. Viewed another way, these shifts have had some democratizing effects in opening up new avenues of audibility for performers who might have otherwise remained restricted to very localized markets. YouTube and other online services as well as increasingly affordable home recording gear have decentralized production and distribution, making music arguably more accessible and potentially better able to attract wider audi-ences to shows. Even with the occasional DIY breakout artist, however, I remain unconvinced that economic prospects for most independent performers have improved much if at all.

This has certainly been the case in Salvador, where despite many undeniable changes in music industries, the working musicians I have come to know have by and large remained engaged in most of the same activities that they pursued prior to the dominance of online streaming and the breakup/consolidation of the majors. Those who live from music have continued to do so primarily by performing music on stages in front of audiences, exchanging their musical labor for payment for services rendered. New avenues of distribution and commodification such as websites, streaming services, and social media are typically addenda, albeit perhaps increasingly important ones, to the same old labors. Likewise, being on the street, making and receiving recommendations, *canjas*, and in-person invocations of QI have remained crucial aspects of working to work even as Facebook, Spotify, YouTube, Twitter, Instagram, and crowdsourcing sites have provided and for some, necessitated, new approaches to pursuing careers in music.

So what of the future? This book has focused primarily on how a particular group of musical workers in Salvador navigated their careers during a period defined roughly by the rise and subsequent fall of Lula's Partido dos Trabalhadores (Workers' Party)—that is, between 2002 and 2014, with a concentration of attention to the period between 2004 and 2007. Return trips as well as phone and Skype conversations and emails up until the present suggest that general patterns of internexus and intergenre flexibility within a macrostructure defined by an annual cycle of music and musical work overarched by racialized musical sensibilities have continued. Evident in my ongoing contact with working musicians such as Farofa, Edni, Laurinha, Luciano Salvador Bahia, and several others is that the economic climates of the circuits continue to ebb and flow; employers appear, vanish, and change strategies; and ensemble nexuses form and end.

A more widely apparent point of change holding tremendous implications for Bahian musicians and audiences has been the expansion of São João. Initially decried for its overt commercialization ("carnivalization"), the magnitude of expansion was affirmed in two articles in *A Tarde* (Leonelli 2013 and Quitéria 2013) that proclaimed that the *festas juninas* had surpassed Carnaval in money earned and visitors attracted. The welcome implication for many Bahian musicians is that São João will likely remain a viable and perhaps improving source of employment.[5] More ambivalent for many is that strong associations with *música nordestina* rather than *música baiana* are holding, as are related hierarchies of esteem. In 2019, several interlocutors complained passionately about the increased presence of *arrocha* at June celebrations. While I saw no indication that accordions and *zabumbas* were destined for obsolescence, I did attend several *forrós* at which large crowds clearly enjoyed singing and dancing to this continuously controversial genre of Bahian music.

Bahian music's main stage and Bahia's most famous event, Carnaval, is not stagnant either. The *camarotization* that I first heard criticized in the early 2000s has shown no signs of abatement, impinging on spaces of free participation and arguably catering to a large, non-Bahian audience at the expense of locals. I am hesitant to posit causality, but in 2014 I heard more non-Bahian artists and genres than I had in the past. Along with the widening gap between stars and local performers that has long been decried by independent musicians, the implication is a further loss of opportunities for maximizing the economic possibilities of the Carnaval circuit peak.

These threats to *baianos'* participation in Bahian Carnaval have not gone either unnoticed or unchallenged, however. For example, a new initiative called Furdunço was begun in 2014 to "revive the 'traditional' celebration with *blocos* without cords and artists closer to the public" (http://carnavalsalvadorbahia .com.br/furdunco-programacao-nos-circuitos, accessed December 9, 2018, my translation). Farofa is among the local, independent musicians who have found work in this alternative space (though local political shifts saw him excluded in 2020). Several *axé* and *pagode* stars have also held parades on the main circuits during the official event without a corded-off area around their *trio* for an exclusive *bloco*, in effect returning Carnaval to the local *povo* (and providing themselves with effective PR).

In spite of other changes, *axé* and *pagode* still reign supreme during Carnaval, and they continue to define the event and Bahian music in general even as members of the cultural elite continue to express disapproval (except during the Carnaval celebration, that is). But *pagode* stars Psirico's 2014 Carnaval hit, "Lepo Lepo," and *arrocha*'s apparent comeback also point to other changes, which, again, have generated a fair bit of debate as well as opportunity. Beyond a simple resurgence of a divisive genre, *arrocha* crossed over between circuits in a manner I had not seen before, claiming space in all three. This multi-circuit-use potential provided employment opportunities for a number of local musicians.

As increased permeability between circuits suggests, the years have seen occasional breaks with the orthodoxies of Bahian musical practice and sensibilities. A few additional examples are Farofa's statement that *axé* is bad music well played, the pursuit and middle-class popularity of Laurinha's MemoriAxé projects, and participants at street parties in (primarily Black) popular neighborhoods saying they had nothing against *pagode*. On the other hand, Farofa did not concede that *axé* is good music, and the (good) musicians who play it well continue to be lauded for their knowledge of MPB, samba, jazz, and the like; Laurinha's *axé* is the *axé* of the past; and the Afro-Bahians who told me that they had *nada contra pagode* also told me that it was not appropriate for the event they were attending when we had the conversation. Perhaps more importantly, MPB still reigns hegemonic as quality Brazilian music par excellence, in no discernable way surrendering its discursive power in the construction and maintenance of musical cultural capital in the Scenes and in Salvador more broadly.

Interestingly, the one context in which I have seen Bahian music accorded more respect has been outside of Bahia. Recently, I'm told, middle-class youth in Rio de Janeiro have been hosting and attending *axé* parties, during which Bahian music is featured. I have also spoken with several Brazilians (not *baianos*) living in Toronto who were more generous toward *axé* and *pagode*, and I saw several sing enthusiastically with *axé* classics in a Toronto Brazilian restaurant. I believe aesthetic distance informs all of this in no small measure. Brazilian immigrants in North America, many of whom are middle class (see Margolis 1994), and bourgeois youth in Rio, are far enough away from the intimacy of Bahian culture that they are free to claim it with plausible deniability. Whether or not their distant embrace will affect sentiments toward Bahian music at home remains to be seen.

Another avenue of national and international recognition of music from Bahia has been much more widely noted and locally significant: the 2006 designation of Bahian *samba de roda* as a UNESCO Masterpiece of the Intangible Heritage of Humanity. The result, I believe, has been a kind of Bahian reclaiming of samba, which I was told repeatedly on initial trips was "from Rio." Though it was rarely difficult to find samba performances in Salvador from the outset of my fieldwork, most that I attended drew heavily on Rio styles. Following UNESCO, there has been a notable amplification of opportunities for audible and paid performances of Bahian versions of Brazil's national music and dance, *samba de roda* and an urban variant, *samba junino*.[6] An afternoon on the Campo Grande Carnaval Circuit is dedicated to samba (local and national); *trio elétrico* parades featuring Bahian sambas and *sambadeiros* have been held during São João; and, as I have noted, Farofa has in the last several years established himself as the leader of a busy samba nexus, which although leaning on Rio-style samba, nevertheless expresses a particular Bahian *cara*.

Despite these changes that suggest greater comfort with the intimacy of Bahian Blackness in Bahian music, little else provides compelling evidence of a radical reconfiguration of long-standing musical sensibilities. Harmonic elaboration, poetic texts, and complex arrangements worthy of contemplation (or purchase for home listening) have remained strong as the primary measures of musical quality while cosmopolitanism or conversely, folk authenticity, continue to provide cultural capital even when the sounds themselves might not. Mastery of these competences, or musics demanding them, and performed associations with genres and people thusly esteemed are, likewise, holding fast in their centrality in the ways that working musicians take positions in the Scenes and live from music. Yet thousands if not millions of people continue to dance and sing enthusiastically to Bahian music, suggesting that it is hardly as disposable as distancing discourse might otherwise suggest.

WHERE ARE THEY NOW? BAHIAN MUSICIANS AND THE *LONGUE DURÉE*

Although I have lost touch with some of the musicians I have discussed, perhaps most significantly, Jorge Elaíde Gois, what remains clear from the many others with whom I have been able to remain in contact over the years is that nearly all of them have continued to make music, with most maintaining it as a central facet of their work lives. However, exemplifying their flexibility and the flexibility necessary to sustain a career, musical or otherwise, few if any are doing now exactly what they were doing when we met. Rather, all of them have navigated ups and downs, and various deviations in and from their musical pathways. Some have continued to work primarily on stages or in studios but in other capacities and/or locations; others refocused their activities to the classroom or teaching studio; and a few have shifted the basis of their livelihood to more conventional work, while still pursuing music avocationally.

In addition to Márcia Castro, who met with her highest level of success by leaving Salvador, others such as Ximbinha have parlayed nonlocal experiences into higher levels of career advancement. After several years of limited success, the guitarist and his wife eventually disbanded Makueto and he accepted a position supporting Angolan pop star Yuri da Cunha. The family left and subsequently returned to Salvador, where among other things, Ximbinha worked again with Farofa in his then nascent samba project. His international exposure, however, facilitated a connection with MPB star Seu Jorge, with whom he has performed for the last several years. More locally, he has made appearances with Laurinha on her MemoriAxé shows and contributed to a Santana tribute and other new projects with a new network of musicians.

Another interesting and somewhat surprising turn was taken by Eugênio, the guitarist-principal from Funk 'n' Roll. For the last ten or so years he has been playing guitar with a Bahian country music band, Seu Maxixe, which has capitalized on the expansion of the São João circuit. At the leading edge of the surging audibility in Bahia of *música sertaneja* (driven by *sertanejo universitario* in São Paulo and the return of *arrocha*), Eugênio's band, in which he is a *socio*, effectively found a niche that situates them as country enough for the June circuit, without limiting themselves to it or trying to force a Bahian face on Forró.

Other collaborators, for instance, Luciano Salvador Bahia, have continued apace with their locally based careers, maintaining similar work patterns and enjoying increased successes built on past efforts and resultant resources. In addition to composing the song that Márcia Castro placed on a *telenovela*, he got his own recording contract with a small Rio-based label—one with significant distribution resources. He has remained in Salvador, where he has built an in-home studio where he continues composing and recording music for his MPB projects as well as film and theater soundtracks. He also uses the studio to produce other artists, a continuation of the freelance musical direction that he has followed for years. He also continues to perform live on occasion, maintaining his focus on MPB and samba, and occasionally hiring Farofa. While the economic and cultural capital he has amassed over the years is significant, perhaps even more important to Luciano's career heights and sustainability has been his professional network, his social capital.

And then there is Farofa. His work has also continued very much as it did for thirty-odd years, lending services to a variety of nexuses, often involving the same people with whom he has worked for the duration. Yet even more satisfying for him—and the focus of most of our recent conversations—has been the slow but rather consistent building up of his samba project, Samba de Farofa.

One reason for his satisfaction is that, ever since I have known him, he has looked toward being part of/having his own samba group as a career aspiration. I have seen his various attempts to pursue this goal too, but owing to the demands of earning a living as a lender of services, the capital necessary to get the project off the ground, the uncertainties of seeing it through, and the less than central placement of samba in the Scenes, most ventures were short-lived. Arguably, the post-UNESCO renewed interest in samba in Salvador provided the right moment for Samba de Farofa. That is hard to prove empirically, but it is clear that the resources of various kinds that Farofa has earned and invested over the years have begun to pay off. The confluence of timing, accumulated capitals, and legwork has led to nonseasonal circuit jobs in clubs, restaurants, and at private events, as well as appearances at Carnaval.

As has been the case throughout his career, flexibility has also been key to

Farofa's accomplishments. As the *dono* of the group, he took on numerous production responsibilities that he could leave to others in other contexts, and he has invested a great deal of his own social, cultural, and economic capital in the project. As a result, it is very much an expression of his musical *cara* despite basing the repertoire largely on well-known tunes. In keeping with the Signifyin(g) sensibilities in the Scenes, the group reworks MPB favorites as sambas, adding his longtime collaborator Dino's accordion as a featured instrument. They take a similar approach to rereading classic sambas, thereby providing a novel take on national music. Their *releituras* also leave little doubt as to the group's Bahianness, an identification that Farofa has always embraced. Enculturated listeners will likely hear their *suingue baiano*; but even the minimally informed can note their use of *timbal*, a distinctly Bahian drum, which is ubiquitous in Bahian Carnaval music and scarcely heard in the more Rio-oriented repertoire that is Samba de Farofa's foundation.

Perhaps most significant about Samba de Farofa is that, whereas Farofa's income has for years been dependent on him exchanging, or more accurately, investing, his labor time in performance as a lender of services, he is the sole principal in Samba de Farofa. In fact, in a recent conversation, he told me that this extends beyond being a musician-leader. With the statement, "é minha" (it's mine), he elaborated that he was well on his way to establishing a core lineup and a network of reliable substitutes to the degree that he did not have to perform in order to earn. Rather, he could, if he chose, book the band, handle production details, send his lenders of services to do the job, and earn the lion's share of the profit. In the years that I have known him, Farofa has moved from being primarily a musician-laborer—a very entrepreneurial one—to laboring as a music capitalist. He continues to lend services and teach since, like any nexus, Samba de Farofa alternates busy and slower periods. But he can now be more selective in the work he does for others provided he maintains his extensive network and his peers' goodwill. One payoff is that this affords him more time with his new granddaughter.

Another unseen, but crucial benefit of Samba de Farofa is that it has put its leader well on his way to being able to maintain some income into retirement. He still has plenty of years of active performance left,[7] but in the past, he lacked sources of revenue to provide a livelihood should he not be able to perform, be it by circumstances or choice. Indeed, he had little set aside in savings and, as an informal employee on most jobs, no access to unemployment benefits. Furthermore, as an independent artist earning below a certain income level, he was not required to contribute to *Prevedência*, the Brazilian pension system. While increasing his take-home pay, this left him minimally vested in the national fund, with few if any rights to retirement income. If not for Samba de Farofa, he would have been almost entirely reliant on what little savings he had, and like so many other musicians in similar circumstances, his family, as a means of support if he were to stop performing for any reason.

Indeed, owing to the economics of musical labor, how to survive in retirement is a pressing concern for numerous musicians, but one that I have discussed only with Laurinha. While she sounded quite serious when she first mentioned it to me in 2014, she continued working in part because MemoriAxé and related projects reinvigorated her career and her legacy to some degree. Her ability and desire to keep working as a singer remains to be seen, as does her ability to stop, though her newfound acting interest may well provide a bridge to the future. We can only hope that should she decide to or need to retire from music, her family, past earnings, and proven flexibility and industriousness over the years, exemplified by her emergent career as an actress, will be enough to provide for her. Certainly her socioprofessional network has supported her well.

Another ongoing aspect of living from music in Salvador, as is the case in other scenes, is working musicians complementing their performance-based earning with teaching. This has been the case for Josehr, Roberval, and Farofa since I have known them—I initially met Farofa when he was recommended to me as a percussion teacher. Others including Pastel and Ximbinha have ventured in and out of teaching, both privately and in schools, over the years.

Whereas Ximbinha moved more definitively away from teaching and toward higher-level performance work, others have left high-profile jobs and taken on more teaching, usually alongside local jobbing. As I have mentioned, Edni left A Zorra several years ago. With numerous contacts in place in Salvador, and a solid reputation as a drummer capable of performing a range of music, he has been able to work as lender of services in the year-round circuits. However, thanks to his undergraduate training in music, he has also been able to secure teaching positions at local schools. In addition, he coauthored a drum method, for which he puts on drum clinics around Brazil. Much of what Edni has accomplished has been facilitated by the fact that during his tenure with an *axé* band, he carefully cultivated relationships and a musical work self that prevented him from being pigeonholed and instead highlighted his versatility and knowledge of multiple and esteemed musics.

In addition to parlaying past training and experience into new avenues of musical work, both in teaching and performance, several musicians I have discussed have returned to school as a way to do so. In addition to Son and Luciano, who completed doctorates in music theory and ethnomusicology, respectively, and took university positions, Roberval capitalized on an initiative to train teachers circa 2008. His intent was to work toward full-time employment in local schools and focus his performing and composition activities on projects that were more musically appealing to him. For a variety of reasons, his progress through his program has been slow, and he has continued to support himself performing, much as he did when we met. As of 2019, he was still pursuing his studies and living from music. Josehr too returned to post-secondary training, completing a second bachelor's degree in lyrical voice. This went hand in hand with a shift away from popular music and into several local choirs and opera productions. His work as a music teacher continues too, but less often with the municipally sponsored programs in which he was seasonally involved when we met and now, on a regular basis with a school for the blind in the Lower City. There he rejoined Katia, one of the background singers from Patua, exemplifying the entangled web of the Scenes. As still another example of the continued importance of social capital, Josehr and Katia brought Farofa into the fold at the school, a job that gave him both increased income stability and tremendous job satisfaction, at least for a time. Unfortunately, he was let go from the position because he did not have a university degree.

Josehr and several other close collaborators have also nurtured career pathways in other facets of the music industries or outside of them altogether. Following Salsalitro, Junior forayed into music production while still lending services to a dance band. At the same time, he pursued a real estate license, worked as a realtor, and subsequently pursued training in architectural engineering. In a January 2019 email, however, he affirmed that he is always playing drums and that he recently jammed with the members of Funk 'n' Roll. Like Junior, Pastel has slowly moved away from playing music full time. As far back as 2007, he was taking classes in graphic design while he supported himself as a drummer and drum teacher. As his graphics career stabilized, he concentrated more of his labor time to design and established himself as less reliant on music for income. Indicative of the importance he still places on music and drums specifically as part of his identity, his online name is dadrummapastel. In a more uniquely Bahian parallel pathway, Josehr has continued his work as a Candomblé *pai de santo*, establishing a *terreiro* just outside of the city.

Common among all of these musicians' pathways is an ongoing ability to utilize their resources and skills flexibly and tactically as needed and possible. Evident too is their ability and willingness to develop new competences and seek out training in pursuit of something different, better, or at times, necessary for survival. Also common to all of their stories is the importance of their networks, which have opened doors for opportunities and on occasion, provided a basis of support to survive tough times. And they keep making music.

NEW MUSICAL CAREERS

In terms of an analysis of musical labor broader than I have provided in this book, it is important to reiterate that the musicians I have been discussing and with whom I am best acquainted are for all intents and purposes part of a particular generation of working musicians in a very particular place. Most were already established on the Scenes when we met, hence their selection for inclusion in the initial study. On various occasions I did encounter a few performers trying to break in—for instance, *pagode* bassist Vando and several other young musicians who circulated in and out of the nexuses in which my central collaborators worked. But my focus has primarily remained on the musicians with whom I developed the closest relationships, moving with them as their positions in the Scenes changed. This mobile lens has strongly shaped my perspectives on musical work, the Scenes themselves, and changes to both.

Nevertheless, the audible and visible shifts I have seen and heard as well as the new musicians I saw working to establish themselves with my particular focus suggest that there might be even more significant changes in how people in Salvador live from music than I have perceived among my closest collaborators. To be sure, new faces have emerged at various levels in each of the circuits, and their practices likely inform emergent sounds, sensibilities, tactics for making do, and perhaps even dominant strategies as well. For instance, writing by scholars such as Hracs (2016) about new modes of musical work in North America such as online marketing point to the probability that the generations of musicians following people such as Farofa, Laurinha, Ximbinha, Márcia Castro, and Luciano Salvador Bahia will make even greater use of new technologies and forms of social media.

Another marked shift even among the generation of musicians with which I worked that might portend wider shifts in the pathways and meanings of living from music is the degree to which they have diversified their activities within and beyond music. Indeed, what may be changing most of all in Salvador and in late capitalism in many places is the way that musicians think about music as a career. While Farofa from time to time suggested that if he were unable to support himself and his family performing music that he liked, he would pursue another line of work, he never made such a move. He did, however, take jobs other than performing to fill in gaps in his income until things picked up. Then he quickly returned to performing and teaching. Unlike Farofa, however, several of his peers who seemed equally committed to living from music did make successful, and apparently satisfying transitions out of being full-time players. Increasing comfort with decidedly mixed, musical and nonmusical ways of earning a living is exemplified by musicians such as Pastel and Junior as well as Zê Mário, who left a headline-level *pagode* job to teach Portuguese and perform samba and *choro* locally, and Márcio, a percussionist from Banda Beijo, who started a trucking firm and occasionally returns to perform with various projects. As much as music and work remain important axes of their identities—none of these people is any less devoted to their music or any less proud of their nonmusical work—music as a sole profession seems to be less important. As gig economies take hold worldwide and increased numbers of workers take on multiple job functions, perhaps newer generations of musicians will view living from music in a manner different from the majority I have discussed here and as I did when I was formulating this study and before, when I tried to live from music. Indeed, while job multiplicity might be new and disconcerting in career paths in locations that were once defined by specialization and stability, flexible work and related precarity in music (and in the Global South) is the old normal. Music at the center of a wide array of jobs in some form or fashion was the constant. That centrality rather than the array may be what is changing most.

While I haven't yet pursued this possibility and related questions to any great extent in Salvador, I do have a nascent sense of them in North America. Los Angeles studio legend and founder of the Los Angeles College of Music, Ralph Humphrey, told me in an interview conducted for another project that most of his students see music as one of several things they will do to earn their living. Moreover, he noted that many of them will not monetize their music making in the same ways that people like him (and my Bahian collaborators) have. Another music educator friend who taught at Musicians Institute, a storied music vocational school in Hollywood, California, told me that many of his students aspired not to play in bands, make records, or perform on stages, but instead to have sponsored YouTube channels in which they do everything from precise covers of hit songs to transcription and analysis of other musicians' perfor-

Jorge Farofa at Carnaval 2014, working with Samba de Farofa
and living from music in Salvador.

mances. As Bahian professional musician turned ethnomusicologist Luciano
Caroso's 2010 dissertation illustrates, such practices have been in place in Brazil
for some time too.

For now, though, most aspects of musical lives in Salvador, from Bahian
Carnaval and its related events to the São João circuit to the wide and changing
array of nonseasonal performance venues suggest that live music in Salvador
will not easily give way to the internet or other avenues of professional musicking. And many of the musicians who I, along with countless tourists and locals,
have had the good fortune to hear on the job continue to make and indeed live
from music. I suspect that I am not alone in hoping that they will continue to
do so in some form or fashion for many more sets to come.

NOTES

INTRODUCTION *Mystique, Myths, and Materialities of Professional Music Making and Bahia*

1. *Blocos afro* are Afrocentric organizations that emerged in the 1970s in response to the frequent exclusion of dark-skinned people from prestigious Carnaval clubs. Samba-reggae is their signature rhythm (see Crook 1993 and Guerreiro 2000).

2. It is the norm in Brazil to refer to people by their first names or a nickname. I follow custom by referring to people in the manner I heard most frequently, using full names to distinguish those sharing similar monikers.

3. The Bahian guitar is a five-string, solid-body electrified modification of the *bandolim* (Brazilian mandolin) that was invented by the creators of the *trio elétrico* for use during Carnaval parades.

4. I wrote little more, but noted that they made heavy use of their drum machine and performed the song "Fame."

5. I would subsequently learn that lunch is typically the largest meal of the day—meaning those of us eating full meals at North American dinnertime stood out as tourists against a few (Brazilian) patrons who were having drinks and eating lightly.

6. As Bahia's capital and largest city, Salvador often serves as a synecdoche for the entire state. This metonymy is supported by a historical tendency to refer to the city as "Bahia."

7. *Orixás* are deities in Afro-Brazilian spiritual practice, Candomblé. The Dique do Tororó is a small man-made lake next to a venerable hillside neighborhood, Tororó.

8. I use the terms work and labor somewhat interchangeably even as scholars such as Hannah Arendt (1958) have parsed a distinction. Arendt links art with the durability and meaningfulness she sees in work, which she distinguishes from labor's necessity and transience. This characterization betrays an investment in art's autonomy, a notion I aim to counter. That said, many musicians in Salvador were involved with musical activities that were effortful but *less directly* tied to economic need and thus more akin to Arendt's "work." On the other hand, many who took musical jobs out of financial necessity found

pleasure and fulfillment in activities that she might view as labor. This points to the hazy, problematic, and ultimately deeply personal nature of this distinction, a recurrent issue in the book. See Hesmondhalgh and Baker (2011) on pleasure and self-satisfaction in creative labor.

9. I use the terms "working musician" and "working player" somewhat interchangeably as glosses for local professionals rather than stars, with the latter usually reserved for instrumentalists. "Musical worker" refers to anyone who works within the music industries.

10. Here I allude to anthropologist Ruth Finnegan's landmark ([1989] 2007) study of amateur musicians.

11. For more on the *malandro*, see Shaw (1999) and Sandroni (2001).

12. Ironically, as their stories remind us, many stars only make it after cutting their teeth locally.

13. As ideas developed by European scholars and firmly rooted in Western epistemologies, it is crucial to account for the particularities of the Bahian context for their application, which I have attempted to do. It is also important to note that these epistemologies and related politics continue to underpin music practice, everyday life, and scholarship about both in Brazil as lingering effects of colonialism and ongoing exchanges with the Global North.

14. My use of the plural is intended to describe a composite formation while also evoking the overlap between the more discrete genre-specific (sub)scenes that comprise it. Bahians frequently use the Portuguese terms for scene, *cena* and *cenário*, as well.

15. I use the term sensibilities in a manner akin to what Appadurai (1986) might call "regimes of value," but in a way that accounts for the embodied way that participants in various scenes know and feel "their" music "to be" as a matter of habitus.

16. Brazilian violonista and education scholar Marco Túlio (Costa 2017) is notable for his application of Bourdieu's notions of cultural captial, habitus, and field in his study of a group of Brazilian guitarists who brought legitimcacy to the instrument and those who played it in a mid-century northeastern Brazilian city.

17. The term "post-Fordism" is often used in conjunction with shifts in labor and manufacturing practices toward flexible employment and niche rather than mass production. With awareness of scholars such as Wood (1989) and Doogan (2009) who problematize the term as overstating the shift, my use of it is to merely acknowledge the post-1980s tendencies toward "portfolio" careers and away from stable, long-term employment, strict divisions of labor, specialization, and concentrated knowledge among managers (see Sennett 2000). Regardless of debates over the spread and significance of flexible labor in more conventional industrial and service sectors, musicians in Salvador, without a doubt, labor under flexible, and I would argue, post-Fordist conditions.

18. Mould's study is focused squarely in the U.S. and Europe.

19. De Certeau's language, while perhaps creating an overly neat distinction, is useful

for calling attention to the relative positions of people engaged in quotidian practice. Relationality is also present in Bourdieu's theorizing, but his universal application of the term "strategies" leaves open the question of specific power imbalances in a given interaction. De Certeau's ideas also aim to highlight flexibility and active agency that he saw lacking in Bourdieu's work (see De Certeau 1984, 52–60), as well as "minor" practices that are less important in Foucault's theorizing of power owing to his focus on "certain foregrounded practices organizing . . . normative institutions" (ibid. 48).

20. Britain is an especially popular location for studies of musical labor and is the focus of monographs by Cottrell (2004), Ehrlich (1985), and Rohr (2001), as well as a (2018) collection edited by Golding.

21. Though not a scholarly monograph, Brazilian pianist and producer Benjamim Taubkin's (2011) collection of interviews with a cross-genre, cross-generational collection of Brazilian musicians is a welcome addition to the literature on musicians' labor. In 2019, Requião published a collection of interviews with Brazilian women who have forged careers as musicians.

22. Noteworthy examples include: Wallis and Malm (1984), Frith (1987), Daley (1998), Negus (1999), Pecknold (2007), Suisman (2009), Scales (2012), Tucker (2013); apropos of Brazil, see articles and chapters by Goldschmitt (2014), De Marchi (2015), and Trotta (2015), as well as Goldschmitt's (2019) monograph.

23. On industries of cultural production more broadly, see Hesmondhalgh (2007) and Hesmondhalgh and Baker (2011), both of which attend to the work practices and related perspectives of a variety of workers.

24. By focusing their work on female musicians Tucker, van Nieuwkerk, Santanna, and Requião are able to engage at length with issues of professional opportunity and constraint women face. Unlike them, any explanations I could offer would be problematically speculative—a problem overcome by Bates, who is able to relate the paucity of women working in Turkish recording studios to issues of space. The variety of work contexts I encountered, however, left me little more than recognition of the weight of historical tendencies and issues of social capital—men tended to hire and recommend other men for instrumental work as an assumed norm. Further, few musicians I met, male or female, queried the status quo. Finally, my focus on musicians who were working rather than those trying to break into the Scenes meant that I did not meet female instrumentalists who were trying but unable to live from music and that I did encounter numerous female singers who had done so successfully.

25. Ickes (2013, 245 n2) traces the appellation "Black Rome" to the 1930s and credits a Candomblé spiritual leader with its popularity. When discussing Salvador and Bahia, North American scholars have used descriptors such as "the heart of African Brazil" (Browning 1995) and "the epicenter of Afro-Brazilian culture" (Dunn 2001) among others.

26. Following recommendations made by the National Association of Black Journalists,

I capitalize the words Black, White, and Brown (https://www.nabj.org/page/styleguide, accessed January 14, 2021). I also capitalize related terms, in particular, Blackness and Whiteness, not to reify any of these constructs, but rather to recognize their complex politics and profound implications for countless people across time and place. Finally, there is significant and productive debate over capitalizing the term White. My decision to do so is rooted in the project of disrupting Whiteness as an unmarked category and recognizing that it too is a *racial* construct. While I am concerned that my choice may resemble practices deployed by racist groups, my rationale and politics are opposed to theirs. In this, I align myself with Kwame Anthony Appiah (2020, https://www.theatlantic .com/ideas/archive/2020/06/time-to-capitalize-blackand-white/613159/, accessed January 14, 2021), who writes, "If the capitalization of *white* became standard among anti-racists, the supremacists' gesture would no longer be a provocative defiance of the norm and would lose all force."

27. This topic is addressed in numerous studies, for instance Sherriff (2001) and Telles (2004). In keeping with practice in Brazil, I do not capitalize color designations or the term "*afro*" in Portugese. This is consistent with the convention of using lower-case letters when writing color designations for people as well as other identifiers such as nationalities that would be capitalized in English.

28. Understandably, Brazilian scholars have been attentive to issues of music and race. See for example, de Andrade ([1928] 1972), Alvarenga ([1947] 1960), Tinhorão (1988), Risério (1991), Lopes (1992), Sansone and Teles dos Santos (1997), Reily (1997, in English), Carvalho (1999), and Guerreiro (2000), as well as many others.

29. A similar mapping was applied to Brazil as a whole during conversations in North America. I also noticed that people from São Paulo think of Rio's residents in much the same way that many in the Global North think about Brazilians and nearly everyone I met seems to think about *baianos*.

30. Livio Sansone (2003) provocatively suggests that stereotypes about the laziness of Black men are rarely heard in Salvador. This has some resonance with my experiences— Black men were not necessarily *singled out* for having a poor work ethic. However, I suspect that this has more to do with the slipperiness of Blackness in the context of extensive mixing and its prominence in notions of Bahian-ness than with a rejection of common stereotypes about Black people's attitudes toward work.

31. I use the phrases "visibly of African descent" and "of visible African descent" to acknowledge the complexities of racial identification in Brazil. I also use the terms African-descended, Afro-Brazilian, Afro-Bahian, and Black, all of which are employed by *baianos*, often with slightly different implications. Importantly, parts of Bahia's interior have higher percentages of people whose bodies reflect Indigenous-European heritage. Yet the audibility and visibility of African-ness in Salvador overshadows such diversity and comes to stand in for the entire state.

32. In February 2016, the Brazilian Institute of Geography and Statistics (IBGE) estimated Salvador's unemployment rate at 12.6 percent in comparison with Rio's 5.2 percent and São Paulo's 9.5 percent. In 2010, Salvador's unemployment rate was estimated by IBGE to be 11.1 percent. *Baianos* I spoke with were uniform in asserting that these numbers are consistently underestimated. In 2005–2006, many put the actual number above 20 percent despite IBGE's estimate of 15 percent.

33. The term for such neighborhoods more commonly used nationally and in scholarship is *favela*.

34. Jair Bolsonaro, 2018 Brazilian president-elect, April 2017; quoted in *The Guardian*, September 6, 2018, https://www.theguardian.com/world/2018/sep/06/jair-bolsonaro-brazil-tropical-trump-who-hankers-for-days-of-dictatorship, accessed December 11, 2018.

35. A small portion of the key scholarship on race in Brazil includes: Bacelar (1999), Butler (2000), Hanchard (1994), Hasenbalg (1999), Marx (1998), Sansone (2003), Sheriff (2001), Skidmore (1992), Telles (2004), and Twine (2001). Scholars such as Collins (2015), de Santo Pinto (2010), Eakin (2017), Ickes (2013), Romo (2010), Sovik (2009), and Teles dos Santos (2006) are but a few of many who continue to contribute to the discussion.

36. See Sheriff (2001) for a particularly convincing discussion of this point.

37. The increasing use of the term *afro-decendente*, as well as affirmative action legislation passed since the turn of the new millennium reserving cherished, free-of-charge spaces in federal universities for students of African ancestry, are two examples of the reappropriation of hereditary racial identification. Both have generated controversy.

38. For a troubling account of this dynamic focused on Salvador's Historic District, see Collins (2015).

39. I did hear musicians speak of "Black music" in English on a few occasions. These references were typically to nonlocal Afro-diasporic musics such as reggae, rap, and especially older R&B exemplified by James Brown.

40. Accounting for the various influences, African, European, and Indigenous, on Brazilian music has been a central concern for scholars and journalists writing on the topic from de Andrade in 1928 (1972) until the present.

41. Foucault (e.g., 1979, 1989) notes that self-regulation engendered through knowledge can become a nonreflexive part of a subject's predispositions for action. In utilizing Foucault's and Bourdieu's ideas, I follow scholars such as Wachs and Chase (2013, 115), embracing the notion that, despite tensions and contradictions in their approaches to theorizing power and subjectivity, "the combination of Foucault and Bourdieu can be done in a productive way, specifically combining Foucault's insights on discourse and Bourdieu's use of practice."

42. *Farofa* is a staple of local cuisine made from manioc flour mixed with food renderings.

43. For several, especially those without strong, usually family-based support net-

works, this made the cancellation of public events due to the 2020 Covid-19 pandemic especially troubling.

44. The reverence paid to MPB across classes and at times independent of active participation points to the importance of discourse in the construction of the cultural capital it can provide. This is a cautious step away from Bourdieu's emphasis on homologies between variously classed people and particular kinds of cultural goods. Peterson and Kern's (1996) article on omnivore taste is an early effort to wrestle with questions of cultural prestige when any one practice is consumed by people from many different class backgrounds and when people of a particular class consume a broad range of practices. Attention to discursive mappings of quality, further, helps reconcile the changing notions of cultural capital astutely addressed in Taylor (2016).

45. Forró refers to a complex of related music and dance practices. Following Fernandes (2005), I use the capitalized form to refer to the umbrella term and the lower case to refer to the subgenre(s) and eponymous events that feature them.

46. Patterns of audience participation in relation to generation were more difficult to discern. Some events seemed to favor certain age groups, usually in relation to the specific artist or venue rather than genre. I saw the same types of music patronized by generationally mixed audiences in some spaces and specific age groups in others. Based on conversations I did gather that younger listeners might hold somewhat more open attitudes toward Bahian music than their elders, albeit usually filtered through their race and class identification and politics.

47. Though genre and venue shaped audience participation to a degree, active singing and dancing were the norm during musical events that might seem "presentational" (Turino 2008) owing to their use of proscenium stages, microphones, curtains, lighting, etc. that distinguish performers from their audience and thus inhibit their participation. See Packman (2010) for an extended discussion of the politics of participation in Salvador.

48. This builds on Crook's (2005) discussion of "the aesthetics of participation" in Brazilian music, which addresses the contours of audience singing and dancing rather than their effect on musicians' production.

49. All quotations from interlocutors are my translations from their Portuguese.

50. In many instances these terms had *brega* (lowbrow or kitsch) connotations. This word and its use, however, are complex (see Araújo 1988). For instance, some members of the middle class enthusiastically consume music said to be *brega*. I heard *dor to cotovelo* most commonly applied to *música sertaneja* (Brazilian country music, see Dent 2009), though it was also applied to other genres, usually with lowbrow associations.

51. Popular music participation was much more commonly referenced in performances of elite identities than Western art music, which nevertheless carried a significant amount of cultural capital. That popular genres are so central to elite identities provides an important deviation from Bourdieu's ideas, which show little interest in popular cul-

ture and situate upper-class habituses in relation to "high art" as well as in the tastes of older generations. Several scholars have subsequently emphasized how notions central to popular and/or youth-oriented practices such as "hipness" (Thornton 1996), the "the hip and the cool" (Taylor 2016), and "aesthetic cosmopolitanism" (Regev 2013) have become central to how participants in contemporary fields of cultural production vie for positions.

52. Brazilian ethnomusicologist Carla Brunet has reminded me that part of the emphasis on poetic lyrics stems from the practice, undertaken by MPB stars such as Caetano Veloso and Chico Buarque, of veiling critiques of the government during the dictatorship.

53. As exemplified by Cusick (1994), music scholars have rightly critiqued the gendered implications of the mind/body duality. However, the racial implications of Cartesian epistemology were explicitly and frequently discussed in Salvador.

54. Noting the racialized aspect of the cultural capital associated with contemplative music in Salvador is an important nuance for Bourdieu's ideas, which, despite their utility for understanding local musical practice, have little to say about a matter that is central to everyday life there.

55. Ulhôa's (1995) chapter also notes this tendency of looking outward for higher musical quality throughout Brazil.

56. It is entirely possible that Forró's biggest stars earn wages comparable with the biggest names in Bahian music. However, few of these artists are based in Bahia.

57. For a foundational economic study of wage determination, see Hamermesh (1986), which also addresses the implications of substitutability.

58. I interviewed the president of the OMB in 2005 and he admitted the weakness of the organization, laying most of the blame on musicians who undermined it by refusing to join and working for low wages.

59. See Tsioulakis (2011), DeWitt (2009), and Taylor (2015) on the building of social ties through music.

60. QI is a pun on the Portuguese word for IQ, *quociente de inteligência*.

ONE *Sounds and Circuits of Musical Work
in the Salvador Scenes*

1. *Afoxés* are another type of Afro-centric Carnaval organization that predates the *blocos afro* and typically parade to the Candomblé rhythm, *ijexá*.

2. See Butler (1998, 28–30).

3. These cities, not coincidentally, were also destinations of European immigrants following the abolition of slavery in 1888 and in the early twentieth century.

4. See Skidmore (1998).

5. At the time I was living in Salvador, the city's daily newspaper, *A Tarde* (August 1,

2004, 17), asserted that 92.2 percent of the poorest residents of the RMS were *negro* (Black) while 76.9% of the richest residents were White.

6. IBGE reported in 2010 that 7.3 percent of children between the ages of 10 and 17 in Salvador worked (https://cidades.ibge.gov.br/brasil/ba/salvador/pesquisa/23/23226?deta lhes=true, accessed January 10, 2021).

This is despite national programs that provide free lunches and even small sums of money to families that keep their children in school. See Hall (2006) on Bolsa Familia, the most notable of the federal programs aimed at keeping children from poor families in classrooms. I should add that, while I have found no official statistics on this, I have no doubt that I have seen children younger than ten years old laboring, for instance, as ambulant vendors or street entertainers, at times between cars stopped at traffic lights on main thoroughfares.

7. "Pelourinho" actually refers to a specific plaza within the Historic District where enslaved workers were publically punished (see Collins 2015). Owing to this history, I use "Historic District" despite local practice.

8. A number of high-rise office buildings are concentrated in Comércio. In comparison to similar Upper City structures, they are in a marked state of disrepair.

9. This statistic is from the Gregorio de Mattos website: http://www.culturatododia .salvador.ba.gov.br/vivendo-area.php?cod_area=6, accessed June 19, 2014.

10. Bus fare in Salvador on a *coletivo*, the most inexpensive option, was R$2.80 in 2014. The federally mandated minimum wage at that time was R$724 per month. When I lived in Salvador in 2004–2005, bus fare and the minimum wage were R$1.75 and R$300, respectively. Many workers require several buses to get to work and each leg requires a separate fare.

11. The term "popular neighborhood" (*bairro popular*) is one that was used by several of my collaborators to describe the working-class areas in which they lived.

12. Samba is the staple of Carnaval in Rio and São Paulo, but not in Salvador.

13. Some members of the middle class took a dimmer view of reggae owing to its associations with Afro-centric politics.

14. *Arrocha*'s rise followed long after Araújo's seminal (1988) article on *brega* and is, thus, not addressed in it. However, the term was frequently applied to *arrocha* along with the "lowbrow" connotations and controversies he discusses.

15. *Pagode* was described by some *baianos* to be an urban variant of *samba de roda* before UNESCO's recognition of the rural practice, directly and via *samba duro* (hard samba, see Leme 2003) and *samba junino* (June samba, see Packman 2012, 2014). After 2007 these links were more frequently discussed and emphasized during performances.

16. Interlocutors differed on whether they considered working at private parties playing at night.

17. In recent years the term *musicista*, technically a female-gendered noun, has been used for both female and male musicians in place of the male-gendered term *músico*. However, save one example, I have only experienced this among academics. Moreover, the musicians and music industry workers I spoke with in Bahia have consistently used the term *músico da noite* to refer to performers working in, for example, bars and restaurants. Thus, I follow their local convention.

18. *Músicos da noite* frequently take advantage of seasonal shifts, although some are more restricted in their options owing to their particular professional identities, reputations, and networks. See chapter 5.

19. Pseudonym used at the singer's request.

20. In this instance, "*pagode*" refers to a samba party and music in the Rio/national style, not Bahian *pagode* (see below).

21. Such work was specialized, somewhat limited, and not necessarily the purview of *músicos da noite*. Some cover artists were featured performers in more concert-like "show" settings.

22. Consumption of "quality music" by members of the *povo* was easily overlooked by elite arbiters of taste since it often took place in out-of-the-way locations that they did not frequent. The result is a rather closed system in which "quality" music in upscale venues contributed to their ambiance and appeal; and the upscale audiences of spaces made exclusive by the cost of attending enhanced the cultural capital of the music presented within, even if it was largely ignored.

23. I discuss these types of adaptations in the context of projects aimed toward a more singular, rather than a "functional" musical vision, in chapter 5 (see as well the following section on "Shows" in this chapter).

24. The cognate for concert, *concerto*, was typically reserved for Western art music performances.

25. Gal Costa is a notable Bahian *intérprete*.

26. I have seen numbers comparable to these over the years. See below.

27. Though anyone can attend parades on the official circuits for free, there are also numerous very costly restricted spaces for participation.

28. The literature on Bahian Carnaval and various means of protesting color-based restrictions on access is vast. Key writing includes Risério (1981), Crowley (1986), Dunn (1992), Crook (1993), Godi (1998), and Moura (2001a, 2001b). For an excellent early history of racial tension in Bahian Carnaval, see Butler 1998 (171–82).

29. One apocryphal explanation of the critique implied in the term is that "*axé*" referred to Africa and "music" referred to the U.S., implying there was nothing "Brazilian" about what Bahian artists were producing.

30. There is a fair bit of slippage in the use of the term *pagode*, which can refer to the

Bahian practice, small-group acoustic samba from Rio, a newer romantic variant also from Rio, and a party featuring any kind of samba. However, when most *baianos* used the word "*pagode*" they referenced the Bahian variant, a convention that I follow.

31. See Hinchberger (1999) and Leme (2003).

32. I have encountered a number of different approaches to the *cavaquinho* part, sometimes within the same song. These include creating a more flowing feel by strumming sixteenth-note patterns with one out of four notes per beat muted, using sixteenth-note arpeggios, or emphasizing the samba timeline to create a more conventional (Rio/national) samba feel.

33. This assertion is supported in de Mello Santos (2006). In contrast, Ari Lima (2011) notes that several *pagode* bands have performed at elite clubs and for prestigious *blocos*. My strong sense is that these are the exceptions rather than the norm and involve a very limited number of ensembles. One band in particular, Harmonia do Samba, was consistently cited by musicians and nonmusicians as the only *pagode* group that was "good."

34. As noted by Lima (2011), homophobic critiques of male *pagode* dancers are also common—and though I did not hear many, I did see male heteronormative disavowals of the music: multiple men told me that it was "fine for watching girls dance."

35. The people who carry the rope (*cordistas*) are paid a small wage for their effort, which all too frequently puts them in harm's way. Apologists for the practice defend it noting that many *cordistas* can be seen dancing and singing, citing this as evidence of "popular participation." Others critique the *cordistas* and assert that some take the job as an opportunity to join/instigate fights at the boundary between *bloco* and onlookers. Elite *blocos* have a second truck (*carro de apoio*) that provides restrooms, refreshments, and a place to sit while the procession continues.

36. Children's *blocos* can involve celebrities as well as less prominent, local performers. For example, in 2005 I attended a parade by famed *bloco afro* Ara Ketu performing for the children affiliated with the organization. In 2014, the group Farofa led was hired by a *bloco infantil*, Todo Menino é um Rei (Every Child Is a King), which provided a celebration space for children whose guardians would normally be unable to afford *bloco* participation.

37. As far as I know, such organizations are less present, if not absent from *micaretas*.

38. Typically, rehearsals are not paid and wages are discussed as a fee for the public performance. Since Laurinha assembled her band prior to Carnaval, I consider the rehearsals part of the labor necessary to earn the fee, a perspective expressed by several musicians I spoke with.

39. Some would argue, not necessarily incorrectly, that decreasing space on the street exacerbates the crowding and potential for violence.

40. A third parade route through the Historic District excludes *trios elétricos* and instead features (often amateur) marching bands, neighborhood *blocos*, and the like.

41. Numerous musicians and managers I spoke with told me that getting a song played

on the radio is often a matter of payola *"jabá,"* which severely limits access for all but the best-financed artists.

42. When talking about a then emergent genre, *sertanejo universitario* (university country), in 2014, composer/*violonista* and now ethnomusicologist Luciano Caroso told me that the designation *"universitario"* typically serves as a marker of gentrification of a music that was previously considered lowbrow (personal communication, Salvador, March 2014).

43. See also McCann (2004).

44. See chapter 5 for more on set planning.

TWO *Musical Work Nexuses and Working to Work*

1. My attention to collectives in their efforts to find work as tactical position takings in a field also builds on Bourdieu and De Certeau, both of whose interests focused primarily on the practices of individuals.

As Brinner (2009, 176) notes, network theorists often treat collectives as a single node in a network, a process called punctualization. While I too am punctualizing, I also wish to problematize uncritical punctualization and point out the tensions and rifts that can be overlooked as a result. In this regard, my approach can be seen as a nuance to the network study of 1960s Brazilian popular music done by business administration scholars Charles Kirchbaum and Flávio Carvalho de Vasconcelos (2007), which traces interactions among and between composers and notable artists in the emergence of *bossa nova, Jovem Guarda,* and *Tropicália.* Their work adds useful insights to the history of the genres' development in relation to the artists' efforts to distinguish themselves and their music in the market (see also Belavitti 2020). Absent from their analysis is attention to the musicians who supported artists discussed and who, as I argue below, can profoundly shape the sound of the music.

2. See also Bates (2016), Hitchens (2014), and Meintjes (2003).

3. Sarah Cohen's (1991) study of Liverpudlian rock culture also provides useful perspectives on this.

4. For useful critiques of the art world concept, see Garcia Canclini (1995) and Brinner (2009).

5. Cottrell (2004: 83) similarly describes groups with whom freelance classical musicians in London work as "nodal points within the larger social matrix." This formulation refers to music- making ensembles exclusively and does not address, for example, venues, production companies, and studios that can also provide ongoing musical work for musicians.

6. As I will discuss, many so-called bands are still based on one or two "core" people who fill out the roster with lenders of services. Thus, the difference between a band and a solo artist can be a fine one.

7. As I discuss in the next chapter, these issues also frame how musicians represented their careers to others in the Scenes.

8. For instance, *baianos* frequently associated certain *blocos* with specific identity groups, and many people wore clothing emblazoned with *bloco* logos well outside of the Carnaval period, as if to publically affirm their identification with their favorite organizations.

9. High-profile work such as this also frequently paves the way for equipment endorsements. Some ensemble *donos* provide equipment for their musicians.

10. Though it might be tempting to detail unfortunate circumstances such as infidelities and relationships lost to long periods of separation, I prefer to keep such aspects of collaborators' private lives private.

11. Principals are under no obligation to pay their lenders of services more if the nexus becomes more profitable. According to several interlocutors, pay raises in such circumstances happened but were not assured.

12. Securing this job in the wake of some success as an independent singer thrust Laurinha into the spotlight as the first woman to perform for a *bloco* on a *trio elétrico*.

13. Following a slightly different but still common path are Banda and Bloco Mel, which were created simultaneously. *Blocos afro* also typically begin in conjunction with their eponymous ensembles. Whereas *blocos do trio* often emerge in the hands of a small group of *socios* with considerable financial resources, *blocos afro* tend to depend on a larger collective effort. Several of these groups, for instance Olodum, Ara Ketu, Timbalada, and Ilê Aiyê, that began as community-based drumming, dancing, and singing for parades, have professionalized, creating smaller groups for touring and theater presentations in complement with other cultural education and outreach efforts.

14. *Blocos* and production companies earned revenues in analogous fashion—they sold entry to performances. Their operations were also usually entangled with any number of other enterprises such as the sale of commodities and advertising. Obviously restaurants, record labels, and studios earn revenue by selling products and services other than live performances, though the endeavors are often related.

15. Parade scheduling is a topic of ongoing debate. A common point of contention is the relegation of *blocos afro* and independent artists to less desirable times.

16. In the following chapter I address analogous working-to-work practices among lenders of services seeking nexus affiliations and improved positions in the field.

17. To my surprise, few individual musicians I met had a demo at the ready.

18. The club was ranked as Salvador's best live-music venue by the national magazine *Veja* in 2004.

19. Performers who do not live from music can also work for less money than full-time music professionals. Several interlocutors noted that their wages had been undercut by "amateurs," both middle-class avocational musicians and members of the working classes who out of financial need also accept low pay.

20. The importance of socio-professional contacts in more "conventional" work sectors has been addressed in a vast literature including Granovetter (1973, 1995), Putnam (1995), Burt (1997), and Lin (2001).

21. As I discuss in the next chapter, this was even more of an issue for individual musicians in relation to their affiliations with specific ensembles and leaders.

22. In addition to being slang for sitting-in, *canja* is a kind of chicken soup.

THREE *Tactical Affiliations and Performances of Musicians' Selves*

1. Tia De Nora's (1995) study of Beethoven's career provides perhaps one of the most provocative examples.

2. For example, string players often aspired to be soloists, which left them unhappy with studio work as part of a section.

3. Despite the currency of the notion, I stop short of equating the individualized working to work discussed in this chapter with "self branding," which Hearn (2008, 196) describes as a "rigorously instrumental set of commercial activities." Rather, much of what I saw struck me as deeply rooted in practices of self-formation far removed from market concerns and in some instances, contrary to (immediate) economic opportunity.

4. Discussions between musicians often involved assessments of who was and who was not a *bom músico*, often in relation to what and with whom they played as well as assessments of how well they did it.

5. A number of the musicians I knew in 1990s Los Angeles who had jobs with prominent performers were paid a retainer to remain available for any work that appeared between tours or recording projects. None of the musicians I met in Salvador had such an arrangement.

6. Edni also suggested that jazz's status as the epitome of good musicianship had diminished to some degree. However, it still carries plenty of cultural capital.

7. This website is no longer active, but the URL was http://tramavirtual.uol.com.br /artistas/ (accessed August 8, 2010; my translation).

8. My categorization was based on multiple references to Olodum as *axé* by interlocutors, in popularly oriented writing on Brazilian music (e.g., McGowan and Pessanha 1998, 131), and at the time of our conversation, in the bins of Salvador's CD vendors. Brazilian scholars such as anthropologist Goli Guerreiro leave room for groups such as Olodum under the umbrella of *axé* even as they recognize the variety of Bahian popular music practices and the distinctions drawn between them. She writes, "the denomination [*axé* music] fits as well for the *blocos afro* ... as for the music made by the *trio elétrico* bands" (1998, 100, my translation).

9. Margareth Menezes embraced a similar tactic with her 2001 CD release, which was titled *Afropop Brasileira*.

10. The other performer of Bahian music mentioned on the site is Carlinhos Brown, whose work has also been called *axé* but who also rejects the term for the group he founded, Timbalada. He also has a very eclectic resumé—much more so than Mercury—that includes collaborations with MPB luminaries such as Marisa Monte as well as North American jazz legends and countless other Bahian artists working in various genres.

11. *Maracatu* is a traditional Carnaval music from the northeastern state of Pernambuco. The project this percussionist described struck me as reminiscent of Chico Science & Nação Zumbi, a group that garnered popular success and critical acclaim with their *maracatu*, funk, rock, hip hop fusion in the late 1990s. See Galinsky (2002).

12. Porco Olho (Marcos de Boa Morte) earns his living as a police officer. However, he is also a prolific lyricist, who contributed several songs included on the first CD by Gera Samba, the group that would eventually become the template for Bahian *pagode* under the name of É O Tchan. Despite this history, Porco Olho referred to himself as a "sambista," not a *pagodeiro*, and he has not composed any more songs for Tchan or other *pagode* artists for many years.

13. This exemplifies conditions discussed by Granovetter (1995, 36, emphasis in original), in which, among the male white-collar workers he surveyed, "it is suspected that those who are searching would not if they didn't *have* to, and wouldn't have to if they were good enough."

14. Fredrickson and Rooney (1993) also note that freelance classical musicians in Washington, DC, often exaggerate their workloads to seem more in demand.

15. Faulkner (1979) notes the importance of this process among studio musicians who "sponsor" younger, less established players, enabling them to break into the Hollywood studio scene.

16. "Punch-in" refers to a common technique used in multitrack recording that allows errors to be fixed by effectively turning on and off the microphone while a track is rolling. This allows for a precise edit of the problematic passage with no effect on the recorded sounds prior to or after it.

17. It was a digital recording.

18. I discuss house and monitor mixes at length in chapter 4.

FOUR *Performance Preparation and Behind-the-Scenes Performances*

1. Eliot Bates (2011) is notable for his attention to this issue in music.

2. It is common for studio musicians, particularly those in the United States, to arrive at recording sessions with no idea as to what they will be playing or with whom

(see Faulkner 1979). This was less common in Bahia, but the amount of preparation still varied considerably.

3. Though books containing lyrics, chords (*cifras*), and notation for classic repertoire were available, such material was expensive and I rarely saw it used at rehearsals.

4. Some MPB, samba, *choro*, and bossa nova performances were delivered with musicians sitting. With the exception of *choro*, larger venues typically meant standing musicians. Nearly all pop/rock, *axé*, *pagode*, and Forró performances I attended—except "unplugged" presentations in small settings—were done standing. This points to another aspect of musicians' flexibility, since the change in bodily orientation can have marked implications for playing certain instruments.

5. It is quite possible that the openness of interpretation embraced by most musicians when rendering recorded music is related to limited literacy in Bahia, not only musical but also linguistic.

6. In Bahia, elements of three modes of composition theorized by Ruth Finnegan (1986) coexist in many contexts. What Finnegan calls the "classical mode" prioritizes canonic compositions and obliges performers to reproduce what is on the written page—*Werktreue*. In Salvador, the primacy of core repertoire in some ways indicates similar canonizing of works, but performers are not expected to reproduce what the "original artist" performed. This approach suggests what Finnegan has deemed the "jazz mode," in which musicians perform pieces from a standard repertoire, but actively change it through improvisation, an approach also evident in Becker and Faulkner's discussion of jazz repertoire (2007). Among Bahian musicians other than *músicos da noite* these changes were more fixed than fluid. This fixity of parts echoes Finnegan's "rock mode." However, her formulation emphasizes original compositions by members of the ensemble, whereas most of the work I saw done through this mode involved music strongly associated with nonaffiliated, recognized composers.

7. A great deal has been written about rhythmic feel, and specifically swing, in the literature on jazz. See for example, Monson (1996) and Progler (1995) among many others.

8. The literature on recording is vast, but key contributions include Faulkner (1973), Goodwin (1992), Porcello (1998), Meintjes (2003), Philip (2004), Porcello and Green (2004), Katz (2010), Scales (2012), Bates (2016), and Hitchins (2016).

9. Hired session players were paid per hour, per track, or in a lump sum for the project; lenders of services usually recorded on spec; and those who were *socios* normally paid for studio sessions.

10. In-ear monitors have become common in the best sound systems used in concert venues worldwide. I rarely saw them in use in Salvador. Rear-facing speakers on the floor or lightweight plastic headphones were the norm and most players used whatever was provided on each job.

11. On occasion during sound check, a walk out to the audience area was possible and several principals and musical directors took advantage of the opportunity. During the show, however, this usually could not be done.

12. Musicians could hurt their cause by making unreasonable demands in undiplomatic ways. However, I rarely saw such behavior, perhaps because most performers were aware of the power engineers had.

FIVE *Staging and Sounding Live Performances*

1. Since this particular location, Largo Quincas Berro d'Água, had several restaurants, this was not always the case.

2. The roots of Bahia's notorious reputation for late-starting performances might well lie, at least in part, with the effects of nasty traffic and the fact that some performers arrive at one job directly following another.

3. He also uses the term "backstage" to emphasize the role of performance in everyday contexts.

4. In contrast to musicians, whose job entails obscuring their labor even as they work onstage, Goffman notes that front-region performances in most labor settings emphasize demonstrating the work being done for managers and other "superiors."

5. Roberval told me that he avoided "playing at night." However, at least some of his work included venues such as restaurants and bars that would typically be regarded as the milieu of *músicos da noite*.

6. This is the most common application of Signifyin(g) in studies of North American musics such as jazz and hip hop.

7. I only saw one instance in which music from a dance genre was adapted in a way that did not serve to engender dancing in a setting different from its usual one. In the early 2000s, a singer recorded and performed acoustic, MPB-like versions of *axé* songs. She enjoyed some limited success, but her project was fairly short-lived and did not inspire similar endeavors.

8. A *versão* is a song in another language reworked with Portuguese lyrics that may or may not be translations of the original text.

9. I thank Rachel Beausoleil-Morrison for reminding me of this state of affairs, one that is changing slowly, evident in the songwriting work of several Brazilian women, including Márcia Castro.

10. I have only encountered the 1959 version, but an earlier recording by Caymmi from 1954 exists.

11. Demonstrative of the importance of composers in Brazil and typical of practices by *intérpretes*, she recorded this version for an album called *Gal Canta Caymmi* (Gal Sings Caymmi).

12. Thanks to noted *cavaquinho* player (and now PhD in ethnomusicology) Henrique Cazes, who told me about this. Silveira (2017) transcribes the song in A major, which is consistent with the chord shapes played but not the sound of the recording. I refer to pitches and chords as sounded on the recording. Note that all chords are fingered in a shape that normally sounds a whole step higher than written—G is fingered as A, C as D, F as G, etc.

13. Across Brazil, Carnaval in Recife, Pernambuco is held up by many as a more authentic alternative to both Bahia's and Rio's festivities. Thanks to Andrew Snyder for reminding me of this.

CLOSING SET *Livings, Living from Music, Music for a Lifetime*

1. The introduction to the 2014 edition of *The Jobless Future* mentions numerous other factors that both evidence and accelerate the kind of job erosion they discussed in 1994.

2. Writing just after Aronowitz and DiFazio, Richard Sennett (1998) expressed similar pessimism about the implications of flexible labor.

3. Crucial here is the distinction between "work" and "labor" as theorized by Hannah Arendt, which Aronowitz and DiFazio reference in writing that work "fuses thought and making in activity that contributes to that which really constitutes freedom" (2010, 334).

4. Technologies such as recording, MIDI, sampling, and file sharing have also changed the ways musicians work. However, rather than eliminate human musical workers in a manner akin to a robotic arm on an assembly line, I would argue that such technologies have changed the nature of what it is to be a musician, eliminating some roles, but also opening up new avenues of work and employment.

5. That is, when São João is reinstated. Nearly all public events, including June *festa* celebrations, were cancelled in 2020 due to the Covid-19 pandemic.

6. See for example Packman 2012 on *samba junino*, and Robinson and Packman (2014) on professional *samba de roda* performance in Salvador.

7. The cessation of all musical work in Bahia due to the Covid-19 pandemic of 2020 has put Farofa's propsects for future income in jeopardy.

BIBLIOGRAPHY

Abe, Marié. 2018. *Resonances of Chindon-Ya: Sounding Space and Sociality in Contemporary Japan*. Middletown, CT: Wesleyan University Press.

Americo Lisboa Junior, Luiz. 2006. *Compositores e Intérpretes Baianos: De Xisto Bahia a Dorival Caymmi*. Ilhéus: Via Litterarum Editora.

Appiah, Kwame Anthony. 2020. "The Case for Capitalizing the *B* in Black" The Atlantic, June 18, 2020. https://www.theatlantic.com/ideas/archive/2020/06/time-to-capitalize -blackand-white/613159/, accessed January 14, 2021.

A Tarde. 2004. Salvador da Bahia, Brazil, August 1, 2004.

Adorno, Theodor W. 1991. "On the Fetish Character in Music and the Regression of Listening." In *The Culture Industry: Selected Essays on Mass Culture*, ed. J. M. Bernstein, 29–60. London: Routledge.

Ahearne, Jeremy. 1995. *Michel de Certeau: Interpretation and its Other*. Stanford, CA: Stanford University Press.

Albuquerque, Carlos. 1997. *O Eterno Verão do Reggae*. São Paulo: Editora 34.

Allen, Roger M. 1999. "Cultural Imperialism at its Most Fashionable." In *The Brazil Reader: History, Culture, Politics*, eds. Robert M. Levine and John J. Crocitti, 447–53. Durham, NC: Duke University Press.

Alvarenga, Oneyda. [1947] 1960. *Música Popular Brasileira*. Rio de Janeiro: Globo.

Andrade, Mario de. [1928] 1972. *Ensaio Sôbre a Música Brasileira*, 3rd ed. São Paulo: Martins.

Appadurai, Arjun. 1986. "Introduction: Commodities and the Politics of Value." In *The Social Life of Things: Commodities in Cultural Perspective*, ed. Arjun Appadurai, 3–63. Cambridge: Cambridge University Press.

Araújo, Clara, and Celi Scalon, eds. 2005. *Gênro, Família e Trabalho no Brasil*. Rio de Janeiro: FGV Editora.

Araújo, Samuel Mello Junior. 1988. "*Brega*: Music and Conflict in Urban Brazil." *Latin American Music Review* 9 (1): 50–89.

————. 1992. "Acoustic Labor in the Timing of Everyday Life: A Critical Contribution to the History of Samba in Rio de Janeiro." PhD diss., University of Illinois, Urbana-Champaign.

Arendt, Hannah. 1958. *The Human Condition*. Chicago: University of Chicago Press.

Aronowitz, Stanley, and William DiFazio. 2010. *The Jobless Future*, 2nd ed. Minneapolis: University of Minnesota Press.

Auslander, Philip. 2006. "Musical Personae." *TDR: The Drama Review* 50 (1): 100–19.

Avelar, Idelber, and Christopher Dunn, eds. 2011. *Brazilian Popular Music and Citizenship*. Durham, NC: Duke University Press.

Azevedo, Ricardo. 2007. *Axé-Music: O Verso e o Reverso da Música que Conquistou o Planeta*. Salvador: Alpha Co.

Baade, Christina, Susan Fast, and Line Grenier. 2014. "Musicians as Workers: Sites of Struggle and Resistance." *MUSICultures* (41) 1: 1–9.

Bacelar, Jeferson. 1999. "Blacks in Salvador: Racial Paths." In *Black Brazil: Culture, Identity, and Social Mobilization*, ed. Larry Crook and Randall Johnson, 85–102. Los Angeles: UCLA Latin American Center Publications.

Baily, John. 1988. *Music of Afghanistan: Professional Musicans in the City of Herat*. Cambridge: Cambridge University Press.

Banton, Michael. 2000. "The Idiom of Race: A Critique of Presentism." In *Theories of Race and Racism: A Reader*, ed. Les Black and John Solomos, 251–63. New York: Routledge.

Barthes, Roland. 1977. "Death of the Author." In *Image Music Text*, ed. and trans. Stephan Heath, 142-48. New York: Hill and Wang.

Bates, Eliot. 2012. "The Social Life of Musical Instruments." *Ethnomusicology* 56 (3): 363–95.

————. 2016. *Digital Tradition: Arrangement and Labor in Istanbul's Recording Studio Culture*. New York: Oxford University Press.

Becker, Howard. 1982. *Art Worlds*. Berkeley: University of California Press.

Bellaviti, Sean. 2020. *Música Típica: Cumbia and the Rise of Musical Nationalism in Panama*. New York: Oxford University Press.

Bennett, H. Stith. 1980. *On Becoming a Rock Musician*. Amherst: University of Massachusetts Press.

Bennett, Jane. 2010. *Vibrant Matter: A Political Ecology of Things*. Durham, NC: Duke University Press.

Bhabha, Homi. [1984] 1994. "Of Mimicry and Man: The Ambivalence of Colonial Discourse." In *The Location of Culture*, 121–31. New York: Routledge.

Bourdieu, Pierre. 1977. *Outline of a Theory of Practice*, trans. Richard Nice. Cambridge: Cambridge University Press.

————. 1984. *Distinction: A Social Critique of the Judgment of Taste*, trans. Richard Nice. Cambridge, MA: Harvard University Press.

———. 1986. "The Forms of Capital." In *Handbook of Theory and Research for the Sociology of Education*, ed. J. Richardson, 241–58. New York: Greenwood Press.

———. 1990. *The Logic of Practice*, trans. Richard Nice. Stanford, CA: Stanford University Press.

———. 1993. *The Field of Cultural Production: Essays on Art and Literature*, ed. Randall Johnson. Cambridge: Polity Press.

———. 1995. *The Rules of Art: Genesis and Structure in the Literary Field*, trans. Susan Emanuel. Stanford, CA: Stanford University Press.

———, and Loïc J. D. Wacquant. 1992. *An Invitation to Reflexive Sociology*. Chicago: University of Chicago Press.

Bradley, Harriet, Mark Erickson, Carol Stephenson, and Steve Williams. 2000. *Myths at Work*. Malden, MA: Blackwell Publishers.

Brinner, Benjamin. 1995. *Knowing Music, Making Music: Javanese Gamelan and the Theory of Musical Competence and Interaction*. Chicago: University of Chicago Press.

———. 2009. *Playing Across a Divide: Israeli-Palestinian Musical Encounters*. New York: Oxford University Press.

Browning, Barbara. 1995. *Samba: Resistance in Motion*. Indianapolis: Indiana University Press.

Buchanan, Donna A. 1995. "Metaphors of Power, Metaphors of Truth: The Politics of Music Professionalism in Bulgarian Folk Orchestras." *Ethnomusicology* 39 (3): 381–416.

Burt, Ronald S. 1997. "The Contingent Value of Social Capital." *Administrative Science Quarterly* 42 (2): 339–65.

Butler, Judith. 1990. *Gender Trouble: Feminism and the Subversion of Identity*. New York: Routledge.

Butler, Kim D. 1998. *Freedoms Given, Freedoms Won: Afro-Brazilians in Post-Abolition São Paulo and Salvador*. New Brunswick, NJ: Rutgers University Press.

Caroso, Luciano. 2010. *Etnomusicologia no Ciberespaço: Processos Criativos e de Disseminação em Videoclipes Amadores*. PhD diss., Federal University of Bahia, Salvador, Brazil.

Carvalho, José Jorge de. 1999. "The Multiplicity of Black Identities in Brazilian Popular Music." In *Black Brazil: Culture, Identity and Social Mobilization*, ed. Larry Crook and Randall Johnson, 261–95. Los Angeles: UCLA Latin American Center Publications.

Carvalho, Marta de Ulhôa. 1995. "Tupi or not Tupi MPB: Popular Music and Identity in Brazil." In *The Brazilian Puzzle: Culture on the Borderlands of the Western World*, ed. David J. Hess and Roberto Damatta, 159–79. New York: Columbia University Press.

Castro, Armando Alexandre. 2010. "Axé Music: Mitos, Verdades, e World Music." *Per Musi* 22: 203–17.

Clifford, James, and George E. Marcus. 1986. *Writing Culture: The Poetics and Politics of Ethnography*. Berkeley: University of California Press.

Cohen, Sarah. 1991. *Rock Culture in Liverpool: Popular Music in the Making*. New York: Oxford University Press.

Collins, John F. 2015. *Revolt of the Saints: Memory and Redemption in the Twilight of Brazilian Racial Democracy*. Durham, NC: Duke University Press.

Cook, Nicholas. 2001. "Between Process and Product: Music as/and Performance." *Music Theory Online* 7 (2). http://www.mtosmt.org/issues/mto.01.7.2/mto.01.7.2.cook.html. Accessed August 18, 2010.

Costa, Marco Túlio Ferreira da. 2017. *Violão Clube do Ceará . . . Os Feitiçeiros da Melodia*. Curitiba: Editora Prismas.

Cottrell, Stephen. 2004. *Professional Music-Making in London: Ethnography and Experience*. Aldershot, UK: Ashgate Publishing.

Crook, Larry. 1993. "Black Consciousness, Samba-Reggae, and the Re-Africanization of Bahian Carnival Music in Brazil." *The World of Music* 35 (2): 90–108.

———. 2005. *Northeastern Traditions: Brazilian Music and the Heartbeat of a Modern Nation*. Santa Barbara, CA: ABC-CLIO.

———. 2009. *Focus: Music of Northeast Brazil*. New York: Routledge.

Crowley, Daniel J. 1984. *African Myth and Black Reality in Bahian Carnaval*. Los Angeles: UCLA Museum of Cultural History.

Cusick, Suzanne. 1994. "Feminist Theory, Music Theory, and the Mind/Body Problem." *Perspectives of New Music* 32 (1): 8–27.

Daley, Dan. 1998. *Nashville's Unwritten Rules: Inside the Business of Country Music*. New York: The Overlook Press.

DaMatta, Roberto. 1991. *Carnivals, Rogues, and Heroes: An Interpretation of the Brazilian Dilemma*, trans. John Drury. Notre Dame, IN: University of Notre Dame Press.

———. 1999. "Is Brazil Hopelessly Corrupt?" In *The Brazil Reader: History, Culture, Politics*, ed. Robert M. Levine and John J. Crocitti, 295–97. Durham, NC: Duke University Press.

Davis, Darién. 2009. *White Face, Black Mask: Africaneity and the Early Social History of Popular Music in Brazil*. East Lansing: Michigan State University Press.

de Certeau, Michel. 1984. *The Practice of Everyday Life*, trans. Steven Rendell. Berkeley: University of California Press.

De Marchi, Leonardo. 2015. "Transformations of the Music Industry in Brazil, 1999–2009: The Reorganization of the Record Market in the Digital Networks." In *Made in Brazil: Studies in Popular Music*, ed. Marta Tupinambá de Ulhôa, Felipe Trotta, and Cláudia Azevedo, 173–86. New York: Routledge.

De Mello Santos, Marcos Joel. 2006. *Esterótipos, Preconceitos, Axé-Music e Pagode*. MA thesis, Federal University of Bahia, Salvador.

De Souza, Tárik. 2003. *Tem Mais Samba Aqui: Das Raizes a Electônica*. São Paulo: Editora 34.

DeNora, Tia. 1995. *Beethoven and the Construction of Genius: Musical Politics in Vienna, 1792–1803*. Berkeley: University of California Press.

Dent, Alexander Sebastian. 2009. *River of Tears: Country Music, Memory, and Modernity in Brazil*. Durham, NC: Duke University Press.

Doogan, Kevin. 2009. *New Capitalism? The Transformation of Work*. Cambridge: Polity Press.

Draper, Jack A. III. 2010. *Forró and Redemptive Regionalism from the Brazilian Northeast*. New York. Peter Lang.

Dunn, Christopher. 1992. "Afro-Bahian Carnival: A Stage for Protest." *Afro-Hispanic Review* 11 (1): 11–20.

———. 2001. *Brutality Garden: Tropicália and the Emergence of a Brazilian Counterculture*. Chapel Hill: University of North Carolina Press.

———. 2007. "Black Rome and the Chocolate City: The Race of Place." *Callaloo* 30 (3): 847–61.

Eakin, Marshall C. 2017. *Becoming Brazilians: Race and National Identity in Twentieth-Century Brazil*. New York: Cambridge University Press.

Ehrlich, Cyril. 1985. *The Music Profession in Britain since the Eighteenth Century: A Social History*. London: Clarendon Press.

Faulkner, Robert R. 1971. *Hollywood Studio Musicians: Their Work and Careers in the Recording Industry*. New York: Aldine Atherton.

———, and Howard S. Becker. 2009. *Do You Know? The Jazz Repertoire in Action*. Chicago: University of Chicago Press.

Fenerick, José Adriano. 2005. *Nem do Morro nem da Cidade: As Transformações do samba e a Indústria Cultural (1920–1945)*. São Paulo: Annablume Editora.

Finnegan, Ruth. 1986. "The Relation between Composition and Performance: Three Alternative Modes." In *The Oral and the Literate in Music*, ed. Tokumaru Yoshiko and Yamatuti Osamu, 73–87. Tokyo: Academia Music.

———. [1989] 2007. *The Hidden Musicians: Music-Making in an English Town*. Middletown, CT: Wesleyan University Press.

Florida, Richard. 2012. *The Rise of The Creative Class*. New York: Basic Books.

Fornet-Betancourt, Raul, Helmut Becker, Alfredo Gomez-Müller, and J. D. Gauthier. 1987. "The Ethic of Care for the Self as a Practice of Freedom: An Interview with Michel Foucault on January 20, 1984." *Philosophy & Social Criticism* 12 (2–3): 112–31.

Foucault, Michel. 1972. *The Archaeology of Knowledge and the Discourse on Language*, trans. A. M. Sheridan Smith. New York: Pantheon Books.

———. 1977. "What is an Author." In *Language, Counter-memory, Practice: Selected Es-*

says and Interviews, ed. Donald F. Bouchard, trans. Donald F. Bouchard and Sherry Simon, 113–38. Ithaca, NY: Cornell University Press.

———. 1979. *Discipline and Punish: The Birth of the Prison*. New York: Vintage Books.

———. 1988. "Technologies of the Self." In *Technologies of the Self: A Seminar with Michel Foucault*, ed. Luther Martin, Huck Gutman, and Patrick H. Hutton, 16–49. Amherst: University of Massachusetts Press.

———. 1991. "Governmentality." In *The Foucault Effect: Studies in Governmentality*, ed. Graham Burchell, Colin Gordon, and Peter Miller, 85–104. Chicago: University of Chicago Press.

Freitas, Ayêska Paula. 2004. "Música de Rua de Salvador: Preparando a Cena Para a Axé Music." *I Enecult*. http://www.cult.ufba.br/enecul2005/AyeskaPaulafreitas.pdf.

Frederickson, Jon, and James F. Rooney. 1993. *In the Pits: A Sociological Study of the Free-Lance Classical Musician*. Queenston, ON: The Edwin Mellon Press.

Freyre, Gilberto. [1933] 1964. *The Masters and the Slaves: A Study in the Development of Brazilian Civilization*, trans. Samuel Putnam. New York: Knopf.

Frith, Simon. 1987. "The Industrialization of Popular Music." In *Popular Music and Communication*, ed. James Lull, 53–77. London: Sage Publications.

Galinsky, Philip. 1996. "Co-option, Cultural Resistance, and Afro-Brazilian Identity: A History of the *Pagode* Samba Movement in Rio de Janeiro." *Latin American Music Review* 17 (2): 120–49.

———. 2002. *Maracatu Atomico: Tradition, Modernity, and Postmodernity in the Mangue Movement in Recife, Brazil*. New York: Routledge.

Garcia Canclini, Nestor. 1995. *Hybrid Cultures: Strategies for Entering and Leaving Modernity*, trans. Christopher Chiappari and Silvia Lopez. Minneapolis: University of Minnesota Press.

Gates, Henry Louis Jr. 1988. *The Signifying Monkey: A Theory of African American Literary Criticism*. Oxford: Oxford University Press.

Geertz, Clifford. 1973. *The Interpretation of Cultures: Selected Essays*. New York: Basic Books.

Gerstin, Julian. 1998. "Reputation in a Music Scene: The Everyday Context of Connections between Music, Identity, and Politics." *Ethnomusicology* 42 (3).

Gilroy, Paul. 1993. *The Black Atlantic: Modernity and Double Consciousness*. Cambridge, MA: Harvard University Press.

Godi, Antonio J. V. dos Santos. 1998. "Música Afro Carnavalesca: Das Multidões para o Sucesso das Massas Elétricas." In *Ritmos en Transito: Socio-Antropologia da Música Baiana*, ed. Livo Sansone and Jocélio dos Santos, 79–93. São Paulo: Dynamis Editorial.

———. 2001. "Reggae and Samba Reggae in Bahia: A Case of Long-Distance Belonging." In *Brazilian Popular Music and Globalization*, ed. Charles Perrone and Christopher Dunn, 207–19. New York: Routledge.

Goehr, Lydia. 2007. *The Imaginary Museum of Musical Works: An Essay in the Philosophy of Music*. New York: Oxford University Press.

Góes, Fred. 1982. *O País do Carnaval Elétrico*. São Paulo: Corrupio.

———. 2000. *50 Anos do trio Elétrico*. Salvador: Corrupio.

Goffman, Erving. 1959. *The Presentation of Self in Everyday Life*. New York: Anchor Books.

———. 1974. *Frame Analysis: An Essay on the Organization of Experience*. Cambridge, MA: Harvard University Press.

Goldberg, David Theo. 2002. *The Racial State*. Malden, MA: Blackwell Publishers.

———. 2008. T*he Threat of Race: Reflections on Racial Neoliberalism*. Malden, MA: Blackwell Publishing.

Golding, Rosemary, ed. 2018. *The Music Profession in Britain, 1780–1920*. London: Routledge.

Goldschmitt, Kariann. 2014. "Mobile Tactics in the Brazilian Independent Music Industry." In *The Oxford Handbook of Mobile Music Studies*, Vol. 1, ed. Sumanth Gopinath and Jason Stanyek, 496–522. New York: Oxford University Press.

———. 2019. *Bossa Mundo: Brazilian Music in Transnational Music Industries*. New York: Oxford University Press.

Goodwin, Andrew. 1992. "Rationalization and Democratization in the New Technologies of Popular Music." In *Popular Music and Communication*, ed. James Lull. Newbury Park, CA: Sage Publications.

Granovetter, Mark. 1973. "The Strength of Weak Ties." *American Journal of Sociology* 78 (6): 1360–380.

———. 1995. *Getting a Job: A Study of Contacts and Careers*, 2nd ed. Chicago: University of Chicago Press.

Gregg, Melissa. 2011. *Work's Intimacy*. Cambridge: Polity Press.

Grenfell, Michael. 2008. *Pierre Bourdieu: Key Concepts*. Stocksfield, UK: Acumen.

Guardian. 2018. "Who is Jair Bolsonaro? Brazil's Far-Right President in his own Words." *Guardian*, September 6, 2018. https://www.theguardian.com/world/2018/sep/06/jair-bolsonaro-brazil-tropical-trump-who-hankers-for-days-of-dictatorship. Accessed December 11, 2018.

Guerreiro, Goli. 1998. "Um Mapa em Preto e Branco da Música na Bahia: Territorialização e Mestiçagem no Meio Musical de Salvador (1987/1997)." In *Ritmos en Transito: Socio-Antropologia da Música Baiana*, ed. Livo Sansone and Jocélio dos Santos, 97–122. São Paulo: Dynamis Editorial.

———. 2000. *A Trama dos Tambores: A Musica Afro Pop em Salvador*. São Paulo: Editora 34.

———. 2011. "Candeal and Carlinhos Brown: Social and Musical Contexts of an Afro-Brazilian Community." In *Brazilian Popular Music and Citizenship*, ed. Idelbar Avelar and Christopher Dunn, 278–90. Durham, NC: Duke University Press.

_____, and Milton Moura, et. al. 2004. *Criatividade e Trabalho no Cenário Musical da Bahia: Relatório de Pesquisa*. Salvador: Universidade Federal da Bahia.

Guilbault, Jocelyne. 2007. *Governing Sound: The Cultural Politics of Trinidad's Carnival Musics*. New York: Oxford University Press.

_____, and Roy Cape. 2014. *Roy Cape: A Life on the Calypso and Soca Bandstand*. Durham, NC: Duke University Press.

Haas, Colleen M. 2010. "The Artistry of Neguinho do Samba: Afro-Brazilian Girls and Samba-Reggae Music in the Local Neighborhood." PhD diss., Indiana University.

Hanchard, Michael George. 1994. *Orpheus and Power: The Movimento Negro of Rio de Janeiro and São Paulo, Brazil, 1945–1988*. Princeton, NJ: Princeton University Press.

_____. 1999. "Black Cinderella? Race and the Public Sphere in Brazil." In *Racial Politics in Contemporary Brazil*, ed. Michael Hanchard, 59–81. Durham, NC: Duke University Press.

Hasenbalg, Carlos. 1999. "Perspectives on Race and Class in Brazil." In *Black Brazil: Culture, Identity, and Social Mobilization*, ed. Larry Crook and Randall Johnson, 61–84. Los Angeles: UCLA Latin American Center Publications.

Hamermesh, Daniel S. 1986. "The Demand for Labor in the Long Run." In *Handbook of Labor Economics*, Vol. 1, ed. Orley Ashenfleter and Richard Layard, 429–71. Amsterdam: North Holland Press.

Harvey, David. 2005. *A Brief History of Neoliberalism*. Oxford: Oxford University Press.

Hayles, Kathleen. 1999. *How We Became Posthuman: Virtual Bodies in Cybernetics, Literature, and Informatics*. Chicago: University of Chicago Press.

Hearn, Allison. 2008. "Variations on the Branded Self: Theme, Invention, Improvisation, and Inventory." In *The Media and Social Theory*, ed. David Hesmondhalgh and Jason Toynbee, 194–210. New York: Routledge.

Henry, Clarence Bernard. 2008. *Let's Make Some Noise: Axé and the African Roots of Brazilian Popular Music*. Jackson: University Press of Mississippi.

Herzfeld, Michael. 2005. *Cultural Intimacy: Social Poetics in the Nation-state*. New York: Routledge.

Hertzman, Marc A. 2013. *Making Samba: A New History of Race and Music in Brazil*. Durham, NC: Duke University Press.

Hesmondhalgh, David. 2007. *The Cultural Industries*, 3rd ed. London: Sage Publications.

_____, and Sarah Baker. 2011. *Creative Labour: Media Work in Three Cultural Industries*. New York: Routledge.

Hillier, Jean, and Emma Rooksby. 2005. *Habitus: A Sense of Place*. Aldershot, UK: Ashgate.

Hinchberger, Bill. 1999. "Bahia Music Story." In *The Brazil Reader: History, Culture, Politics*, ed. Robert M. Levine and John J. Crocitti, 483–86. Durham, NC: Duke University Press.

Hitchins, Ray. 2014. *Vibe Merchants: The Sound Creators of Jamaican Popular Music*. Burlington, VT: Ashgate.

Hofman, Ana. 2015. "Music (as) Labour: Professional Musicianship, Affective Labour and Gender in Socialist Yugoslavia." In *Ethnomusicology Forum* (24) 1: 28–50.

Horkheimer, Max, and Theodor W. Adorno. 1997. "The Culture Industry: Enlightenment as Mass Deception." In *Dialectic of Enlightenment*, trans. John Cumming. New York: Continuum Books.

Hracs, Brian J., Michael Seman, and Tarek E. Virani, eds. 2016. *The Production and Consumption of Music in the Digital Age*. New York: Routledge.

Ickes, Scott. 2013. *African-Brazilian Culture and Regional Identity in Bahia, Brazil*. Miami: University Press of Florida.

Instituto Brasileiro de Geografia e Estatística (Brazilian Institute of Geography and Statistics). 2010. https://cidades.ibge.gov.br/brasil/ba/salvador/pesquisa/23/23226?detalhes=true. Accessed January 10, 2021.

————. 2016. https://www.ibge.gov.br/estatisticas/sociais/trabalho/9180-pesquisa-mensal-de-emprego.html?edicao=9182&t=destaques. Accessed July 3, 2016.

Katz, Mark. 2010. *Capturing Sound: How Technology has Changed Music*. Berkeley: University of California Press.

King, Anthony. 2000. "Thinking with Bourdieu Against Bourdieu: A Practical Critique of Habitus." *Sociological Theory* 18 (3): 417–33.

Kingsbury, Henry. 1988. *Music, Talent, Performance: A Conservatory Cultural System*. Philadelphia: Temple University Press.

Kirchbaum, Charles, and Flávio Carvalho de Vasconcelos. 2007. "Tropicália: Manobras Estratégicas em Redes de Músicas." *Revista de Administração de Empresas* 47 (3): 1–17.

Kondo, Dorinne K. 1990. *Crafting Selves: Power, Gender, and Discourses of Identity in a Japanese Workplace*. Chicago: The University of Chicago Press.

Latour, Bruno. 2005. *Reassembling the Social: An Introduction to Actor Network Theory*. London: Oxford University Press.

Leite, Marcia de Paula. 2003. *Trabalho e Sociedade em Transformação: Mudanças Productivas e Atores Socias*. São Paulo: Editora Fundação Perseu Abramo.

Leme, Mônica Neves. 2003. *Que Tchan é Esse? Indústria e Produção Musical no Brasil dos Anos 90*. São Paulo: Anna Blume.

Levy, Janet M. 1987. "Covert and Casual Values in Recent Writings About Music." *The Journal of Musicology* 5 (1): 3–27.

Lindsay, Shawn. 1996. "Hand Drumming: An Essay in Practical Knowledge." In *Things as They Are*, ed. Michael Jackson, 196–212. Bloomington and Indianapolis: Indiana University Press.

Lima, Ari. 1998. "O Fenômeno Timbalada: Cultura Musical Afro-pop e Juventude Baiana Negro-Mestiça." In *Ritmos en Transito: Socio-Antropologia da Música Baiana*, ed. Livo Sansone and Jocélio dos Santos, 161–80. São Paulo: Dynamis Editorial.

————. 2001. "Black or Brau: Music and Subjectivity in a Global Context." In *Brazilian*

Popular Music and Globalization, ed. Charles Perrone and Christopher Dunn, 207–19. New York: Routledge.

———. 2002. "Funkeiros, Timbaleiros, e Pagodeiros: Notas Sobre Juventude e Música Negra na Cidade de Salvador." *Cadernos CEDES* 22 (57): 77–96.

———. 2011. "Modernity, Agency, and Sexuality in the *Pagode Baiano*." In *Brazilian Popular Music and Citizenship*, ed. Idelber Avelar and Christopher Dunn, 267–77. Durham, NC: Duke University Press.

Lin, Nan. 2001. *Social Capital: A Theory of Social Structure and Action*. New York: Cambridge University Press.

Loenelli, Domingos. 2013. "São João, Turismo, e Economia." *A Tarde* (Salvador), June 18, 2013.

Lopes, Nei. 1992. *O Negro no Rio de Janeiro e Sua Tradição Musical: Partido-Alto, Calango, Chula e outras Cantorias*. Rio de Janeiro: Pallas.

Lysloff, René T. A. and Leslie C. Gay Jr., eds. 2003. *Music and Technoculture*. Middletown, CT: Wesleyan University Press.

MacLeod, Bruce A. 1993. *Club Date Musicians: Playing the New York Party Circuit*. Chicago: University of Chicago Press.

Mahmood, Saba. 2005. *The Politics of Piety: The Islamic Revival and the Feminist Subject*. Princeton, NJ: Princeton University Press.

Marx, Anthony W. 1998. *Making Race and Nation: A Comparison of the United States, South Africa, and Brazil*. New York: Cambridge University Press.

McCann, Bryan. 2004. *Hello, Hello Brazil: Popular Music in the Making of Modern Brazil*. Durham, NC: Duke University Press.

Mello, Erick. 2005. "Exclusivo: Sem Papas na Lingua, Márcia Freire Revela porque sua Segunda Passagem pelo Cheiro de Amor não deu Certo." http://www.carnasite.com .br/noticias/noticia.asp?CodNot=3698.

Meintjes, Louise. 2004. *Sound of Africa! Making Music Zulu in a South African Studio*. Durham, NC: Duke University Press.

Midlej e Silva, Sylvan. 1998. "O Lúdico e o Étnico no Funk do 'Black Bahia.'" In *Ritmos en Transito: Socio-Antropologia da Música Baiana*, ed. Livo Sansone and Jocélio dos Santos, 201–18. São Paulo: Dynamis Editorial.

Millar, Kathleen M. 2014. "The Precarious Present: Wageless Labor and Disrupted Life in Rio de Janeiro, Brazil." *Cultural Anthropology* 29 (1): 32–53.

Miller, Karl Hagstrom. 2008. "Working Musicians: Exploring the Rhetorical Ties Between Musical Labour and Leisure." *Leisure Studies* 27 (4): 427–41.

Moehn, Frederick J. 2012. *Contemporary Carioca: Technologies of Mixing in a Brazilian Music Scene*. Durham, NC: Duke University Press.

Monson, Ingrid. 1996. *Saying Something: Jazz Improvisation and Interaction*. Chicago: University of Chicago Press.

Mould, Oli. 2018. *Against Creativity*. New York: Verso.

Moura, Milton. 2001a. *Carnaval e Baianidade: Arestas e Curvas na Coreografia de Identidades do Carnaval de Salvador*. PhD diss., Federal University of Bahia, Brazil.

_____. 2001b. "World of Fantasy, Fantasy of the World: Geographic Space and Representation of Identity in the Carnival of Salvador, Bahia." In *Brazilian Popular Music and Globalization*, ed. Charles Perrone and Christopher Dunn, 161–76. New York: Routledge.

Mühlbach, Saskia, and Payal Arora. 2020. "Behind the Music: How Labor Changed for Musicians through the Subscription Economy." *First Monday* 25 (4-6). https:// firstmonday.org/ojs/index.php/fm/article/download/10382/9411doi: http://dx.doi .org/10.5210/fm.v25i4.10382. Accessed April 6, 2020.

Napolitano, Marcos. 1998. "A Invenção da Música Popular Brasileira: Um Campo de Reflexão para a História Social." *Latin American Music Review* 19 (1): 92–105.

National Association of Black Journalists. 2020. "Statement on Capitalizing Black and Other Racial Identifiers." June 2020. https://www.nabj.org/page/styleguide, accessed January 4, 2021.

Negus, Keith. 1999. *Music Genres and Corporate Cultures*. New York: Routledge.

Neves de H. Barbosa, Lívia. 1995. "The Brazilian *Jeitinho*: An Exercise in National Identity." In *The Brazilian Puzzle: Culture on the Borderlands of the Western World*, ed. D. J. Hess and R. DaMatta, 35–48. New York: Columbia University Press.

Nucci, João Paulo. 2012. "Carnaval Movimenta R2,7 Bilhões e gera mais Renda que Muitas Empresas." *Brasil Economico*. February 20, 2012. https://globalizar.wordpress .com/2012/02/23/carnaval-movimenta-r-27-bilhoes-e-gera-mais-renda-que-muitas -empresas/. Accessed January 24, 2021.

Odaras Productions. 2017. "Elipdio Bastos." http://odarasprod.com/artist/26/Elpidio_Bastos. Accessed October 6, 2017.

Oliveira, Marcelo Cunha, and Maria de Fátima Hanaque Campos. 2016. "Carnaval, Identidade Negra e Áxe Music em Salvador na Segunda Metade do Século XX." *Textos Escolhhidos de Cultura e Arte Populares*, Rio de Janeiro. 13 (2): 70–84.

Packman, Jeff. 2009. "Signifyin(g) Salvador: Professional Musicians and the Sound of Flexibility in Bahia, Brazil's, Popular Music Scenes." *Black Music Research Journal* 29 (1): 83–126.

_____. 2010. "Singing Together/Meaning Apart: Popular Music, Participation, and Cultural Politics in Salvador, Brazil." *Latin American Music Review*, 31 (2): 241–67.

_____. 2011. "Musicians' Performances and Performances of 'Musician' in Salvador da Bahia, Brazil." *Ethnomusicology* 55 (3): 414–44.

Pecknold, Diane. 2007. *The Selling Sound: The Rise of the Country Music Industry*. Durham, NC: Duke University Press.

Peterson, Richard A. 1982. "Five Constraints on the Production of Culture: Law, Technology, Organizational Structure, and Occupational Careers." *Journal of Popular Culture* 16 (2): 43–153.

Peterson, Richard A., and Howard G. White. 1979. "The Simplex Located in Art Worlds." *Urban Life* 7 (4): 411–39.

_____, and Roger M. Kern. 1996. "Changing Highbrow Taste: From Snob to Omnivore." *American Sociological Review* 61 (5): 900–907.

Perrone, Charles. 1989. *Masters of Contemporary Brazilian Song: MPB, 1965–1985*. Austin: University of Texas Press.

_____. 1992. "*Axé, Ijexá, Olodum*: The Rise of Afro- and African Currents in Brazilian Popular Music." *Afro-Hispanic Review* 11 (1–3): 42–50.

_____, and Christopher Dunn, eds. 2001. *Brazilian Popular Music and Globalization*. New York: Routledge.

Perullo, Alex. 2011. *Live from Dar es Salaam: Popular Music and Tanzania's Music Economy*. Bloomington: Indiana University Press.

Pinho, Osmundo de Araújo. 2001. "Reggae and Samba-Reggae in Bahia: A Case of Long-Distance Belonging." In *Brazilian Popular Music and Globalization*, ed. Charles Perrone and Christopher Dunn, 207–19. New York: Routledge.

_____. "Tradition as Adventure: Black Music, New Afro-Descendent Subjects, and Pluralization of Modernity in Salvador da Bahia." In *Brazilian Popular Music and Citizenship*, ed. Idelber Avelar and Christopher Dunn, 250–66. Durham, NC: Duke University Press.

Pinho, Patricia de Santana. 2010. *Mama Africa: Reinventing Blackness in Bahia*, trans. Elena Langdon. Durham, NC: Duke University Press.

"Pop Azeitado." 2010. http://tramavirtual.uol.com.br/artistas/. Accessed August 8, 2010.

Preston, Katherine K. 1992. *Music for Hire: A Study of Professional Musicians in Washington, 1877–1900*. Stuyvesant, NY: Pendragon Press.

Progler, J. A. 1995. "Searching for Swing: Participatory Discrepancies in the Jazz Rhythm Section." *Ethnomusicology* 39 (1): 21–54.

Putnam, Robert. 2000. *Bowling Alone: The Collapse and Revival of American Community*. New York: Simon and Schuster Paperbacks.

Quitéria, Maria. 2013. "São João na Bahia." *A Tarde* (Salvador), June 18, 2013.

Ransome, Paul. 1999. *Sociology and the Future of Work: Contemporary Discourses and Debates*. Brookfield, VT: Ashgate.

Regev, Motti. 2013. *Pop-Rock Music: Aesthetic Cosmopolitanism in Late Modernity*. Cambridge, UK: Polity Press.

Risério, Antonio. 1981. *Carnaval Ijexá: Notas sobre Afoxés e Blocos de Novo Carnaval Afro-Baiano*. Salvador: Corrupio.

Ritchey, Marianna. 2019. *Composing Capital: Classical Music in the Neoliberal Era*. Chicago: University of Chicago Press.

Reily, Suzel Ana. 1997. "Macunaima's Music: National Identity and Ethnomusicological Research in Brazil." In *Ethnicity, Identity, and Music: The Musical Construction of Place*, ed. Martin Stokes, 71–96. New York: Berg.

Requião, Luciana. 2010. *Eis Aí a Lapa: Processos e Relaçoes de Trabalho do Músico nas Casas de shows da Lapa*. São Paulo: Annablume Editora.

———. 2016. "Festa Acabada, Músicos a Pé!": Um Estudo Crítico sobre as Relações de Trabalho de Músicos Atuantes no Estado do Rio de Janeiro. *Revista do Instituto de Estudos Brasileiros* 64: 249–74.

———. 2019. *Trabalho, e Génro: Depoimentos de Mulheres Musicistas acerca de sua vida Laboral. Um Retrato do Trabalho no Rio de Janeiro dos Anos 1980 ao inicio do Século XXI*. Rio de Janeiro: GECULTE. https://issuu.com/lucianareq/docs/livro_trabalho _musica_genero_fechado.

Robinson, Danielle, and Jeff Packman. 2013. "Authenticity, Uplift, and Cultural Value in Bahian *Samba Junino*." In *Bodies of Sound: Studies Across Popular Music and Dance*, ed. Sherril Dodds and Susan C. Cook, 117–34. New York: Routledge.

———. 2014. "*Chula* in the City: Traditions, Translations, and Tactics in Brazilian *Samba de Roda*." In *Choreographic Dwellings: Practicing Place*, ed. Gretchen Schiller and Sarah Rubidge, 113–35. New York: Palgrave Macmillan.

Romo, Anadelia A. 2010. *Brazil's Living Museum: Race, Reform, and Tradition in Bahia*. Chapel Hill: University of North Carolina Press.

Roque B. de Castro, Janio. 2012. *Da Casa à Praça Pública: A Espetacularização das Festas Juninas no Espaço Urbano*. Salvador: EDUFBA.

Sandroni, Carlos. 2001. *Fetiço Decente: Transformações do Samba no Rio de Janeiro (1917– 1933)*. Rio de Janeiro: Zahar.

Sansone, Livio. 1998. "Funk Baiano: Uma Versão de um Fenômeno Global?" In *Ritmos en Transito: Socio-Antropologia da Música Baiana*, ed. Livo Sansone and Jocélio dos Santos, 219–40. São Paulo: Dynamis Editorial.

———. 2001. "The Localization of Global Funk in Bahia and Rio." In *Brazilian Popular Music and Globalization*, ed. Charles Perrone and Christopher Dunn, 136–60. New York: Routledge.

———. 2003. *Blackness without Ethnicity: Constructing Race in Brazil*. New York: Palgrave MacMillan.

———, and Jocélio dos Santos, eds. 1998. *Ritmos en Transito: Socio-Antropologia da Música Baiana*. São Paulo: Dynamis Editorial.

Santanna, Marilda. 2009. *As Donas do Canto: O Sucesso das Estrelas-intérpretes no Carnaval de Salvador*. Salvador: EDUFBA.

Scales, Christopher A. 2012. *Recording Culture: Powwow Music and the Aboriginal Recording Industry on the Northeastern Plains*. Durham, NC: Duke University Press.

Schaeber, Petra. 1998. "Música Negra nos Tempos de Globalização: Produção Musical e

Management da Identidade Étnica-O Caso do Olodum." In *Ritmos en Transito: Socio-Antropologia da Música Baiana*, ed. Livo Sansone and Jocélio dos Santos, 145–59. São Paulo: Dynamis Editorial.

Schafer, R. Murray. 1994. *The Soundscape: Our Sonic Environment and the Tuning of the World*. Rochester, VT: Destiny Books.

Sennett, Richard. 1998. *The Corrosion of Character: The Personal Consequences of Work in the New Capitalism*. New York: W. W. Norton and Company.

Serravale, Gabriel. 2012. "Fred Dantas: Maestro Guerreiro." *A Tarde*. Salvador, Brazil. http://atarde.uol.com.br/cultura/materias/1466678-fred-dantas-maestro-guerreiro. Accessed July 17, 2014.

Sharp, Daniel B. 2014. *Between Nostalgia and Apocalypse: Popular Music and the Staging of Brazil*. Middletown, CT: Wesleyan University Press.

Shaw, Lisa. 1999. *The Social History of the Brazilian Samba*. Aldershot, UK: Ashgate.

Sheard, Gordon Terrence. 2008. "*O Encontro nos Trios: 'Axé* Music' and Musicians in Salvador, Bahia, Brazil." PhD diss., York University.

Sheriff, Robin. 2001. *Dreaming Equality: Color, Race, and Racism in Urban Brazil*. New Brunswick, NJ: Rutgers University Press.

Shipley, Jesse Weaver. 2013. *Living the Hiplife: Celebrity and Entrepreneurship in Ghanaian Popular Music*. Durham, NC: Duke University Press.

Skidmore, Thomas E. 1998. *Black into White: Race and Nationality in Brazilian Thought*. Durham, NC: Duke University Press.

Souza Pereira, Ianá. 2010. "Axé-Axé: O Megafenômeno Baiano." *Revista África e Africani-dades* 2 (8).

Sovik, Liv. 2009. *Aqui Ninguém é Branco*. Rio de Janeiro: Aeroplano.

Stahl, Matt. 2013. *Unfree Masters: Recording Artists and the Politics of Work*. Durham, NC: Duke University Press.

Stokes, Martin. 1992a. *The Arabesk Debate: Music and Musicians in Modern Turkey*. New York: Oxford University Press.

———. 1992b "Islam, the Turkish State, and Arabesk." *Popular Music* 11 (2): 213–27.

———. 2002. "Marx, Money, and Musicians." In *Music and Marx: Ideas, Practice, Politics*, ed. Regula Burckhardt Qureshi, 139–63. New York: Routledge.

Straw, Will. 1991. "Systems of Articulation, Logics of Change: Communities and Scenes in Popular Music." *Cultural Studies* 5 (3): 368–88.

Stråth, Bo, ed. 2000. *After Full Employment: European Discourses on Work and Flexibility*. New York: P.I.E.-Peter Lang.

Stroud, Sean. 2000. "'*Música é para o Povo Cantar*': Culture, Politics, and Brazilian Song Festivals, 1965–1972." *Latin American Music Review* 21 (2): 87–117.

———. 2008. *The Defense of Tradition in Brazilian Popular Music: Politics, Culture, and the Creation of Música Popular Brasileira*. Aldershot, UK: Ashgate.

Taylor, Timothy D. 2012. *The Sounds of Capitalism: Advertising, Music, and the Conquest of Culture*. Chicago: University of Chicago Press.

_____. 2015. "World Music, Value, and Memory." In *Speaking in Tongues: Pop Lokal Global*, ed. Dietrich Helms and Thomas Phelps, 103–17. Bielfield, DE: Transcript.

_____. 2016. *Music and Capitalism. A History of the Present*. Chicago: University of Chicago Press.

Taubkin, Benjamim. 2011. *Viver de Música: Diálogos com Artistas Brasileiros*. São Paulo: BEI.

Teles dos Santos, Jocélio. 2005. *O Poder da Cultura e a Cultura no Poder: A Disputa Simbólica da Herança Cultural Negra no Brasil*. Salvador: EDUFBA.

Telles, Edward E. 2004. *Race in Another America: The Significance of Skin Color in Brazil*. Princeton, NJ: Princeton University Press.

Thornton, Sarah. 1996. *Club Cultures: Music, Media, and Subcultural Capital*. Cambridge, UK: Polity Press.

Tinhorão, José Ramos. 1998. *História Social da Música Popular Brasileira*. São Paulo: Editora 34.

_____. 2001. *Cultura Popular: Temas e Questões*. São Paulo: Editora 34.

Towse, Ruth. 1993. *Singers in the Marketplace: The Economics of the Singing Profession*. New York: Oxford University Press.

Toynbee, Jason. 2000. *Making Popular Music: Musicians, Creativity, and Institutions*. London: Arnold.

Treece, David. 2013. *Brazilian Jive: From Samba to Bossa and Rap*. London: Reaktion Books.

Trotta, Felipe. 2015. "Samba and the Music Market in Brazil in the 1990s." In *Made in Brazil: Studies in Popular Music*, ed. Martha Tupinambá de Ulhôa, Felipe Trotta, and Cláudia Azevedo, 43–55. New York: Routledge.

Tsioulakis, Ioannis. 2011. "Jazz in Athens: Frustrated Cosmopolitans in a Music Subculture." *Ethnomusicology Forum* 20 (2): 175–99.

Tucker, Joshua. 2013. *Gentleman Troubadours and Andean Pop Stars: Huayno Music, Media Work, and Ethnic Imaginaries in Urban Peru*. Chicago: University of Chicago Press.

Tucker, Sherrie. 2000. *Swing Shift: "All Girl" Bands of the 1940s*. Durham, NC: Duke University Press.

Turino, Thomas. 2000. *Nationalists, Cosmopolitans, and Popular Music in Zimbabwe*. Chicago: University of Chicago Press.

_____. 2008. *Music as Social Life: The Politics of Participation*. Chicago: University of Chicago Press.

Ulhôa, Martha Tupinambá de. 2007. "Categorias de Avaliação da MPB: Lidando com a Recepção da Música Brasileira Popular." https://www.academia.edu/36083522/Categorias_de_avaliacao_estetica_da_MPB. Accessed January 24, 2021.

Van Nieuwkerk, Karin. 1995. *"A Trade Like Any Other": Female Singers and Dancers in Egypt*. Austin: University of Texas Press.

Vianna, Hermano. 1999. *The Mystery of Samba: Popular Music and National Identity in Brazil*, ed. and trans. John Charles Chasteen. Chapel Hill: University of North Carolina Press.

Wachs, Faye Linda, and Laura Frances Chase. 2013. "Explaining the Failure of an Obesity Intervention: Combining Bourdieu's Symbolic Violence and the Foucault's Microphysics of Power to Reconsider State Interventions." *Sociology of Sport Journal* 30: 111–31.

Wallis, Roger, and Krister Malm. 1984. *Big Sounds from Small Peoples: The Music Industry in Small Countries*. New York: Pendragon Press.

Walser, Robert. 1993. *Running with the Devil: Power, Gender, and Madness in Heavy Metal*. Middletown, CT: Wesleyan University Press.

Weber, Max. 1958. *The Rational and Social Foundations of Music*. Carbondale: Southern Illinois University Press.

Weber, William, ed. 2004. *The Musician as Entrepreneur, 1700–1914: Managers, Charlatans, and Idealists*. Bloomington: Indiana University Press.

Weinstein, Deena. 1997. "Art Versus Commerce: Deconstructing a (Useful) Romantic Illusion." In *Stars Don't Stand Still in the Sky: Music and Myth*, ed. Karen Kelley and Evelyn McDonnell, 56–71. New York: NYU Press.

Whitmore, Aleysa. 2020. *World Music and the Black Atlantic: Producing & Consuming African-Cuban Musics on World Music Stages*. New York: Oxford University Press.

Wilde, Oscar. [1891] 2001. "The Soul of Man Under Socialism." In *The Soul of Man Under Socialism and Selected Critical Prose*. London: Penguin Classics.

Williamson, John, and Martin Cloonan. 2007. "Rethinking the Music Industry." *Popular Music* 26 (2): 305–22.

Winant, Howard. 2001. *The World is a Ghetto: Race and Democracy since World War II*. New York: Basic Books.

Wolff, Janet. 1987. "Forward: The Ideology of Autonomous Art." In *Music and Society: The Politics of Composition, Performance, and Reception*, ed. Richard Leppert and Susan McClary, 1–12. New York: Cambridge University Press.

Wood, Stephen. 1989. "The Transformation of Work?" In *The Transformation of Work? Skill, Flexibility, and the Labour Process*, ed. Stephen Wood. London: Unwin Hyman.

INDEX

labor within, 122; position takings within, 12; recent past and near future of, 235–39; relationship ties within, 36; as sole profession, 244–45; success within, 12; supplementation for, 46; tactical adjustment within, 150–51; threats to, 232; types of, 46; value of, 33; working conditions within, 233; work site location importance of, 41

musical literacy, 169–70

musical validation, 150

musicians/musicians' selves: as actualized, 155; discursive performances of, 133–42, 142–47; job-like aspects of, 6; leisure-filled lifestyles of, 6; within the Salvador Scene, 120–24; skill development and, 169–70; sound mixing experience of, 184–85; transparency and, 138–39

nationalization, of samba, 47

Neginho do Samba, 228

negotiations, 33, 143–44, 145–46, 156

neoliberal capitalism, 8

neoliberalism, 5, 10

Nery, Vando, 123, 136–37

networking, 24, 36, 80–81, 113–16

New Year's Eve, 40–41, 190

nexus: bonding capital within, 82; bridging capital and, 82; business-related matters within, 88; business sponsorship within, 104–7; capital within, 113–16; challenges within, 84–85; conditions of, 78; defined, 81; *dono* (owner, master) within, 81; economic capital and, 104–8; ensembles as, 81; government support within, 107–8; independents within, 95–104; motivations within, 84; of musical work, 79–82; networking within, 113–16; node as, 80–81; organization of, 82–84; overview of, 82–85; personal contact within, 111–13; principals within, 81–82, 98–99, 103, 119, 159, 160; rehearsals and, 156–60, 166–72; relationships within, 81; signed, 88–95; *socios* (partners) within, 81, 94; stability within

flexibility within, 85–87; working to sell work of, 108–13

night musicians (*músicos da noite*): adaptations of, 212–14; audiences of, 51–52, 201–2, 212; capital earnings of, 213; earnings of, 52, 210, 213; economic capital of, 113; exploitation of, 112; flexibility of, 209; framing performance challenges of, 201–2; genres of, 211; performance planning of, 209–14; promotion strategies of, 111–12; repertoire of, 210; schedule of, 255n18; self-accompaniment by, 50; volume control for, 209–10; weekly schedule of, 184; working conditions of, 52; work of, 49–53. *See also* "playing at night"

node, 80–81

nonseasonal circuit, 46–55, 78, 95, 105, 106, 163

nonstop labor, as productive, 122

novos roupagens (new clothes), as reworking, 55

Oliveira, Junior, 23–24, 54, 82, 97–98, 102–3, 127, 157, 159, 243

Olodum, 58, 130–31, 134–35, 228, 258n13, 259n8

OMB (Ordem dos Músicos do Brasil), 35

original/unpublished songs (*músicas inéditas*), 55

orixás, 247n7

out-of-season work, 66–67

overt racism, 14

pagode: within the Carnaval Circuit, 27; characteristics of, 59–60, 254n15; chord progressions within, 60; criticism of, 27–28, 31; dancing within, 60; defined, 255–56n30; distancing tactics from, 135, 137; dominant pathway of, 68, 237; earnings within, 32, 61–62; Farofa's viewpoint of, 125–26; history of, 60; overview of, 59–62; participation within, 60; performance locations of, 61; performances of, 49; prejudice against, 123; seasonal work of, 66; viewpoints regarding, 136–37

of, 160–63; harmony, 162, 164, 177; material conditions at, 153; materialities within studios for, 165; negotiations within, 156; nexuses and, 156–60, 166–72; organization of, 157–60, 167; overview of, 155–56; practicing feel within, 173–76; preparation for, 160–63; process of, 33, 154; processual recomposition within, 170–72; recording use within, 168–69; schedule of, 73; sites for, 164–66; structure of, 167, 172; timing of, 160–63, 164Reis, Paulo "Pastel": career pathway of, 23, 85, 242, 243; dance band jobs of, 54; drumming style of, 191–92; "Pescaria (Canoeiro)" (Fishing [Boatman]) and, 223–24; portfolio of, 81; quote of, 147; sound check of, 188–90, 191; viewpoint of, 74, 225

relationships, 79, 81, 95, 121, 230–31

repertoire: adaptations within, 80; flexibility within, 219; learning process of, 169–70; multiple knowledges of, 216–18; within recordings, 109–10, 229; reverence within, 215; reworking within, 215, 219; "right" keys within, 217; sharing of, 214–20; within shows, 55. See also specific musicians

repique, 58

reputation, 124, 131–32, 140

requests, within "playing at night," 212

rereadings (*releituras*), 54

restaurants, musical labor within, 49–53, 52, 86, 201–2, 210

reworking, characteristics within, 215

rhythmic feel, practicing of, 173–76

"right" keys, knowledge of, 217

Rio de Janeiro, Brazil, 1, 42, 47, 238, 251n32

Rio/São Paulo Axis, 42, 47, 76

rock music, 48

romantic music, 30

salsa, 48, 54

Salsalitro, 127, 167–68, 207

Salvador: background of, 41–42; Bahian-ness within, 42; challenges within, 42; classism within, 43; demographics of, 12, 16; education within, 42; employment within, 43, 254n6; income gaps within, 42–43, 44; industrialization within, 42; living conditions within, 42–44; parade routes within, 204; physical and social spaces within, 41, 43; poverty within, 41, 42; rehearsals spaces within, 164–65; slavery history of, 42; soundscape overview of, 39; as synecdoche, 247n6; tourism within, 56; unemployment within, 251n32. *See also specific locations within*

Salvador Scenes, 7, 9

samba, 1, 6, 47, 54, 60, 84, 136, 173, 238

Samba de Farofa, 107, 114, 204–5, 240–42

samba de roda, 49, 238

samba junino, 238

samba-reggae, 2, 3

Sangalo, Ivete, 39, 47, 63, 195

Sansone, Livio, 250n30

Santos, Josehr, 23, 89–91, 116, 243

Santos, Roberval, 115, 212, 230, 243, 262n5

São João, 40, 69, 72–73, 77–78, 105, 199, 236

scratch tracks, 177

self-accompaniment, of night musicians, 50

self-branding, 259n3

self-positioning, 120, 133, 146–47, 234

self-regulation, 251n41

sequenced percussion, within dance bands, 53

sequenced recordings, 162

Seu Maxixe, 239–40

shows, 54–55. *See also* performances

side musicians, 127–28, 159, 168

signal difference, 226

signed nexus, 88–95, 93–94, 95

Signifyin(g), 154, 171, 218–20

slavery, 42

small ensembles, characteristics of, 50–51.
See also ensembles

snare drum, volume control of, 189–90

social capital: career pathways and, 124; defined, 7, 36; of Elpidio Bastos, 131; of Farofa, 114; within lending services, 130; of Márcia Castro, 114; of night musicians, 53,

213; within relationships, 230–31; tactics of, 234; use of, 146; women and, 249n24

social hierarchies, 7

Som Ki Lufa, 96–97

The Song, 154, 171, 193, 215–18

songs/song selection, importance of, 170–71. *See also* repertoire

"sore elbow" (*dor de cotovelo*) music, characteristics of, 30

"The Soul of Man Under Socialism" (Wilde), 1

sound checks, 152–53, 154–55, 183–92, 262n1

sound imperialism, 187

Souza, Kiko, 96–97, 129

specialization, within music, 123

sponsorship, 73, 98, 104–7, 106, 260n15

stages, 199, 203

stars: within Carnaval Circuit, 77, 237; disconnect of, 6; distancing by, 133; earnings of, 34, 63, 67, 73; politics of, 35; race of, 21; schedules of, 74; sponsorship of, 106–7; support for, 105, 200–201. *See also* headliners

subgenres, 70

substitutions/substitutability, 35, 141–42, 155

Subúrbio (Suburbia) (Salvador), 43, 44

supplemental income, 46

surdos, 57, 58

swing (*suingue*), 173, 174, 175, 182, 190

synchronic flexibility, 27

technology, 263n4

technology, recording, 176

Teles, Kadija, 11, 12, 110

temporal frames, of performances, 198–202

theft, within *camarotes*, 65

360-degree deals, 89

timbal, 57, 241

Timbalada, 258n13, 260n10

Torres, Ivan, 138–39

tourism/tourists, 32, 56

trans-Atlantic slave trade, 9

Trio de Ouro, 220

trios elétricos: audiences of, 206, 208; within *axé* music, 39; challenges within, 64–65,

68, 204–5; characteristics of, 64; framing performances within, 200–201; genres of, 214; instruments on, 247n3; overview of, 62–65; performance planning for, 203–9; performances of, 39–40; rehearsals for, 64; repertoire of, 206–7; samba within, 238; schedules of, 63

Tropicália movement, 2

Túlio, Marco, 248n16

unemployment, 251n32

UNESCO, 238

unrehearsed gigs, 155

unsatisfactory performances, effects of, 115, 124

Veloso, Caetano, 1, 47

venues, 46, 185–86, 201. *See also* specific locations

versão, 262n8

versatility, 123. *See also* flexibility

violão, of Márcia Castro, 50

Visi, Carla, 88, 148

volume control, 189, 209–10

wages: within Bahian *pagode*, 61–62; within the Carnaval Circuit, 67–68; cheap labor reputation and, 140; decline of, 34–35; within Forró, 75; within June Circuit, 74; for lending of service, 258n11; of night musicians, 52, 210; within nonseasonal circuit, 46–47; payment timing for, 86; for recording sessions, 178; for rehearsals, 256n38; sacrifice and, 232–33; for shows, 54–55; sources of, 235; stagnation of, 7–8; types of, 104

women, 11, 50, 128, 158, 249n24

work ethic, 121

working conditions, 52, 54–55, 72, 73, 233

working to work, 108–13, 125, 138–39, 197

YouTube, 236, 245–46

zabumba (shallow bass drum), 70

Zarath, Jorge, 168

MUSIC / CULTURE

A series from Wesleyan University Press
Edited by Deborah Wong, Sherrie Tucker, and Jeremy Wallach
Originating editors: George Lipsitz, Susan McClary, and Robert Walser

The Music/Culture series has consistently reshaped and redirected music scholarship. Founded in 1993 by George Lipsitz, Susan McClary, and Robert Walser, the series features outstanding critical work on music. Unconstrained by disciplinary divides, the series addresses music and power through a range of times, places, and approaches. Music/Culture strives to integrate a variety of approaches to the study of music, linking analysis of musical significance to larger issues of power—what is permitted and forbidden, who is included and excluded, who speaks and who gets silenced. From ethnographic classics to cutting-edge studies, Music/Culture zeroes in on how musicians articulate social needs, conflicts, coalitions, and hope. Books in the series investigate the cultural work of music in urgent and sometimes experimental ways, from the radical fringe to the quotidian. Music/Culture asks deep and broad questions about music through the framework of the most restless and rigorous critical theory.

Marié Abe
*Resonances of Chindon-ya:
Sounding Space and Sociality
in Contemporary Japan*

Frances Aparicio
*Listening to Salsa: Gender, Latin Popular
Music, and Puerto Rican Cultures*

Paul Austerlitz
*Jazz Consciousness: Music, Race,
and Humanity*

Christina Baade and Kristin McGee
*Beyoncé in the World: Making Meaning
with Queen Bey in Troubled Times*

Emma Baulch
*Genre Publics: Popular Music, Technologies,
and Class in Indonesia*

Harris M. Berger
*Metal, Rock, and Jazz: Perception
and the Phenomenology
of Musical Experience*

Harris M. Berger
Stance: Ideas about Emotion, Style, and Meaning for the Study of Expressive Culture

Harris M. Berger and Giovanna P. Del Negro
Identity and Everyday Life: Essays in the Study of Folklore, Music, and Popular Culture

Franya J. Berkman
Monument Eternal: The Music of Alice Coltrane

Dick Blau, Angeliki Vellou Keil, and Charles Keil
Bright Balkan Morning: Romani Lives and the Power of Music in Greek Macedonia

Susan Boynton and Roe-Min Kok, editors
Musical Childhoods and the Cultures of Youth

James Buhler, Caryl Flinn, and David Neumeyer, editors
Music and Cinema

Thomas Burkhalter, Kay Dickinson, and Benjamin J. Harbert, editors
The Arab Avant-Garde: Music, Politics, Modernity

Patrick Burkart
Music and Cyberliberties

Julia Byl
Antiphonal Histories: Resonant Pasts in the Toba Batak Musical Present

Corinna Campbell
Parameters and Peripheries of Culture: Interpreting Maroon Music and Dance in Paramaribo, Suriname

Daniel Cavicchi
Listening and Longing: Music Lovers in the Age of Barnum

Susan D. Crafts, Daniel Cavicchi, Charles Keil, and the Music in Daily Life Project
My Music: Explorations of Music in Daily Life

Jim Cullen
Born in the USA: Bruce Springsteen and the American Tradition

Anne Danielsen
Presence and Pleasure: The Funk Grooves of James Brown and Parliament

Peter Doyle
Echo and Reverb: Fabricating Space in Popular Music Recording, 1900–1960

Ron Emoff
Recollecting from the Past: Musical Practice and Spirit Possession on the East Coast of Madagascar

Yayoi Uno Everett and Frederick Lau, editors
Locating East Asia in Western Art Music

Susan Fast and Kip Pegley, editors
Music, Politics, and Violence

Heidi Feldman
Black Rhythms of Peru: Reviving African Musical Heritage in the Black Pacific

Kai Fikentscher
"You Better Work!" Underground Dance Music in New York City

Ruth Finnegan
The Hidden Musicians: Music-Making in an English Town

Christopher Small
Music of the Common Tongue:
Survival and Celebration
in African American Music

Christopher Small
Music, Society, Education

Christopher Small
Musicking: The Meanings
of Performing and Listening

Maria Sonevytsky
Wild Music: Sound and Sovereignty
in Ukraine

Regina M. Sweeney
Singing Our Way to Victory:
French Cultural Politics and Music
during the Great War

Colin Symes
Setting the Record Straight: A Material
History of Classical Recording

Steven Taylor
False Prophet: Field Notes
from the Punk Underground

Paul Théberge
Any Sound You Can Imagine: Making
Music/Consuming Technology

Sarah Thornton
Club Cultures: Music, Media,
and Subcultural Capital

Michael E. Veal
Dub: Songscape and Shattered Songs
in Jamaican Reggae

Michael E. Veal and
E. Tammy Kim, editors
Punk Ethnography: Artists and Scholars
Listen to Sublime Frequencies

Robert Walser
Running with the Devil: Power, Gender,
and Madness in Heavy Metal Music

Dennis Waring
Manufacturing the Muse:
Estey Organs and Consumer Culture
in Victorian America

Lise A. Waxer
The City of Musical Memory:
Salsa, Record Grooves, and Popular
Culture in Cali, Colombia

Mina Yang
Planet Beethoven: Classical Music
at the Turn of the Millennium

ABOUT THE AUTHOR

Jeff Packman is an Associate Professor in the Faculty of Music at the University of Toronto. He holds a PhD in Ethnomusicology from the University of California–Berkeley.